外国语言、文学、文化研究与翻译赏析

主编　马玲　邓兵

副主编　左德雄　张绍菊　李堂英　饶琼珍　刘春燕

云南大学出版社
YUNNAN UNIVERSITY PRESS

图书在版编目（CIP）数据

外国语言、文学、文化研究与翻译赏析：英文/马
玲，邓兵主编.-- 昆明：云南大学出版社，2018
ISBN 978-7-5482-3255-1

Ⅰ.①外… Ⅱ.①马… ②邓… Ⅲ.①外语教学—教
学研究—高等学校—文集—英文 Ⅳ.① H09-53

中国版本图书馆 CIP 数据核字 (2018) 第 291938 号

策划编辑：王翌沣
责任编辑：王翌沣
封面制作：王婳一

外国语言、文学、
文化研究与翻译赏析

主　编　马　玲　邓　兵
副主编　左德雄　张绍菊　李堂英　饶琼珍　刘春燕

出版发行：云南大学出版社
印　　装：廊坊市海涛印刷有限公司
开　　本：787mm×1092mm　1/16
印　　张：22.5
字　　数：573 千
版　　次：2018 年 12 月第 1 版
印　　次：2021 年 7 月第 2 次印刷
书　　号：ISBN 978-7-5482-3255-1
定　　价：68.00 元

社　　址：昆明市一二一大街 182 号（云南大学东陆校区英华园内）
邮　　编：650091
电　　话：（0871）65033244　65031071
网　　址：http://www.ynup.com
E－mail：market@ynup.com

若发现本书有印装质量问题，请与印厂联系调换，联系电话：0316-2516002。

编者的话

　　云南大学外国语言文学学科具有悠久的历史，英语专业始建于 1942 年。此后，学院汇聚了诸多国内英语学界精英和知名翻译家。1972 年，云南大学成为国内较早、云南省最早设立法语专业的院校；1988 年成为云南省开设日语专业最早的学校。1984 年和 1993 年，我院英语语言文学和法语语言文学专业先后获得硕士学位授权点；2010 年学院成为外国语言文学一级学科硕士学位和翻译硕士学位授权单位。近年来，在国家"一带一路"倡议的鼓舞下，同时又占有与南亚东南亚国家相邻的地缘优势，我院先后开设了亚非语言文学的缅甸语、泰语和越南语等本科专业。2013 年和 2014 年增设了日语语言文学和亚非语言文学（缅甸语、泰语）二级学科硕士学位点。同时，英语和法语开始招收翻译硕士（笔译方向）。2018 年，我院又开设了印地语本科专业（印度语言文学），并将于 2019 年增设印度语言文学（印地语）和亚非语言文学（越南语）二级学科硕士学位点。目前，学院已形成了多语种、多层次的办学局面。

　　近年来，云南大学外国语学院围绕国家"一带一路"倡议和云南省"两强一堡"建设需求，以云南大学"双一流"的建设为契机，致力于加强学科建设，不断提高人才培养的质量，培养了一批高层次、专业型、创新型多语种外语人才，促进了云南省社会经济的发展。

　　云南大学外国语学院的全体教师在完成教学任务的同时，积极投身于科研，产生了一大批有影响力的科研成果。有些教师还积极探索用外语撰写学术论文，目的在于扩大国际视野，增加国际交流，目标瞄准国外的学术刊物和国际学术会议。为鼓励广大教师科研积极性，我们组织编写了这部用外语撰写的论文集。

　　该论文集共收录了云南大学外国语学院教师撰写的 25 篇论文，涵盖了英语、日语、法语、德语、越南语、缅甸语、泰语等 7 个语种，涉及语言学、外语教学、翻译学、外国文学、外国文化等多个领域。论文集体现了语种和内容的多样性，体现了各个语种教师在各领域用外语进行科研的成果。可视为冲击国外刊物的一次练兵。

　　最后，希望这本论文集能成为云南大学外国语学院教师科研的有效平台，

充分展示教师们的科研成果，促进学院的科研发展，进一步提升教师的科研水平，激励更多的老师投身科学研究，以产生更多更好的科研成果，并且使科研成果走向国际，为云南大学的"双一流"建设做出应有的贡献。

编　者
2018 年 8 月

目　录

Literary Studies

Linguistics and Translation Studies

Studies on Language Teaching

Culture and National Conditions

Literary Studies

A Textual Analysis of the Psychological Development of the Nameless Narrator in James Welch's *Winter in the Blood* *

Xie Ping**

School of Foreign Languages, Yunnan University,

Kunming　Yunnan

Abstract: James Welch's first novel *Winter in the Blood* is noted for its surrealistic description of the psychological development of the nameless narrator/protagonist whose psychological world is frozen solid after the death of his beloved brother and father. After some aimless shuffling between his home and the "white town", he finally attains his self-salvation and the "winter" in his blood begins to show signs of thawing. By means of textual analysis, this paper is to detect from the haphazard details of his wandering the clues to his psychological world so as to reveal that his self-salvation is achieved as a result of both his retrieving the Indian tradition and his acceptance of life reality.

Key words: psychological development; nameless narrator; *Winter in the Blood*

It is fair when Shanley comments on the unnamed protagonist/narrator of James Welch's *Winter in the Blood* that "while we are led to believe we are getting to know him, we can not be sure what we ought to believe" (238). With the surrealist abrupt transition of scenes, multiple parallelisms of episodes and hard-edged descriptive style, James Welch presents in his first novel a tight-lipped narrator who allows us little access to his inner world. Frustrating as it appears to be, by close-examining whatever scarce clues he drops us consciously or unconsciously, it is possible for us to trace his psychological development so as to find out about the freezing and thawing of

---

　* 论文题目: 简析《血中冬日》中无名氏男主人公的心理发展。

　** 作者简介: 谢萍(Xie Ping), 云南大学外国语学院副教授, 研究方向: 美国印第安文学。

his psychological winter.

Different from Tayo in Silko's *Ceremony*, whose personal healing process is closely related to, and therefore significant for, the communal recovery of tribal culture, the unnamed narrator in Winter in the Blood is, in a larger sense, putting up a struggle of his own. Different from the stereotypical image of "tough" Indian men who are incapable of any "soft" feelings and emotions, Welch's protagonist is first of all an ordinary individual at the sway of emotional ups and downs. Even though he manages to evade any sentimental revelation in his narrative, he impresses us just by his rather comical habitual peeing at the moments of emotional turbulence that he can easily get emotionally worked up and is truly what his mother Teresa terms "too sensitive" (16). For him, the meaning of life is first and foremost established upon effective emotional ties.

Unfortunately, twenty years after the death of his brother Mose, and ten years after the death of his father First Raise, the narrator is still psychologically alienated. He remains a "servant to a memory of death," and finds it hard to anchor his feelings in his actual life (30). Devoid of any emotional energy, his factual existence is no more than a listless void. Even though he is ambivalent about many things, at the beginning of his first home-coming he is quite articulate and definite when translating the metaphorical "winter" in his blood, or rather his psyche, into some overwhelming "distance" that "came from within [him]" and "that had grown through the years" (2). Transfixed by winter of such depth and dimension, life for him is frozen. His psychological winter has encroached upon his initiative, depriving him of any agency to live a life that means something to him.

The impotence to make life meaningful plunges the narrator into the haphazard reality where he gets lost and becomes in a sense a "wanderer" as Teresa calls him. His indulgence in emotional trauma has drained him of any active control over life. He is either easily manipulated by others or drifts wherever his random life takes him. He can hardly settle down, shifting frequently between home and bars in town. He finds no good reason for his actions and goes to look for his girlfriend just because his family expects him to. His judgment is obviously impaired when he is easily tricked into helping Dougie rob the white man but is afterwards troubled by the dreadful consequences he fabricates in his mind. He seems confused when on one hand he violates the law by agreeing to help the fugitive airplane man, but on the other hand states clearly when the airplane man buys a hunting knife that by law "[p] art of that knife has to show"(78). He allows vanity to take over him when he lies to Malvina about his job as a foreman on the railroad and enjoys the untruthful impression that he is a rich man. Despite the fact that he keeps reminding and correcting other people that he is thirty-two, the funny picture of his carrying a big teddy bear down the street is indicative of his being an adult-child psychologically. His naivety, which is out of proportion to his age, testifies to some stagnation in his psychological development. Such psychological stagnation is the winter that has frozen him, preventing him from a life of purpose he should have enjoyed at the age of thirty-two.

The winter comes and takes dominance after the deaths of Mose and First Raise — "the only ones[he]really loved"(135). He is stuck in the emotional mire not only because his emotional ties are severed with the deaths of Mose and First Raise, but because his memory of them is, in the first place, plighted with the burden of guilt and ambiguity. Just like the tall cupboard with glass doors that holds"mementos of a childhood, two childhood, two brothers,"his mind is occupied by the memory of his time together with Mose(30). Even though Mose's death is an accident, as the narrator has come to see their lives as connected and inseparable, to live alone in a world where Mose is forever gone brings him an irrevocable feeling of guilt. The sharp pain that comes with the death memory when"Mose was fourteen, [he]was twelve" weighs so much on his mind that on one hand his memory of their life together is one of the few things he can fall back on in his emotional barrenness, but on the other hand the unbearable pain embedded in it makes it"a memory[he]had tried to keep away" (87). If the death of Mose has been a detrimental blow to the narrator, the death of First Raise finally freezes him up. Compared with Teresa who tends to practical living, First Raise dreams about hunting elk in Glacier Park, but it is First Raise to whom the narrator feels emotionally related. Love abounds in his memory of him, and the narrator is quite explicit in saying that First Raise is the person who"loved us"and who "enjoyed the way we grew up"(84, 17). While Teresa has always been"Teresa"in his narrative, First Raise is his"father". However, apart from love, the father should also be the role-model the son looks up to, and here the narrator's memory of First Raise is jeopardized. First Raise took him to visit Yellow Calf, trying to connect him to his cultural and ancestral roots, but he also drunk with the white men and made them laugh; he is a capable mechanic who can"fix anything made of iron,"but is also"a wanderer"who"was always in transit"(5, 16, 17). Even more confusing is Teresa's contradictory statements that"your father wasn't ever around"and that"he was around enough. When he was around he got things accomplished" (14, 15). The ambiguity as for how he should feel about First Raise catalyzes his near-verge nervous breakdown when the family discovers the body of First Raise. Overwhelmed by the mixed feeling of confusion and denial he remembers clearly that" [they] had come upon him first," but insists" that was a different figure in the ditch, not First Raise" (15, 16). Living in the memory but also tortured by it has thus become the life reality which the narrator has to deal with. While memory is inadequate to furnish him with the emotional support he needs to move on psychologically, people around him prove to be even less helpful.

Teresa may not be a bad mom in the eyes of other people, but the narrator's declaration that" I never expected much from Teresa and I never got it" speaks of the emotional alienation that has typified the mother-son relationship. Compared with emotion-oriented First Raise, Teresa is practical. It is her who takes cares of the household while First Raise wanders in and out of home. Even though it is not clear why she gets married with Lame Bull who has literally nothing in his name, their union is probably out of her consideration for the 360 acres of land in her possession. Teresa keeps a good record of the things they own, and the moment the narrator comes back home, she tells him clearly that his girlfriend has run away with his gun and electric razor. She maintains some" friendship" with the priest from Harlem when First Raise is absent from her life, and she is the one who kills Amos for Christmas dinner. Different from First Raise and the narrator, the" wanderers" who have gone down in the world, Teresa has tight control over her life so much so that she has" grown handsome, more so every year," and her eyes " seemed to grow darker, more liquid, as the years passed" (26).

However, instead of evoking some resonance in her son to her prosperous attitude towards life, her practical way goes against the emotional temperament of him. Amos, the only survivor of the ducks First Raise won at a game, is of symbolic significance to the narrator. To a certain degree, he identifies with the duck because he is also the one who survives the deaths of Mose and First Raise. After Teresa tells him that it is her who kills Amos, he dreams about Teresa giving birth to Amos with" one orange leg cocked at the knee" (42). The cocked knee of the duck is reminiscent of his own knee which gets hurt at the time when Mose dies. Thus, the fact that Teresa kills Amos in reality but gives birth to it in his dream implies both his conscious disappointment that their mother-son emotional connection is not functional and his subconscious desire that some remedy, or even rebirth can be brought into place.

Contrary to his wish, reality always gets the upper hand of dream. Also in this dream, Teresa "raged at [him] in several voices" while his mouth is "dry and hollow of words" (42). No matter how he wants to establish some emotional communication with Teresa, their relationship is one of Teresa taking dominance over him. Except for the occasional verbal challenges he puts up against her and she chooses to ignore, he opts to escape and evade any tension between them. He is obviously not comfortable about Teresa having a priest friend "who refused to bury Indians in their own plots, who refused to set foot on the reservation," but he remains silent about it (4). When he gets the letter from the priest to her, he hesitates for a while but finally decides to tear it up so that he doesn't need to face the emotional uneasiness the letter brings him and as he doesn't have to deliver it he can also avoid facing Teresa.

To make things worse, Teresa's new husband Lame Bull sets out both literally and figuratively to " [hold him] down by the neck so that [he] couldn't get up" (61). Lame Bull's motto is money and power. He is first married to Teresa's 360 acres of land and then to her. When he looks at the field, "he was counting bales, converting them into cows and the cows into calves and the calves into cash" (23). Only money rings true in his ears, and therefore he can be cruel when his economic gains are threatened. He does not hesitate to punch Long Knife brutally on the face when the helper wants to stop working and go to town to get a drink. With Teresa's property coming into his possession after their marriage, his obsession with the idea that he is the proprietor goes to such extremes that he behaves in a rather comical and absurd way. Although he is too short to drive the bull rake and has to "slide forward to reach the brake and clutch pedals," he still makes a point of driving it because "it was the proprietor's job," and the result, unfortunately, is that he " [breaks] two teeth in the bull rake and [screws] up the hydraulic lift" (20). To live up to his new image as the head of the house, he treats old grandma with some slight and regards the narrator as no more than a cheap helper. Obviously, the money-and-power motto of Lame Bull leaves no place for any consideration of the narrator's emotions; together with the practical attitude of Teresa, home dominated by the couple has become the least possible place for the narrator to find any emotional nourishment, and home-coming has thus become " a torture" to him (1).

Having failed to get emotionally connected to people around him after the deaths of Mose and First Raise, the narrator is left alone in an emotional wasteland and his psychological growth is almost terminated. He is thus " as distant from [himself] as a hawk from the moon" and has "no particular feelings toward my mother and grandmother," the two people with whom he shares his ancestry(2). He drifts further and further away from his life which in turn makes less and less meaning to him. However, compared with the confusion of his present life, the story his grandmother has told him about the Starvation Winter of 1883—1884 stands out as something of significance. Therefore, even though it is not clear why he goes to visit Yellow Calf when his attempt to get his girlfriend back fails, he is probably turning to the past subconsciously in search of meaning his present life denies him. Unfortunately, as he has long been estranged from Indian tradition, he cannot fully appreciate the wisdom in his dialogue with Yellow Calf. Even so, their talk does draw his attention to some traditional Indian views concretized in Yellow Calf's remarks that deer are not happy and that the world is cockeyed. Moreover, he even exerts some energy and initiative in directing the conversation, which sets off a sharp contrast to his otherwise listless self. His account about this visit is one of the rare occasions when his narrative appears coherent, and his promise that he will bring some wine next time preconditioned the crucial visit which leads directly to the thawing of his emotional winter. Subtly but undeniably, even though what this visit informs him is not enough for his psychological revival, Yellow Calf's inclusive but meaningful life looms as a potential inspiration for him to reclaim his Indian origin and thus prepares him to a certain degree for the thawing of his psychological winter.

Except for such vague clues in the epilogue of the novel as the narrator's thinking of his girlfriend and his consideration for the possible operation on his knee, Welch is rather implicit as for the narrator's recovery from his emotional winter. However, it is almost universally acknowledged that the novel ends with a positive note that the emotional winter of the narrator has thawed and his psychological development has resumed its momentum. Paradoxically, his recovery first arises from his naivety, for while naivety bespeaks the immaturity of his mentality, it also implies that like an innocent child he still retains some clean conscience in his bleak emotional world. Life without emotional communication is disappointing, but the corrupted outside world is even more formidable. Its ugliness impinges on the narrator's conscience and finally wakes him up from his indulgence in his emotional tragedy.

In the collage of his narrative, his relationship with women can be pinned down as leading to his epiphany. Except for his girlfriend Agnes, his experiences with the other three women can be summarized as his attempt to fill his emotional void with sexual gratification. However, guarded by his conscience, instead of using sex to kill his mental agony, he is brought to confront face to face with his degradation. The barmaid from Melta has no name in his narrative; likewise, his impression of her is also dominated by some nameless confusion. He is repulsed by the lies and flirtation between the airplane man and the barmaid, but at the same time feels sexually attracted to her and the image of "the button of her blouse strained between her breasts" keeps surging in his mind (46). However, despite the sexual attraction he "felt uneasy about the barmaid, a feeling almost of shame" (46). He has no way to explain the shame he feels, but it is possible that the shame arises from his conscience and is both for the barmaid and for himself because they have both given themselves up to their sexual desires. Such feeling of shame brings with it some subconscious denial to their sexual relationship which contributes to his confusion as to what has actually happened between them. Thus, instead of using sexual gratification as a distraction from his empty life, the narrator is further troubled by the feeling of shame and confusion. His first adventure with woman suffers defeat.

Malvina is the second woman he encounters in town. Despite his initial curiosity about her background, their relationship also ends up as sexual attraction, but this time his sexual desire is extinguished first by Malvina's abrupt order and then by his consideration for the presence of her young son. Such abstaining may be the result of his subconscious equation of Malvina to Teresa prompted by the bubble-bath globes which both women have, but it can also be interpreted as the working of his conscience which reminds him of the inappropriateness of sex in the particular situation. Whatever the case, his sexual encounter fails again and leaves him a feeling of uneasiness.

Different from the barmaid from Melta or Malvina whose relationship with the narrator is a sheer game, Marlene shows him some sincerity and care. For once, their harmonious love-making seems to imply that the narrator has finally got what he desires from a woman and their relationship begins to mean something to him. However, either confused by his experience with the previous women or waking up suddenly from his sexual delusion, the narrator slapped Marlene in the middle of their love-making. This slap is more a slap on the narrator himself than one on Marlene. While his conscience does not stand in his way this time and he is finally able to get some sexual gratification from a willing woman, he is brought to witness the degraded existence of his own. He stares at the sobbing Marlene "as though [he] were watching a bug floating motionless down an irrigation ditch, not yet dead but having decided upon death"(99). He sees in Marlene his own reflection, and this sudden realization induces his epiphany that his life has been reduced to the hollowness of a near-death bug. It dawns on him how his life will end up when he surrenders to the indulgence in his emotional agony, when he gives life up to aimless wandering. What comes into his mind afterwards is"the kind of peace that comes over one when he is alone, when he no longer cares for warmth, or sunshine, or possessions, or even a woman's body, so yielding and powerful" (99). Drained of any desire, the peace the narrator is experiencing at this moment is in fact his declaration of psychological independence, the turning point towards his psychological maturity. Different from his previous self who has to depend on the emotional communication with other people to make sense of his own life, the narrator now begins to appreciate the peace when he is alone, when he becomes the master of his own life, when the meaning of his life no longer dwells on either material possessions, or more importantly, emotional consonance.

If the narrator's experiences with the three women indicate his degradation but function at the same time as the epiphany that wakes him up to his stark reality, he sees in Agnes what he wants in his life. He defines Agnes as"just a girl[he]picked up and brought home,"but she is actually the one who harbors some promise for his life (18). Agnes has the innocence of"a grade-school girl", "a child caught roaming the halls in school"(88, 81). Her eyes"held the promise of warm things, of a spirit that went beyond her miserable life of drinking and screwing and men like me"(90). Such innocence and warmth are in sharp contrast with the ugliness around the narrator and are what he needs to begin his new life with. When he helps the airplane man to flee he is intrigued by a"warmth"at seeing her and feels some"sadness"at his prospective departure from a life with her (82). However, he is yet to experience more antagonism before he can start a life of such"warmth".

The antagonism and rough world holds against him soon emerges in the form of his being beaten up by Dougie and barely missing being caught by the police when the airplane man was cuffed. He feels"helplessness"in the white world, but"those Indians down at Gable's were no bargain either. [He] was a stranger to both and both had beaten[him]"(96). He is clear and eloquent about the overwhelming disappointment he feels:

I had had enough of Harve, enough of town, of walking home, hung over, beaten up, or both. I had had enough of the people, the bartender, the bars, the cars, the hotels, but mostly, I had had enough of myself. I wanted to lose myself, to ditch these clothes, to outrun this burning sun, to stand beneath the clouds and have my shadow erased, myself along with it(100).

Under the combined influence of his epiphany and his total disappointment with the world around him, the narrator finally bids farewell to his wandering in town and sets off once again on his way home.

Contrary to the profound emotional alienation that makes his first home-coming a "torture", he feels "good to be home" this time (105). The determination and initiative he shows right from the beginning when hitchhiking with the family from Michigan indicate that the psychological winter that features his first home-coming has begun to thaw. Not only does he give reason for eating the peach that the sick girl gives him, but the reason itself("out of loyalty toward the sick girl")marks his change from waiting for other people's emotional care passively to actively generating care to other people. The first thing he does when he gets back home is to take a near-ceremonial bath to purge himself of"the invisible[dirt]that coats a man who has been to town"so that"the weariness[he]had felt vanished from[his]bones" (105). He is ready to sever from his old self and turn on a new leaf in his life. The death of the old lady forces him to face death again and gives him at the same time the chance to compromise with his feeling of guilt at the death of Mose. For the first time in many years, he brings himself to face the grave of Mose, and his reasoning of his accident with old Bird implies that he has come to accept Mose's death as an accident. He cries silently and mumbles"What use, what use, what use..." (116)The unsolved"what use..."is too heavy for him to specify and he is whispering it for his soul"as though the words would rid it of the final burden of guilt, and[he]found himself a child again, the years shed as a snake sheds its skin, and[he]was standing over the awkward tangle of clothes and limbs"(116). Emotional burden heavy as the death of his brother is not easy to be absolved but the fact that he can now confront his guilt-ridden feelings signals that he has become emotionally strong enough to depart from his previous attitude of evasion.

It is then his visit with Yellow Calf enlightens him on his ancestry. His understanding that Yellow Calf is actually his biological grandfather means more than clarifying his bloodline. By connecting to Yellow Calf, the individual struggle of the narrator is placed against the general background of his tribal history and tradition. Annihilated by white colonization, Yellow Calf and his grandmother have once suffered the Starvation Winter but have also lived in "a world as clean as the rustling willows, the bark of a fox or the odor of musk during mating season" (118). Like Yellow Calf, the narrator is also part of such history and tradition, a member of his tribal people who have lived, are still living, and will continue to live on this land. His personal life is thus given gravity and for the first time in his narrative the narrator laughs—"it was the laughter of one who understands a moment in his life" (124). Like warm sunshine, the laughter disperses the clouds over his heart and the love it brings that reminds him of the time when First Raise has taken him to visit Yellow Calf. There has always been the distance of three miles between their house and Yellow Calf's shack, but instead of a distance of emotional alienation, the three miles is one of love and connection; it is the distance Yellow Calf has travelled to care for his grandmother and the same distance First Raise has traveled to visit Yellow Calf. Now the three miles is to connect him to his ancestry, to a tradition of love which gives him energy and prepares him for the total thawing of winter in his blood.

His fight to save the spinster from the sucking mud declares the end of his psychological winter. It is with elaborate details that the event is narrated, and the determination and courage involved in it testify to the fact that the narrator has not only overcome his emotional trauma but has grown into a person capable of handling any difficulty in his life, either in the past or in the future. The first test put to him in this rescue mission is the choice whether to save the spinster that has caused the death of Mose. Metaphorically, to save the spinster is to save the narrator himself. The spinster has got stuck in the mud out of its own stupidity just like the narrator has got engulfed in his life because of his own resignation; the spinster is to blame for causing the death of Mose just as the narrator has always blamed himself for the same reason. The crazy hatred he sees in the spinster resonates with "a quick hatred in [his] own heart" (131). When hatred won't make a change, to forgive the spinster and save it from its own stupidity is to compromise with his own past and save himself from his present mire of life. Thus, the choice the narrator makes to save the spinster indicates his determination for his own self-salvation. More importantly, the narrator is all alone in this fight of life and death. Contrary to his previous passive self alienated from and born down by the hypocrisy and indifference of people around him, he is now courageous enough to ignore and despise them and take his fight in his own hand. As rain is usually taken as having generating power in Indian tradition, the "clean rain" accompanying his fight through the rescue mission washes away his past and brings about his rehabilitation, and his victory in the end demonstrates that he has matured into a man with independent character and a good control over his life(135).

There are other incidents marking the narrator's maturity. He corrects the disrespectful misdoing of Lame Bull by stamping the cigarette butt Lame Bull throws into the grave of his grandmother; he lies to the wife of Ferdinand Horn to keep the busybody from prying into his life. At the end of the novel, he throws the pouch into the grave of his grandmother. No matter how we interpret this action, one thing we can be sure of is that compared with the fashionable Teresa and the hypocritical Lame Bull, the nameless narrator has got a better understanding about life, not only about life of himself but about life in general.

Works Cited

Shanley, Kathryn W. "James Welch: Identity, Circumstance, and Chance." *The Cambridge Companion to Native American Literature*. Ed. Joy Peter and Kenneth M. Roemer. New York: Cambridge University Press, 2005. Print.

Welch, James. *Winter in the Blood*. New York: Penguin Books, 2008. Print.

References

[1] Allen, Paula Gunn. *The Sacred Hoop*. Massachusetts: Beacon Press, 1986.

[2] Erdoes, Richard and Oritz, Alfonso. *American Indian Myths and Legends*. New York: Pantheon Books, 1984.

[3] Fleck, Richard F. *Critical Perspectives on Native American Fiction*. Washington: Three Continents Press, 1993.

[4] Garroutte, Eva Marie. *Real Indians: Identity and the Survival of Native America*. Berkley: University of California Press, 2003.

[5] Gill, Jerry H. *Native American Worldviews: An Introduction*. New York: Humanity Books, 2002.

[6] Hibib, Rafey. *Literary Criticism from Plato to the Present: An Introduction*. West Sussex: John Wiley & Sons Ltd, 2011.

[7] Lyons, Scott Richard. *X-marks: Native Signatures of Assent*. Minneapolis: University of Minnesota Press, 2010.

[8] Owens, Louis. *Other Destinies: Understanding the American Indian Novel*. Oklahoma: University of Oklahoa Press, 1992.

[9] Porter, Joy and Roemer, Kenneth M. *The Cambridge Companion to Native American Literature*. Cambridge: Cambridge University Press, 2005.

[10] Teuton, Sean Kicummah. *Red Land, Red Power: Grounding Knowledge in the American Indian Novel.* Durham: Duke University Press, 2008.

[11] Tillett, Rebecca. *Contemporary Native American Literature.* Edinburgh: Edinburgh University Press, 2007.

[12] Vine Deloria, Jr. *Custer Died for Your Sins: An India Manifesto.* New York: Macmillan Publishing Company, 1969.

The Interdependence of Femininity and Masculinity in *Song of Solomon*[*]

Wang Jinmei**

Abstract: *Song of Solomon* is Toni Morrison's first novel with a male protagonist. Although the novel develops in depth Morrison's vision of masculine archetypes, the portraits of the women are as strong and compelling as her more centrally feminine previous novels. Through the textual analyses of the characters, this paper aims to explore the gender issue in the novel and throw light on the significance of interdependence of femininity and masculinity to African-Americans' survival.

Key Words: Femininity; Masculinity; Interdependence; *Song of Solomon*

Song of Solomon differs from Morrison's other novels in its use of a male central character. With its publication, Morrison radically shifts the focus of her familial portraits to men. It greatly enhanced Morrison's literary reputation and broadened her reading audience. In this novel, Morrison "scrutinizes friendship, marriage, family, and relationship to community, primarily (but not exclusively) from men's points of view." (Bloom 1999: 195)

The novel's project is to work through the dominance of the paternal and to confront paternal affiliations with other relational paradigms, so as to discover a balance between the extremes of familial interaction, between intimacy and absence, closeness and distance. Yet this novel adds fathers to mothers and explores the viability of a dual masculine-feminine legacy. Although the novel's protagonist is male, he is finally redeemed by the strength and spirituality of several women in his family and the witch figure Circe, whom he meets on his journey south.

---

* 论文题目:《所罗门之歌》中阴柔与阳刚之相互依赖性。

** 作者简介: 王锦梅(Wang Jinmei), 云南大学外国语学院英语系副教授, 研究方向: 英美文学。

Some critics believe that men in the novel are not linked to or grounded in nature or the feminine. The major symbol of the book is flying, men out of touch with the ground. They are also alienated, isolated from and rejected by masculine white culture, so they exist in a sort of vacuum.

The flying counterpoints the other archetype of masculinity, the image of power through dominion by ownership. Milkman's father drives to own things. Macon is described as existing like a volcano, ready to erupt, his anger and bitterness drying up even the watery feminine, in the women around him; his daughters are "boiled dry from years of yearning", and his wife's feminine nature is also completely dried up. His son is corroded with self-doubt and his material. Morrison uses the peacock imagery several times to develop the masculine narcissism of Macon. Macon's keys to all the houses is that he owns lock him out of the Black world and into isolation.

The unconnected flying and the folly are, in other words, twisted and inversed masculine ambition, all that is left to the black male. Flying is dynamic, frontier breaking, if it is grounded in some kind of psychic anchoring in the real world, as Milkman finally learns from Pilate, his strong aunt. Flight and dominion are polarized forces in these men's world.

Michael Awkward reads the novel as Morrison's radical revision of classical male myth. In contrast to the dominant critical focus on male consciousness, Awkward shows that Morrison is really just as interested in a female perspective that calls attention to women's exclusion from traditional male narrative(Furman 2003: 13). Morrison's male epic does not represent a break from the female-centered concerns of works such as *The Bluest Eye* and *Sula* but is a bold extension of these concerns in a confrontation with the tenets.

Song of Solomon is based around the search of a young black man, Milkman Dead, for his legacy. He has been brought up in a family where his father has shunned his own community while striving to become a small businessman respected by white people. His mother has been ostracized by her husband because he believes he has discovered her in a abnormal relationship with her father. Milkman's adolescence and early adulthood are years of irresponsibility and of indifference to the emerging civil rights movement of the time. But his quest for the lost family gold eventually becomes a search for spiritual values and for the black ancestry in which he shows previously no interest and which is also denied by his father. His spiritual mentor in this search and the guardian of the lore he hopes to find is his aunt, Pilate.

The young Milkman Dead is, for much of his childhood and youth infantilized by his mother and indulged to the point of satiety by women who adore him and prostrate themselves on his behalf. Accustomed to receiving without giving, he is, like many of the males in Morrison's fiction, allowed to stretch his carefree boyhood out for thirty-one years. At the same time he is belittled by his cold father and patronized or deeply resented by his elder female siblings, who loathe his privileged maleness. Milkman's search for gold indicates further the similarity between his father's vision of the world and his own. He thinks that leaving his hometown, his past, and his responsibility will guarantee him a sense of his own identity.

In the community of Shalimar, the home of his ancestors, Milkman is still the ignorant, irresponsible, passive adolescent. Milkman senses that his life is "pointless, aimless". To gain the knowledge of responsible adulthood, he must leave behind the fixed boundaries of his old, immature self and experience the chaotic, liminal, near-death experience of initiation. The bobcat hunt that the older men invite him to join is more accurately a male initiation rite at the hands of the elders and wise men of African tribal cultures. Before Milkman leaves Michigan, he perceives the world in much the same way that his father does. His steadiness of vision and lack of compassion allow him to abuse remorselessly and unself-consciously the people around him. For instance, his letter to Hagar reveals his inability to understand her feelings and psychology despite their years of intimacy. He fails to accept responsibility for ending their relationship; instead, he writes little more than a business letter suggesting that he leaves her for her own best interest.

Not only actions, but also words are early reflections of Milkman's lack of consciousness in regard to women. He tells Hagar, "If you keep your hands just that way and then bring them downstraight, straight and fast, then you can drive the knife right smack in your cunt. " (Morrison 1977: 135) Such backwards, genocidal acts committed and words voiced against the mothers of his race can only find life in a society that promotes profit above human welfare, the individual above the group. It is this priceless treasure of knowledge that Milkman gains by the end of the novel.

In many ways Milkman's journey from his home in Michigan to Pennsylvania to Virginia and back home conforms to the classical male monomyth of the heroic quest. The journey south introduces the first of Milkman's new set of teachers and helpers. Milkman perceives these teachers as instruments to bring him closer to the gold, but as the quest for gold becomes a quest for identity, their meanings change. Milkman's search for identity soon takes the shape of a spiritual quest because it is guided by a woman, Pilate, and it moves toward embracing the funkiness of black cultural identity. By the fourth chapter Milkman has "taken his place in the world of male power"; he has defied and struck his father, been told his father's story— "You want to be a whole man, you have deal with the whole truth"—He has rejected his mother in response to his father's story and his own remembering of her late nursing of him. Significantly, after his discussion with his mother he goes in search of Guitar and finds him in a company of men. From chapter 4 on we witness Milkman's growing dissatisfaction with his masculine identity.

　．　　Milkman is emotionally estranged from Ruth Dead as he is from all women with whom he interacts. As his nickname suggests, he milks women, pilfering their love and giving evident by his inability to distinguish his sisters from his mother. From Pilate, as from Hagar, he receives a love both free and abundant. Wallowing in it, Milkman feels for "the first time in his life that he remembered being completely happy." Most important, it is because of Pilate—the pilot—that he is steered in a conscious direction. Through her acknowledgement of, dignity in, and proudness of her Africanness, despite her lack of material wealth, Milkman gets his first lesson in race and class consciousness. Like Pilate, Milkman must learn to respect his African self and to realize that money does not ensure happiness. It is she who first forces him to confront his identity as the living dead who sucks the life force from his people; from her he learns the essence of life. His nickname, Milkman, foreshadows the fullness of self that he will find through the feminine principle and women themselves. In his realization of his love for Pilate and Ruth, Milkman begins his first steps towards true adulthood.

　　It is not until Milkman has stripped himself of the ruling class's views of race and class superiority that he is able to see women as his equals. This rite of passage is not complete until the Shalimar hunt, during which Milkman first becomes conscious, then ashamed of his exploitation of Hagar, "whom he'd thrown away like a wad of chewing gum after the flavor was gone—she had a right to try to kill him too." (Morrison 1977: 246) The central relationship Morrison uses to show Milkman's evolution from selfish to selfless is his connection with Sweet, the woman he stays with in Shalimar. After being bathed by Sweet, Milkman offers to bathe her. She demurs, saying the tank is too small and there isn't enough hot water left. But he persists, saying, "then let me give you a cool one." The following passage demonstrates

Milkman's growing ability to give and take, instead of just take; it is only after this event that he fully understands the reciprocal nature of human relationships: "She (Sweet) put salve on his face. He washed her hair. She sprinkled talcum on his feet. He straddled her behind and massaged her back. She put witch hazel on his swollen neck. He made up the bed. She gave him gumbo to eat. He washed the dishes. She washed his clothes and hung them out to dry. He scoured her tub. She ironed his shirt and pants. . . " (Morrison 1977: 289)

Milkman, as a result of his spiritual awakening, is in a position to see just how badly he has treated Hagar. In keeping with his new awareness of others and of his personal past, Milkman, insensitive to Hagar and unwilling to accept responsibility for her in life, understands her posthumously and assumes the burden of her death. He acknowledges the inappropriateness of his letter to her and realizes that he has used her. His new connected and caring self is signified by the box of Hagar's hair that Milkman takes home. Milkman brings home the box to mark both his commitment to, and responsibility for the life that he has taken. The hair is also an icon of his black consciousness and his love. Milkman moves from a selfish and juvenile immaturity to a complex knowledge of adulthood. Milkman's conversion occurs on multiple levels. He senses his connection with his ancestry, he learns domestic harmony with Sweet, he commits himself to the community at Danville, and he feels guilt at his treatment of Hagar. He learns to love Pilate.

In Shalimar, after the hunt, a transformed Milkman engages a woman's generosity with his—for the first time in his life and without hesitation. His unselfish attentions to Sweet are a striking contrast to his inattention to the other women in his life, especially his cousin, Hagar. The new Milkman is a striking contrast to the other male characters in the novel, who are they have no control. Each reacts to his helplessness with a compulsive and unremarkable will to conquer.

Having learned to respect the natural world more than the material one and having gained the ability to laugh at himself, Milkman has become a psychologically balanced individual. While previously he had dehumanized his friends and relations, he now empathizes with his parents and feels shame for having robbed Pilate: "The skin of shame that he had rinsed away in the bathwater after having stolen from Pilate returned. But now it was as thick and as tight as a caul. How could he have broken into that house—the only one he knew that achieved comfort without one article of comfort in it. No soft worn-down chair, not a cushion or a pillow—but peace was there, energy, singing, and now his own remembrances. " (Morrison 1977: 304)

Perhaps the most significant evidence of Milkman's awareness of the principle of reciprocity as related to women is his commitment to guide Pilate to Shalimar to bury her father's bones, just as she has guided him to bury the Dead in him. In fact, with his revolutionized consciousness—which prizes humanism and egalitarianism—he becomes the pilot, the source of life. The protagonist becomes the milkman who is capable of carrying the source of life for those in need.

Flight in *Song of solomon* signifies both freedom and abandonment; while Solomon may have freed himself from enslavement, he leaves others, his family, behind. *Song of Solomon* emphasizes the cost of the freedom of this masculine flying: " The children of the flying men suffer discontinuity of every kind. They lose their homes, a sense of their fathers, a sane and stable mother, and even their racial roots in this case of the boy raised by the Indian" (Morrison 1977: 88). Susan Byrd tells Milkman that while the myth says Ryna lost her mind because she couldn't live without her man, Byrd thinks " it was trying to take care of children by herself" that caused Ryna's despair and eventual insanity. In Morrison, children need to be parented so that they may know their history and grow up with a strong and proud sense of self. By flying back to Africa, Solomon not only abandons his children, but he also breaks the children's connection to the motherline and ancestral memory.

The flying men in *Song of Solomon* are emotionally cut off and thus are unable to nurture themselves or others. When Milkman learns that his granddaddy could fly he becomes once again one of Morrison's flying men. He sees Solomon's flight as triumph and transcendence and does not concern himself with those that were left behind. It is not until Milkman returns to Pilate that his relational sense of self is restored. When Milkman comes to after being knocked unconscious by Pilate he realizes that Hagar is dead. Milkman accepts responsibility for Hagar's death. When Milkman discovers his great-father's flying abilities, he has two options. He can continue the path of Solomon (celebration without commitment), or he can use the kinship as a sign to renew his ties to his family. When he accepts Pilate's teachings that " you just can't fly on off and leave a body" he has chosen kinship over flight. (Morrison 1977: 336)

Under the tutelage of Pilate and other women, Milkman comes to learn of the limitations of flight as a mode of survival. By the end of the novel, Milkman is beginning to remake himself as a new kind of man. He begins to show consideration toward a woman for the first time when he responds to Sweet's generosity. The alternating actions suggest that Milkman is beginning to practice the reciprocity that his sister Lena had found lacking in him. He learns from her reciprocity in male and female relations.

Guitar is one of Morrison's most appealing male characters. He can't put his great energy and passion into mature love relationships; instead he turns them to hate. He is an artist without a constructive form, a medium. He stays ready to fly and can kill with equanimity, much more easily than he can love, because of his very lack of connections. His soul and intelligence finally shrink to only a cunning compulsion to stalk and murder. Guitar and Milkman are opposite sides of a single fabric, and Morrison constructs their friendship from the threads of male life—street fights, barbershop talk, pool hall banter, sexual conquest, adventure. In Guitar's view, the African-American man is the supreme marginal figure, silenced not only by whites, but undermined and unmanned even by African-American women. Guitar joins The Seven Days, which epitomizes patriarchal organization. The group is all male and does not permit its members to marry or to form permanent attachments with women. The unrecognized mission of the Seven Days seems to be the following: if white male violence works to keep African-American men from white women, then African-American men need to organize to ensure continued property rights in African-American women.

As Milkman's best friend, Guitar plays a complex role. He functions as a teacher as well as an enemy. He removed from the well-heeled world of Not Doctor Street, acts as Milkman's guide to the wilderness of Southside, where the African-American underclass live. The novel's opening underscores the importance Guitar will have as Milkman's guide and mentor. When Milkman's mother, goes into labor, Guitar was sent around to the emergency room to fetch help. Later at age seventeen, Guitar befriended the twelve-year-old Milkman, and from that time on, Guitar is always there for his young friend. As a teacher, Guitar pushes Milkman to recognize his weaknesses, his flawed priorities, and finally his identity. Guitar repeatedly reminds Milkman of his alienation and aimlessness, of his failure to commit himself to person or place, and he forces Milkman to acknowledge his boredom and inability to risk himself.

When Milkman began to doubt his father, his mother, himself. He told Guitar his father's story about Ruth and her father's corpse; Guitar advised him to "forget it." As to the origin of Milkman's name, Guitar remarks, "Niggers get their names the way they get everything else—the best way they can" (Morrison 1977: 88). "You think because he doesn't love you that you are worthless, "Guitar says to Milkman. "If he throws you out, then you are garbage. . . he can't value you more than you value yourself" (Morrison 1977: 305 – 306).

Milkman's father, Macon Dead, one of the few male characters in Morrison's work who imitates the dominants model of masculine power, is a quintessential self-made man. Orphaned and disinherited in his adolescence, he wheels and deals his way into his position as the richest black man in town. Debasing the intimate and productive connection to land enjoyed by Milkman's grandfather, Macon Dead conceives of ownership as acquisition and exploitation. Erotic love, so essential in bringing men and women together in Morrison's novels, is missing in the Deads' marriage.

Like all the members of the Macon Dead household, Macon is dead. "A dead man ain't no man. A dead man is a corpse. " (Morrison 1977: 101) At this point in his life, Milkman Dead is neither a man(exploiting all women with whom he comes into contact), nor a human being in general. He is both psychologically and emotionally dead. While he seems bombarded with images of flight and imbued with a sense of flying, he experiences feelings of flying blindly. Not knowing his past, he is unsure of the future: "Infinite possibilities and enormous responsibilities stretched out before him, but he was not prepared to take advantage of the former, or accept the burden of the latter. " Unconscious of the fact that responsibilities are an integral part of life, Milkman lives turn back. "His face reveals the confusion he feels, for" it was all very tentative", and" it lacked a coherence, a coming together of the features into a total self. " (Morrison 1977: 128)

Macon Dead, has lost this essential freedom; he has traded it for wealth under the mistaken belief that " money is freedom. . . The only real freedom there is. " (Morrison 1977: 101) Macon advises his son to" own things. And let the things you own other things. Then you'll own yourself and other people too. " (Morrison 1977: 103) But despite his thinking so, property does not elevate Macon, above other blacks or earn him respect from whites. In truth, blacks do not hold him in high esteem; they merely fear his ruthless exercise of power. A lifetime of acquiring property, collecting rents, and making deals has rendered Macon, a greedy, self-absorbed, unforgiving man who is incapable of showing love or receiving it. Hating his wife, Ruth, ignoring his daughters, Lena and First Corinthian, and disowning his sister, Pilate, are the sum of Macon's family connections. Family for Macon is just another category of personal wealth.

Macon, who dons the mask of exhibitionistic self-importance and prideful arrogance, teaches Milkman to fear and respect him. As an adolescent, Milkman expresses his inherited false pride through his posture and style of walking. The legacy that Macon hopes his son will inherit is the one built by power and property in order to move the sociopolitical boundaries so that the family will one day become integrated with white society. In the nation's ideology, material poverty became an indicator not of a social problem but of individual spiritual poverty. The effect of this ideology on Macon Dead is evident in the way in which he is ashamed of Pilate.

Macon's teachings are subverted from two directions—by his sister Pilate and by Milkman's friend Guitar—and their presence together seems to constitute a play on Sam Fathers. Both act as Milkman's guides to ostensibly different world pictures—Pilate, the part-Indian advocate of the rights of ghosts, and Guitar, the materialist who wishes to awaken Milkman to African American's real conditions of existence.

Song of Solomon focuses on the maternal transmission of shame and it is also concerned with the dangers of excessive mothering. It explores the black patriarchy through the figure of the stern, greedy, unloving Macon Dead. Macon terrorizes his wife and daughters in private, yet he indulges in proud public displays of his family. "First he displayed us, then he splayed us", the adult Lena remarks of Macon's treatment of her and her sister. "All our lives were like that: he would parade us like virgins through Babylon, then humiliate us like whores in Babylon" (Morrison 1977: 216)

Weak and pathetic as she is, Ruth finds subtle methods of objectifying the members of her family as well. She retaliates against her husband's cruelty by manipulating him. She remarks that her son has never been "a person to her". Before he was born, Milkman was "a wished-for bond between herself and Macon, something to hold them together and reinstate their sex lives". (Morrison 1977: 13). After she realizes that her husband will never again gratify her sexually, she uses Milkman to fulfill her yearnings by breast feeding him until he is old enough to talk, stand up, and wear knickers.

Similarly estranged from the community are Milkman's sisters, Lena and Corinthians, whose narrow lives result from their father's insistence that they keep apart from others to illustrate the family's superior status. The two sisters occupy their time in the pointless manufacture of artificial roses that Corinthians comes to view as the portent of "a smothering death". To escape this narrow existence, she gradually gives up her pretentions to being a "lady" and accepts Porter as her lover, a step down in terms of her parents' values but a passage from death to life in the logic of the novel.

Milkman's two elder sisters serve as twin status symbols for Macon to dress up and parade in the family car around other black people, almost all of a lower economic class than Macon. When not on parade in the public, they sit in their rooms and make roses out of red velvet. They are a true, bitter, virulent portrait of what happens to the sisters who are made subservient body-servants to a selfish, adored brother simply because he is male.

Macon's world is the material one, but he provides additional links to the past. Macon tells his son about Circe, the black woman servant whose employer, Butler, killed his father... Milkman's mother, Ruth, also provides information that he will understand only much later. She tells Milkman about his conception, about Pilate's early devotion to him, and about the sexual deprivation that Milkman eventually sees and how it "would affect her, hurt her in precisely the way it would affect and hurt him" (Morrison 1977: 303). His sister, Lena, is another teacher, confronting Milkman with his irresponsibility and selfishness, reminding him that he has been "using us, judging us: how we cook your food, how we keep your house" (Morrison 1977: 216). Her final condemnation, that he is a "sad, pitiful, stupid, selfish, hateful man", will serve him later when he realizes that "hating his parents, his sisters, seemed silly" (Morrison 1977: 218, 304).

Black female psychic health can be achieved without the cooperative participation of both females and males in its creation and nurturance no more than black male psychic can. Male participation helps to provide the novice female with a sense of balance between the "best of that which is female and the best that which is male" without which gendered and tribal health is, for Morrison, quite unlikely. Morrison's male epic does not represent a break with the female-centered concerns of works, but a bold extension of these concerns.

Solomon flies off, and Ryna, his wife, is left to take care of the children. Milkman and Hagar reenact this tragedy of abandonment. Hagar is constructed as a traditional dysphoric romantic heroine—a woman who makes the man the center of her life and thus feels an utter sense of loss and despair when her love relation fails. She is also presented as a potentially violent underclass woman. Having internalized hegemonic beauty standards, which link skin color and hair texture to class status and construct dark-skinned women as the racially inferior and stigmatized other, Hagar feels unworthy, dirty, spoiled, undesirable. When Milkman leaves, Hagar loses all capacity to think rationally, and she dead, as the euphemism goes, of a broken heart.

Hagar is bound for disappointment as the promises of cosmetic beauty are washed away. Morrison's heroic characters must resist; they must be transformed, not cosmetically, but internally by their own lives.

Relationships between sisters, female friends, mothers, and daughters are central in Morrison's novels, but there is also an enduring concern with the problem of heterosexual love. If the black community is to endure, men and women must survive together. Only male children coexist with powerful women who assume mythic dimensions in the masculine imagination.

Pilate is the other heroic character in *Song of Solomon*. Her journey to self-knowledge having been completed, she knows, from the beginning of the text, what Milkman discovers in the end, and as her name suggests, Pilate is Milkman's spiritual guide throughout his passage. During Milkman's infancy and even before, she shields him from Macon's angry attacks, and later, during Milkman's adolescence, she catalyzes his course of self-discovery. In her presence, at age twelve, he discovers a woman, who without property and social position, is taller and wiser than his father. That " was the first time in his life that [he] remembered being completely happy. " (Morrison1977: 175) Pilate's stories about her life on the arm, about her father's bravery, about her brother's love, and her refusal to adopt the meaningless rituals that occupy most people—these counter Macon's stories about conquest, ownership, and dominion.

Pilate Dead, Macon's younger sister, provides a marked contrast to her brother and his family. Like Macon, Pilate presides over a household which is predominantly female. But while Macon's love of property and money determines the nature of his relationships, Pilate's sheer disregard for status, occupation, hygiene, and manners enables her to affirm spiritual values such as compassion, respect, loyalty, and generosity.

If the Macon Deads seem barren and lifeless, Pilate's family bursts with energy and sensuality. Pilate, Reba, and Hagar engage ceaselessly in collective activity, erupting spontaneously into harmonious song. On his way to his own emotionally empty house one evening Macon Jr. peeks through the window of his sister's home in search of spiritual nourishment. He hears the three women sing one song, Pilate stirring the contents of a pot, Reba paring her toenails, and Hagar braiding her hair. Macon is comforted both by the soothing and unending motion of each character in the vignette and by the harmony and tranquility of the music they make together.

Pilate's house reflects her African heritage in other ways. Her house appears to her in-law Ruth as "an inn, a safe harbor", and "true to the palm oil that flowed in her veins," (Morrison1977: 150) Pilate offers both food and hospitality to all who enter. Even Macon, who deserted his sister, sees the house as a place of music, warmth, and caring, not realizing that he has destroyed the music in his own house. The two houses stand in stark contrast. In the Dead's house, built by Ruth's acerbic and bourgeois father, the women cower and Milkman is bored. Ruth suffers under Macon's rule, her creativity stunted, her flowers dying. The two daughters pine for lack of love and life, since no man in the community is good enough for Macon Dead's daughters. In contrast to this "dead" house, three generations' worth of women in Pilate's house can live and breathe and sing in harmony.

Pilate's role as conjurer is well documented throughout the book. Revealingly, she is also the one who attempts to rebuild her extended family as well as pass on the knowledge of her heritage to her nephew so that he can recover their roots. Much of the focus of generational continuity has centered on the mother-daughter relationship, so it is interesting, in light of this context, that Morrison chooses the son to make the search rather than any of the daughters of the novel. This choice may illustrate the dominant role the female ancestor plays in passing on cultural knowledge and values to both male and female children in the family. Pilate, in this case, also reflects practices in many West African cultures where the education of the children—until the boys' initiation—is done by the women.

Pilate alone teaches him the true meaning of flying without ever leaving the ground. Pilate is not the selfish flight of Solomon, who leaves everyone behind. When Milkman leaves Hagar, it is Pilate who locks him in her cellar and upon his return, forcing his dawning realization that Hagar is dead, that "it was his fault and Pilate knew it." His punishment by Pilate's reckoning is to carry with him "something that remained of the life he had taken." (Morrison 1977: 206) That evening Milkman returns home with a box of Hagar's hair as a healing reminder that with freedom comes responsibility.

Ancestral, mythic, free, Pilate embodies traits of character that give form to the major theme of Morrison's work: spiritual transcendence. Born without a navel, which evidences the common birth of one human from another, Pilate seems ageless, immortal. As a natural healer whose "compassion for troubled people" and "respect for other people's privacy" are her passport, she has no fear of life. Neither does she have the familiar terror of death: "she spoke often to the dead [and] ... knew there was nothing to fear. " (Morrison 1977: 176) At the end of life, Milkman wonders if there is another like Pilate. As ancestor Pilate bears a major share of the novel's work in passing on cultural knowledge to Milkman.

Dominating men and emotionally dependent women come in for harsh scrutiny. Her women are imperfect too, in their "smothering possessiveness. " Milkman rejects his mother and Hagar, the two women intent on owning him, but Pilate is a different sort. She flies and sings, though her flight is not the flight of male abandonment and her song is not of the female blues variety. Pilate reflects Morrison's fundamental ambivalence toward conventional gender scripts.

Milkman's quest is to learn to fly and to find his name—in his pursuit, then, he straddles the two roles of father and son. But it is his aunt Pilate who exemplifies the combination of self-invention and responsibility, symbolized when Milkman realizes at her death that "without ever leaving the ground, she could fly". (Morrison 1977: 340) As in many traditional male quests, Milkman seeks his origins through his paternal lineage. Pilate is, for Milkman, like the "black thread", "Milkman followed in her tracks" (Morrison 1977: 145). Milkman's quest has been guided by women. His search for Pilate's gold is what brings Milkman to Danville and it is Circe who tells him how to find the cave. Circe also tells Milkman the name of his paternal grandmother, learn the leg-end of his ancestors, and become reconnected to the motherline. The next two significant occurrences in Milkman's quest take the form of rites of initiation and are performed by men.

Pilate is a personification of Morrison's maternal standpoint; namely, that black women are ship and harbor, inn and trail. The fruits associated with Pilate—oranges, peaches, and grapes—composed as they are of both seed and juice, couple the feminine and masculine principles to convey the ancient properties of ship and harbor, inn and trail of Pilate's character. In *Song of Solomon*, Milkman's survival is made possible through Pilate's function of cultural bearer; she not only embodies, in her connection to motherline, the ancient properties, funk, and ancestral memory of her people, she also conveys these values to her people, through the stories she tells and the songs she sings.

Pilate's lack of attachment stems not from choice but from people's rejection of her as "something God never made" (Morrison 1977: 144). While her alterity isolates her from others, it also allows her to invent herself. She discards habits that are destructive or meaningless, and she focuses on what she deems necessary to life. Settling in the town where her brother lives, she founds another of the Morrisonian three-women households. In contrast to the deadening environment that her brother has created, Pilate's home offers Milkman a haven. Restful, though devoid of material amenities, sustaining even though barely subsisting, this household offers a vital alternative to the one that Macon's influence has made dead.

When Milkman disobeys his father's prohibitions and visits his aunt for the first time, he finds her to possess a beauty and fascination that confound his expectations. Rather than imitating received patterns of self or family, she originates her own models. In Pilate, Morrison imagines an alternative to the dominant ideals of femininity that prove so restrictive to her imitative women characters. Confounding stereotypes of female fragility, Pilate is as strong as any man.

Pilate is omnipresent in the novel, and many of her values and powers are passed on to her daughter and granddaughter. For all her powers, she is unable to bring her extended family back together as a force to confront racial oppression, nor is she able to save Hagar from the imposition of the white dominant culture's definition of beauty after Hagar and Milkman's incestuous relationship ends in disaster.

Milkman's true inheritance, black cultural identity and ancestry, is provided by the women and particularly his aunt, Pilate. Although the epigraph mentions only the male forefathers in the novel and the book is dedicated to "Daddy" Morrison creates a space in which the women may be recognized and may assume importance. In many respects, the women are outside the soulless material-oriented, patriarchal world in which the men—Macon Dead and Dr. Foster—are locked. She becomes quite literally Milkman's pilot or guiding force. She challenges his indifference and initiates him into the legacy. Pilate's perfect, soft-boiled eggs symbolize a balance of which Macon and herself seem separated spheres.

Historically, the political and physical experiences of settling and exploring a wilderness have required powers that have commonly been granted to men rather than women. However, in this respect, *Song of Solomon* casts women in a better light than the men: Macon Dead, Ruth's father and Milkman himself are selfish, uncaring people. Macon Dead is ruthless with delinquent tenants, wants to "own" people and worships wealth. Ruth's father is seen as a "miracle doctor" by whites, but, obsessed with caste, he does little for African-Americans. Milkman deserts Hagar and most of the men violate family bonds. It is some of the women in the novel who have, or stand a better chance of acquiring, the qualities and values necessary for establishing a true sense of community.

Evidently, Morrison reminds us that the man flying away leaves people behind, most often women and their children. Both Ryna, Solomon's wife, and Hagar, Milkman's spurned lover and cousin, cannot function after being left and basically die of broken hearts.

Although the protagonist is male, the novel reassesses the legacy of the forefathers from Pilate's—a daughter's—perspective. Morrison describes *Song of Solomon* as "a journey from stupidity to epiphany, of a man, a complete man." (Grewal 1998: 74) Crucial to this development is Milkman's learning to respect black women and to establish a relationship of reciprocity with them. Focusing on fathers and sons, the novel offers a different evaluation of the individualist, self-reliant model of male heroism celebrated in American society. Relying on a number of women, Milkman does not achieve selfhood on his own—he is coached by Pilate, loved by Ruth and Hagar, cared for by his sisters, guided by Circe, and healed by Sweet.

Women and children are essential to Milkman's achievement of flight—his freedom and literacy. The women are, in many ways, the sustenance and ground from which Solomon and Milkman leap—like the promised land, they contain the milk of the mothers and the honey of the lovers (embodied by Ruth and Sweet). Pilate acts as Milkman's pilot, a guide, a mentor, and a model of the desired balance of strength, wisdom, and love. With the interdependence of femininity and masculinity, Milkman achieves a successful journey to completeness.

References

[1] Bloom, Harold. *Modern Critical Interpretations of Song of Solomon* [C]. Philadelphia: Chelsea House Publishers, 1999.

[2] Bouson, J. Brooks. *Quiet As It's Kept* [M]. Albany: State University of New York Press, 2000.

[3] Furman, Jan. *Toni Morrison's Song of Solomon* [C]. Oxford: Oxford University Press, 2003.

[4] Gates, Henry Louis. *Toni Morrison——Critical Perspectives Past and Present* [C].

New York: Amistad Press, Inc. , 1993.

[5]Grewal, Gurleen. *Circles of Sorrow, Lines of Struggle* [M]. Baton Rouge: Louisiana State University Press, 1998.

[6]Harding, Wendy. *A World of Difference: An Inter-Cultural Study of Toni Morrison's Novels*[M]. Westport: Greenwood Press, 1994.

[7]McKay, Nellie Y. *Approaches to Teaching the Novels of Toni Morrison*[C]. New York: The Modern Language Association of America, 1997.

[8]Middleton, David L. *Toni Morrison's Fiction Contemporary Criticism*[C]. New York: Garland Publishing, Inc. , 1997.

[9]Morrison, Toni. *Song of Solomon*[M]. New York: Plume, 1977.

[10]O'Reilly, Andrea. *Toni Morrison and Motherhood: A Politics of the Heart*[M]. Albany: State University of New York Press, 2004.

[11]Peach, Linden. *Toni Morrison* [M]. Hampshire: Macmillan Press Ltd, 2000.

[12]Rigney, Barbara Hill. *The Voices of Toni Morrison* [M]. Columbus: Ohio State University Press, 1991.

James as an Evil Portrait Painter:
Evil in Henry James's *The Portrait of a Lady*[*]

Xu Sha^{**}

School of Foreign Languages, Yunnan University,

Kunming Yunnan

Abstract: Evil, the opposite of good, frequently appears as a major theme in literary works. Literary men of all times draw on this eternal theme repeatedly. Henry James's way of portraying evil is unique. It is not only in line with his American predecessors, but also focus on the harmful suffering of one person over another. This paper mainly discusses Henry James's sense of evil and its manifestations in one of his representative novels *The Portrait of a Lady*, and finally concludes that evil brings experience and intellectual maturity to the protagonists, maturing them through the encounter with the dark side of lives. Only through this process can they become intellectually mature, and have the confidence and courage to continue life.

Keywords: sense of evil; Henry James; *The Portrait of a Lady*; international theme

1. Henry James's Sense of Evil

As an American writer, Henry James's sense of evil is in line with his American predecessors. As a modern writer, however, his sense of evil is different.

When the early American writers started to present the eternal theme in their works, they found the gothic theme favorable to them. In *Rip Van Winkle* and *The Legend of Sleepy Hollow*, one could see how Washington Irving paid his homage to the

* 论文题目: 刍议亨利·詹姆斯的小说《一位女士的画像》中的罪恶。

** 作者简介: 徐莎(Xu Sha), 云南大学外国语学院讲师, 博士; 研究方向: 英语诗歌与诗学理论; 19 世纪英国文学。

thrilling and horrifying gothic tradition. Yet, this technique, borrowed from their British counterparts, satisfied little, for the newly founded land proved unable to provide such a literary atmosphere to back up a theme that needs the cultivation of a long history. In order to alter the awkward situation, Hawthorne then traced back the America's puritan past to invoke evil. In work like *The Scarlet Letter*, he explores the innermost heart of people and unfolds the latent evil inside every individual. For him, the most sinister evil is the abuse of the sanctity of human heart. Henry James, a literary man who lived two centuries later, would not accept the didactic means to unfold evil in his own time. Besides, as one of the most important figures in the era of literary realism, James's concerns are the embodiments of evil itself. This difference distinguishes Henry James from others. If we consider Hawthorne's works as "romance", and characters like Roger Chillingworth in *The Scarlet Letter* as "personified evil that is the special realm of American romance" (Freedman, 2000: 113), then James's villains, on the contrary, have an air of actuality, for they are not Satan like figures and they do not personify evil. They are motivated by common desires—pride, greed, revenge and so on. To put it in another way, they are not in a condition of entire depravity. They just submit to their innermost desires and unaware that these desires can be harmful to others.

Besides, Henry James's sense of evil, quite different from that of Hawthorne, does not exist beyond human relationship. "It is centered in the human soul and manifests itself in the harmful domination of one person over another" (Ward, 1961: 11 – 12). That is to say, James's evil originates in the individual's will and reflects itself by making others suffer. This is another difference that lies between Hawthorne and James—the difference of focus. What Hawthorne concerns is the evildoer, the villain himself. In his work like *The Scarlet Letter*, Arthur Dimmesdale is obsessed with his own guilt and depleted by his past unforgivable sin. His sin rarely has anything to do with others. While Henry James is by no means the same. What he tends to concentrate on is the victim's reaction to evil. In James's eyes, evil is not evil without the existence of its victim. Therefore, the protagonists in James's novels are always doomed to encounter some kind of experiences. These experiences—with the illusion or imagination at the beginning, through the process of exploration and falling, and finally with the rise or the spiritual enlightenment at the end—ultimately give the sin-against a sense of intellectual maturity. To put it more specifically, Henry James, not like his predecessors who dealt with the villainy alone, endows his characters with a self-consciousness, an intellect, and a wisdom after the encounter with real life, thus combining their imagination with a sense of experience. It is this sense of evil that defines Henry James as a writer in literary realism, for he adds into reality an existence of experience and knowledge.

In short, the evil that Henry James reveals is inside human mind rather than the outside. As far as this is concerned, James is in line with his American predecessors and contemporaries. However, James's evil is unique, of no repetition. It lies in the fact that his evil, the embodiments of a sin, does not exist beyond human relationship. It originates in the human soul and reveals its force by bringing sufferings to those who are not physically but emotionally and psychologically hurt.

2. Henry James's Sense of Evil and the International Theme Novels

Henry James's fame as a man of letters is largely built on a series of novels dealing with the encounter between Americans and Europeans. This theme—international marriages and American tourists in Europe—prevails repeatedly in his works. Although James might not be the first to write works with such a theme[①], there is no doubt that no one else has ever dealt with this theme in such an acute sense and reached such a height as he does. "Through his repeated use of the international theme he gave cultural and national embodiment to the oppositions of innocence and experience, self and society, and good and evil which provide the dramatic tensions in all his works" (Ward, 1961: 18). Indeed, the international theme offers Henry James a chance to explore the dazzling perfection and the sordid reality of his time.

Henry James's international theme is mainly concerned about the international marriages and Americans in Europe. However, it is far from that simple. The Americans have, in James's eyes, an instinctive love of freedom, a nature of innocence and a sense of morality. Yet they are not provided with access to experience and evil. When they are in Europe, the Americans are exposed to a reservoir of art, history, manners, as well as an evil indispensable from the decadent civilization they pursued. Therefore, the Americans react either too much or too little to it. For those who react too much, they, in order to accept the seemingly brilliant though otherwise decayed European manners, violate everything even their own instinctive merits to

---

① Henry James is often thought to be the inventor of the international theme novels. This idea is questioned and challenged by Oscar Cargill in his paper. "The First International Novel". *Modern Language Association*. Nol. 73. No. 4(Sep. 1958), pp. 418 – 425.

fulfill their desires. While for those who react not enough, they, pitifully influenced by their American pride and ignorance of the value of foreign experience, misfortunately fall into the "snares" already woven ahead of them.

2.1 The Innocent and Arrogant Victims

It is quite clear that the one who reacts not enough to the European experience are very likely to become the victim. On the one hand, the merits, namely the love of freedom, the nature of innocence, and the sense of morality, are the natural endowments possessed by the Americans. This is what James speaks highly of—the value of being an integral and Emersonian individual. On the other hand, however, the other side of the merits usually accompanies provincialism. The provincialism leads them to be narrow-minded and blind to experience and the European manners. This is what Henry James cannot bear, or at least looks down upon. Thus, when confronting with the Europeans manners, those Americans who retain much of their Americanism were often betrayed by the European experience, and finally become the victims.

2.2 Europeanized Americans: the Selfish and Shameless Evildoers

If the arrogant and ignorant Americans are merely targets of which James doesn't speak highly or even pities, then the Europeanized Americans are definitely those who are the agents of evil. The Europeans, with the consideration of respecting their own conventions, would, at least, be more restrained in treachery, and prohibit any overt grossness due to their aesthetic sense; the Europeanized Americans, however, influenced greatly by their belief of freedom and individualism, would put aside their unrighteousness and morality when self-interests are concerned. Consequently, if the Europeans' intrigue may have some codes of conduct in it though they appear as ridiculous and amoral, and then the Europeanized Americans' have no codes at all. In order to fulfill their desires, they are very likely to lose the native integrity and the moral sense. Therefore, they are the real evildoers in James's international themenovels.

2.3 The Significance of the Sense of Evil in Henry James's International Theme Novels

If Henry James only portrays the encounter of good and evil, of innocence and experience in his international theme novels, then we don't have to fatigue ourselves so much to discuss the meaning and significance of his works here. Besides, he will be Henry James no more. Behind the disparity between good and evil, there lies a more important issue to consider—the consequence of the encounter. To put it another way, what influence or result does the encounter of good and evil actually bring to both sides? Henry James believes that real knowledge is learned from experience. So, experience poses a comparatively important status in his literary career. In his critical essay "*The Art of the Novel*", he discussed experience in length:

"Experience is never limited and it is never complete; it is an immense sensibility... The power to guess the unseen from the seen, to trace the implication of things, to judge the whole piece by the pattern, the condition of feeling life, in general, so completely that you are well on your way to knowing any particular corner of it—this cluster of gifts may almost be said to constitute experience, and they occur in country and in town, and in the most differing stages of education. If experience consists of impressions, it may be said that impressions are experience, just as (have we not seen it?) they are the very air we breathe" (James, 1984: 52 – 53).

What Henry James tries to convey here in the lengthy and obscure essay is that experience is of great importance to the existence of people, especially to a writer. Moreover, experience can be acquired only from real life. In his opinion, the ideal life should be the combination of intrinsic virtue and learned experience. The intrinsic virtue, or the merits endowed to an individual, alone is not the desirable state of life, for it lacks the real knowledge. While life filled with learned experience is neither worth praising at all, for it requires the cultivation of intrinsic virtue and morality. Thus the one who loses nothing of his intrinsic virtue and remains his moral sense when coming across the setback of life, and who finally acquires the real knowledge of life through the painful experience is the real winner in the end. The victims in Henry James's international theme novels usually belong to this type. Though they expose their innocence to the tact evil, their ultimate consciousness and intellectual maturity finally define them as victors.

3. Evil in *The Portrait of a Lady*

The Portrait of a Lady is one of Henry James's renowned novels, and the representative of his international theme novels. This novel, told with James's inimitable poise, unfolds the genuine tragic story of Isabel Archer, an innocent American girl. The protagonist of this novel is, as Henry James tells us, endowed with candor, beauty, intelligence, an independent spirit and a marked enthusiasm for life. Hence she, like other American girls at that time, becomes quite popular among all her friends after her arrival in Europe from her native America. However, she turns down twice the proposals of an English Duke, Lord Warburton and a young man from her native country, Casper Goodwood, in order to experience life. An unexpected inheritance not only gives her freedom to do so, but also pulls her into a carefully woven "snare" as well. Despite all her natural advantages, she makes one disastrous mistake of judgment—she falls into the scheme of her long-time friend and mentor Mme. Merle and marries her lover Gilbert Osmond, an extremely selfish dilettante. The result is genuinely tragic. Isabel finally experiences the failure of her marriage and the death of her cousin Ralph Touchett who has been kind to her all the time.

Like other Henry James's international theme novels, *The Portrait of a Lady* also presents the victims and the sinners to its reader. However, the line between the two groups of people is not obvious. Each character in Henry James's novel is some kind of combination. Even the evildoer does not commit any real crimes. Yet, the suffering that the sinners bring to the sin-against not only matures them and fills their lives with precious life experience, but also purifies their own souls, thus giving them both the courage to go on.

3.1　Isabel: the Triumphant Victim

Like most American protagonists in Henry James's novels, Isabel comes to Europe with her creed of freedom and individualism, as well as her admiration and curiosity of the old Continent. We know from the novel that she is fond of knowledge, and reads many books. Besides, the *London Spectator*, the music of Gounod, the poetry of Browning, and the prose of George Eliot which were in fashion then at the Continent appeal to her much. In short, she is the admirer of the refined culture. Though deeply attracted, her knowledge and interests about the European culture are mainly from books. She has hardly any experience of life. Thus her eagerness to see life is as keen as her love for it. She is, just as what James said of her, "too young, too impatient to live, too unacquainted with pain" (James, 1996: 58).

In order to acquire the experience of life, Isabel, deeply influenced by her belief of freedom and individualism, thought that there is no harm in her wish not to tie herself. Just as Ralph says, "She'll please herself, of course; but she'll do so by studying human nature at close quarters and yet retaining her liberty, she has started on an exploring expedition" (James, 1996: 240). So, she turns down several times the proposals of her American admirer Caspar Goodwood, for she wants to see life. Marrying someone will definitely put an end to this journey, and shut all her accesses to experience. Therefore, Lord Warburton's proposal is, at least it seems to Isabel, an obstacle for her to experience life, for what Warburton represents is merely a system behind him. To accept his proposal means to accept the system, and to accept his social relationship which, in the eyes of Isabel, is a hinder for her to see life. Thus, when Lord Warburton propose to her, she felt, "a territorial, a political, a social magnate had conceived the design of drawing her into the system in which he rather invidiously lived and moved. A certain instinct, not imperious, but persuasive, told her to resist—murmured to her that virtually she had a system and an orbit of her own" (James, 1996: 98). In fact, What Isabel wants is to be herself, to represent herself, and to master her life rather than to become someone who could only be measured by the title or status that the society forcefully imposes upon her.

Her thoughts and ideas about being oneself make her become vulnerable, and even suffer the failure of her marriage and the betrayal of her long-time friend and mentor. Her knowledge of life is acquired, to some extent, through the sacrifice, or the loss of her previous keenness, boldness, dreams and illusions. In another word, her deepened consciousness and matured intelligence is the result of her painful failure.

Just like what J. A. Ward says, "when Isabel partakes of the tree of knowledge in the world of experience she is made forcefully aware of the presence of evil, but in a sense her earlier ambitions are fulfilled" (Ward, 1961: 47). Thus, the 42nd chapter of this novel secures the position of Isabel's famous retrospection of herself. In this chapter, Isabel sits in the still drawing-room, near the fire, and gives up to her meditation. She constantly feels, thinks, and weighs. She recalls her own past, and finally has an understanding of it. In just a few hours, she sees what is blind to her before. In the end, she has a deeper and more thorough understanding of those who surround her, and of her own life. She realizes that it was her imagination that enabled her to love Osmond. Brought up across the ocean in a land where freedom and value of one's life are much appreciated and cherished, Isabel would not subject to her husband's expectations and requirements. Though she could act in a harmonious relationship with him outside, inside she will never agree, for her strong moral identity and her belief in pure truth will not submit to, or carter to her husband's taste. She now admits—as James employs pages of the stream of consciousness to reveal her monologue—her encounter with hardship in life. From the beginning, Isabel always wishes to see life and to taste the flavor of it. Now, at the price of her failure in marriage, she eventually acquires the precious experience of life.

Isabel, though endowed with an instinct innocence and moral sense, is by no means offered any experience. When she travels to Europe, she is open to the civilization as well as the evil accompanied. Thus, it seems very likely for her to become the prey of other evildoers. Her final intellectual maturity in pain seems to reveal that though filled with dangers and pains, it is indispensable and very important for an innocent American to experience the pains that most people would suffer. Only through this process, can one turn from a victim to a victor; and can one succeed spiritually though otherwise fails.

3.2　Gilbert Osmond: the Selfish Evildoer

The name of Gilbert Osmond and Mme. Merle is, in terms of the novel or Henry James's novels as a whole, often connected with the notorious word "evil".

Indeed, the debut of Osmond is told by Mme. Merle who mentions that "he lives in Italy, that's all one can say about him or make of him... No career, no name, no position, no fortune, no past, no future, no anything" (James, 1996: 176). For Isabel, Osmond fits pretty well with her imagination, for he, unlike Caspar Goodwood and Lord Warburton who are restraint by the social status and title, is absolutely free from being involved in any system. Thus, our protagonist mistakenly considers this to be Osmond's great advantages. Yet, no one including Isabel will realize that this man, disguised by his good-humor, knowledgeable, tasteful and easy-to-live-with mask, is someone who would sacrifice everything around him to fulfill his ambitions and goals and ultimately bring sufferings and miseries to them. Though not clearly pointed out, Osmond, together with his one-time lover Mme. Merle, has been, from the very beginning, designed the scheme of marrying Isabel in order to get her money. If money is the solely concern, then Osmond in turn would not be Osmond, and he would only fall into the common money-hunters' type. Besides, it doesn't conform to Osmond's tact and "savoir-faire". Osmond, just as what Ralph says of him as the incarnation of taste, has an inclination for the pursuit of rarities, exquisiteness and arts. However, he does not collect them for their own sake. He "collects treasures for the sake of owning them and making it impossible for others to own them" (Ward, 1961: 52). It gives him an idea of being admired and well thought, as well as a sense of superiority. One can still recall the scene when he unexpectedly finds that the women whom he is going to marry had once declined the proposal of a Duke. He has no reasons not to consider this incident a perfect match for his idea. In his opinion, Lord Warburton is the fine sample of a British Duke of whom he conceives as exquisite and superior. And his marriage with a lady who had once turned down such a Duke would undoubtedly raise his own status and reputation. Moreover, it has an underlined meaning—Isabel has qualified herself as being a rare art in his collection of selected objects. He, Osmond, the collector of this collection, should certainly treat these objects at will, for they are his possessions. Among these objects, there is Isabel "whom he marries for money"; there is his daughter "whose love for Edward Rosier he suppresses"; and there is Mme. Merle "whom he uses as a piece of machinery to better his position" (Ward, 1961: 51). It is reasonable to state that Osmond is, indeed, an extremely selfish person, an egoist. Everything he does is to please himself, to let the world think well of himself, to involve others to agree that everyone is obsessed with himself, and to present himself as superior as possible in front of those who surround him. The only less vulgar thing he does is that except his motive that is as vulgar as the art itself, his means are by no means vulgar. No wonder Ralph says, "everything he did was pose— pose so subtly considered that if one were not on the lookout one mistook it for impulse" (James, 1996: 338).

3. 3　Mme. Merle: the Pitiful Evildoer

If Osmond lives for art, for rarities and for the exquisite, Mme. Merle then, lives definitely for society. Society to Mme. Merle is what art to Osmond. It exerts an overwhelming force to enslave its admirers and subjugate them to be his loyal followers who, like the chancellor of the old, would spare no efforts to contribute everything including their lives to their Majesty Mme. Merle, therefore, is such a faithful follower. She travels almost without a stop between the Continent and the island to guest in the house of a multitude of friends who willingly treat her as their intimate guest. She exists, just as what Isabel thinks of her, only in her relations with her fellows. It should be mentioned that it is Mme. Merle's social ability that makes her the most comfortable and amenable person to live with. Or at least, these are the merits that Isabel attributes to her when the young protagonist first saw her. Besides, Mme. Merle emits an aura of matured beauty. She never acts as being vulgarly good-natured or as being restlessly witty. She strikes people with her reposeful and confident manner which is from years of experience. Just as what Isabel says, "her nature had been too much overlaid by custom and her angles too much rubbed away. She had become too flexible, too useful, and was too ripe and too final. She was in a word too perfectly the social animal that man and woman are supposed to have been intended to be" (James, 1996: 171). For such a perfect figure, who would have thought that she would design a scheme to trap a constant admirer of herself, especially someone who adores her so much? When she is informed by Isabel's aunt that the lucky young lady has inherited a large sum of money, her seemingly docile yet otherwise fiery temperament starts to display itself. A plan of sacrificing Isabel for the benefit of her daughter comes into play. Not having anything to gain in this intrigue, she, however, helps Osmond in marrying Isabel even though he has dried up her tears and sucked up her souls, for she knows that the money will guarantee her daughter a dowry and a prominent husband. It is important to notice that she is not without conscience. In the end, she acknowledged her guilt and left for America. Actually, one could realize that Mme. Merle is, in some sense, a victim as well. Partaking the evil doing from the beginning to the end, yet she is merely a tool for Osmond to steady his position, fulfill his ambition, and realize his goal. So, she also suffers.

4. Conclusion

As a modern American writer, Henry James's sense of evil is unique. He inherits Hawthorne's tradition by adding into it some necessary changes. His sense of evil centers on the human soul and manifests itself in the harmful suffering of one person over another. The sense reflects itself mainly in his international theme novels in which James sent his innocent Americans abroad to encounter the European evil or experience. The protagonists in these novels, do not, obviously, commit any real crimes. However, evil consists of an important part in their life experiences. Evil purifies their soul and secures them a sense of reality.

The Portrait of a Lady, one of James's representative works, is such a fine example. With the encounter of evil, Isabel not only matures, but also obtains the real experience of life. It is the suffering which Osmond brings to her that fills her life with precious experience and, in the same breath, gives her courage to continue life—the reason why, at the end of the novel, Isabel returns.

In short, the significance of evil in Henry James's novels, especially in *The Portrait of a Lady*, lies in the fact that it brings experience to the protagonists, maturing the innocent and idealistic people through the encounter with the dark side of lives. Only through this process can they become intellectually mature, and have the confidence and courage to continue life. And this is, in my opinion, the lesson that

Henry James wishes to give to all our modern people.

References

[1] Cargill, Oscar. *The First International Novel* [J]. PMLA. Vol. 73. No. 4 (Sep. 1958),
pp. 418 – 425.

[2] Freedman, Jonathan. *The Cambridge Companion to Henry James* [C]. Cambridge:
Cambridge University Press, 1998.

[3] James, Henry. *Literary Criticism Vol. 1: Essays on Literature, American Writers,
English Writers* [M]. Ed. Leon Edel. New York: The Library of America, 1984.

[4] James, Henry. *The Portrait of a Lady* [M]. London: Wordsworth Editions
Limited, 1996.

[5] Ward, J. A. *The Imagination of Disaster: Evil in the Fiction of Henry James* [M].
Lincoln: University of Nebraska Press, 1961.

Robert Browning and the Philosophy of Imperfection

——With textual analysis of *The Last Ride Together* and *Adrea del Sarto* [*]

Xing Ling[**]

School of Foreign Languages, Yunnan University,

Kunming Yunnan

Abstract: This paper analyzes the Victorian poet, Robert Browning's philosophy of imperfection(as is concealed in most of his dramatic monologues), and the poet's special position brought by this philosophy in the history of literature. Two pieces of the dramatic monologues by Robert Browning *The Last Ride Together* and *Andrea del Sarto* are used to illustrate his philosophy, which is followed by a compare and contrast with other literary schools before and after Browning, namely, from Homer to the Romantics, and existentialist Camus. This paper holds that Robert Browning's philosophy of imperfection is quite significant in that it plays a transitional role in the change of ideology in the realm of literature.

Key words: Browning; dramatic monologue; imperfection; ideal; *Adrea del Sarto*

Introduction

The poetic style of Robert Browning of the Victorian Age has long been taken as barbaric, grotesque and unintelligible. Few readers manage to overcome the difficulties in reading through and comprehending his many poems, for Browning's choices of diction and subjects are so original and conspicuously at variance with his

---

* 论文题目：论勃朗宁的不完美哲学——基于对《最后一次同骑》和《安德烈·裁缝之子》文本分析。

** 作者简介：邢凌(Xing Ling)，云南大学外国语学院讲师，研究方向：英美文学；美学；哲学。

contemporaries whose stock in trade is a diluted Romanticism; and his deliberate adoption of the mechanism of dramatic monologue by all means increases the difficulties of reading, demanding the reader's strenuous efforts to figure out the relationships between the speaker and the implied interlocutor, the understanding of which is just the first step to get a hint for grasping the whole poem's intention. All the seemingly awkwardness is in fact Browning's greatness in disguise. His speculation as a philosopher and sensibility of the world's tendency urge him to produce *Paracelses*, *Sordello*, *La Saisiaz*, and many well-known pieces in *Men and Women*, *Dramatic Personae* and other collections. A labor demanding study of the deep level of Browning's poems reveals a surprising and long hidden fact that Browning indeed deserves a unique and important position in the development of literature. Great poets, say Homer, Dante. . . no matter how different their subjects and artistries are, have one thing in common, that is, they all yearn for an ideal world where perpetual happiness ends injustice and evil; similarly many philosophers strive after the absolute truth which would be able to explain both the natural world and the spiritual world, therefore, to provide an ultimate "order" and to realize all and all dreams of human kind. The ideal shares a spirit with Browning's conception of "perfection". But Browning, with the ultimate concern and aspiration to ideal in the bottom of his heart, shows a far more objective and practical attitude toward this life, and he is more engaged in the reality. He described life so vividly and profoundly that some critics compared him with Chaucer and Shakespeare. Besides, Browning summons the courage to tell in most of his pieces a poignant truth: imperfection pervades and will forever pervade. However, Browning never shows pessimism which is the characteristic of many modern poets and philosophers. Browning advocates the idea and practice of "noble failure", the glory for one who strives for dream and agonizes to do, and fails in doing. He denies all perfection in life because the attainment of perfection would become stagnation and death of the soul. Constant efforts and unattainment of the goal are frequently emphasized. To Browning, even the existence of the "evil" is positively welcome in the sense that it provides the raw material for processing the development of human soul which is of the utmost significance in his philosophy.

1. The Spirit of the Victorian Age and the birth of Browning's dramatic monologue

Darwin's publication *The Origin of Species* in 1859, along with many other scientific discoveries, brought drastic changes in ideology of the Victorian people. There arose a collision between their religious convictions and the rapid development of science and technology. Tennyson expressed those doubts in his *In Memoriam* "*I stretch lame hands of faith, and grope, and gather dust and chaff, and call to what I feel is lord of all, and faintly trust the larger hope*" (M. H. Abrams 1986: 1147 volume II). But Browning has a radical difference from all other poets of the nineteenth century and almost promptly and decisively changed from a subjective poet to an objective poet.

Browning was born on 7th May 1812 in Camberwell, one of the southeasten suburbs of London. Young Browning declared himself a follower of Shelly and started to read Keats and other Romantic poets. But his early attempts in poem writing were unsuccessful and brought forth mocks by some critics. They forced the poet to develop a literary form that suited him best and actually gave full swing to his genius, i. e. the dramatic monologue.

Browning did not invent the dramatic monologue, but he perfected a distinctive form of it. The requirements of the genre(not all of them observed in every Browning's monologue) call for a single speaker, addressing a silent listener or one whose words must be imagined, in a concrete situation that either represents a crisis in the speaker's life or brings out through the circumstantial setting his or her personality and values. The person portrayed often reveal more about themselves than they are aware of doing, and they sometimes touch on ideas Browning himself felt strongly about. Much of the fascination of the dramatic monologues arises from our sense of tension between different sides of the protagonist, between his or her values and Browning's, and between the characters' limited visions and implicit fuller visions of reality. The monologues make stringent demands on the reader, who is expected to know a good about history and special subjects(about statuary stone, for example, in *The Bishop Orders His Tomb*) and to have the mental acuity to piece out what is happening—not to mention sensing the psychological implications and appreciating the artistry.

It is safe to assume that dramatic monologue enabled Browning to best exemplify his talents as well as to play his interest in a vast room. His interest lay in interior, or psychological probing into souls under pressure, twisted minds and hearts, while careful dissection of motive and act are emphasized throughout Browning's literary life. Browning affirmed in the preface to *Sordello*, that his "... stress lay on the incidents in the development of a soul: little else is worth study. " (Norton B. Crowell 1972: 10) Usually his characters are set in concrete situations of the real but imperfect world, facing various problems in their lives, speaking out their psyches both consciously and unconsciously.

2. Browning's philosophy of imperfection shown in his poetry

In the year of 1855, nine years after his marriage life in Italy, Browning published his best-known and most popular work, *Men and Women*. It contained fifty-one poems, most of which are now to be found dispersed under other headings in complete editions of his works. In these works Browning brought the form of his poetry, i. e. the dramatic monologue, to its full maturity and portrayed a variety of speakers so vivid and impressionistic, such as *Andrea drea del Sarto*, *Fra Lippo Lippi*, *A Grammerian's Funeral*, *Bishop Blougram's Apolog*. Unquestionably, in these works we have the very flower of Browning's genius. As it is said, the distinguishing feature of these monologues is "the monologue brought to perfection. Such monologues as *Andrea del Sarto*, or *the Epistle of Karshish*, never have been, and probably never will be, surpassed, on their own ground, after their own order. " (Edward Berdoe 1891: 272)

Usually, Browning's dramatic monologue has three progressive levels leading to the overall understanding of the poem: the plot level, the psychological level and the philosophical level. Only when the reader manages to figure out the plot and comprehend the speaker's psychology, can he get a clue to the philosophical meaning which reveals something of Browning.

2. 1 Analysis of the philosophy of imperfection in *The Last Ride Together* and *Andrea del Sarto*

The story is simple in *The Last Ride Together*: The rejected lover earnestly asks his beloved to have a last ride with him. The request is accepted and he has the last ride together with her when the dusk falls. At the very beginning of the monologue, the rejected lover displays a manly self-restraint in accepting his beloved's refusal. He shows no wounded pride or indignation rather than the firm loyalty to the ideal. As he helps her to mount, there arises a momentary rapture in him and he begins to measure his achievement mentally in the riding. With all past hopes turn out to be impossible, the unrevealed bitterness of his heart can be imagined. In the dusk, there is a natural view of splendor: some western clouds carrying the brightness of the setting sun and rising evening star at once. At that moment, his soul—"a long-cramped scroll" is smoothed itself out, even his lover leans on his breast in joy and fear. Though she does not love him, he is neither angry with her nor annoyed that she fails to estimate him as highly as he estimates himself. He has the ideal in his heart; it shall be cherished as the occupant of his heart's throne for ever—of the ideal he, at least, can never be deprived. He will not question how he might have succeeded better had he said this or that, done this or the other. She might not only not have loved him, she might have hated. Rather, he reflects that all men strive, but few succeed. He begins to ponder life instead of his lost love only, and sees other regions in his mind: statesman, soldier, poet, musician, and sculptor. None of them can bridge the gap between ideal and realization, hope and fruition. Imperfection is the truth. Being aware of the truth, he contrasts the petty done with the vast undone.

> "What hand and brain went ever paired?
> What heart alike concened and dared?
> What will but fell the fleshly screen?
> What act proved all its thought"（飞白，汪晴 2013: 186）

And admits that he himself is a case illustrating the truth of imperfection in life: he hoped that she would love him, but what he achieves is ride together with her.

However, there is no shadow of despair over him; rather, he is in silent ecstasy when finds the ride itself so wonderful that even the dim-descried heaven is no better than it.

> "Earth being so good, would heaven seem best?
> Now, Heaven and she are beyond this ride"（飞白，汪晴 2013: 190）

It seems to him also that heaven is now, or the present joy eternalized. The monologue shows that his ideal of personal love is elevated to boundless aspiration for life and human love. In the riding, his soul gets advanced and becomes almost divine.

> "Who knows but the world may end tonight?"（飞白，汪晴 2013: 182）

If the unusual significance of the ride was suggested there, it becomes obvious at the end of the monologue that the force of the hour, the value of the quintessential moment are crucial factors in the development of the soul.

Impressed by the process of this development, the reader may find himself appreciating the personality of the speaker as well as in sympathy for him. Consequently, the philosophical meaning of the poem becomes quite self-evident. In brief, it includes the following two points:

First, man should have a noble ideal in life. Though in the imperfect world, his quest may be impossible and he may not achieve the goal, he nevertheless has his glory so long as he carries grace under pressure and failure. What's more, the higher his goal is, the more arduous his process of striving, and the greater progress his soul may get. Here is the theme running throughout Browning's poems: the meaning of it all. The reason for struggle, and the prize for the effort are in the process rather than in the end.

Secondly, the imperfection of earthly life is not dreadful but valuable. The speaker's monologue reveals the poetic vision of Browning: life is to be lived first, to be thought about second, and being transcends essence. It is the imperfect but real world provides room for man's ideal as well as joy and sorrow, success and failure which intensify life and make possible the development of his soul. It is for this reason that Browning always celebrates imperfection earnestly.

Browning develops this reasoning through the mind of Andrea in *Andrea del Sarto*. *Andrea del Sarto* appeared in volume two of *Men and Women* and is perhaps the most celebrated among Browning's dramatic monologues. It is a poem which lies very close indeed to the center of Browning's philosophy of imperfection, combining his view of art career, love, and marriage. It best exemplifies Browning's poetic ability to interpret life, at the same time reveals Browning's spirit, his vigor, energy and ideal of life. Before we look into *Andrea del Sarto* the poem, we had better first have a knowledge about Andrea del Sarto (1487 – 1531) the man. He was a contemporary of Raphael (1483 – 1520) and Michelangelo (1475 – 1564) and was called "the faultless painter". His *Nativity of the B. V. Mary* is a grand fresco, the characteristics are noble and dignified, and draped in the magnificent taste which distinguished Andrea. Those who have roamed the galleries in Italy might find Andrea's many paintings conspicuously lacking in soul, demonstrating the fatal consequences of over adherence to photographic realism, the excellence of his productions comes as a surprise.

Andrea was a middle-class artist, with no great aspirations to fame, but with considerable taste and great powers of execution. He loved social preeminence and finally fell in love with a socialite, Lucrezia del Fede, wife of a hatter named Carlo Reeanati, who conveniently died, permitting the pair to regularize the liaison. Lucrezia, according to Vasari, was shallow and faithless—but surpassingly beautiful. In 1518, Andrea was invited to visit the French court at the invitation of Francis I. Leaving his wife at Florence, Andrea went to Fontainebleau, where he was royally entertained and handsomely remunerated for his artistic service. Upon the request of his restless wife to return to Italy, he obtained leave from the king and departed, carrying with him a substantial treasure entrusted to him by Francis for the purchase of art treasures which would adorn the royal gallery. Perhaps at the instigation of his wife—certainly to gain favor in her eyes—Andrea spent the king's money and some of his own as well in building a house in Florence Although he lost the favor of the beneficent king and lived in fear for his life thereafter, Andrea suffered no direct reprisal at the royal hand. Andrea spent the remaining years of his life in Florence and died at forty-three of plague, which was then rampant, on January 22, 1531. His wife, for whom he had sacrificed his honor and much of his artistic career as well, failed to tend him in his illness, fearing the pestilence, and she survived her husband for forty years. He was buried unceremoniously in the church of Servi. It was generally agreed that he lacked invention notwithstanding his great technical skill. He had no inward impulse toward the high and noble: he was a man without fervor and had no enthusiasm for the true and good. It is said that Michelangelo once remarked that if he had attempted greater things he might have rivaled Raphael, but Andrea was not a man for the mountain-top—the plains sufficed for him.

Andrea del Sarto the poem is a "translation" from the self portrait of Andrea and his wife Lucrezia. John Kenyon, Mrs. Browning's cousin requested that Browning supply him with a copy of the picture of Andrea and his wife Lucrezia in the Pitti palace, Browning, apparently being unable to comply with the request, wrote the poem instead, hence framed his greatest and unique art-poem. Browning, on the bare historical facts, as recorded by Vasari in his life of Andrea del Sarto, tries to read from the self-portrait the painter's complicated feeling, and to find the answer why "Faultless but soulless" is the verdict of art critics on Andrea's works.

The dramatic monologue happens in the autumn of 1525, five years after the death of Raphael ("Yonder's a work now, of that famous youth/ the Urbinate who died five years ago. ") (飞白, 汪晴, 2013: 204), when Andrea's golden time has gone. One evening, after a quarrel, Andrea and his wife sit before the window of his painting room in Florence. Looking out at Fiesole at dusk. Andrea tries to talk with his wife while the wife is impatient and indifferent. So, the whole monologue is a one-sided talk revealing Andrea's complex and tortured soul.

Andrea is the "Faultless Painter," with the sharp eye of an artist for beauty, he aspires for perfection in every detail. In order to please his beautiful wife, Lucrezia, he makes himself a painting-machine for her to make money

> "I'll work then for your friend 's friend, never fear
>
> Treat his own subject after his own way, fix his own time, accept too his own price,
>
> And shut the money into this small hand
>
> When next it takes mine Will it? Tenderly?" (飞白，汪晴 2013：196)

For Andrea, Lucrezia, the surpassingly beautiful woman, is the embodiment of perfection. He even couldn't bear her pierced ear lobs, the solitary spots on the white radiance of her beauty. So is with his paintings. He himself is the "Faultless Painter", who has reached the heaven of technical perfection. When he sees other painter's works, namely, Raphael's, he cannot bear the wrongly put arm and attempts to alter it several times.

Then, what kind of situation does "perfection" bring Andrea? Andrea's inner world changes in this monologue, from seemingly satisfaction to obvious sense of lost, from self-deception to self-exploration, his heavily-coasted sick soul is tearing open layer after layer. The reader thus finds himself is getting more and more involved in Andrea's self-introspection, and the initial attitude of a simple disparagement changes into a general sympathy and deep speculation of his own life.

Roughly, Andrea's psychology in the monologue experiences four stages:

The first stage is at the beginning of the monologue. The weary painter bribes his wife to sit with him for a while at the window of his painting-room, looking at "the yonder sober pleasant Fiesole", with the company of the "serpentining beauty" by his side, though she is seemingly absent-minded, Andrea gets very much pleased and excited. He just couldn't help remembering people's praise for his painting and boasting his talent proudly:

> "Behold Madonna, I am bold to say
>
> I can do with my pencil what I know,
>
> What I see, what at the bottom of my heart
>
> I wish for, if ever I wish so deep—
>
> Do easily, too—when I say perfectly
>
> I do not boast, perhaps: yourself are judge,

......

at any rate this easy, all of it,

No sketches first, no studies, that's long past—"（飞白，汪晴 2013：200）

It is a big irony for Andrea to ask his wife, Lucrezia, who neither understands nor cares to understand about his art, to judge his painting, since Lucrezia, the model for his "Madonna", is likely to be a biased judge and sing high praise for it because of her sheer vanity. Here, a scrupulous reader will wonder to what degree could he trust the painter's boast. Indeed, when Andrea says he can do easily what many dreams of others', he knows deeply in his heart that truly successful art works should be the combination of both technique and ideal. His success is an easy and fake one. Then a cool question is raised:

"—Dream? Strive to do, and agonize to do

And fail in doing. "（飞白，汪晴 2013：200）

This voice belongs more to Browning the poet than to Andrea the painter. There is no more perfect statement in Browning of the essence of success than this, not failure. The essence of success to Browning lies in these lines: the dream of illimitable growth in artistic vision and power, the struggle to attain the ever-receding heights, and-most important-the failure to attain the vision of dream. This is Browning's concept of success, for "the prize is in the process." This truth lies deep in the heart of Andrea like a sickness.

Then comes the second stage of Andrea's psychology. While realizing this, Andrea's self-satisfaction and proud turns into a gloomy sense of lost. He ruefully admits there is a "truer light" in the works of his rivals whose blundering efforts rush them onward to the supreme. His pride of technical dexterity is in fact a shame demonstrating the lack of soul. Their works may drop downward, but in contrast they themselves rise to heaven; his works rise toward heaven—perfection—but he sits in the dust. They are volatile, alive; their blood boils at a word of praise or blame, but he has abdicated from life, and is impervious to praise or blame either.

"Well, less is more, Lucrezia! I am judged.

There burns a truer light of God in them,

In their vexed, beating, stuffed and stopped-up brain,

Heart, or what'er else, than goes on to prompt

This low-pulsed forthright craftsman's hand of mine. "（飞白，汪晴 2013: 202）

While referring himself as a craftsman, he knows exactly what he can do and how it will turn out—a mark of dead perfection:

> "All is silver-gray
> Placid and perfect with my art: the worse!"（飞白，汪晴 2013: 204）

Andrea the artist was not born without aspiration. On the contrary, he is so infatuated with Lucrezia who is a human personality in the most dazzling body that all his enthusiasm and energy are expended on courting and pleasing this serpentining beauty. However, her shallowness disperses any possibility of her to reward Andrea with inspiration or encouragement.

Recognizing his now fractured, imperfect spirit, Andrea cries for Lucrezia to supply the missing half of his soul needed to provide his wholeness:

> "Had I been two, another and myself,
> our head would have overlooked the world!"（飞白，汪晴 2013: 204）

On the impulse, this yearning instantly changes into reproaching:

> "But all the play the insight and the stretch—
> Out of me! Out of me! And wherefore out?
> Had you enjoined them on me, given me soul,
> We might have risen to Rafael, I and you!"（飞白，汪晴 2013: 204）

If in this indignation a wreck of manhood is remained with Andrea, it slips away even faster than when it comes. For at these unusually direct words of recrimination, Lucrezia, it may be safely assumed, bridles in anger. The pathetic painter, straightway frightened and abused, utters words that form a singular contrast with his foregoing sentiment:

> "Nay love, you did give all I asked. I think—
> More than I merit, yes, by many times. "（飞白，汪晴 2013: 204）

This timely modification of his previous words may work well in calming Lucrezia down, thus, Andrea dares to finish his illusion:

"But had you—oh, with the same perfect brow,

And perfect eyes, and more than perfect mouth,

And the low voice my soul hears, as a bird.

The fowler's pipe, and follows to the snare—

Had you, with these the same, but brought a mind!"（飞白，汪晴
2013：204，206）

In the word "perfect" used thrice, the reader may get a revelation in the poem to attain
is to lose.

Knowing clearly the impossibility of his request that Lucrezia supply him with
spiritual power, Andrea just couldn't sustain this illusion any more and his psychology
reaches the third stage. So, fancy for a bright future turns into nostalgia of good old
days in France. The glorious days at Fontainebleau, with the King's golden look and
his golden chain and the gold that filled his life, should have promised him a
successful career had he not come back on the call of the restless Lucrezia. At
Fontainebleau, he made the irrevocable and fatal decision, from where there is no
returning. What's more, he followed what Lucrezia prompted him to steal he King's
gold and built their house to be gay with, therefore, to live in fear and with
shame. The painful contrast between the golden days at Fontainebleau and the present
ashen-gray desolation makes him lament：

"And I'm the weak-eyed bat no sun should tempt.

Out of the grange whose four walls make his world. "（飞白，汪晴，
2013：208）

To console himself, Andrea likes to fancy that he gave up all for love, like Antony,
who cast the world aside for Cleopatra with a noble gesture："You called me, and I
came home to your heart. " But this is an ingenious fiction for he never came home to
her heart at all. If he ever fancied that he possessed her heart, time disabused him of
his error. When he requests permission to "let my hands frame your face in your hair's
gold", he utters the greatest forlorn wish of his life："You beautiful Lucrezia that are
mine. " Of all the things, he aspires to or wishes for, nothing is so little his as
Lucrezia.

Throughout the poem there are signs of his ennui, a creeping enervation and
despair, the result of endless frustration and failure. In art Andrea has set his sights
low to accommodate Lucrezia's avarice and in so doing has gained the reputation of

being "the faultless painter" and in love he has done much the same thing. To him Lucrezia represents perfection of body, perhaps a perfection that should remain inviolate, virginal. One is tantalized by the degree of Andrea's syndrome: How far does he carry the belief that perfection—even in things mechanical or physical—is a sufficient substitute for an imperfect but alive, searching, growing spirit?

In the forth stage, Andrea couldn't help complaining for his tragedy. His complaints first go to God who leads his fate and fetters him so fast, next to Lucrezia who exhausts his zeal and ruins his artistic pursuit, but finally he ruefully admits that "incentives come from the soul's self." Indeed. if he cannot succeed, he has also deliberately chosen it. Granting another chance in the next life, he will again be unable to narrow the distance that separates him and Raphael, Angelo, because he will still choose Lurcezia:

> "In Heaven, perhaps, new chance, one more chance—
> Four great walls in the New Jerusalem
> Meted on each side by the angel's reed,
> For Leonard, Rafael, Angelo and me
> To cover—the three first without a wife,
> While I have mine! So—still they overcome
> Because there's still Lucrezia, —as I choose. " (飞白, 汪晴 2013: 216)

This is his own predict of his future, a hopeless future. In a very real sense, Andrea is aware that his obstinate chase of perfection is stupid enough to be fruitless. For as he perceives in the monologue:

> "In this world, who can do a thing, will not—
> And who would do it, cannot, I perceive. . .
> . . . And thus we half-men struggle. At the end. " (飞白, 汪晴 2013: 206)

Such is life, imperfect as it is. No matter what your choice is, there is always something missing, something needing your strenuous efforts to reach.

2. 2 Browning's view of life and his understanding of the philosophy of imperfection

Here is Browning's life long assertion in the monologue:

"Ah. but a man's reach should exceed his grasp,

Or what 's Heaven for?" (飞白，汪晴 2013：202，204)

Browning insists on the nobility of high aims, even if unattainable. To him, a man who is living as he should be, doing his best to use his powers in a world that offers no possibility of absolute attainment, will be distinguished by his activeness and resilience. Holding this conception of a "glorious failure", Browning feels coolly toward the man who aspires only to what he was certain he could achieve. Andrea is such a man who relinquishes his noble ideal and degrades himself to be a safe winner. In doing so, he shuts out the trials and dangers of life and life's opportunities of growth and fulfillment as well. What his title "the Faultless Painter" and his Lucrezia, the paragon of beauty bring him are frustration and stagnation of soul rather than any real sense of achievements. Browning never conceals his denial of the attainment of "perfection". To Browning, who held that in life all perfection is denied, that to be perfect is the hallmark of easy and ignoble aspirations, Andrea is the surest indication of failure, for absolute attainment is stagnation and death of the soul. Only through endless growth and struggle toward unattainable goals can man achieve success.

There are some differences between the two heroes in *The Last Ride Together* and *Andrea del Sarto*. The former, a loser of love as he is, is not desperate or disheartened at all, but loyally and royally keeps his ideal deep him. In the process of his examination on life, he gets the clue of the truth of imperfection and finds felicity of his actual circumstances. The latter, a seemingly winner, suffers a fractured spirit that is close to schizophrenic brought by self-constructed situation which is of "perfection" achieved by lowering his aim in life and career. He lives in gray and finds no hope for the future.

Browning's objective presentations of the rejected lover and Andrea are really infecting enough to promote one's recognition of the imperfection of life and evoke the aspiration to a life not for absolute attainment but for constant striving. One may consciously and naturally judge the rejected lover a glorious failure, and Andrea a shameful winner, at the same time comprehend that Browning's philosophy of imperfection is not for comforting but for encouraging as he sees human life is imperfect, the qualities which make up this world are not all comforting. Far from taking shelter from life, he has not even his back to the wall; he stands forward with life all around him. He flings his mind wide to it and absorbs it, delighted with its staring colors, fascinated by its grotesque shapes and contrasts. Browning is completely engaged in the battle of life and urges "Let a man contend to the uttermost/ For his life's set prize, be it what it will!" (飞白, 汪晴 2013: 176)

There is a group of Browning's poems dedicating to encouraging people to fight against the evil, to overcome the obstacles in the way of life, to make constant efforts for progress but not absolute attainment, to name a few: *Love in a Life*, *How They Brought the Good News from Ghent to Aix*, *A Grammarian 's Funeral*... these are all poems that are designed to bring home to the reader the power and hope of the real and imperfect life.

3. Browning's philosophy of imperfection as a transition in the history of literature

In order to get a full view and correct understanding of the uniqueness of Browning's philosophy of imperfection, its special position in the development of literary trends, and its profound influence to modernism, let us now have a brief review of the representation of perfection or idealism, which can be regarded as enjoying the same essence with Browning's conception of perfection, in the legacy of preceding Western literature. When poetry got its embryo in the rites of religions, man has begun using it to carry dreams and express his mysterious feelings.

First, let us have a look at Homer's epics. They seem to embody the spirit of an age of ancient heroes, who lived earnestly for honor and dream, fought nobly in fire and war. In Homer's epic world gods and human lived together. The gods were seen as behaving very much like mortal humans and with all the foibles of humans. They descended frequently from Mount Olympus where all gods lived, and involved themselves in human affairs, or created disturbances. The gods had the superhuman strength and immortality both of which were dreamt of by mortals. At the same time, many heroes in the epics were recorded as divine descendants, for example, Achilles, whose mother was the sea-goddess, Thetis. Obviously, there was in the epics an obliteration of the definite division between gods and men. This homogeneity brought a lighter tone to the narration of the arduous life and cruel heroic experiences, thus, the heroic ideal no longer seemed to be a dream remote. While manifesting this romantic aspect of the heroic ideal, Homer's epics showed a naive hue of it as well.

The rise of Christianity created distinctive political and cultural forms. Christian faith generally became the dominant power affecting the spiritual world. Dante's *Divine Comedy* was a product under the influence of Christianity. It was an account of a privileged journey taken by Dante the character(who should be distinguished from the Dante who wrote the poem). He traveled the three worlds of afterlife: Inferno, Purgatory and Paradise. It was called a comedy mainly because its movement was from sadness to joy, expressing Dante's desire for the ideal world in a vicious, corrupt and benighted age. In the *Comedy*, descriptions of punishment and beatitude were combined with comments on earthly life through the journey. The journey was a pilgrimage of Dante's soul into perfection and made Dante's belief confirmed that the perfect afterlife was there waiting for those who could get the way. To Dante, all of the three worlds of afterlife existed in reality. When the moment of death occurred and God's judgment made, one of the three worlds, to which one belonged, would have its vestibule open to him. Salvation and damnation depended on one's soul. One could make the perfect afterlife almost certain by living this life under the guidance of human reason and Christian faith.

We can see that Dante's ideal was in afterlife and the Christian faith was a prerequisite. While during the Renaissance whose essence was humanism, idealism took on an entirely new look. Humanism sprang from the endeavor to restore a reverence for the antique authors and is frequently taken as the beginning of the Renaissance on its conscious, intellectual side, for the Greek and Roman civilization was based on such a conception that man was the measure of all things. Through the new learning, humanists not only saw the arts of splendor and enlightenment, but the human values represented in the works. In the medieval society, people as individuals were largely subordinated to the feudalism rule without any freedom or independence, and in medieval theology, people's relationships to the world about them were largely reduced to a problem of adapting to or avoiding the circumstances of earthly life in an effort to prepare their souls for a future life. But Renaissance humanists found in the classical works a justification to exalt human nature and came to see that human beings were glorious creatures capable of individual development in the direction of perfection, and that the world they inhabited was to question, explore, and enjoy. Thus, by emphasizing the dignity of human beings and the importance of present life, they voiced their beliefs that man did not only have the right to enjoy the beauty of this life, but had the ability to perfect himself and to perform wonders. One typical illustration of humanist's idea is Hamlets monologue: "What a piece of work is man! How noble in reason! How infinite in faculties! How like a god! The Beauty of the world! The paragon of animals. "(G. Blackmore Evans 1974: 1156)

The Enlightenment Movement was a furtherance of the Renaissance. Its purpose was to enlighten the whole world with the light of modern philosophy and artistic ideas. The en-lighteners celebrated reason or rationality, equality and science. They held that rationality or reason should be the only, the final cause of any human thought and activities. They called for a reference to order, reason and rules. They believed that when reason served as the yardstick for the measurement of all human activities and relations, every superstition, injustice and oppression was to yield place to "eternal truth", "eternal justice" and "natural equality". In his *An Essay on Man*, Alexander Pope states the en-lighteners' view that man is in the process toward "perfection":

"Then say not man's imperfect, Heaven in fault;

Say rather, man's as perfect as he ought:

His knowledge measured to his state and place,

His time a moment, and a point his space. " (M. H. Abrams 1986: 2265, 2266 Volume I)

The en-lighteners of the eighteenth century predicated that a harmonious society of ideal would soon be established once the feudal one was destroyed. However, this was far from the truth. Take England as an example: With the British Industrial Revolution coming into its full swing, the capitalist class came to dominate not only the means of production, but also trade and world market. Though England had increased its wealth by several times, it was only the rich who owned this wealth; the majority of the people were still poor, or even poorer. As a result of the cruel economic exploitation and desperation, there were frequent large-scale worker disturbances. Here Romantic Movement began in such a turbulent social situation. The Romantics felt that the society denied people their essential human needs. So under the influence of the leading romantic thinkers like Kant and the post-Kantians, they demonstrated a strong reaction against the dominant modes of thinking of the 18th century writers and philosophers. Romanticism actually constitutes a change of attention from the outer world of social civilization to the inner world of the human spirit. It places the individual at the center of art, making literature most valuable as an expression of his or her unique feelings and particular attitudes, and valuing its accuracy in portraying the individual's experiences. Although Romantics were often mutually unsympathetic and seems openly at war and their themes and styles of their poetry were different, they were united in the sense of the poet himself as the most important element of his art. They had a belief in the supreme importance of the individual and hence in the primacy of the personal will and intuition over the dictates of external authority. The belief was what Shelley said that they were "the unacknowledged legislators of mankind." As Wordsworth defines poetry as "the spontaneous overflow of powerful feelings, which originates in emotion recollected in tranquility"（张伯香，1998：166）, the Romantic poets poured energy to show in their poems the inner world of their feelings, emotions and imaginations from where there arose respectively their highest ideals. The Romantics' ideal is in the exaltation of their individual spirit. In this sense, Romanticism is itself idealism as well as the loudest song for idealism in the history of literature.

So, it is evident that idealism had always been a constant theme in different stages of literary history before Browning's time. The aspiration to the perfect state of man is at no time frittered away. It is from this literary tradition that Browning shows a different color. Browning is surely an idealist in the sense that he earnestly advocates the advance toward one's noble ideal and the development toward perfection of one's soul. But his idealistic creed is different from those of his predecessor of or contemporaries in that, to him, "perfection" is the ideal to be strived for, not to be realized. "Perfection" is more of the nominal than of the factual in Browning's case, it is, in the essence, but the traction to carry the process of this life. His philosophy of imperfection proves him to be a poet who is preoccupied with the concern for the real world of men and women. Browning comprehended the imperfect nature of life and saw its desirability simultaneously. Facing the imperfect life, Browning never took refuge in religion or anything else. He held that man should feel inspired and impelled rather than deflated in the process of constant striving and progressing. To Browning, there could be achievement even in defeat. A good balance between reality and spirit, between the secular life and lofty aim occurs here in Browning.

Browning's profound understanding of the imperfect world was inherited but carried further on the way by modern literature of the 20th century.

Modern literature affirms "ennui", and "absurdity", an existential state void of meaning, which seems to be the disillusion from idealism and surrender to imperfection. The balance in Browning's philosophy is lost.

Albert Camus, the typical absurdist, published his essay *The Myth of Sisyphus* in 1942, which brought him international fame. It explores the concept of absurdism, and displays Camus's concern about the understanding of the human condition, showing the changes that occur in man's perception of himself, his life, and his world as the individual process of existence runs its course. *The Myth of Sisyphus* is a clear statement of the idea of absurdity in which a vestige of Browning's spirit could be discovered. For Camus, life, like Sisyphus's task, is senseless. One must recognize that life is "absurd", that is, irrational and meaningless and then surmount this condition. Sisyphus is the absurd hero who takes personal fate as inevitable. The absurd man says yes to this sterile world and henceforth makes unceasing efforts in the endless struggle in life. He lives in the absurd, without hope, and without resignation either. If he has any "passion", it is not for any "ideal" in life, but for the awaiting death ahead of him, and this fascination liberates him to grasp the whole of his life as a process completed in itself. Sisyphus triumphs over his fate by accepting its inherent meaninglessness. We could not deny that there is a grace in the absurd hero, which is somewhat like the dignity displayed by the lost lover in Browning's *The Last Ride Together*. The difference is that the rejected lover still has his world and even a bigger world after his contemplation in the last ride, while Sisyphus would not look at the world around him because he understands it as absurd first and foremost.

Conclusion

Robert Browning, the Victorian poet, is a poet of great originality. Both the form of his poetry, i. e. dramatic monologue, and his philosophy of imperfection help to earn him a special position in the history of literature. Browning cares little more than man and this world. He has a firm denial of perfection or the ideal world, which can be easily observed in most of his poems. Browning treasures the enjoyable chances provided by the imperfect world for the soul's development, and thinks that the attainment of perfection means stagnation and is beyond this world. Facing up challenges from life, he nevertheless pours all his love and passion to this world. He is a lover of as well as a fighter against life. Browning's poems are not meant to entertain the readers with the usual acoustic and visual pleasures: they are supposed to keep them alert and thoughtful, and bring them hope and power for life. His philosophy of imperfection shows a cleavage with the literary tradition and anticipated the literary tendency toward modernism. It is this transitional function that much explains Browning's greatness and uniqueness.

References

[1]飞白, 汪晴译. 勃朗宁诗选[M]. 北京: 外语教学与研究出版社, 2013.

[2] 张伯香. 英美文学选读[M]. 北京：外语教学与研究出版社，1998.

[3] Edward Berdoe. *The Browning Cyclopaedia——A Guide to the Study of the Works of Robert Browning*[M]. London：George Allen Unwin Ltd, 1891.

[4] Norton B. Crowell. *A Reader's Guide to Robert Browning* [M]. Albuguerque：University of New Mexico Press, 1972.

[5] G. Blackmore Evans. *The Riverside Shakespeare volume II*[M]. Boston：Houghton Mifflin Company, 1974.

[6] M. H. Abrams. *The Norton Anthology of English Literature volume I* [M]. New York：Norton & Company, Inc. , 1986.

[7] M. H. Abrams. *The Norton Anthology of English Literature volume II* [M]. New York：Norton & Company, Inc. , 1986.

An Analysis of W. B. Yeats' *The Celtic Twilight* From An Ecocritical Perspective*

Yang Mi, Liu Yuezhi**

School of Foreign Languages, Yunnan University,

Kunming Yunnan

Abstract: William Butler Yeats is regarded as one of the greatest Irish poets in the 20th century. His great creativity in prose writing, which has long been neglected, also worth a further study. *The Celtic Twilight*, published in 1893, is a representative prose collection of Yeats. The fairy tales, the beautiful natural landscape, and the mysterious fantasy world reflected by Yeats in the book convey his love for nature. In order to explore Yeats' insight into the relationship between human beings and nature, the focus of this study lies in non-anthropocentrism from an ecocritical perspective. It is studied through the following aspects: firstly, nature is depicted as a beautiful and peaceful harbor for human beings to escape from annoyances in their daily lives; secondly, the spirits are personified to have human skills, characteristics and emotions; thirdly, most human behaviors in the book show the author's awareness of non-anthropocentrism. At present, with the deterioration of the natural environment, the awareness of ecological protection is to be increased. Thus, an analysis of *The Celtic Twilight* from an ecocritical perspective is carried out to help readers review and understand Yeats' prose and have a reevaluation of his avant-garde ecological ideas.

Key Words: Yeats' prose; non-anthropocentrism; ecocriticism

William Butler Yeats, one of the most famous Irish poets of the 20th century,

---

 * 论文题目: 生态批评视角下的《凯尔特的薄暮》。

** 作者简介: 杨汨(Yang Mi), 云南大学外国语学院副教授, 研究方向: 英美文学; 刘悦之(Liu Yuezhi), 云南大学外国语学院 2014 级本科生, 研究方向: 英美文学。

was awarded the Nobel Prize in 1923. He is known all over the world for his poems, but his creativity in prose writing has regretfully long been neglected. *The Celtic Twilight*, written by W. B. Yeats, is a romantic prose collection based on Irish fairy tales and his extraordinary fantasy. According to the *Oxford Advanced Learner's Dictionary*, "His book of stories, *The Celtic Twilight*, created a lot of interest in traditional Irish stories." And "*The Celtic Twilight* is the romantic and mysterious atmosphere that many people associate with the Irish people and their literature, including their brief in fairies, ghosts, etc." Traditionally, this book is always considered by the literary critics as a kind of expression of his loyal love for his native Ireland. At present, with the deterioration of the natural environment, the awareness of ecological protection has been increased. Yeats' love for nature has been discovered and regarded as prominent as his love for his native country in this book. Thus, an analysis of *The Celtic Twilight* from an ecocritical perspective is carried out to help reevaluate and understand the human-nature relationship and other relevant issues in his proses.

In order to explore Yeats' insight into the relationship between human beings and nature, the focus of this study lies in anthropocentrism and non-anthropocentrism conveyed in *The Celtic Twilight* from an ecocritical perspective. It is also closely related to the relationship between mythology and ecologism and the relationship between the feature of romanticism and ecologism in *The Celtic Twilight*. The respective roles of nature and human beings are analyzed in details to help the readers realize that the ecological ideas and concepts are a major contribution that Yeats has made to literature, besides his other achievements ideas.

There are several pieces of research on Yeats at home and abroad from the ecocritical perspective. Gan Wenting finds in Yeats poem "The Sad Shepherd" (Gan Wenting, 2009: 207 – 208), is an appeal for the harmonious relationship between human and nature. The shepherd is laughed at by the stars, shells and seas because of his arrogant attitude toward nature. The non-human objects in nature can also make their voice to call for respect. Zhang Minglan concludes Yeats' ecological thought reflected from his poems lies in "his pursuit of an ecological balance among human beings." (Zhang Minglan, 2010: 131) However, since its publication, *The Celtic Twilight* has attracted almost no attention from Chinese scholars, except for Sun Zhaoling's article on the appreciation of *The Celtic Twilight* by focusing on symbolism, mysticism and Yeats' obsession with Irish traditional and folk culture (Sun Zhaoling,

2013: 4 – 6). There are also some ecocritical analyses of works of Yeats made by some foreign scholars. For instance, Sabine Lenore Müller compares works of R. M. Rilke and W. B. Yeats, and concludes "Yeats' works performs a shift towards a deconstruction of the concretely delineated self and goes hand in hand with explorations in occultism and environmental thought. " (Müller, 2017: 39 – 59) Moreover, both Chinese and foreign literary studies of Yeats' works from an ecocritical perspective are limited in the dualism between human and nature.

First of all, to analyze *The Celtic Twilight* from an ecocritical perspective, it is necessary to figure out the definition of "ecocriticism". American scholar Karl Kroeber introduced the concept of "ecology" and "ecological" to literary criticism in his article published in PMLA. (Kroeber, 1974: 132 – 141) And the word "ecocriticism" first appeared in "Literature and Ecology: An Experiment in Ecocriticism" (1978) written by William Rueckert.

> What then is ecocriticism? Simply put, ecocriticism is the study of the relationship between literature and the physical environment... ecocriticism takes an earth-centered approach to literary studies. (Glotfelty, 1996: 114)

According to *Merriam-Webster Third New International Dictionary*, anthropocentrism means "considering human beings as the most significant entity of the universe", and "interpreting or regarding the world in terms of human values and experiences". According to the definition of anthropocentrism, the core of this perspective is human beings. It refers to the assumption that human social activities are the central focus of the planet. Due to the countless pollution and damages human beings have made to the environment. More and more people begin to agree to the belief that this concept does not meet the requirement of keeping a sustainable development of the environment and protection of ecology today.

On the contrary, the dominance of human beings as the center of the earth is denied by non-anthropocentrism. " It is necessary for us to establish an overall awareness of the relationship between human and the world. " (Roger 1982: 248, cited in Chen Xiaohong, trans, 2013: 14 – 19) So all elements in nature, including human beings, other creatures and non-human objects in the eco-system on the globe should be equally respected by non-anthropocentrism, which is the opposite of anthropocentrism. And non-anthropocentrism meet the acquisition of sustainable development of our earth today. According to this concept, all of the factors in *The Celtic Twilight* including human beings, nature itself and miraculous creatures and spirits in it should be listed into consideration when we do the analysis of this book from an ecocritical perspective.

The Celtic Twilight is one of the representative works of Yeats classified as a piece of romantic writing and the fascinating Irish fairy tales in it. It has built up a relationship between ecology and romanticism and the relationship between ecology and fairy tales firstly. Yeats is among the "numerous authors and artists (who) have attempted to render nature as a speaking subject, not in the romantic mode of rendering nature an object for the self-constitution of the poet as speaking subject, but as a character with texts with its own existence." (Hochman, 2000: 187)

The basic characteristics of Romantic writing are described in Wikipedia as the following, "Romantics were distrustful of the human world, and tended to believe a close connection with nature was mentally and morally healthy." It implies that there are ecological thoughts in romantic literature. And it also implies that the yearning and praise for nature from romantic authors are contained in their romantic works. According to this standard, *The Celtic Twilight* is undoubtedly has some ecological thoughts in it. In addition to that, *The Celtic Twilight* is based on Irish fairy tales. As we all know, fairy tales are originated from the ancient society, where the ancient people made their livings by hunting and gathering. "And one of the functions of myth is to arouse our respect and fear of the power of nature." (Liu Yong and Zhang Fenghua, trans, 2011). As has been found in many former researches, the close relationship between human beings and nature is usually contained in fairy tales or myths. Just like "Human are correlated with the universe and other creatures by mythologies." (Deng Disi, trans, 1994: 310) And "Mythology can be regarded as the origin of ecological literature." (Wang Nuo, trans, 2003: 81) *The Celtic Twilight* is based on Irish fairy tales, and the ecological philosophy such as fear of and respect to nature has become one of the major components of it.

There are three main subjects of study in *The Celtic Twilight*: nature, miraculous creatures and spirits, and mankind. Firstly, the beautiful landscape of the natural environment conveys Yeats' aesthetic interest and love for nature. For instance, there is a description of the scenery in *Dust Hate Closed Helen's Eye*.

There is sweet air on the side of the hill/ When you are looking down upon Ballylee; / When you are walking in the valley picking nuts and blackberries, / There is music of the birds in it and music of the Sidhe. (40 −41).

This is a popular classical poem among the Irish local people. According to the poem, nature is described as a wonderful place, which implies mankind's affection and praise of nature. For Yeats, nature is exclusively beautiful in itself, never the stuff of labor and the reproduction of life, let alone the concept of something profitable or useful to mankind. Just by " looking down ", " picking nuts and blackberries " and enjoy the " music of the birds ", a person can feel great joy.

And there is another poem in *The Celtic Twilight* about nature. "Though hope falls from thee or love decay/ Burning in fires of a slanderous tongue. / Come, heart, where hill is heaped upon hill, / For there the mystical brotherhood... " (234) According to this poem, nature is regarded as a harbor for mankind to protect their heart from annoyances. And it suggests the author's yearning for the escape from the social world of human groups. Like other romantic pieces of work in literature, nature does function as a heaven for people to calm down and have a rest.

Yeats deliberately personifies nature in this book. Trees, stars, shells, mountains... can possess human abilities, emotions and wisdom. For example, in *Dust Hath Closed Helen's Eye*,

> He was standing under a bush one time, and he talked to it, and it answered him back in Irish. Some say it was the bush that spoke, but it must have been an enchanted voice in it, and it gave him the knowledge of all the things of the world(47).

In this example, this individual" he" is willing to talk with a bush, which shows that he admits that nature is equal to him. It implies that wisdom is contained in nature. And mankind acquires wisdom and knowledge from nature, so nature deserves the respect of human beings, which suggests the ecological concepts of Yeats.

Besides personification, nature is also regarded as the origin and end of human beings by Yeats in *The Celtic Twilight*. In" Earth, fire, and water", Yeats says that "And I am certain that the water, the water of the seas and of lakes and of mist and rain, has all but made the Irish after its image. " (135) Yeats implies that he believes that mankind is the progeny of other elements on earth. And in *Enchanted Woods*, Yeats expresses that" All nature is full of people whom we cannot see... and we shall be among them when we die if we but keep out natures simple and passionate. " (107 – 108) According to the idea, only individuals with pure souls can return to nature to join the team of spirits. And in these two instances mentioned above, Yeats displays his attitudes toward nature in that human beings are closely connected to nature. Yeats' ecological thoughts are embodied in these details, which accord with non-anthropocentrism.

Moreover, in *The Celtic Twilight*, spirits and miraculous creatures come from and live in nature. For example, "Drumcliff is a wide green valley, lying at the foot of Ben Bulben, the mountain in whose side the square white door swings open at nightfall to loose the fairy riders on the world. "(148) This detail proves that fairies or spirits are considered to have an equal position in nature like human beings. And there is a description in *Miraculous Creatures* as the following: "There are marten cats and badger and foxes in the enchanted woods, but there are of a certainty mightier creatures, and the lake hides what neither net nor fine can take. " (109) These examples about "faerie rider" and "mightier creatures" imply Yeats' ecological ideas to represent nature and environment in the imaginary spirits and to place mankind besides them as a companion to each other. These descriptions are to reinforce the impression upon the readers that nature and the environment is of great importance to the sphere as well as human beings.

Not only the non-human spirits have higher positions than those in traditional human-centered literary works, but also they have abilities and qualities of mankind in *The Celtic Twilight*. Firstly, they possess some abilities of mankind, such as dancing and singing. "His eyes were opened and he saw the ground thick with them. Singing they do be sometimes, and dancing. . . " (75) Singing and dancing are no longer limited to the human world. The spirits can also enjoy music on their own. Secondly, they have different characters. Such as "The house ghost is usually a harmless and well-meaning creature. " (32) And "These H—spirits have a gloomy, matter-of-fact way with them. " (33) Thirdly, they have emotions like human beings. For example, in "A Remonstrance with Scotsmen for Having Soured the Disposition of their Ghosts and Faeries", the "kelpie" begs a cruel Scottish for fear (177), and the "faerie" is sad because of the betrayal of his lover (178). According to these two examples, fairies and miraculous creatures have emotions of human beings, such as fear and sadness. Therefore, it can be inferred that spirits and miraculous creatures are not something inferior to mankind, which implies Yeats' respect paid to other creatures on the earth.

In a word, the spirits and miraculous creatures in *The Celtic Twilight* are similar and equal to human beings, because they share the same origins and abilities, which suggests that they should be respected by mankind. And according to the analysis of nature and the spirits and miraculous creatures in *The Celtic Twilight*, an overall perspective of Yeats has be shown in accord with non-anthropocentrism.

According to non-anthropocentrism, all of the factors including nature, miraculous creatures and human beings should be listed into the analysis. The behaviors of mankind should not be an exception. Yeats arranges punishment and criticize against those selfish individuals in *The Celtic Twilight* who care about nothing but their own benefits. In the meanwhile, some comparisons, especially comparisons between different types of human beings, are carried out in *The Celtic Twilight* by Yeats to emphasize its romantic style. For example, there are two distinct pairs of comparison of mankind in *The Celtic Twilight*: the farmers who believe in the power of nature and the farmers who do not believe in the power of nature, and the Irish and the Scottish. They will be analyzed one by one in following parts.

Miraculous events and fairy tales recorded in *The Celtic Twilight* always happen in the countryside. Just like what shows in *Village Ghosts*:

> In the great cities, we see so little of the world, we drift into our minority. In the little towns and villages, there are no minorities; people are not numerous enough. You must see the world there, perforce... The ancient mapmakers wrote across unexplored regions, "Here are lions." Across the village of fishermen and turners of the earth, so different are these from us, we can write but one line that is certain, "Here are ghosts." (23)

According to this description, fairy tales happen in the rural areas because miraculous creature and spirits always appear in the places far away from cities. And it is the people who live in the rural areas who have an opportunity to get in touch with the real world or the real nature.

Farmers are the people who live in the countryside. And in *The Celtic Twilight*, except the "gleeman" in *The Last Gleeman* and the "sailors" in *The Religion of a Sailor*, the major appearance of human beings are related to farmers in this book. And all of them live in the rural areas such as "the village of Grange" (8), "barony of Kiltartan in County Galway" (35), "Ben Bulben" (117) and so on. Therefore, it is necessary to analyze farmers in *The Celtic Twilight*.

Yeats draws a distinction between farmers who fear and respect the power of nature and farmers who do not believe or respect the power of nature. Different fates of farmers are caused by different attitudes of them towards the power of nature.

Most of the farmers in *The Celtic Twilight* fear and respect the power of nature.

Firstly, these farmers in *The Celtic Twilight* tend to believe that the creatures in nature possess the similar abilities to mankind. For example, it can be easily seen in the following paragraph from *Enchanted Woods*:

> An old countryman... had thought much about the natural and supernatural creatures of the wood... he is certain too that the cats, of whom there are many in the woods, have a language of their own-some kind of old Irish. He says, "Cats were serpents, and they were made into cats at the time of some great change in the world. That is why they are hard to kill, and why it is dangerous to meddle with them." (101 – 102)

According to this description, the old farmer believes that creatures in the forest have their own language just like mankind has its own language. And animals like cats can change or evolve themselves for protecting themselves from danger. In a word, other creatures in nature possess ability of human beings in this countryman' mind. Lots of similar events can be found in *The Celtic Twilight*. And these details suggest that this kind of farmer in *The Celtic Twilight* believe that nature is equal to human beings, which shows their respect to nature.

Secondly, this kind of farmers fears the power of nature. There is a typical example in *Kidnappers*:

> A little north of town of Sligo, on the southern side of Ben Bulben, some hundreds of feet above the plain... It is the door of fairy land... the unearthly troop do not always return empty-handed. Sometimes a new-wed bride or a new-born baby goes with them into their mountains... a woman, Ormsby by name, whose husband had fallen mysteriously sick... now he was a good-looking man, and his wife felt sure the "gentry" were coveting him..." (117 – 119)

According to this example, fairies come from nature. And Ormsby believes that the illness of her husband is caused by spirits from nature. Her fear of death is transferred into fear of spirits from nature. Similarly, many farmers prefer to explain the normal phenomenon with the power of nature. And their fear of nature is implied in these details.

Thirdly, this group of farmers believes that they will get benefits if they respect other creatures on earth. For example, a folklore is recorded in *Village Ghosts* as following:

> I remember two children who slept with their mother and sisters and brothers in one small room. In the room was also a ghost. They sold herrings in Dublin streets and did not mind the ghost much, because they knew they would always sell their fish easily while they slept in the "haunted" room. (32 – 33)

According to this description, this group of farmers allows ghosts to live in their house instead of dislodging them, which embodies their respect for other creatures. And their behavior accords with non-anthropocentrism since they take the feeling of other creatures into consideration.

In a word, according to Yeats, most of the farmers respect and fear the power of nature in *The Celtic Twilight*, so that they can benefit from it.

On the other side, there are a few farmers who do not believe in the power of nature in *The Celtic Twilight*, and they are punished by the power of nature for it. For instance, it can be testified in *The Man and His Boots*:

> There was a doubter in Donegal, and he would not hear of ghosts orsheogues... the man came into the house and lighted a fire in the room under the haunted one... for a time he prospered in his unbelief... they jumped along towards him, and then one got up and hit him, and afterwards the other hit him... in this way he was kicked out by his own boots, and Donegal was avenged upon its doubter. (141 – 142)

As has been mentioned before, spirits come from nature. Although the punishment from spirits in this example is similar to a mischief, it will be unforgettable for a person who never believes in the power of the nature like the "doubter in Donegal" to suffer from a mysterious event. And this example proves that people who doubt the power of nature will be punished by spirits from nature. And since the core of anthropocentrism is that human is the dominant power in the relationship between nature and mankind, it is impossible for human beings to be punished by nature in anthropocentrism. So this fact in *The Celtic Twilight* disaccords with anthropocentrism, which suggests the opposition to anthropocentrism of Yeats.

In summary, there are two kinds of farmersin *The Celtic Twilight*. The different results of these two groups of farmers imply that Yeats has realized the significance of respecting the power of nature. Most of them fear and respect for the power of nature. According to the details above in *The Celtic Twilight*, their behaviors accord with non-anthropocentrism rather than anthropocentrism, because they admit the equal state of nature and human and respect nature. And they benefit from it. Whereas, some of them suspect the power of nature and do not establish an awareness of fairness and respect in the relationship between nature and themselves. These farmers' behaviors disaccord with non-anthropocentrism. That is the reason why Yeats arranges punishments for them by nature. They deserve them.

Except for farmers, there is another comparison of human beings between the Irish and the Scottish in *The Celtic Twilight*. In *The Celtic Twilight*, and different situations of relationships between human and spirits in Ireland and Scotland are caused by different attitudes of the Irish and the Scottish towards the spirits in nature.

On one hand, the attitude of the Irish towards nature and spirits and miraculous creatures in *The Celtic Twilight* influences the behavior of spirits and the relationship between human and nature in Ireland.

In *The Celtic Twilight*, the attitude of the Irish towards nature and spirits and miraculous creatures is friendly. For example, it can be proved in "A Remonstrance with Scotsmen for Having Soured the Disposition of Their Ghosts and Faeries", "In Ireland, there is something of timid affection between men and spirits. They only ill-treat each other in reason. Each admits the other side to have feelings. There are points beyond which neither will go." (176) Under this description, the Irish "exchange civility" (182) with the spirits from nature in Ireland. Both of them are sane and calm when they debate on something. And the Irish admit their favorable emotion of Irish spirits. Therefore, the Irish are friendly to nature and spirits and miraculous creatures in it in *The Celtic Twilight*. And it also implies that the Irish deny the dominance of human beings between the relationship of other members of nature and themselves, which disaccords with anthropocentrism but accords with non-anthropocentrism.

Moreover, the behavior of spirits in Ireland is influenced by the amicable attitude of the Irish towards them in *The Celtic Twilight*.

These two different ways of looking at things have influenced in each country the whole world of sprites and goblins. For their gay and graceful doings, you must go to Ireland... our Irish faerie terrors have about them something of make-believe(179 – 180).

It demonstrates that the behaviors of Irish spirits are harmless and pleasant because of the friendly attitude of the Irish towards them.

Additionally, the friendly attitude of the Irish towards Irish spirits influences the relationship between the spirits and themselves in *The Celtic Twilight*. "In Ireland, war like mortals have gone amongst them, and helped them in their battles, and they, in turn, have taught men great skill with herbs, and permitted some few to hear their tunes. " (179) It suggests that the relationship between the Irish and spirits in Ireland is harmonious. And in the meanwhile, it implies that the amicable attitude of the Irish towards Irish spirits is beneficial to keeping the peaceful relationship between the spirits and themselves. In *The Celtic Twilight*, it is the peaceful atmosphere among human and the other creatures in nature in Ireland that accords with the non-anthropocentrism.

In a word, the Irish are friendly to nature and spirits or miraculous creatures in *The Celtic Twilight*, so spirits and miraculous creatures behave appropriately in Ireland in return. And friendly attitudes of both mankind and spirits in Ireland keep the relationship of them harmonious, which suggests that Yeats has discovered the benefits of mankind for getting on well with other creatures in nature.

On the other hand, confronted with nature and spirits and miraculous creatures in it, the attitude and behavior of the Scottish are different from that of the Irish *The Celtic Twilight*, which influences the behavior of spirits and the relationship between human and nature in Scotland.

Firstly, in *The Celtic Twilight*, the attitude of the Scottish towards nature and spirits and miraculous creatures is unfriendly. A description in this book about how a Scottish tortures a miraculous creature in this book can prove it.

> He caught a kelpie and tied her behind him on his horse. She was fierce, but he kept her quiet by driving an awl and a needle into her. They came to a river, and she grew very restless, fearing to cross the water. Again he drove the awl and needle into her... (177)

According to the above illustration, this Scottish tends to control the kelpie in a cruel manner. And there is another story about a group of naughty Scottish boys cut a hand of the fairy who help their sister finish her housework quickly for envy (177 – 178). These two examples imply that mankind is indifferent to feelings of other creatures in Scotland in *The Celtic Twilight*. Nothing is important than human beings in anthropocentrism.

Similarly, mankind in Scotland hurt or torture other creatures for their own desire. These kinds of behaviors and attitudes should be criticized and abandoned in our daily life.

Additionally, the behavior of spirits in Scotland is influenced by the unfriendly attitude and behavior of the Scottish towards them in *The Celtic Twilight*. There is a Scottish folklore in this book about a greedy Scottish killed by a monster who guards the treasure in a cruel manner, "In a little while his heart and liver floated up, reddening the water. No man ever saw the rest of his body. " (181) According to this folklore, the behaviors of miraculous creature and spirits in Scotland are horrible. "These two different ways of looking at things have influenced in each country the whole world of spirits and goblins... for their deeds of terror to Scotland. " (179 – 180) It proves that terrible behaviors of Scottish spirits are caused by terrible attitudes of the Scottish in *The Celtic Twilight*. And the importance of keeping friendly and appropriate attitude in association with the others is emphasized by these facts in *The Celtic Twilight*.

Furthermore, the unfriendly attitude of the Scottish towards spirits in Scotland influences the relationship between the spirits and themselves in *The Celtic Twilight*. "You—you will make no terms with the spirits of fire and earth and air and water. You have made the Darkness your enemy. " (182) This illustration implies that the relationship between human and nature is terrible in Scotland in *The Celtic Twilight*. And it also suggests that this situation is caused by the Scottish, for they regard the spirits and miraculous creatures in nature as the enemy.

The Scottish are unfriendly to nature and spirits or miraculous creatures in *The Celtic Twilight*, which causes the terrible behavior of spirits and miraculous creatures. And the relationship between human beings and nature is destroyed by the wrong attitudes of both of them towards each other, which implies that Yeats has realized that it is the inappropriate attitudes that cause the deteriorative relationship between mankind and nature.

In summary, in *The Celtic Twilight*, there is a comparison between the Irish and the Scottish according to their different attitudes towards spirits and creatures in nature. The Irish are friendly to nature, while the Scottish is unfriendly to it. And the relationships between mankind and nature are different in Ireland and Scotland due to it. The relationship between human and nature is peaceful in Ireland, while it is terrible in Scotland. Mankind, other creatures, and natural environment influence each other in *The Celtic Twilight*, which implies the advanced ecological concept of Yeats.

According to the analysis above, *The Celtic Twilight* is an ecological literature not only because that it is a romantic work based on Irish folklore but also because that the details in it accord with non-anthropocentrism.

Firstly, according to the analysis of nature in *The Celtic Twilight*, nature is the place where mankind originates from at the beginning of the world and belong to after death, nature is the place where mankind can enjoy the rosy landscape and forget annoyance, and nature is the place where mankind can acquire wisdom. Therefore, the yearning and praise of the author for nature in *The Celtic Twilight* can be inferred from these details.

Secondly, miraculous creatures and spirits possess abilities and qualities of human beings, which implies the ecological idea of Yeats that other creatures are equal to human beings.

Thirdly, according to the analysis of two comparisons of human beings in *The Celtic Twilight*, most of individuals respect other creatures and nature and believe in the power of nature. Although there are some exceptions among human beings in *The Celtic Twilight*, they are punished by other creature or mysterious power of nature in the end.

In conclusion, there are three elements in *The Celtic Twilight*: nature, the miraculous creatures and spirits, and mankind. According to the analysis of this book, they are influenced by each other. And it proves that there is an overall perspective in *The Celtic Twilight*, which accord with non-anthropocentrism. Therefore, *The Celtic Twilight* is an ecological literature, which contains the advanced ecological ideas of Yeats.

References

[1]陈小红主编. 什么是文学的生态批评[C]. 上海: 上海外语教育出版社, 2013.

[2]邓迪斯, 朝戈金等译. 西方神话学论文选[M]. 上海: 上海文艺出版社, 1994.

[3]甘文婷. 从生态批评的角度解读叶芝的《悲哀的牧羊人》[J]. 安徽文学, 2009(10).

[4]刘永安、张凤华. 中美生态文学思想起源探析[J]. 文学教育(上), 2011(07).

[5]孙兆玲. 爱尔兰的紫色风铃——品《凯尔特的薄暮》[J]. 名作欣赏, 2013(14).

[6]王诺. 欧美生态文学[M]. 北京: 北京大学出版社, 2003.

[7]王诺. 生态批评: 发展与渊源[J]. 文艺研究, 2002(03), 0257 – 5876

（2002）03 – 0048 – 08.

[8] W B. 叶芝，颜爽译. 凯尔特的薄暮[M]. 北京：新星出版社，2013.

[9] 张明兰. 叶芝诗歌生态观解读[J]. 长江师范学院学报，2010(9).

[10] Glotfelty, Cheryll & Fromm, Harold, *The Ecocriticism Reader*：*Landmarks in Literary Ecology*[C]. Athens：The University of Georgia Press，1996.

[11] Hochman, Jhan. "Green Cultural Studies", *The Green Studies Reader*[C]. Laurence Coupe. Oxon：Routledge. 2000.

[12] Jones, Roger. "On Seeing the Universe Freshly". *Southwest Review*[J]. 67 (02)，Spring，1982.

[13] Kroeber, Karl. "Home at Grasmere"：Ecological Holiness, *PMLA* 89 [J]. 1974.

[14] Müller, Sabine Lenore. Environmental Modernism：Ecocentric Conceptions of the Self and the Emotions in the Works of R. M. Rilke and W. B. Yeats. *Nature, Culture&Literature*[J]. Dec. 2017(13).

[15] Snyder, Gary. *No Nature*：*New and Selected Poem*[M]. New York：Pantheon，1992.

[16] Yeats W B. *The Celtic Twilight*[M]. Colorado：Create Space Independent Publishing Platform，2017.

[17] *Oxford Advanced Learner's Dictionary*https：//www. oxfordlearnersdictionaries. com/

[18] *Merriam-Webster Third New International Dictionary* https：//www. merriam-webster. com/dictionary/anthropocentrism

[19] https：//en. wikipedia. org/wiki/Romanticism

Une écriture spontanée et poétique

——*L'Amant* de Marguerite Duras[*]

Sun Fang[**]

Résumé: «Pourquoi écrit-on sur les écrivains ? Leurs livres devraient suffire» avait dit Marguerit Duras. Vraiment, *L'Amant* est sans doute une de ses oeuvres méritant d'être éduiée, pour laquelle elle a gagné le prix Concourt en 1984. En relativement peu de pages, et sans intrigues parasites, avec peu de personnages, elle échappe à toute classification et déroute le lecteur non averti. Cependant la lecture profonde nous révèle son charme et son originalité, se manifestant, entre autres, dans son écriture spontanée et poétique munie de six facteurs: rythme, lyrisme, jeu d'échos, images, style épuré et ambiguïté.

Mots clés: Marguerit Duras; *l'Amant* ; poétique; écriture spontanée; ambiguïté; échos; lien intime

Introduction

L'Amant est une oeuvre autobiographique de Marguerite Duras, écrite dans sa vieillesse. Ce récit, ayant pour thème central la rencontre avec l'amant chinois-un éblouissement éphémère de l'amour - , évoque en même temps la vie de la famille de l'auteur-une société à part - , en Indochine dans les années 30, à l'époque coloniale qui allait toucher sa fin.

De tous les thèmes de la littérature française, l'amour est sans doute celui dont la

---

[*] 论文题目：自然而诗性的写作——玛格丽特·杜拉斯的"情人"。

[**] 作者简介：孙芳(Sun Fang)，云南大学外国语学院法语系副教授。研究方向：语言学，文学，翻译。

fortune reste la plus grande et la plus durable. *De Tristan et Iseut* du Moyen Age à *Partage de Midi* de Paul Claudel, ce mythe de l'amour fatal a été beaucoup traité de manières différentes par de nombreux écrivains depuis des siècles. Quels qu'ils soient, les écrivains se rejoignent sur un point commun : la mise en scène des aspirations contradictoires de l'homme(conflit entre chair et esprit)et le tragique cheminement de la rédemption à travers le péché. Ce thème occupe encore une place entrale dans la littérature contemporaine, tel que le thème du salut de l'oeuvre claudélienne, où le conflit entre chair et esprit se résoudra dans un dépassement de soi-même et la reconnaissance de l'amour Sauveur de Dieu.

Contrairement à ces oeuvres, l'*Amant* se distingue d'abord par sa vision nouvelle de l'amour. C'est-à-dire que, en trouvant l'harmonie entre le désir et l'esprit, l'amour durassien s'épanouit dans la passion qui requiert l'être entier : charnel et spirituel, et donne sens à l'existence de l'homme dans un univers sans Dieu ni grâce. Etant autobiographique, l'*Amant* paraît cependant moins l'évocation nostalgique d'un passé innaccessible que la découverte progressive de la seule vérité, celle qui se cristallise dans la mémoire et qui se cache derrière des souvenirs obsédants. Ici l'*Amant* dirait cette vérité qu'*Un Barrage Contre le Pacifique* avait évoqué de façon romancée.

Si la première lecture peut nous dérouter, en approfondissant, on comprend que le désordre n'est qu'apparent, ce sont l'état d'âme, la conscience de Duras, qui donnent l'unité intérieure de l'oeuvre. Avec un langage poétique et un flou suggestif, elle nous emmène au-dehors du livre, plus loin vers l'imaginaire.

L'*Amant* reste alors une oeuvre originale en révélant particulièrement, à côté de sa vision personnelle sur l'amour et sur les rapports des êtres, son écriture spontanée, que nous essayons de mettre en lumière selon les six plans suivants.

I. Le rythme

Des images reviennent régulièrement dans le texte lui donnant un rythme poétique. Par exemple, celle de la petite fille sur un bac pendant la traversée du Mékong est reprise maintes fois aux premières pages du récit. La répétition de «Quinze ans et demi» sonne comme un refrain et donne son rythme à l'oeuvre en nous ramenant à chaque fois au thème de la rencontre.

II. Le lyrisme

On trouve que le «je» ambigu de la narratrice s'efface souvent pour évoquer, de façon lyrique, « la petite » ; le lyrisme réside aussi dans la recherche du pathétique. Le départ de la jeune fille et la séparation des deux amoureux ne constituent pas le point d'arrêt, car M. D. fait ressortir le pathétique dans le sursaut où l'amour perdu est retrouvé au fond du coeur de la jeune fille: «elle avait pleuré parce qu'elle avait pensé à cet homme de Cholen et elle n'avait pas été sûre tout à coup de ne pas l'avoir aimé d'un amour qu'elle n'avait pas vu parce qu'il s'était perdu dans l'histoire comme l'eau dans le sable et qu'elle le retrouvait seulement maintenant à cet instant de la musique jetée à travers la mer. » [1] Cela comme plus tard, elle retrouve l'éternité du petit frère à travers la mort.

III. Un jeu d'échos

L'oeuvre est construite sur un jeu d'échos complexe qui parfois déborde le cadre du livre pour envoyer à des oeuvres antérieures, telle qu'*Un Barrage Contre le Pacifique*. Plustôt création que représentation, le roman tend alors à s'organiser comme une série de variations sur des thèmes obsédants. *L'Amant De la Chine Du Nord*, une réécriture de l'*Amant*, nous en donne un bon exemple en chantant la mélodie, d'une façon théâtrale, de la même rencontre. On dirait que l'oeuvre de Duras est en écho: la variation autour d'un même thème. C'est ainsi qu'on retrouve l'image de *La Femme du Gange*(Gallimard, 1973) chez«la folle de Vinhlong» dans l'*Amant*.

Ce jeu d'échos ouvre aussi au sein du roman les champs nous permettant de retrouver les liens intimes à travers les apparences disparates: «Mais le plus souvent je n'ai pas d'avis, je vois que tous les champs sont ouverts, qu'il n'y aurait plus de murs, que l'écrit ne saurait plus où se mettre pour se cacher, se faire, se lire, que son inconvenance fondamentale ne serait plus respectée... » [2] Elle n'a pas d'avis, c'est qu'elle ne réclame pas son idée, ne se soucie pas des règles. Son oeuvre n'est pas faite pour fonder une morale. Elle ne cherche pas à plaire, à instruire, ni à convaincre. Son oeuvre nous livre plutôt une intelligence qu'une connaissance, l'auteur n'analyse pas, ne raisonne pas. En bref, elle n'est pas au service d'une idée ou d'une propagande quelconque. Privé du didactisme, l'*Amant* incarne une souplesse, une fluidité qui laisse le champ libre au psychologique où les choses et les êtres s'appellent et se coordonnent par un lien intime, il n'y aurait ansi plus de murs ni de

---

① L' Amant, p. 138.
② L' Amant, p. 15.

cloisonnement.

Ayant levé les obstacles que posent les soucis de la bienséance, les personnages de l'*Amant* représentent un idéal qui disqualifie toute civilité et un être qui se laisse aller à sa nature. «la petite blanche», «l'amant chinois», «la folle de Vinhlong», «la Dame de Savannakhet», même«la mère» sont des gens qui s'abandonnent à leur bon plaisir.

Si on dit que M. D. continue, dans l'*Amant*, à reposer sur une visée traditionnelle: explorer les rapports entre les êtres, elle explore ces rapports sous l'angle d'une spontanéité créatrice, d'une vision originale. Toute grande oeuvre témoigne d'une vision originale, différente de toute autre, qui fait de son auteur ce qu'il est. Et particulièrement, pour Duras, la mise en évidence de la parenté des choses se lie étroitement avec elle, avec son expérience, avec ses sentiments vecus. Ce qui explique aussi pourquoi elle confond le temps de la guerre avec le règne de son frère aîné. La mort de petit frère, pour elle, est un drame comparable qui l'a ouverte à tout autre drame, et la méchanceté de son frère aîné l'a conduite à accéder à l'absolu du mal.

On voit clairement qu'il n'y a jamais de seuls événements fortuits dans son oeuvre. Il lui faut partir d'elle pour écrire. Elle essaie toujours de donner une image vivante qui puise dans ses souvenirs obsédants, pour mettre en lumière les événements étant en résonnance avec celle-ci et en tirer leur équivalence. A ses yeux, «l'équivalence est absolue, définitive. »[1] Sous cet angle se fonde l'homologie entre «moi», les Fernandez et Marie-Claude. De même, l'amant chinois s'apparente à Hélène Lagonelle: «je la vois comme étant de la même chair que cet homme de Cholen[...], elle est la femme de cet homme de peine qui me fait la jouissance si abstraite, si dure, [...]. Hélène Lagonelle est de la Chine. »[2] Ainsi tous les deux, Hélène Lagonelle et l'homme de peine sont-ils devenus inoubliables pour elle.

IV. Les images

M. D. confronte l'imagination aux forces et aux éléments de l'univers. Par exemple, l'amour lui rappelle la mer, «Sans forme, simplement incomparable. »[3] Le torrent symbolise la force du désir. La passion est le seul partage entre l'amant chinois,

---

① L' Amant, p. 85.
② L' Amant, p. 92.
③ L' Amant, p. 50.

riche et déja adulte et la jeune fille adolescente, issue d'une famille française mais pauvre. Ecart de l'âge, contraste entre pauvreté et richesse, différence de race, tant d'éléments constituent le contexte où se situe leur rencontre. Cependant le désir et l'attraction réciproque unissent au fond ces deux êtres sans préjugé raciste ni de rang social. Cette force pousse la jeune fille à se révolter contre l'autorité de sa mère et aussi contre la discrimination raciale. «Je me demande comment j'ai eu la force d'aller à l'encontre de l'interdit posé par ma mère. » [1] Pour eux, la rencontre amoureuse, le désir et la passion deviennent l'échappatoire de la condition humaine qu'ils refusent pour retrouver l'être entier. «Quand on laisse le corps faire et chercher et trouver et prendre ce qu'il veut, et là tout est bon, il n'y pas de déchet, les déchets sont recouverts, tout va dans le torrent, dans la force du désir. » [2]

Ici, l'antagonisme s'évanouit entre chair et esprit, entre amour et haine, entre beauté et laideur, entre bonheur et douleur. Ils coexistent dans un chaos des émotions. Ainsi, en rétablissant la coexistence du désir et de l'amour, la vision de Marguerite Duras s'oppose à une philosophie dualiste où âme et corps sont divisés. Dans l'*Amant*, cette coexistence du désir et de l'amour s'épanouit dans la passion qui requiert l'être entier et donne sens à l'existence: «si l'on n'est pas passé par l'obligation absolue d'obéir au désir du corps, c'est-à-dire si l'on n'est pas passé par la passion, on ne peut rien faire dans la vie. » dit justement Marie Claire. Dans cette passion elle trouve l'issue de se révolter contre le désespoir et le malheur. «Dans la famille je ne pleure pas. Le jour-là dans cette chambre les larmes consolent du passé et de l'avenir aussi. » [3]

De même, l'image de la nuit se présente plusieurs fois dans l'oeuvre: «la présence de l'assasin des enfants de la nuit, de la nuit du chasseur. » [4] Ici, la mer, les eaux, les forêts, le désert, la chaleur, le vacarme, le crépuscule, la nuit, en apportant leur symbole, tracent les frontières intérieures sur lesquelles se fonde l'homogénéité des espaces de l'oeuvre.

Selon Pierre Reverdy, «le propre de l'image forte est d'être issue du rapprochement spontané de deux réalités très distantes, dont l'esprit seul a saisi les

---

① L' Amant, p. 51.
② L' Amant, p. 55.
③ L' Amant, p. 58.
④ L' Amant, p. 12.

rapports. » ① Dans l'*Amant*, le glissement d'image d'une époque à une autre décèle aussi ces rapports intimes, ainsi le visage dévasté de sa vieillesse et l'image de sa jeunesse à dix-huit ans, à quinze ans, restent toujours la même, au-delà du temps, sur un point commun : le désir. L'essentiel est que «le visage de l'alcool m'est venu avant l'alcool. L'alcool est venu le confirmer [...] De même que j'avais en moi la place du désir. J'avais à quinze ans le visage de la jouissance et je ne connaissais pas la jouissance. » ② Ici Duras dresse le portrait de la jeune fille : visage voyant, exténué, les yeux cernés en avance sur le temps. C'est une image clée, parce que tout a commencé de cette façon pour elle ; à quinze ans et demi, elle est avertie déjà, elle sait quelque chose, elle sait que la beauté d'une femme ne dépend pas des vêtements, elle sait que problème est ailleurs. «Il était l'intelligence immédiate du rapport de sexualité ou bien il n'était rien. » ③

Voyons encore ces images montrant sa façon de s'habiller : elle porte un chapeau d'homme, rose à bords plats et au large ruban noir, une paire de chaussures à talons hauts en lamé or. Cette tenue insolente maintes fois reprise trahit d'une part la volonté de la «petite » qui veut se réclamer et se révolter contre les conventions sociales, d'autre part la pauvreté de la famille, puisque ces habits qu'elle a portés sont des «soldes soldés ».

V. Le style épuré

«Pas de vent au-dehors de l'eau. Le moteur du bac, le seul bruit de la scène, celui d'un vieux moteur déglingué aux bielles coulées. De temps en temps, par rafales légères, des bruits de voix. » Voilà un bon exemple qui illustre son style dépouillé. Ces phrases sont réduites à leur plus simple expression par l'exclusion du verbe. Comme si l'auteur avait extrait de son souvenir, en rayant les éléments superflus, une image pure et éternelle, celle de «Quinze ans et demi» lors de la traversée du fleuve. Ainsi dépouillée, l'expression durassienne révèle la portée symbolique de cette rencontre sur le bac pour en dégager l'universalité et l'éternité : «J'ai quinze ans et demie, il n'y a pas de saisons dans ce pays-là, nous sommes dans une saison unique, chaude,

---

① Collection littéraire Lagrade & Michard, P. 683.
② L'Amant, p. 15.
③ L'Amant, p. 28.

monotone, nous sommes dans la longue zone chaude de la terre, pas de printemps, pas de renouveau. » ①

VI. L'ambiguïté

L'incarnation de l'ambiguïté est une autre caractéristique de la manière d'écrire de Duras. L'auteur laisse dans l'*Amant* des phrases, des paragraphes où le réalisme et le symbolisme sont difficiles à démêler. Autrement dit, on peut en discerner de différents sens. Ainsi, elle écrit«L'histoire de ma vie n'existe pas. Ça n'existe pas. Il n'y a jamais de centre. Pas de chemin, pas de ligne. Il y a de vastes endroits où l'on fait croire qu'il y avait quelqu'un, ce n'est pas vrai il n'y avait personne. » ② A la première lecture, on erre un peu dans le brouillard, à la recherche d'un fil conducteur qui n'existe pas.

L'oeuvre est autobiographique, destinée à décrire une tranche de vie, voire toute la vie, pourquoi dit-elle que son histoire n'existe pas ? Qu'il n'y avait personne ! Littéralement, cela peut signifier que l'auteur est nihiliste. Cependant, vu sous un autre angle, on peut penser qu'elle considère que l'histoire personnelle n'existe pas, chaque être n'étant qu'une goutte du torrent historique qui anime la société. C'est l'histoire sociale qui préside le destin et l'avenir de chacun, il n'y a donc ni ligne ni chemin objectif.

Dans *l'Amant*, on ne trouve ni l'antagonisme entre le bien et le mal, ni le contraste de l'amour et de la haine, ni le conflit chair esprit. L'auteur n'expose pas les règles de jugement, ne traite pas un sujet déterminé, elle laisse parler ses souvenirs, naturellement. L'histoire donne la matière, le lecteur prend ce qu'il peut. Chacun peut avoir sa propre compréhesion.

Pour la même raison, on peut interpréter de façon différente la phrase la plus énigmatique de l'*Amant* : «Je n'ai jamais écrit, croyant le faire, je n'ai jamais aimé, croyant aimer, je n'ai jamais rien fait qu'attendre devant la porte fermée. » ③ Cet énoncé fait de doute, d'attente, de désarrois, exprime peut-être une fusion de sentiments : l'écriture-sa carrière, toute sa vie, son amour ne sont peut-être qu'une attente perpétuelle, et la porte devant laquelle elle attend est toujours fermée. Elle n'a vécu qu'un amour inachevé et une carrière non accomplie. La perfection de l'amour et

---

① L' Amant, p. 11.
② L' Amant, p. 14.
③ L' Amant, p. 35.

l'accomplissement de la carrière ne se trouvent que dans l'illusion. Cette phrase mélancolique explique peut-être une autre compréhension de la vie, comme les poèmes de Li ShanYin, un poète de la dynastie des Tang, qu'on peut interpréter de façons différentes, en laissant libre cours à l'imagination. En cela réside le prestige de l'oeuvre, qui devient alors une «partition» exécutée par l'âme et l'esprit du lecteur. Et Marguerite Duras commenta elle même ainsi: «Cette phrase[...]veut dire que j'étais à la porte de la famille, devant la porte du sanctuaire qui contient mon corps même, celui où elle se trouvait, elle, la mère qui avait interdit d'écrire des livres. » [1] Son commentaire nous fait penser à Paul Valéry qui dit «Une fois publié, un texte est comme un appareil dont chacun peut se servir à sa guise et selon ses moyens: il n'est pas sûr que le constructeur en use mieux qu'un autre. » [2] Chacun, alors, peut s'approprier l'oeuvre.

Cependant, ambiguïté et obscurité ne sont pas des artifices de style. Duras n'essaie pas de mettre en lumière ces choses obscures, mais de les laisser dans leur état naturel-le chaos du monde. En avouant qu'il y a des choses qui échappent encore à son entendement, M. D. écrit, à l'état brut, de façon indéterminée, avec des phrases parfois ambiguës. D'une part, elle prend conscience de l'incompabilité des mots à rendre les virtualités innombrables de la sensation ou même de la pensée profonde. D'autre part, elle trouve la beauté de l'ombre. Elle dit en 1959: «Ce qui m'intéresse dans une situation romanesque, c'est son ombre ou celle qu'elle projette sur les êtres alentour. Chacun de mes romans se présente comme un négatif [...] Je n'avance qu'avec incertitude. » [3] Donc, elle écrit avec indétermination suggestive, au gré de l'écriture, et elle s'exprime par la spontanéité créatrice. Parrallèlement, l'écriture devient plus allusive, fait une large part à la suggestion et à l'implicite. Comme ce que dit Christiane Blot-Labarrère «Chez elle, elle représente non pas ce qui viendrait après coup troubler la raison, mais la pensée originelle où la raison n'a nulle action, la dénégation de l'analyse intellectuelle, la préférence pour le chaos des émotions, le développement de la sensibilité sur l'intelligence, une intelligence nouvelle. » [4] En fait, dans l'*Amant*, il n'y a ni raison stricte, ni analyse

---

① Marguerite Duras par Christiane Blot-Labarrère, p. 57.
② XXᵉsiècle Collection Littéraire Lagarde & Michard, p. 309.
③ Les nouvelles littéraires, 18 juin 1959.
④ Marguerite Duras Par Christiane Blot-Labarrère, p. 120.

intellectuelle, l'oeuvre reflète sa pensée originelle, sa sensiblilté et sa sagesse.

Conclusion

L'évocation des périodes cachées de sa jeunesse révèle non seulement l'amour durassien-échappatoire de la condition humaine à la recherche de l'être entier: charnel et spirituel, et fait vivre aussi ses propres impressions, ses propres sensations sur une époque particulière, sur des gens particuliers. Par son regard particulier, elle relie en résonnance les choses disparates, les êtres dispersés, les moments éloignés qui se cachent derrière ses souvenirs obsédants et en a tiré leur parenté essentielle. L'exploration des rapports entre les êtres est faite par Duras sous l'aspect d'une spontanéité créatrice qui la caractérise.

Nourri de la substance intime de l'auteur, l'*Amant* marque un univers intérieur d'une grande cohérence, dans son organisation fantasmatique. Avec rythme, lyrisme, jeu d'échos, image, style dépouillé et la beauté de l'ombre, l'oeuvre a donc trouvé une structure propre qui forme une unité signifiante, cohérente et poétique. De plus, cette structure permet à l'écrit de s'affranchir des entraves posées par l'architecture stéréotypée et de laisser le champ libre à l'imagination.

Bibliographie

[1] Marguerite Duras. *L'Amant* [M]. Ed. de Minuit, 1984.

[2] Marguerite Duras. *Un barrage contre le Pacifique* [M]. Gallimard, 1950.

[3] Marguerite Duras. *Hiroshima mon amour* [M]. Gallimard, 1960.

[4] Marguerite Duras. *Nathalie Granger*, suivi *de la Femme du Gange*. [M]. Gallim – ard, 1973.

[5] *L'Amant de la Chine du Nord* [M]. Gallimard, 1991.

[6] Christiane Blot-Labarrère. *Marguerite Duras* [M]. Ed. du Seuil, 1992.

[7] Duras Romans. *Cinéma*, *Théâtre*, *Un parcours* 1943 – 1993 [M]. Gallimard, 1997.

[8] Bordas. *XXe siècle Collection Littéraire* [M]. Lagarde & Michard, 1973.

[9] SUN Fang. *L'Amant—à la découverte d'une «intelligence nouvelle»*, mémoire de master sous la direction du professeur XU Feng, 1999.

L'ambiguïté et la clarté dans
Les Liaisons dangereuses[*]

Zhou Shanshan, Xie Ting[**]

Résumé：*Les Liaisons dangereuses* de Choderlos de Laclos reste son seul roman et le chef-d'œuvre de la littérature française du XVIIIème siècle, où l'auteur fait gloire de l'ambiguïté et de la clarté. Dès la parution du roman, les moralistes et l'Église ne cessent pas de le critiquer à cause de la description des scènes érotiques ou de la vie corrompue de l'aristocratie. L'auteur et son oeuvre restent pendant longtemps méprisés et il est considéré comme un écrivain libertin. Cependant, à travers sa carrière d'écriture et l'équivoque chez les personnages qu'il a peint, on arrive davantage à redéfinir ses *Liaisons* et Laclos lui-même.

Mots-clés：*Les Liaisons dangereuses*；Laclos；ambiguïté；clarté

Introduction

Choderlos de Laclos est officier de carrière et écrivain amateur. *Les Liaisons dangereuses* est son seul roman épistolaire qui a été terminé au cours de sa garnison en tant qu'officier. Dès que ce roman composé de 175 lettres a vu le jour, il surgit de la dispute, certains le trouvent débauché, tandis que les autres l'admirent.

Voilà un roman plein de controverses. On voit l'abomination et à la fois l'admiration. D'une part, pour les moralistes ou l'Église, il s'agit d'un roman à interdire à cause de ses personnages dépravés et des intrigues pleines d'érotisme. Ils le

---

[*] 论文题目：小说《危险的关系》中模糊性与清晰性研究

[**] 作者简介：周舢杉(Zhou Shanshan)，云南大学外国语学院助教。研究方向：法语文学。解婷(Xie Ting)，云南大学外国语学院讲师。研究方向：法语文学。

trouvent corrompu pour avoir décrit les détails de la vie dissolue des libertins. Non seulement en France, mais aussi à l'étranger, il existe des critiques sévères contre cet ouvrage. D'autre part, en revanche, aux yeux des admirateurs, Roger Vailland par exemple, cette oeuvre mystérieuse reste toujours un des chefs-d'œuvre les plus importants durant l'histoire de la littérature française. En un mot, les lecteurs qui adorent ce roman par lettres l'interprètent d'un tout autre point de vue. On en a déjà fait plusieurs adaptations cinématographiques ou théâtrales.

D'où vient ces opinions complètement opposées? C'est par suite de l'ambiguïté mise en relief par Laclos dans son ouvrage. Il a transposé son talent militaire sur "le champs de bataille de l'amour" dans ce livre. Chaque personnage paraît en ordre et possède son propre style de l'écriture. On pense qu'on les voit nettement, l'écrivain a pourtant toujours l'intention de les peindre d'une manière équivoque. Là où se trouve la stratégie de guerre. Pourtant, plus Laclos met l'accent sur l'ambiguïté, plus il veut que ses lecteurs mettent en valeur la clarté de ses *Liaisons* et chez lui.

I. Un roman difficile à définir

En tant qu'un des écrivains les plus mystérieux dans l'histoire de la littérature française, Choderlos de Laclos et *Les Liaisons dangereuses* restent depuis longtemps contestables. Tant critiqué qu'admiré, Laclos atteint le but en faisant de son seul et premier roman un vrai agrément aux lecteurs.

Lors d'un séjour à Londres, Laclos écrit dans une lettre à son ami Tilly: "[...] je résolu de faire un ouvrage qui sortît de la route ordinaire, qui fît du bruit, et qui retentît encore sur terre quand j'y aurai passé" (GRESHOFF C. J. 2013: 383). On peut dire qu'il a réussi avec ses *Liaisons*.

Il est en bonne justice de déclarer son ambition littéraire. *Les Liaisons dangereuses*, sous titré *lettres recueillies dans une société et publiées pour l'instruction de quelques autres*, est le chef-d'œuvre de Laclos. De plus, c'est un inattendu tant pour la littérature que pour sa vie comme écrivain amateur. Il n'arrive probablement jamais à prévoir toutes les conséquences: les critiques ainsi que les admirations après sa parution. Dans ce cas-là, d'où vient cet ouvrage aimé des uns et en revanche détesté des autres? On ne peut pas parler de ce roman sans parler de son auteur.

Né à Amiens le 18 octobre 1741, Pierre Ambroise François Choderlos de Laclos est officier de carrière, politicien et écrivain amateur. Sorti d'une famille de petite noblesse, Laclos s'engage très jeune dans l'armée de l'artillerie. Sous l'Ancien

Régime, sa carrière en tant qu'artilleur est bien restreinte, il n'a jamais connu une vraie bataille pendant son service militaire à l'armée. Ainsi commence-t-il la création littéraire tout en changeant sans arrêt de lieux de garnison. Il s'adonne à l'écriture et termine plusieurs pièces de théâtres sans grand succès. Finalement en 1782, en profitant d'une permission de six mois à Besançon, Laclos achève *Les Liaisons dangereuses.*

L'écrivain prend un genre littéraire très à la mode de son époque: le roman épistolaire, dans lequel il laisse libre cours de son talent militaire sur le champ littéraire: il replace la guerre dans le salon et déclenche la guerre amoureuse. Le genre épistolaire est exactement favorable pour Laclos à la manipulation de cet échiquier d'amour grâce à la distanciation entre ces correspondants, soit un décalage temporel et géographique. Avec toutes ces descriptions minutieuses des émotions de chaque personnage principal, on voit clairement leur développement sentimental de jour en jour. Les différents points de vue s'offrent aux lecteurs avec les correspondances intercalées. En outre, les affrontements mutuels n'éclatent discrètement qu'entre les correspondants, sous la forme de l'écriture. Ces personnages interagissent même s'ils ne se voient pas directement, la lettre devient chez Laclos une arme. C'est juste par là que se produit l'intrication des relations interpersonnelles et enfin le double sens du roman.

En renforçant un effet de réel pour cet effet d'équivoque, l'auteur s'efforce de, au début du roman, dans la préface du rédacteur et l'avertissement de l'éditeur(il est en fait à la fois le rédacteur fictif et l'éditeur imaginé), convaincre ses lecteurs de croire ce qu'écrivent les correspondants dans ces *lettres recueillies dans une société et publiées pour l'instruction de quelques autres.* "Cet ouvrage, ou plutôt ce recueil, que le public trouvera peut-être encore trop volumineux, ne contient pourtant que le plus petit nombre des lettres qui composait la totalité de la correspondance dont il est extrait... j'avais proposé des changements plus considérables, et presque tous relatif à la pureté de dicton ou de style... on m'a objecté que c'étaient les lettres mêmes qu'on voulait faire connaître, et non pas seulement un ouvrage fait d'après ces lettres[...]" (DE LACLOS Pierre Choderlos 1869: 7)

Il met en premier lieu l'authenticité des lettres, et en même temps il indique que les corrections sont inévitables, car on y trouve "beaucoup de fautes". C'est ainsi qu'on est persuadé du réel de la source des lettres: elles sont effectivement écrites par certains correspondants qui commettent parfois des fautes quand ils s'écrivent.

Cependant, dans l'avertissement de l'éditeur, cet éditeur imaginé le considère comme un roman complètement inventé par l'auteur, en disant que "plusieurs personnages qu'il met en scène ont de si mauvaises mœurs, qu'il est impossible de supposer qu'ils aient vécu dans notre siècle", parce que c'est un siècle de "philosophie" avec les "lumières", qui ont "répandu de toutes parts", "ont rendu [...] tous les hommes si honnêtes et toutes les femmes si modestes et si réservées" (DE LACLOS Pierre Choderlos 1869: 5). Ce qui se passe dans ce recueil ne doit paraître que dans "d'autres lieux" ou bien dans "d'autres temps".

"Nous croyons devoir prévenir le Public que, malgré le titre de cet ouvrage et ce qu'en dit le rédacteur dans sa préface, nous ne garantissons pas l'authenticité de ce recueil, et que nous avons même de fortes raisons de penser que ce n'est qu'un roman" (DE LACLOS Pierre Choderlos 1869: 6).

Ici, comme ce que font les épistoliers, Laclos pose une énigme, il met en évidence une contradiction apparente. Auquel doit-on se fier, le rédacteur ou l'éditeur? Là où est la stratégie du doute de l'écrivain.

À partir de sa publication, *Les Liaisons* attirent et fascinent de plus en plus de lecteurs. Il faut savoir que c'est un roman à la fois critiqué et admiré, voire interdit, pour l'atteinte à la moralité publique. Il a été en outre prohibé de voir le jour suivant le jugement d'un tribunal parisien sous prétexte de l'outrage publique. Au cours du XIXème siècle, Stendhal est, parmi les écrivains, le seul qui lui accorde du respect. Laclos reste ainsi en liaison avec la débauche et la corruption des mœurs. C'est jusqu'au début du XXème siècle, en particulier avec la publication des notes de Baudelaire, un de ses lecteurs, et après la deuxième guerre mondiale, avec l'admiration de Gide, de Malraux, de Giraudoux et de Roger Vailland par exemple, qu'on redécouvre et reconnaît Laclos et ses *Liaisons*. Et ce qui fait de lui un des écrivains phares du XVIIIème siècle, c'est par lui-même, un style caractérisé par l'ambiguïté et la clarté.

II. Paradoxe chez les personnages du jeu d'amour

Lors de la lecture de ce roman épistolaire, on ne voit que les correspondances interposées entre les personnages. Chacun a son propre style d'écriture et parle pour soi-même. La personnalité et la pensée se manifestent et se développent de jour en jour par lettres. Il devient difficile de les étiqueter simplement.

Cécile Volanges est la première qui entre en scène. C'est une naïve qui sort du couvent à l'âge de 15 ans et vit plus tard avec sa mère. Celle-ci veut l'épouser au comte de Gercout sans que sa fille le sache. Jeune et innocente, Cécile éprouve des ennuis de toutes sortes auprès de sa mère. Elle commence à écrire à son amie au couvent, Sophie Carnay, pour lui raconter ce qui se passe autour d'elle. Ce qu'il lui faut faire chaque jour, c'est de rester à la maison avec sa mère, sans amis de son âge ni activités sociales intéressantes. Même peu de personnes lui parle pendant la soirée chez sa mère, car selon les hommes "il faut laisser mûrir, nous verrons cet hiver" (DE LACLOS Pierre Choderlos 2005: 7). Chez Mme de Merteuil, elle rencontre le chevalier Danceny dont elle tombe immédiatement amoureuse. Dans la lettre 7, elle écrit à Sophie Carnay: "Il est extrêmement aimable. Il chante comme un Ange, et compose de très jolis airs dont il fait aussi des paroles[...]il me semble que s'il se mariait, sa femme serait bien heureuse[...]il a une douceur charmante. Il n'a jamais l'air de faire un compliment[...]lui et Mme de Merteuil sont les deux personnes que je trouve aimables"(DE LACLOS Pierre Choderlos 2005: 18).

Les deux jeunes s'écrivent et tombent bientôt amoureux l'un de l'autre. Tout cela est dans la maîtrise de la marquise de Merteuil. Elle leur donne des conseils, séparément par lettres, comme une vieille amie sincère. Cécile compte sur Mme de Merteuil, avec laquelle elle se sent même plus intime qu'auprès de sa mère qui ne s'occupe que de la suffisance matérielle de sa fille. Le vicomte de Valmont profite plus tard d'une occasion et la viole. Quand elle sollicite des avis de la marquise, celle-ci continue à la manipuler et lui conseille de bénéficier de sa liaison avec les deux hommes, même de s'éloigner de sa mère. Finalement, la jeune fille se retire de nouveau au couvent.

Comme une jeune naïve de quinze ans, Cécile Volanges écrit avec beaucoup de fautes de syntaxe et de la gaucherie. L'écrivain saisit parfaitement ce caractère et lui donne un style maladroit. Tout au début, on la considère comme une fille très innocente qui va épouser un homme qu'elle ne connaît point. C'est une jeune fille ingénue qui n'est pas capable de se protéger de l'intention vicieuse d'autrui. Après la manipulation malveillante de la marquise de Merteuil et du vicomte de Valmont, elle perd sa virginité. Autrement dit, elle est corrompue dans le milieu qu'elle vit. C'est ainsi qu'on voit un changement chez elle causé par les dépravés. L'avortement qu'elle subit est un signe que Laclos fait, c'est à dire que l'innocence peut être facilement détruite dans une certaine société pleine de ruse et de duperie. Ce sera pourtant un nouveau commencement pour elle en se reculant au couvent.

La présidente de Tourvel est une dévote de vingt-deux ans et se sent heureuse en mariage. Selon la marquise de Merteuil, c'est une femme moins séduisante que Cécile Volanges, cet "bel objet". On se reporte à la lettre 5 : "[...] des traits réguliers si vous voulez, mais nulle expression : ensablement faite, mais sans grâces : toujours mise à faire rire! Avec ses paquets de fichus sur la gorge, et son corps si remonte au menton! [...] donnant la main à ce grand échalas en cheveux longs, prête à tomber à chaque pas, ayant toujours son panier de quatre aunes sur la tête de quelqu'un, et rougissant à chaque révérence" (DE LACLOS Pierre Choderlos 2005 : 12).

Pour conclure, ce n'est pas une femme désirable d'après Mme de Merteuil, soit aux yeux des libertins. À l'avertissement de la mère de Cécile Volanges, la présidente évite avec effort toutes les rencontres privées avec Valmont. Mais ce dernier est déterminé à la rendre esclave. "J'ai bien besoin d'avoir cette femme, pour me sauver du ridicule d'en être amoureux" (DE LACLOS Pierre Choderlos 2005 : 10). Il s'agit d'une phrase érotique pour les moralistes, mais selon ses propos à Mme de Merteuil et ce qu'il fait, on se rend compte que Valmont tombe amoureux de Mme de Tourvel.

À mesure qu'ils ont plus de contact et de communication, Mme de Tourvel n'est plus sur ses gardes contre Valmont grâce au déguisement et à la manifestation amoureuse imperceptible. Elle se met à croire qu'elle est capable de le sauver et de le rendre pieux. Elle fait de vains efforts. Lorsque Valmont lance une attaque de l'amour, elle est prise de panique et demande son départ. Elle refuse de lire les lettres de Valmont, mais ce dernier ne cesse pas de lui écrire. La présidente commence à réfléchir si elle est contente de son mariage. Elle insiste particulièrement sur sa condition de vie et conclut qu'elle doit être heureuse. Ce qu'elle ignore, c'est que son amour pour Valmont s'accroît davantage. Plus elle résiste, plus elle s'enfonce dans le piège que dresse Valmont. Et évidemment, elle succombe et avoue à la fin sa passion pour lui.

Pourtant Valmont obéit à Mme de Merteuil et écrit une lettre de rupture à Mme de Tourvel qui sombre dans le désespoir. Elle choisit aussi de se retirer au couvent. Néanmoins, sa passion pour Valmont devient de plus en plus forte et sa santé va de mal en pis. Après avoir eu la nouvelle de la mort de Valmont, elle meurt tragiquement. Mme de Tourvel est sûrement dévote devant ses convictions religieuses. Elle essaie de ne pas accepter l'amour de Valmont quoiqu'elle échoue. La passion pour un autre homme que son mari est complètement immorale et intolérable dans la société qu'elle se situe. Certains la trouve la plus positive des personnages féminins du roman. Même après avoir avoué sa passion pour Valmont, elle ne reste en contact avec lui que par lettres. Elégante, pieuse et douce, elle mène une vie tout autre que celle des Merteuil ou des Valmonts, selon les moralistes de son temps, elle doit être femme idéale du XVIIIᵉᵐᵉ siècle. Citons les descriptions de Valmont: "[...] elle n'a point, comme nos femmes coquettes, ce regard menteur qui séduit quelquefois et nous trompe toujours. Elle ne sait pas couvrir le vide d'une phrase par un sourire étudié; et quoiqu'elle ait les plus belles dents du monde, elle ne rit que de ce qui l'amuse. Mais il faut voir comme, dans les folâtres yeux, elle offre l'image d'une gaieté naïve et franche! comme, auprès d'un malheureux qu'elle s'empresse de secourir, son regard annonce la joie pure et la bonté compatissantes!" (DE LACLOS Pierre Choderlos 2005: 15)

Danceny est un jeune chevalier qui tombe amoureux de Cécile Volanges après quelques rencontres. De toute façon, il est entraîné également dans la machination de Mme de Merteuil et de Valmont. Pour commencer, son style d'écriture est factice. Il emploie souvent avec l'antithèse voire l'ironie. On se reporte à la lettre 28: "[...]je n'ose plus me flatter d'une réponse[...]" (DE LACLOS Pierre Choderlos 2005: 74), mais en fait, il demande une réponse de Cécile en exprimant son engouement pour elle ainsi que sa souffrance. Il écrit ensuite: "L'amour l'eût écrite avec empressement, l'amitié avec plaisir, la pitié même avec complaisance: mais la pitié, l'amitié et l'amour sont également étrangers à votre cœur" (DE LACLOS Pierre Choderlos 2005: 74). Sa passion le pousse à satiriser son amour Cécile, simplement pour implorer une réponse par lettre.

Il éprouve pourtant une émotion inextricable pour la marquise de Merteuil, certes, c'est le résultat de la manipulation de Mme de Merteuil. À cause de la provocation de celle-ci, il se bat en duel avec Valmont qui, avant sa mort, lui confère des lettres pour dévoiler le machiavélisme de la marquise.

Il n'est pas difficile de voir que Danceny est vraiment un débutant dans son milieu. Il semble qu'il finit par rien perdre, soit la fortune soit le statut social. Les gens de son milieu vont lui montrer de la sympathie voire glorifier son courage de dénoncer Mme de Merteuil en publiant ses lettres.

Mme de Rosemonde, la plus âgée parmi les correspondants du roman, est censée être lucide et sage. Elle se retire dans un château et est éloignée des vicissitudes du monde. Certes, elle ne s'occupe pas trop de ce qui se passe sous ses toits, la séduction de Valmont, par exemple. Tout de même, elle représente les valeurs sous l'Ancien Régime: la rigidité, la douceur et le zèle. La sage donne à son neveu

Valmont un amour maternel en voulant lui laisser tout son héritage. C'est sans doute pourquoi elle choisit de négliger les faits qui crèvent les yeux.

Lorsque la présidente de Tourvel lui a confié sa passion pour Valmont, Madame de Rosemonde se rend compte de tout et lui montre de la compassion et compréhension. Cette vieille dame a eu probablement la même expérience quand elle était jeune pour qu'elle comprenne ce que sent la présidente. En outre, Mme de Rosemonde est la seule qui connaisse l'ampleur de ce désastre, elle écrit dans sa dernière lettre à Mme de Volanges : "[...] laissons-les dans l'oubli qui leur convient ; et sans chercher d'inutiles et d'affligeantes lumières, soumettons-nous aux décrets de la Providence, et croyons à la sagesse de ses vues, lors même qu'elle ne nous permet pas de les comprendre" (DE LACLOS Pierre Choderlos 2005 : 456). Elle fait l'ignorance de ce qui se passe et elle espère que la Providence mettra fin à cette tragédie.

Le Vicomte de Valmont est doué pour séduire les femmes, on le comprend immédiatement lorsqu'il poursuit sa proie Mme de Tourvel. Dans ses lettres, il manifeste une partie de ce qu'il pense, le reste est à cacher. Il la connaît davantage. C'est pourquoi il réussi à la captiver. Voilà ses quatre phases de séduire : choisir, séduire, chuter et rompre. Il s'attache plus tard à Mme de Tourvel sans qu'il le sache. Quand la marquise se moque de son choix, il ignore et réplique avec une affection pour la présidente. On se reporte à la lettre 6 : "De quels traits vous osez peindre Mme de Tourvel ! ... pour être adorable il lui suffit d'être elle-même. Vous lui reprochez de se mettre mal ; je le crois bien : toute parure lui nuit ; tout ce qui la cache la dépare : c'est dans l'abandon du négligé qu'elle est vraiment ravissante". (DE LACLOS Pierre Choderlos 2005 : 15).

Il nie tout le temps dans ses lettres à Mme de Merteuil d'être vraiment amoureux de la présidente et s'imagine avoir dressé un piège d'amour pour celle-ci, toutefois ses écritures trahissent son secret. Pour la marquise, tout ce que fait Valmont est par l'amour. Il est "sans principes", "au caprice" et "amant langoureux". Pour Valmont, la conquête est son destin. Il s'efforce de séduire les deux femmes, Cécile Volanges et Mme de Tourvel. La première est facilement à tromper avec l'aide de la marquise, tandis que la seconde lui paraît plus difficile à approcher. D'une part, elle est pieuse en face de son mari et de l'amour de Dieu, elle ne se permet pas de tomber amoureux d'un autre homme. Elle ne lui donne jamais d'occasion de rester ensemble. D'autre part, Valmont est fasciné par elle tout en se trompant soi-même.

À la fin du roman, il accepte le duel proposé par Danceny et meurt sous l'épée de celui-ci. Ce qui est étonnant, c'est qu'il remet les lettres de Mme de Merteuil avant son dernier souffle. Il se peut que Valmont regrette d'avoir trahi la présidente en disant la vérité. Sa passion pour celle-ci est sans contredit. C'est l'amour qui le délivre.

La marquise de Merteuil est une femme de tête. Dans la lettre 81, elle parle à Valmont de son histoire autodidacte dans son milieu. Mme de Merteuil relate les connaissances de se comporter en public et de s'entendre avec les autres, surtout avec le sexe opposé. C'est vraiment un livre classique pour apprendre les techniques qui favorisent les activités sociales. Laclos détaille un art de conduite dans la vie sociale, pas seulement dans la société mondaine.

Pour la marquise de Merteuil, c'est important de ne pas exprimer ses sentiments sur le visage, la joie, la tristesse ainsi que la colère. Les femmes, selon elle, ne doivent notamment pas être esclaves de l'amour ou de l'homme. Il faut jouir du plaisir quand on est amoureux. Mais il est évident que dans cette bataille de l'amour, les femmes sont moins puissantes que les hommes. "En effet, ces liens réciproquement donnés et reçus, pour parler le jargon de l'amour, vous seul pouvez, à votre choix, les resserrer ou les rompre: heureuses encore, si dans votre légèreté, préférant le mystère à l'éclat, vous vous contentez d'un abandon humiliant, et ne faites pas de l'idole de la veille la victime du lendemain" (DE LACLOS Pierre Choderlos 2005: 198).

Quoi qu'elle soit cruelle et impitoyable, on voit également chez la marquise l'indépendance matérielle et spirituelle. L'indépendance matérielle, c'est de l'héritage de son mari qui est mort. L'autre provient de ses expériences dans sa jeunesse. "Entrée dans le monde dans le temps où, fille encore[...]j'ai su en profiter pour observer et réfléchir" (DE LACLOS Pierre Choderlos 2005: 201). A mesure qu'elle observe les autres pour saisir leur sentiment, elle reste pendant longtemps au silence. Elle arrive à mieux manipuler les techniques des activités sociales, même dans la relation avec ses amants. "Profondes réflexions: je les ai créés, et je puis dire que je suis mon ouvrage" (DE LACLOS Pierre Choderlos 2005: 201), affirme-t-elle. Elle est sûre de ses gestes et de ses discours. Le plus important, c'est qu'elle est sûre d'elle-même, ce qui est la plus importante qualité d'une femme réussi dans son milieu. Après des années d'écouter, d'imiter et d'apprendre, Mme de Merteuil devient habile tant dans la vie amoureuse que dans l'activité sociale. Elle tend toujours à se perfectionner dans la relation interpersonnelle.

Pourtant, il se peut qu'on observe d'une autre manière les personnages principaux dans le roman. Cécile Volanges n'est jamais une innocente, toutes les instructions méchantes de la part de Mme de Merteuil sont simplement un réveil de ses désirs. Elle s'ennuie au début chez sa mère, et succombe même une fois à la soirée. C'est pour qu'elle ne rencontre pas encore ses semblables, c'est-à-dire les Merteuil et les Valmont. Elle accepte avec plaisir les conseils de la marquise d'entretenir de bons contacts avec Danceny et Valmont. Ce n'est pas parce qu'elle est naïve, mais elle a l'intention. Pour Danceny, il perd l'aspiration à l'amour pur. Son premier amour est prise au piège, il devient un sacrifice et une pièce sur l'échiquier du jeu d'amour des Merteuil et des Valmont. Il ne peut jamais se reculer sain et sauf de ces événements tragiques. Mme de Rosemonde n'est pas aussi sage qu'on ne le croit. Elle est sourde et muette de ce que fait son neveu. Et Mme de Tourvel, est-elle tellement dévote et prude? Si elle était toute pieuse, elle resterait ferme même devant sa passion pour Valmont. Tout comme Cécile Volanges, elle aspire en effet aux aventures amoureuses avec Valmont. Les confessions ou les secrets qu'elle confie à la mère de Cécile Volanges sont peut-être des déguisements. Plus on se dissimule, plus on se démasque.

Valmont est considéré comme un vétéran dans les aventures galantes, les gens qui le connaît croient que c'est impossible pour lui de tourner sur "le droit chemin". De toute façon, il déclare la guerre à Mme de Merteuil: "[. . .]le moindre obstacle mis de votre part sera pris de la mienne pour une véritable déclaration de guerre: vous voyez que la réponse que je vous demande n'exige ni longues ni belles phrases. Duex mots suffisent" (DE LACLOS Pierre Choderlos 2005: 418). Il meurt et finit par détruire la réputation de la marquise qui a été autrefois son amant, et il a gagné la bataille. C'est juste sa conviction: "conquérir est notre destin" (DE LACLOS Pierre Choderlos 2005: 9). Certains prétendent que c'est la victoire qu'il poursuit, à n'importe quel prix et jusqu'à la mort. Il n'aurait jamais pu se convertir à l'amour de Mme de Tourvel, parce que c'est lui qui recopie la lettre féroce de rupture rédigée par Mme de Merteuil et l'envoie à Mme de Tourvel.

Mme de Merteuil est une femme dure au cœur mais bienveillante à l'apparence. Personne ne connaît son vrai caractère jusqu'après avoir lu ses lettres. On la trouve élégante, délicate et décente. Mais cette femme est décidée depuis très jeune à venger son sexe. Au cours de ses aventures amoureuses, elle apprend toute seule des techniques de captiver et de manipuler les hommes. C'est écrit dans la lettre 81, une lettre autobiographique, citons-en les phrases ci-dessous: "[. . .] plus souple avec les autres, l'art de les rendre infidèles pour éviter de leur paraître volage, une feinte amitié, une apparente confiance, quelques procédés généreux, l'idée flatteuse et que chacun conserve d'avoir été mon seul amant, m'ont obtenu leur discrétion" (DE LACLOS Pierre Choderlos 2005: 205).

La marquise est une excellente manipulatrice. Elle se perfectionne dans le monde de l'aristocratie et forme ses propres principes du libertinage sans lui nuire. Ce n'est plus une femme traditionnelle du XVIIIème siècle, tout comme l'image de Mme de Tourvel. C'est une rusée qui jouit de manipuler son sexe opposé, même les femmes, en déclarant qu'elle est née pour venger son sexe.

"Quand j'ai à me plaindre de quelqu'un, je ne le persifle pas; je fais mieux: je me venge" (DE LACLOS Pierre Choderlos 2005: 430). C'est ce qu'elle fait envers le comte de Gercourt qui l'a trahi pour une autre femme. La marquise complote de l'humilier par détruire la chasteté et la pureté de sa fiancée Cécile Volanges. C'est pourquoi Mme de Merteuil met beaucoup de temps à l'instruire et voire sollicite l'aide de Valmont.

Les lettres chez elle deviennent véritablement une arme destructive. En manipulant la langue, elle cache ses émotions réelles et reste décente et calme tout le temps. On remarque que la marquise incite Cécile Volanges de s'éloigner de sa mère et de rester en liaison avec deux hommes. Après avoir rompu avec Valmont, elle provoque un duel entre celui-ci et Danceny. Mme de Merteuil perd enfin la fortune et la beauté et fuit de Paris, de sa société. Disgracieuse et dépourvue d'argent, elle n'a plus ses armes importantes: belle apparence et richesse.

Il est difficile d'étiqueter catégoriquement les personnages dans *Les Liaisons dangereuses*. Ils ont un aspect positif et à la fois négatif. Cécile Volanges et Mme de Tourvel ne sont pas simplement innocentes; Mme de Rosemonde, la plus sage du roman, regarde les complots et les malheurs sans rien dire; Valmont et Mme de Merteuil, les deux dépravés aux yeux des autres, l'un perd la vie pour remords, l'autre perd sa beauté et l'argent pour vouloir venger son sexe.

III. Ambiguïté et clarté dans *Les Liaisons dangereuses*

Dès sa parution, *Les Liaisons dangereuses* et son auteur reçoivent des critiques les plus sévères notamment venant des moralistes et de l'Eglise, et en même temps les admirations des écrivains français contemporains. Ceux qui le critiquent voient l'immoralité. Ils prétendent que ce n'est qu'un roman libertin à interdire, car il y a des mots de légèreté et des scènes corrompues de l'aristocratie. Ce serait un outrage public si le roman se repandait parmi les lecteurs. Cependant, ce roman est si populaire que bien des ouvrages d'alors choisissent les mots " liaisons " ou " dangereux " comme titre. Pour ceux qui l'admirent, c'est un roman réaliste même révolutionnaire. Certains y lisent même le féminisme.

Né d'une famille de petite noblesse, Laclos s'engage à l'armée mais sans grands exploits comme artilleur. Puis il s'éprend d'une grande passion pour la création littéraire et après quelques essais, il parvient à achever cette oeuvre pleine de controverse. Pour " [...] faire un ouvrage qui sortît de la route ordinaire, qui fît du bruit, et qui retentît encore sur terre quand j'y aurai passé ", Laclos emploie le genre littéraire bien populaire de son époque, comme tous les épistoliers. " C'est le défaut des Romans; l'Auteur se bat les flancs pour s'échauffer, et le Lecteur reste froid " (DE LACLOS Pierre Choderlos 2005 : 75).

Dans *Les Liaisons dangereuses*, il semble que l'auteur n'intervient pas dans le déroulement de l'histoire, et on a l'impression qu'il s'agit d'une ambiguïté du début jusqu'à la fin du roman. Il n'est pas facile d'étiqueter les personnages. Valmont est-il encore libertin ou un enfant prodigue qui se repent? Mme de Merteuil est-elle un personnage machiavélique ou un avatar du féminisme? Est-ce un roman libertin ou moraliste? Laclos montre toutefois clairement son dessein par les 175 lettres.

Il ne doit pas être classé dans les écrivains des romans libertins, comme le marquis de Sade, Crébillon fils et Restif de la Bretonne. Comme la description des scènes érotiques ne compose pas tout le roman. Il faut encore voir ce que veut dire l'auteur par son roman, comme le précise premièrement dans le sous-titre de l'ouvrage : *lettres recueillies dans une société et publiées pour l'instruction de quelques autres*. Il est clair que l'instruction est son engagement initial, en particulier celle des femmes. " Toute femme qui consent à recevoir dans sa société un homme sans mœurs, finit par en devenir la victime " (DE LACLOS Pierre Choderlos 2005 : 7). Laclos rédige même trois textes inachevés sur le statut de la femme, sous le titre *De l'éducation des femmes*. Il dénonce l'esclavage des femmes qui manquent d'instruction par la société et la soumission aux hommes. Et à travers la lettre 130 écrit par Mme de Rosemonde, on voit une victoire des femmes : " Plaire, n'est pour lui qu'un moyen de succès; taudis que pour elle, c'est le succès lui-même " (DE LACLOS Pierre Choderlos 2005 : 360).

Conclusion

Parmi les ouvrages du XVIIIème siècle, *Les Liaisons dangereuses* se trouve dans une place importante, tant pour l'histoire de la littérature française, que pour son auteur Laclos. Quelques-uns font la critique car il existe la description des scènes érotiques ou de la débauche de l'aristocratie. Les autres le trouve réaliste même révolutionnaire, parce qu'ils voient le féminisme, par exemple.

Laclos cherche un exploit dans sa carrière militaire sans aucun résultat. En revanche, il réussit dans sa carrière littéraire pour son seul ouvrage plein d'énigme qui provoque la dispute après sa mort. Il se détermine à faire une oeuvre prestigieuse, alors il connaît bien le caractère d'un tel roman: un roman non univoque au sujet de son genre, de ses personnages et de ce que veut dire l'auteur. Cette ambiguïté se met au service de la charté. Un roman caractérisé par l'ambiguïté attire davantage l'intention du public, de là on est prêt à l'entendre attentivement.

On se reporte à la préface du rédacteur: "Les jeunes gens de l'un de l'autre sexe pourraient encore y apprendre que l'amitié que les personnes de mauvaises mœurs paraissent leur accorder si facilement, n'est jamais qu'un piège dangereux, aussi fatal à leur bonheur qu'à leur vertu" (DE LACLOS Pierre Choderlos 2005: 7).

L'auteur tend à "[...]faire un ouvrage qui sortît de la route ordinaire, qui fît du bruit" afin que son roman soit instructif et mette en garde les jeunes gens contre les pièges tendus par ceux qui ont de mauvaises intentions et contre leur hypocrisie. Ce but précis qui s'enracine dans le roman devient explicite, et il ne faut plus, avec négligence, prendre l'auteur pour un des écrivains des romans libertins. Il parvient à ses fins et on n'arrête pas de parler de ses *Liaisons* jusqu'à nos jours.

Bibliographie

[1]BLUM Carol, *A Hint from the Author of Les Liaisons dangereuses?* [J/OL]. http://www.jstor.org/stable/2908179, 2013.

[2]CREPIN Annie, *Choderlos de Laclos l'auteur des Liaisons dangereuses* [J/OL]. http://ahrf.revues.org/1853, 2006.

[3]CAMON Clémence, *Résumé des Liaisons dangereuses* [DB/OL]. http://www.alalettre.com/laclos-oeuvres-liaisons-dangereuses.php, 2013.

[4]DE LACLOS Pierre Choderlos, *Les Liaisons dangereuses* [M]. Paris: Gallimard, 2011.

[5]DE LACLOS Pierre Choderlos, *Les Liaisons dangereuses* [M]. http：//www. inlibroveritas. net/auteur340. html, 2005.

[6]DE LACLOS Pierre Choderlos, *Les Liaisons dangereuses* [DB/OL]. http：// fr. wikisource. org/wiki/Les_ Liaisons_ dangereuses, 2011.

[7]GRESHOFF C. J. , *The Moral Structure of ' Les Liaisons dangereuses '* [J/OL]. http：//www. jstor. org/stable/384626, 2013.

[8]LEBEUF Sophie et MONGOUR Aurélie, *Les Liaisons dangereuses de Pierre Choderlos de Laclos： suprématie féminine* [DB/OL]. http：//www. evene. fr/livres/ actualite/liaisons-dangereuses-choderlos-laclos-bac – 2437. php, 2009.

[9]MALRAUX André, *Le Triangle noir*[M]. Paris：Gallimard, 1970.

[10]VAILLAND Roger, *Laclos par lui-même* [M]. Paris：Editions Du Seuil, 1953.

[11]金恒杰译. 危险的关系[M]. 上海：华东师范大学出版社, 2011.

[12]钱培鑫，陈伟. 法国文学大手笔[M]. 上海：上海译文出版社, 2010.

Linguistics and Translation Studies

Henry James's Grandly Vague and Abstract Periodic Style as a Creative Adaptation of Both John Milton's and Samuel Johnson's Periodic Styles[*]

Wang Ling[**]

School of Foreign Languages, Yunnan University,

Kunming, Yunnan

Abstract: Henry James's periodic syntax in *The Ambassadors* reflects the characteristics of both John Milton and Samuel Johnson. It resembles Milton's Latin periodic syntax in the length and complexity of his left-branch and embedding. James also echoes Johnson's preferences for abstract Latinate terms, nominalisation, stepped structure, and cohesive periodic structure by the foregrounding of balance and parallelism. He makes use of the length and complexity of Miltonian syntactic embedding to realise the thematic grandeur and reflect the protagonist's long-standing vague vision and complex mental process. He also imitates Johnsonian abstractness to represent his major concerns about the qualities of social relationships and his characters' psychological states. James adopts Johnsonian rhetoric to enhance formal grandeur and lessen the difficulty of long periodic structures. All the Jamesian lexical and syntactical idiosyncrasies are fully justified by the emphases he creates and the

  * 论文题目：亨利·詹姆斯对约翰·弥尔顿和塞缪尔·约翰逊圆周文体创造性改编而成的庄重地模糊而抽象的圆周文体。本文系 2017 年度国家社科基金艺术学项目"中国西南民族音乐舞蹈图像研究"（17EH248）、2015 年度国家留学基金出国研修项目（201507035007）、2015 年度云南省哲学社科艺术科学规划重点项目"云南民族音乐舞蹈图像文化艺术的资源保护、产业开发与国际交流研究"（A2015ZDZ001）、云南大学首批"青年英才培育计划"培育对象人才项目、2013 年度云南大学研究生优秀教材《英语跨文化交际：理论与体验》建设项目、2016 年度云南大学教改研究项目"国际化课程开发研究——以《跨文化交际》课程为先导"（2016Y01）、2015 年度美国圣路易斯大学国际合作科研项目"Multidisciplinary Approaches to the Study of Interculturality"的阶段性成果之一。

  ** 作者简介：王玲（Wang Ling），云南大学外国语学院教授，研究方向：英语语言文学与文化、跨文化交际与文化传播。

symbolic significance they convey, and contribute to the suspense in the plot and the vagueness of the characters' personalities. Periodic postponement, as a constant in the syntax, plot and characterisation in the novel, contributes to James's grandly vague and abstract periodic style. His success lies in his combined application of Miltonian periodic syntax and Johnsonian rhetorical devices and cohesion.

Keywords: John Milton; Samuel Johnson; Henry James; *The Ambassadors*; periodic style

1. A Review of the Stylistic Characteristics of English Periodic Syntax

It is generally accepted that both John Milton(1608 – 1674) and Samuel Johnson (1709 – 1784) are masters of the English periodic style. Why, however, is it that Milton's periodic sentences are difficult to understand, whereas Johnson's are much easier and more readable? Either author's focus on specific aspects of the English periodic syntactic pattern creates distinctive syntactic and stylistic effects. A discussion of the contrasts between their sentences calls for first a review of the syntactic and stylistic features of English periodic sentence patterns.

In the seventeenth century, John Milton made extensive use of the typical Ciceronian periodic sentences, which are long, involved and embedded. As a result of the Enlightenment in the eighteenth century, the size of the reading public increased. The middle class came into being and made up the majority of the reading public, but the Miltonian complex embedding was difficult for many middle-class readers to understand. Then Samuel Johnson's innovative use of the periodic sentence pattern made concessions to the comprehension level of the ordinary readers. Johnson led them to follow his reasoning process and rendered his meanings more accessible by simplifying the periodic structure. Johnson's popularity was largely due to his innovative use of the simplified periodic sentence pattern adapted to the balanced structure codified by Quintilian. Syntactic balance or parallelism refers to the repetition of the same syntactic form(e. g. tense, voice, phrase or clause structure) in two or more neighbouring clauses or sentences. The meanings in the two parts of a balanced structure may be similar or contrastive. The similarity in syntactic form is a device of emphasis. The balanced structure reinforces its meaning by similarity, contrast or antithesis, or helps to build up an emotional climax. As a great exponent of Latinate prose after Milton, Johnson used a strongly cohesive and controlled periodic style appropriately in both his argumentative discourse and his fiction. In his time, the novel, which was par excellence a mode of writing that represented people in relationship to society, was established as a prose form utilising a variety of strategies of representation.

Syntax is the organisation of words in phrases, clauses and sentences. By the nineteenth century periodic syntax had come to be regarded by English grammarians as the ultimate form of good prose, thanks to Johnson's modification, popularisation and successful use of it. It was adopted by early novelists such as Henry Fielding(1707 – 1754)in the eighteenth century, and then by the grand novelist Henry James(1843 – 1916)of the late nineteenth and early twentieth centuries.

By dictionary definitions, the term"periodic"can either refer to many subordinate clauses or denote a sentence ending with the main clause. "A period,"says Alistair Campbell, "is a complex sentence wherein the meaning remains suspended till the whole is finished... The criterion of a period is as follows: if the reader stops anywhere before the end, the preceding words will not form a sentence, and therefore cannot convey any determined sense"(Minto 1872: 4).

If Campbell's definition were rigorously adhered to, the term"periodic syntax" could be applied only to sentences that keep the reader in suspense up to the very last word. A periodic sentence in a strict sense is one that saves its main clause to the end. As a matter of fact, the term is applied much more widely and loosely. Any sentence can be said to have a periodic structure if anticipatory constituents play a major part in it. An anticipatory constituent is any subordinate or dependent one that is non-final(Leech and Short 1981: 225). Parenthetical dependent constituents(those occurring in medial positions)belong to the anticipatory category. The corresponding dependent elements in final position are generally called trailing constituents, which include final dependent and non-initial coordinate constituents. In summary, anticipatory elements can be identified as initial dependent and medial parenthetical constituents. Relatively speaking, a periodic sentence can be divided into a former anticipatory part and a latter or even final realisation(Leech and Short 1981: 225). The reader has to bear in mind points of the former part until he or she gets to the essential point at the end. If positioned before the predicate verb and delaying its appearance, a subject in a periodic sentence is considered anticipatory and heavy-headed if it is realised by a long and complex noun phrase which may embed one or more subordinate clauses, whereas the predicate is much shorter, simpler and postponed to the very end of the sentence. Adverbials or subordinate constituents positioned before the subject or before the verb are also anticipatory constituents of a periodic sentence.

Generally speaking, the periodic sentence pattern has five main characteristics. First, subordination is involved, and the subordinate clause or clauses precede the main or principal clause. Second, it is massive in length but controlled by inner coherence. Third, the heavy-headed subject is often separated from its delayed predicate verb by a long distance because of a long and complex insertion. Fourth, medial insertions or parenthetical constituents can be periodic elements. Two other kinds of periodic constituents are final extension to provide further new information, and stepped structure to reach a climax. Fifth, because the main clause and the predicate verb are delayed, the structure and sense of a periodic sentence are not complete until the latter part or even the very end is reached (Gordon 1966: 73).

2. An Analysis of John Milton's and Samuel Johnson's Distinctive Periodic Styles

With its skillful intricacy and artful, rhythmical devices, classical Latin periodic syntax was readily imitated in the seventeenth century. John Milton and Samuel Johnson resorted to different features of the periodic syntactic pattern and brought about different stylistic effects. Gordon thus comments on Milton's sentence pattern: "The normal sentence structure is the Ciceronian period, sustained with considerable virtuosity through interlocked subordinate clauses in some of the longest sentences in English" (Gordon 1966: 106). Extreme length and interlocking of subordinate clauses are two prominent features of Milton's Ciceronian-style periodic syntactic pattern.

In Milton's prose, the syntax is more Latinised than the lexical choices. Part of one sentence from Milton's *Doctrine and Discipline of Divorce* (1644) will be used as a brief illustration of the Latin periodic aspect of his prose. For the sake of analysis, the first few lines of the extract, which give the context, are set out as normal prose, but, after the colon, the remainder is set out in numbered clauses or clause-equivalents to bring out the complexity of the structuring, which may be masked by the syntactic ordering of the text; the principal clause is capitalised; balanced words are linked together vertically.

Love if he be not twin born, yet has a brother wondrous like him, called Anteros, whom while he seeks all about, his chance is to meet with many false and feigning desires, that wander singly up and down in his likeness:

1a   by them in their borrowed garb,

2   LOVE,

3a   though not wholly blind,

4   as poets wrong him,

3b   yet having but one eye,

5   as being born an archer aiming,

6   and that eye not the quickest
      in this dark region here below,

7   which is not Love's proper sphere,

1b   partly out of the | simplicity
                  | and credulity

8   which is native to him,

1c   often deceived,

2b | embraces
      | and consorts him with these
      | obvious
      | and suborned striplings,

9   as if they were his mother's own sons;

(Stephens and Waterhouse 1980: 70)

The extremely long and elaborated sentence is complicated and embedded with entangled prepositional phrases, participial phrases and subordinate clauses. From the long distance between the components of the same clause, one can see that Milton's extreme Latin tendency contorts the syntax in such a way as to issue a challenge to the reader's intellect, making no concessions that might render the structure of the sentence easier to follow. The dominance of monosyllabic and disyllabic over polysyllabic words in the extract proves that Milton's diction is less Latinised than his syntax. His lexical choices are not heavily Latinate, but what creates the impression of Latinity is his syntax, with its inversions, contortions, and splitting up of the clauses in the way that Latin does.

The three parts of Clause 1 explain why and how love is deceived by desires: because he is naturally simple and credulous, and because they are deceptive. However, the three are placed far apart one from another. The sentence is highly convoluted, left-branching in the extreme and very difficult to follow because its major part lies on the left of the predicate "embraces and consorts". As a result, the reader's anticipation of the predicate is evoked intensely and held for a long time. The subject of the principal clause, "Love", is separated from its predicate by subordinate clauses running as long as fifty-one words. A long left-branching structure precedes the predicate verbs of the principal clause "embraces and consorts", but only a brief and light-weighted right-branch follows the predicate verbs. Clause 1, which is tripartitely divided and provides the explanation for the deception, occurs before the actual term "deceived". Clause 3 after the subject is a heavily-weighted explanation for the poor eyesight of love. All the explanations precede and postpone the pair of principal predicate verbs which relate love's affectionate responses towards the deceivers. The suspense and the reader's curiosity regarding the anchor of the explanations are evoked. In developing the periodic structure, an explanation is elaborated before the reader knows the actual element for which the explanation is given.

The late placement of the main predicate verb and the jungle of parentheses and subordinate clauses in Milton's extremely convoluted periodic structure are typical of Latin, and pose great difficulty to the reader. If the English writers were to abandon their native parataxis and coordination to imitate the indirectness and complexity of the Ciceronian periodic sentence, something to mitigate the Latin periodic structure would be required to lessen the complexity. The answer lay in the rhetoric of Quintilian (Gordon 1966: 78). In the eighteenth century, Johnson's combination of the Ciceronian periodic structure with the rhetoric of Quintilian led to a periodic syntax which was less complex in structure and easier to understand, but more intensive in meaning.

Johnson reduced the length of his periodic sentences and controlled their complexity by using more conjunctives or connectives. The manifestation of inner coherence within his periodic sentences guides the reader's logical and reasonable understanding of his arguments. Johnson's periodic elements lie mainly in final extension, which provides more and more information to explain or reinforce the former context, and balanced stepped structure, which takes the form of parallel phrases or clauses, but with a build-up of semantic tension and a final realisation or resolution. The sense of a periodic sentence with extension and stepped structure is usually incomplete until the very end, which provides new information or a climax.

Consider a typical Johnsonian periodic sentence in his *Letter to Lord Chesterfield*:

Seven years, my Lord, have now past, since I waited in your outward rooms, or was repulsed from your door, during which time I have been pushing on my work through difficulties, of which it is useless to complain, and have brought it, at last, to the verge of publication, without one act of assistance, one word of encouragement, or one smile of favour.

(Wang and Li 1983: 443)

The sentence contains both extension and the stepped structure. The two clauses: "... during which time..." and "... of which..." are extensions to provide further information on the basis of preceding noun phrases. The stepped structure: "... without one act of assistance, one word of encouragement, or one smile of favour...", contains two groups of parallel words implying degradation or declining of actions: act—word—smile, assistance—encouragement—favour. In collaboration with the preposition "without" preceding the stepped structure, the gradation in meaning and emotion rises to its climax at the end of the sentence. The author's meaning and emotion are incompletely expressed until the final noun phrase of the stepped structure.

Consider another passage by Johnson:

(1) I cannot forbear to flatter myself that prudence and benevolence will make marriage happy. (2) The general folly of mankind is the cause of general complaint. (3) What can be expected but disappointment and repentance from a choice made in the immaturity of youth, in the ardour of desire, without judgement, without foresight, without enquiry after conformity of opinions, similarity of manners, rectitude of judgement, or purity of sentiment? (4) Such is the common process of marriage. (5) A youth and maiden meeting by chance, or brought together by artifice, exchange glances, reciprocate civilities, go home, and dream of one another. (6) Having little to divert attention, or diversify thought, they find themselves uneasy, when they are apart, and therefore conclude that they shall be happy together.

(Stephens and Waterhouse 1980: 80)

Johnson's lexical choices are distinctive with regard to his mixture of Latinate and native terms. The proportion of polysyllabic Latinate words in the passage by Johnson is higher than that in Milton's prose. The combination is seen in Sentence 5: "exchange glances, reciprocate civilities, go home, and dream of one another". The two verbal phrases " exchange glances " and " reciprocate civilities " belong to Latinate lexical choices, and their native alternatives would be "look at each other" and "speak to each other". The former two Latinate verbal phrases expressing social behaviour form a sharp contrast with the latter two native verbal phrases denoting natural inner emotions. Johnson preferred more abstract, Latinate, nominalised words to native adjectives. Instead of "proper judgement" and "pure sentiment", Johnson resorted to the more abstract noun phrases "rectitude of judgement" and "purity of sentiment". Abstractness is part of the effect of Latinate prose. The use of Latinate, especially polysyllabic words is characteristic of formal style.

The last two sentences in this extract are typical of the periodic left-branch. However, Johnson's left-branching structure is shorter and less embedded than Milton's complex formulation. In Sentence 3, a what-cleft sentence, the long and complex logical subject with its modifiers is postponed and replaced by an abstract subject clause with the pronoun " what " questioning and delaying the real logical subject. There are many balanced words, phrases and clauses in the passage. In Sentence 2 the repetition of "general" underlines the balancing of cause and effect in the relationship of " folly " and " complaint ". In Sentence 3 the number of balanced phrases increases progressively along the syntactic chain: two balanced "in the..." phrases, three parallel " without... " phrases, and four parallel " ... of... " phrases. Finally there are two balanced coordinate clauses.

The use of the balanced structure and logical connectives in Johnson's prose is partly shaped by his social background. Britain in the eighteenth century was intellectually enhanced by the Enlightenment, which advocated reason and logic. The people's harmonious mental states and enlightened and careful ways of thinking found expression in balanced structures and elegant periodic sentence patterns. The emphasis on reason and logic was embodied in Johnson's use of such logical connectives as " ... so... that... ", " ... neither... nor... ", as in his " Letter to Lord Chesterfield": "... but I found my attendance so little encouraged, that neither pride nor modesty would suffer me to continue it" (Wang and Li 1983: 442). His balanced structure and logical connectives within and between sentences intermittently relieve the reader from the burden of the periodic structure. By making his periodic sentences appear partly regular in form, logical in connection, and repetitive or contrastive in sense, Johnson guides the reader's comprehension and imparts his ideas in periodic sentences much more directly and obviously than Milton.

In sum, Johnson's Latinism, in contrast to Milton's, lies predominantly in more abstract Latinate nouns and shorter, simpler periodic structure. While both Milton and Johnson can be regarded as Latinate periodic writers, they differ totally in the way that they apply the lexical and syntactical aspects of the Latin prose style. Johnson's periodic syntax is foregrounded by his balance and parallelism. The stylistic impression of formality, elevation and distance in Johnson's prose is very differently achieved from that in Milton's prose. Johnson paid more attention to the lexical and rhetorical aspects, whereas Milton stressed the syntactical aspect by his persistent naturalisation of complicated Latin syntax in English. As contrasted with Milton, Johnson marked the cohesion and logical relationships within and between sentences much more clearly and directly. His sentences are less left-branching, and he was less inclined to embed deeply and locate the components of the same clause far apart from one another. Johnson's repetition of subordinators and recurring use of semantically related terms lend cohesion to his text and clearly mark the logical and grammatical relations within his sentences.

3. Henry James's Grandly Vague and Abstract Periodic Style as a Creative Adaptation of Both John Milton's and Samuel Johnson's Periodic Styles

According to Alistair Campbell's criterion, writers whose works contain periodic sentences may be considered as having a periodic style even though complete periodic sentences are few in their works (Minto 1872: 6). Analogously, the term "periodic" may still be retained for a periodic sentence whether rigorously complete or nearly so. "Periodic" is now generally accepted as a term referring to anticipatory constituents, and is adopted to refer to any style in which anticipations habitually occur.

In *The Ambassadors* (1903), one of the three late novels by Henry James, such anticipations recur successively in the syntax, and have their counterparts in the plot and the characterisation. James uses long parenthetical constituents here and there in his periodic sentences to delay the subjects, the predicate verbs or their objects, and the referents' names. Some sentences include more than one such parenthesis. The long delay in completion and specification in his periodic sentences makes the sense vague until the final appearance of the main grammatical components and the final identification of the referents. Furthermore, the periodic delay of revelation and the consequent vague sense are also realised on a larger scale in the plot-building and personality-portraying of the characters in *The Ambassadors*. Suspense is always present as to the characters' relationships and their characteristics. The vague sense resulting from the syntactic delays is cumulative and underlies the vagueness in the plot-building and characterisation.

One major concern of James is to examine the qualities of the characters in his novels. In *The Ambassadors* nearly all the characters' qualities are difficult to define, and their responses are often unexpected. Even after long acquaintance, Lambert Strether, the protagonist, comments on the impenetrability of Chad Newsome's character as follows: "I'm not altogether sure what he thinks. I'm not sure of anything that concerns him, except that the more I've seen of him, the less I've found him what I originally expected. He's obscure and that's why I'm waiting" (James 1986: 493). Chad's reactions are so capricious and unexpected that his character is vague to Strether, who himself is also characterised as "grandly vague" (James 1986: 493) even at the very end of the novel. Also vague-ness are Strether's impressions of Madame de Vionnet: "She was an obscure person, a muffled person one day, and a showy person, an uncovered person the next" (James 1986: 256). Even Strether's old friend Waymarsh becomes vague and impenetrable to him: "Waymarsh had been slightly ambiguous" (James 1986: 408).

Another major concern of James is to reveal the interpersonal relationships. Many times James assures the reader that his novels represent relationships rather than objects or even people. R. W. Short distinguishes three orders of relationship emphasised constantly throughout the later writings by James. The first order—a simple, rhetorical one—consists in explicit statements of relationship (Short 1946: 77). In the beginning of *The Ambassadors*, Strether does not worry about the difficulty of his errand, although there are "early signs in him that his relation to his actual errand might prove none of the simplest" (James 1986: 56). The statement of Strether's relation to his errand is an example of the first order. The reader must agree at once that, however remarkable the relation is as the subject of *The Ambassadors*, there is nothing remarkable at all about this means of expressing it.

The second and third orders may be called structural because they are expressed by grammatical means. The second order is simply the expression of relationship between the parts of the sentence. It is true that without relationship, no sentence exists, but here again it is a matter of emphasis. James secures great emphasis for these relating elements by his two favourite devices: italicising the relating words and the unconventional organisation of his sentences. The first device is frequently employed, as a casual inspection of any of James's later writings will reveal (Short 1946: 77 – 78). The occurrences are not all of equal interest, for example, " . . . he should have been there with, and as it might have been said, for Chad" (James 1986: 65). To distinguish the second preposition "for" from the first "with" and give it some emphasis, James italicises it, particularly because he wrote before emphatic italics went out of fashion. Even more frequent than this employment of italics is James's use of abnormal sentence order to secure emphasis on words denoting relationship. His sentences often seem to have been unthreaded and restrung for the sole purpose of removing emphasis from the active verbs and throwing it instead onto nouns and humbler words of connection. The third order of relating expressions common in James consists in expressions within a sentence that relate that sentence to what has gone before and what will come after. Numerous transitional expressions of this kind are employed in the form of parentheses or interjections by James. They frequently interrupt the periodic sentences in which they occur and contribute heavily to the unusual texture of James's writing.

In *The Ambassadors* the interpersonal relationships are multiple but always vague because the writer delays their specification or revelation. The central concern of the protagonist Strether later turns to the relationship between Chad and Madame de Vionnet. Along with Strether, the reader is kept in suspense as to the true nature of their friendship up to Chapter IV, Book XI, nearly the end of the novel. Around the central thread of that relationship, other interpersonal relationships are interwoven but not specified even at the novel's conclusion. For example, Miss Maria Gostrey and Madame de Vionnet turn out to be former classmates and good friends, but it is puzzling that Miss Gostrey goes out of town when Madame de Vionnet is coming to present herself in Paris, leaving their attitude toward each other evasive and vague. Then after the first presentation of Madame de Vionnet and her daughter Mademoiselle de Vionnet, it is difficult for Strether to figure out to which one Chad is attached. It vaguely comes to Strether's mind that Mademoiselle de Vionnet loves Chad, but it is surprising at the end that she is marrying another man mediated through Chad to show her love to her mother. Strether gradually comes to realise that the central relationship is that between Chad and Madame de Vionnet.

The vague affection between Chad's friend little Bilham and Mamie Pocock, who is supposed to be Chad's fiancée, is vaguely perceived by sensitive Strether. At last little Bilham goes after Mamie when she is leaving for Switzerland. However, the result is not easy to anticipate since Chad seems inclined to go home and accept Mamie. The reader is kept in the dark as to their future. The multiple and entangled relations are beyond Strether's anticipation and control. Later in the novel, Waymarsh seems to be close to Chad's sister Sarah, while Madame de Vionnet appears to be approaching Sarah's husband Jim Pocock in order to defy Sarah. So many vague and complex interpersonal relationships delay and confuse Strether's attention to the central relationship between Chad and Madame de Vionnet. The clouded interpersonal relationships are represented through the embedded periodic structure to maintain a sense of vagueness until a resolution point.

At first Strether enjoys the delay in meeting Waymarsh, and then he enjoys the absence of Chad because he can delay his mission and prolong his connection with Paris and the Parisian residents. Toward the end of the novel he tries to postpone Chad's departure for the United States by asking him to stay and reproaching his irresponsibility. The whole novel is a process of delay made up of numerous dilatory actions and events. The writer uses the strategy of delay, which is typical of the periodic style, to convey vagueness, to open up wide possibilities and potentialities, and to prolong the protagonist's free imagination, mental process, and experience in Paris.

The periodic style implies the use of long periodic sentences, which are elaborately constructed and hold a flock of clauses in suspense. James's style reflects the characteristics of both John Milton and Samuel Johnson, two famous writers of the periodic style. James's periodic syntax resembles Milton's Latin periodic syntax in the length and complexity of his left-branch and embedding. He also echoes Johnson's preferences for abstract Latinate terms, nominalisation, stepped structure, and cohesive periodic structure by the foregrounding of balance and parallelism.

Two illustrations will demonstrate James's absorption of the syntactic idiosyncrasies of both Milton and Johnson. "At the end of the ten minutes he was to spend with her his impression—with all it had thrown off and all it had taken in—was complete" (James 1986: 248). In the sentence, "he was to spend with her" is embedded to modify "the ten minutes". The subject is separated from its delayed predicate by the parenthetical constituent marked off by two dashes. The final word "complete" resolves the vagueness about the sense of the rest of the sentence. The subject is delayed by the adverbial which embeds a restrictive attributive clause, and the predicate "was complete" does not appear until the very end of the sentence. The meaningful elements are interdependent. The rest of the sentence cannot be interpreted until the reader reaches the final word"complete", and the full implication of"complete"depends on the understanding of its preceding part. The form and content fit perfectly in the periodic sentence. Besides the periodic structure, James weaves an antithesis: "all it had thrown off and all it had taken in". The sentence is an illustration of James's periodic style, combining Milton's Ciceronian-style periodic syntax with Johnson's Quintilian-based rhetoric of balanced structure.

The following sentence is another instance of similar combinations: "Strether meanwhile continued to hold off from Miss Gostrey, keeping her till tomorrow, so that by evening his responsibility, his impunity, his luxury, had become—there was no other word for them—immense" (James 1986: 474). Like Johnson's frequent use of logical connection, "so that" is used here by James to indicate the causative relationship. In the adverbial clause of result, the subject is composed of three parallel phrases, and the predicate is interrupted by a parenthesis of explanation and comment. The final word"immense"is part of the predicate and immensely postponed until the very end of the sentence.

Consider another example:

A young girl in a white dress and a softly plumed white hat had suddenly come into view, and what was presently clear was that her course was toward them. What was clearer still was that the handsome young man at her side was Chad Newsome, and what was clearest of all was that she was therefore Mademoiselle de Vionnet, that she was unmistakeably pretty— bright gentle shy happy wonderful—and that Chad now, with a consummate calculation of effect, was about to present her to his old friend's vision. What was clearest of all indeed was something much more than this, something at the single stroke of which—and wasn't it simply juxtaposition? —all vagueness vanished.

(James 1986: 217)

Similar to Johnson's syntactic pattern, James's four parallel what-cleft sentences are periodic sentences because they arouse the reader's anticipation of and attention to the contents of the real subjects replaced, questioned and delayed by the beginning "what". Three other parallel that-clauses are embedded within the second sentence after"and what was clearest of all was that. . . ". The stepped structure and cohesive link between the sentences are realised through the adjective"clear". "Clear"develops from the positive, the comparative to the superlative degree and reflects a reasonably gradual process of perception and cognition. In the last sentence, the repeated part "what was clearest of all" with further modification of "indeed" brings the reader's anticipation and attention to the climax. However, the last sentence is ironical in that the long-awaited clearest thing is "something" vague and unspecified. The climactic point still keeps the reader in suspense and vagueness. Strether's vague impression and realisation are vividly portrayed by the periodic syntax which contains the parallel and stepped structure to reach a climactic point and achieve its characteristic stylistic effect of irony.

James is similar to Milton in presenting this long periodic structure with complex embedding, which is realised in the second long sentence with sixty words made up of two what-cleft subject clauses, four that-clauses as the predicative, and a parenthesis marked off by two dashes. Johnson's idiosyncrasies of repetition, parallelism, and the periodic stepped structure are also prominent in this extract. James's use of the balanced structure creates two specific stylistic effects in *The Ambassadors*. First, it contributes to the elegance, grandeur and refinement of the periodic style and the well-known grandiose image of belle-époque Paris with its social beauty and refined residents. Second, related to Strether's peculiar nature, it is a manifestation of his effort to see the world about him and classify his impressions into neat and well-defined categories.

The grandeur of James's style is shaped by the long and complex periodic structure modified by balance and parallelism. Because they are elaborately prolonged and embedded with insertions, the senses of his periodic sentences are always vague and incomplete until their ends. The protagonist's long-standing vague knowledge of Paris and the portrayed interpersonal relationships finds expression in the vague effect of the periodic structure. James's periodic length and complexity in combination with balance and parallelism make his style look grand in form. His postponement of specification and completion prolongs anticipation and makes the senses of the periodic sentences, the plot and the characters' personalities vague until the final revelation point of the sentences and the plot. Linguistically and thematically, James creates the image of Strether, who always resorts to the strategy of delay or postponement, just as he comments on the protagonist, "He had been great already, as he knew, at postponements" (James 1986: 488). In this sense, therefore, James's style can be called a grandly vague periodic style.

In following the stylistic idiosyncrasy of elegance and vagueness through the texture of *The Ambassadors*, the present inquiry can offer an account of the sense of unity in multiplicity. Grandeur and vagueness, two concepts characterising the periodic style, can be found to operate at various linguistic levels in the novel. All the aspects of James's language serve and contribute to the grandly vague and abstract periodic style and reflect the characters' personalities and the substances of the plot. All or at least nearly all the idiosyncrasies of James's diction and syntax are fully justified by the emphases he creates in the novel.

Henry James's style, far from being a surface eccentricity, exactly embodies his intentions. All of the Jamesian linguistic idiosyncrasies have stylistic implications in the plot-building and personality-portraying of the characters in *The Ambassadors*. The common assessment of James is that his language is difficult, abstract and indirect. Abstractness and complexity of lexis and syntactic embedding are indeed characteristics of James's periodic style. It is also these characteristics that give rise to the complex vision that James creates in *The Ambassadors*.

Sentences can be prolonged with a good many subordinate clauses and parentheses. James's long periodic sentences are punctuated with frequent qualifications and parentheses, for instance, "Slowly and sociably, with full pauses and straight dashes, Strether had so delivered himself" (James 1986: 216). The reader's attention is drawn to the ways in which familiar actions or events are defamiliarised by being slowed down or interrupted. The effect of postponement and protraction is achieved by the separation of the subject from the predicate verb, and the separation of a transitive verb from its object. James's long sentences, composed of word groups linked together, with many insertions and parentheses, form a complexity that is not of idea, but of relationship between ideas. They throw into relationship a number of ideas, each of which may have, within the sentence, its own finite grammatical structure.

In *The Ambassadors*, James's style reaches its highest point of development. The writer has arrived at a periodic style in which he shows more interest in playfully exploring the connotative possibilities generated by the surface of his vague vocabulary and periodic structure than in conveying a definite meaning. He has created a narrative and expositive syntax which mirrors that grandly vague and abstract periodic style by perpetually postponing predication and escaping any conclusion in order to protect the plot's abstractly infinite potential. Supplied by the periodic structure, the plot is vague because the story is replete with tendencies to pause or hesitate, to anticipate or reminisce through the screen of modal verbs and the subjunctive mood, to convert sensations and observations into abstractions and generalisations.

The long periodic sentences can create a dramatic effect, which James foreshadows by repeating the word "drama". The protagonist Strether is referred to as "the hero of the drama" (James 1986: 402). The final river scene of revelation is climactic and dramatic. Apart from its dramatic quality, James's periodic structure has the related virtue of concentrating significance at a later point in both the sentences and the plot because the interpretation of anticipatory constituents is delayed in the periodic sentence. The enlightenment regarding his sentences and the whole plot comes retrospectively at the end, where all the elements of meaning and scene fit synoptically into a complete whole. Thus an apparent complication of James's grandly vague and abstract periodic style, especially his predilection for parenthetical constructions, may find its justification in the integral and comprehensive implications, and the surprising and ironical effects that it creates.

The periodic structure always postpones to its end most new, relatively important and climactic element. This feature is congruous to the arrangement of the plot in *The Ambassadors*. The climactic revelation is set in the river scene in Chapter IV, Book XI, nearly the end of the novel. By the agency of the merest coincidence, admittedly the stuff of fiction or farce, Strether's months of surmises are resolved in the instant of his shock at witnessing the illicit sexual liaison between Chad and Madame de Vionnet. The periodic structure is also embodied in the arrangement of the climactic scene toward the end of the novel.

James inherits the characteristics of John Milton and Samuel Johnson, his two famous predecessors in the periodic style, and applies them to *The Ambassadors*. The periodic strategy of postponement in structure and sense is extended on a larger scale to the plot-arrangement and characterisation in the novel. The protagonist Strether always postpones action in order to prolong his stay in Paris as an ambassador. James makes use of the length and complexity of Miltonian syntactic embedding to realise the thematic grandeur and vagueness and reflect the long-standing vague vision and complex mental process of the protagonist as the central sensor in the novel. He also imitates Johnsonian abstractness to represent his major concerns about the qualities of social relationships and his characters' psychological states. James adopts Johnsonian rhetoric to enhance formal grandeur and lessen the difficulty of long periodic structures. In a word, all the Jamesian linguistic idiosyncrasies, which are manifold but unified, contribute to the suspense in the plot and the vagueness of the characters' personalities. The Jamesian lexical and syntactical features are justified in all respects by the symbolic significance they convey in *The Ambassadors*.

Periodic postponement is a constant in the syntax, plot and characterisation in the novel, and contributes to its grandly vague and abstract periodic style. In this sense, the success of James as a successful periodic master lies in his combined application of Miltonian periodic syntax and Johnsonian rhetorical devices and cohesion, the main components of the periodic style as traditionally understood. At the same time James is a modern writer in terms of his literary initiatives. David Lodge summarises the characteristics of modern English writing as follows: formal experiment, dislocation of conventional syntax, radical breaches of decorum, disturbance of chronology and spatial order, ambiguity, polysemy, obscurity, myth-poetic allusion, primitivism, irrationalism, structuring by symbol and motif rather than by narrative or argumentation(Lodge 1981: 70). Many of those characteristics are embodied in *The Ambassadors*, such as dislocation of the conventional subject + verb + object syntax in his periodic structure, especially parenthetical constituents; disturbance of chronology and spatial order by means of preview and retrospect; interplay of mental and physical spheres; ambiguity and obscurity of diction. In a word, as seen from *The Ambassadors*, Henry James is a great modern periodic master in terms of his literary and stylistic initiatives.

References

[1]Gordon, I. *The Movement of English Prose*[M]. London: Longman Group Limited, 1966.

[2]James, H. *The Ambassadors*[M]. Middlesex: Penguin Books Limited, 1986.

[3]Leech, G. , and M. Short. *Style in Fiction*[M]. London: Longman Group Limited, 1981.

[4]Lodge, D. *Working with Structuralism: Essays and Reviews on Nineteenth-and Twentieth-Century Literature*[C]. Boston: Routledge & Kegan Paul Ltd. , 1981.

[5]Minto, W. *A Manual of English Prose Literature: Biographical and Critical, Designed Mainly to Show Characteristics of Style* [M]. London: William Blackwood & Sons, 1872.

[6] Short, R. The sentence structure of Henry James [J]. *American Literature*,

1946, 18(2).

[7] Stephens, J. and R. Waterhouse, *Literature, Language, and Change: From Chaucer to the Present*[M]. London: Routledge, 1980.

[8] Wang Zuoliang and Li Funing *An Anthology of English Literature Annotated in Chinese*[M]. Beijing: Commercial Press, 1983.

Lexical Differences in Chinese Translations of *Auguries of Innocence*: A Cultural Perspective[*]

Yin Kexiu[**]

School of Foreign Languages, Yunnan University,

Kunming, Yunnan

Abstract: The translations of the first four lines of *Auguries of Innocence* are popular in China. Based on the analysis of ten widely accepted Chinese versions, this paper explores how cultural connotations are conveyed by the nouns. Four religious or philosophical traditions are included in the analysis, namely, Buddhism, Taoism, Christianity and non-religion. Factors that contribute to the popularity of these translations are also examined. It is hoped that the paper can have practical and theoretical implications to literary translation.

Keywords: Buddhism; Taoism; Christianity; non-religion; literary translation

1. Introduction

William Blake, a forerunner Romanticist English poet in the 18th and 19th centuries, has struck the reader with the strong religious belief and philosophical undercurrent of his works. The first four lines of his poem *Auguries of Innocence* and the corresponding translations have received great popularity in China. The translation of the four lines appeared in the early 20th century by the Chinese poet Li Shutong and the translation efforts have never stopped since then. A number of Chinese translations can be found not only in literary publications but also in the mass media such as online

---

* 论文题目:《纯真的预言》多译本词汇特点赏析。

** 作者简介: 尹可秀(Yin Kexiu), 云南大学外国语学院英语系副教授, 研究方向: 翻译理论与实践; 应用语言学。

forums and magazines. Both the popularity of the poem and its translations have aroused wide academic interest. Interpretations of the poem have been conducted on its narrative modes(An, 2014a, 2014b), the image(Shen & Zhang, 2015; Jingjing Li, 2013a; Bi, 2009) and the appeal for and complex of innocence(Jingjing Li, 2013b). Research perspectives include culture(Zixin Li & Zhengshuan Li 2017; Ling Li, 2017) and cognitive poetics(Mao & Zhao, 2011). These studies either analyze one of the translations or make a comparison between the translations in rhetorical or grammatical means or on the sentence and discourse levels. As the basic component of a language, words are shaped by culture and thus convey distinct cultural connotations. The poem *Auguries of Innocence* was created by the recognized pious Christian William Blake, and its translators in China include poets or writers of diverse backgrounds like the Buddhist poet Li Shutong. It may be interesting to compare different translations on the lexical level from a cultural perspective. Hence the present study. Since the 132-line poem *Auguries of Innocence* is mostly known to Chinese readers for its translations of the first four lines, this paper will focus on the four lines only. For brevity, "the poem" refers to the first four lines of *Auguries of Innocence* in this paper. The following three questions will be answered:

Research question 1: What are the Chinese translations of the English nouns in the first four lines of the poem?

Research question 2: What cultural connotations can be found in the Chinese translations?

Research question 3: How can the Chinese translations shed light on literary translation?

2. Translations of the Poem

As is mentioned above, the poem has been translated into different Chinese versions. For the purpose of the study, a total of ten popular Chinese translations are collected from publications and websites. For the ease of reference and comparison, the original English poem and the ten Chinese translations are provided below.

The original poem:

To see a world in a grain of sand,

And a heaven in a wild flower,

Hold infinity in the palm of your hand,

And eternity in an hour.

The ten Chinese translations are produced either in the form of quatrain or prose poem. Translations ① to ⑤ are quatrains.

①一花一世界，一沙一天国。君掌盛无边，刹那含永劫。（by Li Shutong）

②一沙一大千，一花一桃源。乾坤执掌心，永恒一瞬间。（by You Keqiang）

③一沙一世界，一花一天堂。无限掌中置，刹那成永恒。（by Xu Zhimo）

④粒沙窥天地，朵花藏乾坤。无极掌中握，万古一瞬间。（by an anonymous writer）

⑤一沙窥海，一花报春。须弥纳芥，刹那永恒。（by an anonymous writer）

Translations ⑥ to ⑩ are prose poems.

⑥一粒沙里见世界，一朵花里见天国。手掌里盛住无限，一刹那便是永劫。（by Feng Zikai）

⑦从一粒沙看世界，从一朵花看天堂；把永恒纳进一个时辰，把无限握在自己手心。（by Wang Zuoliang）

⑧从一粒细沙看世界，从一朵野花窥天堂。以你的手掌执持无限，以一小时把握恒常。（by Mou Zongsan）

⑨在一颗沙粒中见一个世界，在一朵鲜花中见一片天空，在你的掌心里把握无限，在一个钟点里把握无穷。（by Zhang Chiheng）

⑩一颗沙里看出一个世界，一朵野花里一座天堂；把无限放在你的手掌上，永恒在一刹那里收藏。（by Liang Zongdai）

Despite grammar differences such as the sentence mood and structure between the original poem and the translations, it can be seen that four nouns in the original poem are all translated as nouns in the ten Chinese versions. Table 1 presents the four English words and their Chinese translations.

Table 1. English Nouns in the Poem and their Chinese Translations

Number \ Nouns	world	heaven	infinity	eternity
①	世界	天国	无边	永劫
②	大千	桃源	乾坤	永恒
③	世界	天堂	无限	永恒
④	天地	乾坤	无极	万古
⑤	海	春	须弥	永恒
⑥	世界	天国	无限	永劫
⑦	世界	天堂	无限	永恒
⑧	世界	天堂	无限	恒常
⑨	世界	天空	无限	无穷
⑩	世界	天堂	无限	永恒

A comparison of the translations in Table 1 reveals that most of these words are associated with specific sets of beliefs. As is pointed out by Lefevere, translation never takes place in the language vacuum but is influenced by the target culture(2006: 6). A cultural perspective is thus applicable in the interpretation of the translations. By examining the source of these Chinese words, it seems that the ten translations can be classified into four groups indicating four beliefs(see Table 2).

Table 2. Beliefs in the Chinese Translations of the Poem

Belief	No. of Translation
Buddhism	①⑤⑥
Taoism	②④
Christianity	③⑦⑧⑩
None of the Above/Non-Religion	⑨

In table 2, the ten Chinese translations are categorized into four groups according to the appearance of words with distinct cultural connotations. When a word associated with a specific belief is found, the translation is grouped accordingly.

It is worth mentioning that none of the ten translations comprises of two or more beliefs. How the four beliefs are presented by these words, or, how these words contribute to the cultural connotation of the translations, is to be analyzed in the next part.

3. Cultural Connotations of the Words in Chinese Translations

The four beliefs embodied in the translations are Buddhism, Taoism, Christianity and non-religion.

3.1 Buddhism

Buddhism has shaped Chinese culture since the Han dynasty around the first century through missionaries from India. Three of the ten translations, namely, translations ①, ⑤ and ⑥, convey the Buddhist connotations.

The Buddhist implications can be seen in the nouns. In translations ① and ⑥, the words "无边 (meaning boundless, unlimited)" and "永劫 (meaning endless)" brings the reader into a Buddhist realm. The word "无边" generates the association with such typical collocations or expressions as "无边佛土 (boundless Buddha land)", "佛法无边 (unlimited powers of the Buddha)" and the great vow made by the Amitabha Buddha recorded in *Aparimitayur Sutra* that reads "all the Buddhas with unlimited powers shall be honored and worshiped" [1]. Meanwhile, the word "劫" is a Buddhist term, referring to an extremely long period which can not be measured in secular sense, or billions of years, or the endless time. The Chinese words "无边" and "永劫" represent the words "infinity" and "eternity" with the construction of Buddhist time and spacial images in the translations.

Similarly, the third line of translation ⑤ that reads "须弥纳芥" employs two Buddhist terms. The word "须弥" refers to Mount Meru, the center of all the physical, metaphysical and spiritual universes (Madan 1990: 78). A back translation of "须弥纳芥" is that Mount Meru, while too immense to imagine by the secular, can be held in a tiny seed of mustard ("芥子") without any distortion or change of the universes' size. The translation is partly quoted from a Buddhist saying [2], which tells that Mount Meru can hold a tiny seed of mustard, and vice versa. The saying suggests that the broadest is the mind, which, as tiny as the seed of mustard, can hold everything.

It is worth noting that other words originally borrowed from Buddhist scriptures can

---

① 原文为"常供无量无边一切诸佛", 出自《无量寿经》。
② 原文为"以至芥子纳须弥, 须弥纳芥子之类亦非假于他术", 出自《大慧普觉禅师普说·卷十八》。

be found in the ten Chinese translations such as"世界(literally meaning the world)", "刹那(literally meaning instant)" and "瞬间(literally meaning transient)". These words are not analyzed in the present study, because they have been assimilated into the Chinese lexicon for everyday use. In sum, the three translations ①, ⑤ and ⑥ have featured the words of distinct Buddhist connotation.

3.2 Taoism

Taoism is a traditional native Chinese religion or philosophical system, which dates back at least to the 4th century B. C. The keystone works of the Taoist tradition are *The Book of Changes* (Yijing), *Tao Te Ching* (Daodejing) and the writings of Zhuangzi. Taoism has a profound influence on the Chinese culture, which can be seen in two translations of the poem.

Translations ② and ④ present the recreation of the poem with Taoist connotations. The notion "Tao" (道) is the fundamental idea of Taoism, denoting the source and principle of everything, as is described in the sentence that reads "one is the child of Tao, after one comes two, after two comes three, and after three come all things" ①. The notion of Tao is also conveyed by other words such as "无(literally meaning the formless, intangible)" and "无极(transliterated as *Wuji*)". The former is seen in the sentence that reads "all things in the world come into being with a form and the form comes from the formless"②. And the latter appears in the Taoist conception of the world that reads "*Wuji* generates *Taiji* (i. e. , *yin* and *yang*), *Taiji* generates two complementary forces, two complementary forces generate four aggregates, four aggregates generate eight diagrams, and eight diagrams determine myriads of phenomena"③. The fundamental notion "无极" in translation ④ brings the reader into a Taoist world.

Apart from the words embodying the fundamental notion, the two words "天地" and "乾坤" in translations ② and ④ are also markers of Taoism. Both words literally refer to the world or the universe, and they are compounded in the same way with the first character referring to the heaven and the second character referring to the earth. In all the 81 chapters of *Tao Te Ching*, the word "天地" appears nine times in seven chapters, for example, in the sentence that reads "in the beginning heaven and earth

---

① 原文为"道生一，一生二，二生三，三生万物"，出自《道德经·第四十二章》。
② 原文为"天下万物生于有，有生于无"，出自《道德经·第四十章》。
③ 原文为"无极生太极，太极生两仪，两仪生四象，四象生八卦，八卦生万物"，出自《易传》。

are nameless"① and in the sentence that reads"there was chaos before the existence of heaven and earth"②. In addition, the noun"桃源"in translation ② is associated with a Taoist allusion, which is an imaginary paradise where people contentedly follow the hermit and seclusion life style as a practice of the leading ethical concept in Taoism called"无为(Wuwei, literally meaning effortless action)".

In short, both translations use the words conveying the fundamental notion of Tao, construct Taoist images such as heaven and earth, and generate the association of the poem with the classical allusion. In doing so, the translations have substituted Taoism for the original religion or tradition in the poem.

3.3　Christianity

Christianity was first introduced into China in the Tang dynasty around the 7th century, according to the official record, but it is not until the late 19th century that Christianity has greatly influenced the Chinese literature with the translation boom exposing Chinese readers to works from western countries.

Four of the ten translations, namely, ③, ⑦, ⑧ and ⑩, present Christianity by employing the same word"天堂(literally meaning the heaven)". Although the words"世界", "无限"and"永恒/恒常"appear in all the four translations, they are used as everyday words generating little religious association. Thus, in the four translations, "天堂"is the sole word to be analyzed. What the word"天堂"brings to the contemporary Chinese reader may be the image of a western heaven, where the God, angels, saints or venerated ancestors are said to live. Interestingly, this Chinese word does not seem to have originated from translations of Christian works; instead, it first appeared in *The Platform Sutra of the Sixth Patriarch* of the Tang dynasty, which teaches that the mind is everything, good and evil, the heaven and the hell③. Despite occasional appearance in history books such as *Book of Song*④ or dramas like *A Tumbledown Cave*⑤, the word was not widely used until a great number of Christian teachings, works and their translations became available and popular in China since the late 19th century. In contemporary Chinese lexicon, the word"天堂"seems to have

---

① 原文为"无名天地之始"，出自《道德经·第一章》。
② 原文为"有物混成，先天地生"，出自《道德经·第二十五章》。
③ 原文为"一切草木、恶人善人、恶法善法、天堂地狱，尽在空中"，出自《六祖坛经》第二十四节。
④ 书名原文为《宋书》。
⑤ 书名原文为《破窑记》。

been accepted as a proper noun of Christianity (Wang 2006: 40). The immediate association of the word to the Chinese reader may be the heaven in the Christian belief.

Christianity has developed as one of the five major religions in China. No matter whether it is out of the purpose of presenting the belief expressed in the original poem or serving the reader open to the Christian culture, the four translations unanimously adopt the same word, making it explicit that a Christian worldview is taken in the lines.

3.4　None of the Above or Non-Religion

Different from those translations with Christian, Taoist or Buddhist connotations, translation ⑨ can be hardly identified with any of the three beliefs. It is thus categorized as non-religious. The term non-religion in the present study is not to be interpreted as atheism. It suggests that no markers of any religion can be found, whereas atheism rejects the belief that any deities exist.

All the words in translation ⑨ are non-religious daily words. Take four words in the translation. The first word "世界", as is analyzed above, is a common word for everyday use in contemporary Chinese and embodies little religious belief. The other word "天空", literally meaning the sky or the space around the earth, is more of a reference of a natural existence than a cultural system. It does not create the same image as those generated by the Taoist terms "天地" and "乾坤" or the Christian word "天堂". Besides, the unit noun in the word group "一片天空" in the translation indicates that the word "天空" is uncountable, which is distinct from the countable word "a heaven" in the original poem. In comparison, the heaven is countable in Chinese Taoism, which is described by such words as "九霄/九天 (literally nine heavens)". Another word "无限", referring to infinity as a frequent word for literary creation, is also employed in other translations such as ③, ⑥ and ⑦. The fourth word "无穷" is widely adopted in Chinese poetry such as "惟天地之无穷兮，哀人生之长勤"① and "平生不下泪，于此泣无穷"②. The tradition of not taking a clear theism or atheism standpoint may be related to the fact that there are no clear boundaries between folk religions, Confucianism, Taoism and Buddhism in the Chinese culture. In Confucius and Taoist teachings and works, discussions about supernatural beings should be laid aside. For example, Confucius refused to talk about

---

① 出自屈原《远游》。
② 出自李白《江夏别宋之悌》。

matters on ghosts and gods①, and Zhuangzi, an important Taoist figure, held that beings beyond human cognition may exist and people should not speak about them②. Since the three major cultural systems share similarities and do not claim to be exclusive, the Chinese culture may feature fuzziness and indeterminacy in their belief.

It seems that translation ⑨ tries to minimize or remove the Christian overtone of the original poem. Since no markers of any religion or philosophical traditions can be found in the four lines, the translation is regarded as a non-religious version.

4. Discussion

The ten Chinese versions have been included in literary anthologies(Zong, 1981; Fan, 2015), used in commercial advertisements and quoted in essays or online writings. They can be taken as representative translations of the poem for their popularity in China. Their success is worth analyzing in the hope that the analysis may contribute to literary translation.

The wide acceptance of these translations may be attributed to at least two factors. First, the images created by the nouns in each translation are consistent in conveying the religion or philosophical traditions of Buddhism, Taoism, Christianity or non-religion. Each translation features a distinct tradition and forms its own aesthetic value, thus winning the readership of different beliefs. This indicates that the cultural connotation of the original poem may be represented in more than one way. The point is that the consistency in the cultural system within a translation has to be ensured no matter it follows or differs from that of the original. Second, the original poem gets recreated either in the form of a quatrain or a prose poem, which provides the reader with the option of different literary genres. Quatrains are effective in producing the aesthetic value of sound and highlighting the profoundness of the thoughts(Chen 2004: 81), while prose poems may generate the reader's empathy for the narrative style close to daily discourse. A diversity of genre ensures a wide readership of varied preference for the literary form.

With regard to the theoretical implication, the popularity of the translations corroborates the views on the importance of culture in translation studies. Bassnett compares translating a poem to transplanting a violet, in which the task of the translator is to determine and locate that seed and to set about its transplantation

---

① 原文为"子不语怪力乱神"，出自《论语·述而》。
② 原文为"六合之外，存而不论"，出自《庄子·齐物论》。

(2001: 58). The seed of the poem was introduced into China in the early 20th century, and since then the transplantation efforts from the Christian land to the Chinese soil have produced a number of Chinese versions. As is described by Benjamin, "the life of the original attains in them to its ever-renewed latest and most abundant flowering" (1968: 71). Many of these translations have changed the original cultural images in the original poem, for example, from Christianity to Buddhism or Taoism. The practice illustrates a transplantation step that "the seed can be placed in new soil, for a new plant to develop" (Bassnett 2001: 58). These Chinese translations are the new plants, and they are, obviously, of great vitality. In this way, the original poem, although changed in the form, continues its life in a foreign culture.

In sum, the success of the translations shows that a recreated text can have its own life vigorously once it takes root in the cultural soil and develops a distinctive feature.

5. Conclusion

Based on the analysis of the translations of *Auguries of Innocence*, it can be seen that the employment of different nouns between the versions presents different religious or philosophical traditions. The four words "world", "heaven", "infinity" and "eternity" in the original poem convey the religious belief in Christianity. While translating the poem into the Chinese culture in which theism and atheism coexist in harmony, a variety of translations seem necessary for readers of different beliefs. The profoundness of the poem is the seed, and the images in Christian terms may be represented by Buddhist, Taoist or non-religious words. The popularity of these translations shows that the Chinese soil is suitable for the "new plants" (Bassnett 2001: 58) which have developed from the seed of the original. In these vigorous translations, the original poem continues its life and thrives in a foreign culture.

References

[1]安然. 并置的艺术—威廉·布莱克诗集《天真和经验之歌》的空间蒙太奇叙事[J]. 文艺争鸣, 2014 a, (3): 190-195.

[2]安然. 布莱克诗歌《天真和经验之歌》的对话与复调[J]. 边疆经济与文化, 2014b, (4): 107-108.

[3]毕鹏晖. 见微知著—谈布莱克诗中意象之哲理[J]. 时代文学月刊, 2009

（8）：55 – 56.

[4]陈玉兰. 论绝句的结构艺术[J]. 文艺研究，2004(6)：81 – 88.

[5]范存忠. 英国文学论集[M]. 南京：译林出版社，2015.

[6]李玲. 布莱克《天真的预言》汉译的文化解读[J]. 外国语文，2010(5)：92 – 94.

[7]李菁菁. 一花一天堂—布莱克诗歌中的花意象解读[J]. 通化师范学院学报，2013a，(11)：66 – 69.

[8]李菁菁. 从《天真之歌》到《天真之兆》的天真之旅—布莱克诗歌中的"天真"情结[J]. 吉林化工学院学报，2013b，(10)：61 – 63.

[9]李子馨，李正栓. 威廉·布莱克诗歌中的宗教思想[J]. 燕山大学学报(哲学社会科学版)，2017(6)：58 – 62.

[10]毛雪青，赵明炜. 从认知诗学的角度解析布莱克的《天真与经验之歌》[J]. 名作欣赏，2011(1)：128 – 130.

[11]申霖，张晓鹏. 论布莱克诗中的意象[J]. 语文建设，2015(36)：69 – 70.

[12]王克非. 翻译文化史论[M]. 上海：上海外语教育出版社，1997.

[13]王永聘. 基督教对中国文化语言的影响[J]. 三峡大学学报(人文社会科学版)，2006(28)：39 – 42.

[14]周融. 天真与想象—威廉·布莱克诗歌中的童真诉求[J]. 海外英语，2015(15)：183 – 186.

[15]宗白华. 美学漫步[M]. 上海：上海人民出版社，1981.

[16] Bassnett, S. and Lefevere, A. *Constructing Cultures*. Shanghai：Shanghai Foreign Language Education Press，2001.

[17] Benjamin, W. "The Task of the Translator". In H. Ardent(ed.)。*Illuminations*. New York：Schocken Books，1968：69 – 82.

[18] Lefevere, A. *Translating Literature*：*Practice and Theory in a Comparative Literature Context*. Beijing：Foreign Language Teaching and Research Press，2006.

[19] Madan, G. *India through the Ages*. New Delhi：Publication Division，Ministry of Information and Broadcasting，Government of India，1990.

Traduction terminologique

—— À l'exemple du *Marbre*[*]

Ou Yu[**]

Résumé：Le marbre fait partie des pierres ornementales, ou pierres de taille, défini comme des roches ayant des qualités esthétiques et mécaniques qui les rendent propres à un usage de construction et de décoration. Dans le langage d'aujourd'hui, nous parlons de toute roche susceptible de prendre un beau poli, et d'être utilisée en décoration, dans cette acception, le mot n'a pas de sens pétrographique précis, même s'il s'applique le plus souvent à des marbres calcaires. La Chine d'aujourd'hui est à la fois un exportateur significatif et un importateur incontournable du marbre. Sur le sol chinois, nous pouvons trouver des gisements très prospectifs où se cache de belles matières. Mais sur le plan technique de chaque étape de production, il lui reste beaucoup à faire pour rattraper les fleurons européens, tels que l'Italie, dont la moitié de la production est exportée, la France, la Grèce, l'Espagne, etc. Avec l'intensification des échanges internationaux économiques et techniques, la Chine a eu besoin et continuera à avoir un grand besoin des technologies de l'industrie marbrière. Un grand intérêt se présente ainsi dans le champ de la traduction.

Mots-clés：marbre; veine; Mohs; découverte; bloc brut

---

　* 论文题目：术语翻译——以"大理石"为例。本文为 2016 年度全国翻译专业学位研究生教育研究项目"法译汉教学案例库建设初探——职业译者的素养"（MTIJZW201619）的阶段性成果之一。

　** 作者简介：欧瑜（Ou Yu），云南大学外国语学院法语系讲师。研究方向：翻译实践，翻译教学。

Introduction

Le mot Marbre (01) vient du grec (*marmarein*), qui signifie reluire, briller. Cette étymologie indique que ce mot conviendrait à toutes les espèces de pierres pouvant être polies. Ainsi les anciens comprenaient-ils dans la catégorie des marbres, les granits, les porphyres et les albâtres, tandis que les minéralogistes modernes n'admettent, eux, au nombre des marbres, que les pierres calcaires pouvant être polies. Quant aux architectes et aux constructeurs, ils ne considèrent ordinairement les marbres que par rapport à l'effet qu'ils produisent, et ils peuvent très bien ranger dans cette classe toutes les espèces de pierres que les anciens y faisaient entrer.

Cette appellation marbre recouvre donc une grande variété de pierres ornementales, le plus souvent de nature calcaire souvent métamorphisée, prenant un bel aspect au polissage mais dont les caractéristiques physico-chimiques (dureté, résistance, porosité, etc.) varient dans des proportions considérables d'un matériau à l'autre.

Jusqu'au milieu du XIXème siècle, sous le nom de marbre, ont été rangées toutes les roches prenant le poli, en incluant les granits, les porphyres, les serpentines. Les marbriers ont perpétué cette acception du terme marbre: ils travaillaient indistinctement toutes les roches ornementales. Par contre, les géologues ont restreint le nom de marbre aux carbonates métamorphiques, formés de grains visibles de calcite ou de dolomite. Il y a donc contradiction entre la classification des roches selon les marbriers et les connaissances géologiques acquises depuis deux siècles.

D'une façon générale, le mot marbre correspond à toutes les roches susceptibles de prendre un beau poli et d'être utilisées pour la décoration (marbrier). De ce fait, aujourd'hui, notamment dans l'industrie, nous tendons à inclure toutes les pierres ornementales, silicatiques, et dans certain cas, même des roches difficiles à polir comme les travertins.

En chinois, le mot « marbre » signifie la pierre de *Dali*, ville du Yunnan, région située dans le sud-ouest de la Chine. En 937, le conquérant de *Dali*, *Duan Sicheng*, a accordé le nom de *Dali* à la ville. C'était après l'année de *Jia Jing* (1522 – 1566) sous la dynastie des Ming que le mot de *Dalishi* a fait sa première apparition, remplaçant les appellation de *Diancangshi* (点苍石), *Chushi* (礎石) et *Wenshi* (文石). Sous le règne des Qing, l'appellation de *Dalishi* a été généralisée au fil du temps. Cette pierre a même voyagé jusqu'au Japon où les habitants ont gardé l'écriture et la prononciation originales de ce mot.

D'ailleurs, nous parlons des pierres marbrières① qui sont souvent confondues avec le marbre dont les caractéristiques géologiques sont détaillées plus haut. Elles méritent toutefois d'être décrites car leur caractère esthétique est largement exploité dans les mêmes domaines que le marbre.

1. Coup d'œil d'histoire

1.1 Le marbre en France

La France n'est pas aussi riche en marbre que l'Italie(carrière de Carrare), et ne possède pas de grands sites d'extraction. Elle possède toutefois une grande variété de pierres, on peut ainsi dénombrer une centaine de marbres différents allant du bleu au rouge en passant par le vert, l'uni, ou avecveines(02).

Cette roche noble a inspiré les marbriers français qui en ont tiré un style propre, tant pour les pavements, les revêtements muraux que le mobilier.

D'après les connaissances actuelles, nous devons l'existence du marbre sur le territoire français à la domination romaine, qui avait importé, en même temps que ses armes, les premières œuvres d'art, statues, vases, stèles, etc., de l'Italie. Puis, le Romain s'étant fixé sur le sol gaulois pour très longtemps, sinon définitivement, il importa d'Italie l'ornementation de sa Villa, sous forme de pavements ou de revêtements.

Plus tard, est venu le besoin d'orner l'habitation, par le marbre, et c'est de cette époque que date l'introduction de la mosaïque, d'importation italienne toujours. Aujourd'hui, la plupart des carrières historiques françaises sont fermées, en raison du coût élevé de leur exploitation ou de leur épuisement. Certaines carrières, ouvertes au XVIIe siècle pour Versailles, sont toujours en activité: brèche du Bénou jaune(Pyrénées), brocatelle jaune de Jura...

Après avoir privilégié le marbre blanc, les Romains se sont mis à apprécier les marbres polychromes de la Gaule. Après des dizaines d'abandon et de reprises, le marbre a retrouvé faveur à la Renaissance. Sous l'impulsion de son épouse Catherine de

---

① La distinction essentielle entre un marbre et une pierre marbrière est que le premier contient un ramage qui produit des dessins attirant le regard(sauf dans le marbre blanc et le marbre noir), tandis que la pierre marbrière a plus d'uniformité et que lorsqu'elle contient des dessins, ils ne sont pas capricieux comme dans le marbre(Noël 1994: 232).

Médicis, le roi Henri II a imposé des revêtements de marbres polychromes issus des carrières françaises, lors de la construction du Louvre et des Tuileries. Egalement époux d'une Médicis, Henri IV s'est intéressé de très près à la production du marbre national. Louis XIV, quant à lui, a fait ouvrir de nouvelles carrières dans les Pyrénées, les Alpes, le Languedoc et en Provence. La dynamique qu'il a apportée à cette industrie a fait de la France, à l'époque, le premier producteur de marbres. Le château de Versailles est la vitrine de cette richesse marbrière: cour de Marbre, colonnes des façades du château, portiques et façades du Grand Trianon[①], buffet d'eau...A l'intérieur, les salons de la Paix et de la Guerre, le Salon d'Hercule, l'escalier de la Reine, la galerie des Glaces et des marqueteries baroques décorent le pavement de la Chapelle royale.

Le Second Empire était une époque florissante pour l'industrie marbrière française, avec l'abondante production de copies du mobilier XVIIIème et le retour aux revêtements de marbres polychromes. Les vestibules des hôtels particuliers de la Plaine Monceau et des immeubles haussmanniens sont revêtus de marbres et de stucs d'imitation. Les nouvelles fortunes d'aujourd'hui affectionnent la profusion de ce matériau, symbole de richesse et de rareté.

1.2 Le marbre en Chine

La première dynastie connue, celle des Shang, remonte à la période −2500 à −1027, elle est connue pour ses vases de bronze à ornementations basées sur les motifs Taotie(masque, 饕餮) et Gui(龟), mais n'a construit que des cités d'argile et de bois selon les fouilles de Xiaotun; on travaillait déjà le jade importé(de Birmanie). Sous les Zhou(vers 1046 av. J.-C) et les Han(−1027 à +221) rien de remarquable n'est signalé en pierre. Les maisons étaient de pisé, bois et tuiles, avec des charpentes étonnamment compliquées: elles pouvaient atteindre plusieurs étages comme l'indiquent des modèles réduits en céramique. Vers la fin de ces dynasties, la pierre commence à être employée. A l'époque des Qin(221 à 206 av. J. C.)la Grande Muraille est revêtue de pierres, sauf dans l'Est. Sous les dynasties suivantes (Wei, Tang, Song, Ming, Qing), la pierre et le marbre n'ont été employés

---

① Le Grand Trianon ou Trianon de marbre est un palais que Louis XIV fit construire à proximité de Versailles en France. L'extérieur du bâtiment est construit en marbre d'où son nom de «Trianon de marbre». Il est aujourd'hui inscrit au patrimoine mondial de l'UNESCO depuis 1979 (Pascal 2006: 25).

qu'occasionnellement ; les constructions, souvent très élaborées, étaient pour la plupart en briques et bois, ce qui s'explique peut-être par la concentration des habitants dans les plaines alluviales et les collines de lœss, et par la distance des affleurements. L'utilisation de la pierre et du marbre était réservée aux constructions impériales. Les techniques du travail de la pierre étaient pourtant bien connues des architectes et artisans chinois, puisqu'ont été réalisés quelques monuments remarquables, comme des soubassements de temples et de palais, avec larges rampes d'escaliers, quelques ponts à grande portée, des portes monumentales, le bateau de marbre du Palais d'Eté à Pékin avec une proue carrée et des superstructures à deux étages avec colonnes (XVIIIème siècle). Des tombes souterraines en pierre de taille avec murs décorés ont été édifiées dès le IIème siècle dans le *Shandong*. Les lions gardiens de temples et de palais sculptés en marbre sont un élément constant de la civilisation chinoise, de même que le travail du jade (disques divinatoires *bi* (璧), vases, ornements, pendentifs...), qui a fourni des chefs d'œuvre dans maints musées.

Etant une matière relativement coûteuse, le marbre a été petit à petit identifié au cours des civilisations comme un symbole de sacralité, de puissance, de beauté et de luxe. Cette pierre est utilisée très largement comme matériaux de construction, qu'ils soient fonctionnels ou décoratifs, et est destinée à se transformer en représentations figurées, sacrées ou commémoratives. En Chine d'aujourd'hui, les marbres sont aussi bien utilisés à couvrir les façades du gratte-ciel commercial qu'à décorer l'intérieur de l'appartement privé. Les Chinois tentent de bâtir pour l'éternité, en adoptant les matériaux et les procédés qui permettront de résister le mieux à l'érosion du temps. Cette matière, avec toutes ses vertus, est l'espace multiple des différences, des mélanges, des infinis.

2. Aspects techniques du marbre

2.1 Formation du marbre

Les bancs de marbres ont été formés, comme les autres bancs calcaires, par le mouvement et le dépôt des eaux de la mer, qui a transporté les coquilles et les matières pierreuses réduites en petits volumes, en graviers, en galets, et les a stratifiées les unes dans les autres.

Il semble que l'établissement local de la plupart de ces bancs de marbres d'ancienne formation a précédé celui des autres bancs de pierres calcaires, puisqu'on les trouve presque toujours au-dessus de ces mêmes bancs et que, dans une colline composée de vingt ou trente bancs de pierres, il n'y a, ordinairement, que deux ou trois bancs de marbre, souvent même un seul, toujours situé au-dessous des autres, à peu de distance de la glaise qui sert de base à la colline. Habituellement, le banc de marbre porte immédiatement sur cette argile ou n'en est séparé que par un dernier banc, qui paraît être l'égout de tous les autres, et qui se trouve parfois mêlé de marbre, de pyrites et de cristallisation spathique d'un assez grand volume.

2. 2 Propriétés du marbre

Tous les marbres sont des roches et partagent donc avec les composés minéraux qui forment les parties superficielles de la Terre de nombreux caractères fondamentaux. Ils présentent une bonne résistance aux sollicitations mécaniques et à l'usure du temps, se prêtent donc à être utilisés comme matériaux de construction pour des ouvrages de grandes dimensions, non seulement ornementaux mais également portants. Les marbres se présentent en couches de la croûte terrestre et peuvent être ainsi traités dans des carrières«à ciel ouvert», différemment des minerais métalliques, par exemple, qui existent dans des veines et des filons et doivent presque toujours être traités«en galerie».

La dureté peut être définie par la résistance que la surface d'une substance offre à la corrosion. Un marbre de carbonate de chaux pur peut, en général, être facilement rayé au canif. Il a une dureté de 3 dans l'échelle de Mohs(03). En se rapportant à cette classification les verres à vitre ont une résistance de presque 6. Les marbres sont plus durs que la plupart des pierres calcaires, bien qu'ils puissent être constitués par les même matières-carbonate de chaux-mais les grains des calcaires sont en général cémentés entre eux d'une façon moins ferme et la dureté d'une roche granuleuse est mesurée par le degré de cohésion des grains qui la composent plutôt par la dureté du matériau. Les marbres dolomitiques ont une dureté classée entre 3, 5 et 4. La présence d'impuretés, comme la présence de silicates peut augmenter considérablement la dureté des marbres.

Les vides dans les marbres sont en général si minimes que le poids réel ne diffère sensiblement pas de celui calculé par le poids spécifique. Le marbre pèse en général entre 165 et 180 livres par pied cube. Un ouvrier qui connaît le poids spécifique de son marbre, en le cubant peut calculer le poids du bloc avec une approximation très suffisante et très proche du poids exact. L'indication économique du poids est surtout en connexion avec la résistance nécessaire des appareils de levages et de transports. Le poids par pied cube permet aussi de calculer dans les hautes constructions le poids que les fondations auront à supporter.

La solubilité du marbre doit être prise en sérieuse considération surtout lors qu'il doit être utilisé à l'extérieur, car la totalité des roches se dissolvent et se désagrègent plus ou moins lentement du fait des agents atmosphériques. En général, la marche de cette dissolution est très lente mais elle peut être largement activée sous certaines conditions; il est donc nécessaire de bien connaître la roche destinée à la construction. Le degré de solubilité varie avec chaque marbre car elle dépend de sa composition chimique, de sa texture et de sa porosité. Dans les grandes villes, divers acides provenant des fumés et transportés par la pluie augmentent considérablement la dissolution. Donc, un matériau perméable se désagrègera plus rapidement que celui plus imperméable. Le carbonate de chaux se dissout plus vite que la dolomie sous les mêmes conditions et similitude de texture.

La couleur du marbre est une de ses principales propriétés physiques. Elle présente la principale nature de ses constituants. Les marbres formés de carbonate de chaux pur ou de dolomie sont blancs; dans le Vert Antique①, le vert domine en raison de la présence de la serpentine, parfois mêlé de rouge. Les variations de ton dans les marbres blancs sont toujours dues à l'immixtion de substances étrangères. Certaines impuretés peuvent être uniformément distribuées et donnent une coloration uniforme, ou bien, elles peuvent se présenter en bandes ou taches, donnant ainsi une coloration tantôt nuagée, tantôt diversement colorée. On peut obtenir des effets magnifiques d'ondulations en sciant les marbres de certaines manières.

Parfois les causes de la coloration des marbres sont facilement déterminées. Des nuances noires et grisâtres sont dues à des matières carbonacées souvent présentes en fins sédiments de graphite; le rouge, le rose, le brun-rougeâtre sont causés par la présence d'oxydes de manganèse ou par de l'hématite; le brun-jaune et le jaune, sont le fait de grains imperceptibles d'oxydes hydratés de fer et de limonite.

Les grains de carbonate de chaux ou de dolomie qui forment une masse de marbre sont cristallins et possèdent un clivage défini, montrant des faces à éclat brillant sur une surface brisée. En général, le clivage apparaît avec d'égales saillies dans toutes les directions. Dans certains marbres toutefois, les grains sont allongés en une seule

---

① Marbre en provenance de la Grèce. Les verts intenses et vibrants du marbre thessalien connu sous le nom de vert antique. Ces marbres ont été utilisés en grande quantité pour décorer les revêtements de Rome antique(Pascal 2006: 36).

direction suivant les sens des plissements, direction qui est celle dans laquelle le marbre se fend le plus facilement.

La vitesse de propagation du son exprimée en m/s, c'est la mesure du temps de passage à travers un échantillon de pierre d'une impulsion recueillie à une distance connue de la source émettrice. Elle est fonction des propriétés élastiques du matériau et de son état comme la porosité, le taux d'humidité, les micro-fissures.

2. 3 Classification du marbre

Au point de vue pétrographique, nous ne parlons que des calcaires cristallins métamorphiques en employant le mot«marbre» ; mais dans le commerce et l'industrie, le terme est doté d'un sens plus large, c'est-à-dire en se référant à toute pierre ornementale en mesure de devenir polie et brillante. Dans ce cas, nous pouvons établir trois groupes principaux qui respectent les diverses genèses et réunissent des matériaux dont la composition, la structure et le comportement ont des caractéristiques similaires.

2. 3. 1 Classifications par couleurs

La couleur compte non seulement au point de vue esthétique, mais aussi en ce qui concerne le rendement, la durée dans le temps et parfois la dureté et dégradabilité du marbre même dans les milieux atmosphériques. Certaines pierres ne gardent pas leur couleur étant exposées à l'air, et ne peuvent donc pas être utilisées comme marbre, malgré la valeur de leurs couleurs originales.

2. 4 Technique du travail

2. 4. 1 Prospection des gisements

Nous ne devons pas ouvrir une carrière sans bien nous assurer tout d'abord que la masse à extraire est non seulement intéressante au point de vue attractif, mais qu'elle est saine, que sa qualité reste uniforme et qu'elle existe en quantité suffisante pour rendre son exploitation profitable. Nous devons consulter avec soin les cartes géologiques, étudier les failles, l'étendue, l'épaisseur, l'aspect, la solidité afin de bien nous rendre compte de ce que le gisement pourra éventuellement fournir. Lorsque le banc est très recouvert, nous pouvons nous rendre compte de ces données nécessaires à l'aide de perforatrices bien orientées ou par quelques tranchées. Ces essais nous permettront d'être fixés sur la couleur, l'uniformité et l'aspect général du matériau comme de son extension et de sa formation.

Avant l'ouverture d'une nouvelle carrière, les sondages en profondeur et les tests sont nécessaires pour vérifier la consistance du gisement, la qualité du marbre, la possibilité d'exploitation et l'orientation de l'éventuelle schistosité métamorphique, afin de choisir l'orientation du front d'excavation. Quelques critères sont à considérer : aspect esthétique, caractéristique physique, fracture du massif, homogénéité des réserves.

Il est rare que la roche affleure le sol, elle est généralement recouverte de ladécouverte (04). Suivant l'épaisseur et la composition de la découverte, il est préférable soit de procéder à son enlèvement soit d'exploiter la carrière en galerie. En général, les matériaux issus de la découverte vont être stockés sur le site même de l'exploitation. Ils peuvent être réutilisés lors du réaménagement de la carrière. Une découverte jugée trop importante peut entraîner une perte de rentabilité et la fermeture de la carrière.

Après la localisation probable du gisement, on effectue un sondage, pour lequel toute une série de méthodes ont été développées pour la reconnaissance des massifs de roche. Seules les plus répandues dans la pratique seront mentionnées dans cette partie : la méthodes de l'analyse structurale qui nécessite des outils simples, dont les données collectives nous permettent d'obtenir un schéma structural du gisement ; la géophysique de surface qui demande un matériel plus sophistiqué fournit une information sur le sous-sol sans aucun forage ; le sondage carotté, une technique chère, mais qui peut être nécessaire pour étudier sur des échantillons représentatifs la couleur, la taille et l'uniformité de grain de la roche, la présence de minéraux défavorables, comme la pyrite, et pour analyser la hauteur de la découverte, la hauteur des bancs, la position dans le sol, etc. ; les diagraphies, méthodes moins coûteuses que le sondage carotté ont été développées, fondées sur l'emploi de la diagraphie.

2. 4. 2 Extraction

Cette phase constitue l'essentiel du travail en carrière. L'objectif de l'extraction est de séparer un bloc de la masse en évitant les cassures, tout en produisant ces blocs à la dimension la plus proche de leur utilisation pour éviter les reprises ou les déchets. Les méthodes d'extraction peuvent être différentes, chaque méthode est plus spécialement adaptée à une qualité de matériau et/ou à un type de gisement.

L'emploi de l'explosif est plus rare que les autres méthodes dans les carrières de marbres, car les risques de destruction du matériau sont trop importants. Des explosifs déflagrants sont ainsi choisis à priori pour éviter des fissures dans la roche. Le principal explosif de cette catégorie est la poudre noire.

La mise en œuvre de la poudre noire est bien adaptée à l'exploitation de gisements très fissurés, quant aux gisements massifs où la première difficulté est de désenclaver de grandes masses afin de procéder au débitage secondaire (production deblocs bruts (05), cette méthode se montre beaucoup plus délicate. Une évolution de l'utilisation des explosifs a cependant permis une adaptation de la charge à la nature des roches en réalisant un tir doux, ou à charges découplées dit «Smooth Blasting». L'objectif est de séparer des masses très importantes (plusieurs centaines de tonnes) simultanément sur 1 à 4 faces, à l'aide d'une méthode de tir évitant un couplage roche-explosif générateur des phénomènes de fissuration. Les avantages sont multiples : la masse rocheuse à découper est disloquée sans être brisée ; le débitage secondaire est alors facilité.

3. Utilisation du marbre

Le marbre assume une multi-fonction dans les constructions : portantes (colonne, piliers), d'usure (marches d'escaliers, seuils de portes), d'ameublement (salle de bain, cheminée) et ornementales (sculptures, revêtements internes). Etant donné que le marché est en forte expansion et que les gisements marbriers s'épuisent progressivement, la recherche sur les matériaux alternatifs s'intensifiera, d'autre part, baisser les prix de revient et améliorer la fonction des équipements seront toujours l'enjeu pour l'industrie. Nous allons citer ici quelques usages principaux de marbre dans le bâtiment.

Conclusion

Les recherches exposées montrent que dans l'industrie marbrière, les coûts (d'extraction, de production et de transport) sont élevés et qu'en outre, il ne semble pas qu'ils puissent être abaissés. Par conséquent, seuls les gisements d'une qualité exceptionnelle, c'est-à-dire étendus, uniformes et où la structure facilite l'extraction des blocs, sont susceptibles d'être exploités. Les roches les plus saines seront exploitées en tant que pierres ornementales et les autres ainsi que les déchets seront utilisés pour produire des agrégats.

Aujourd'hui, l'évolution économique mondiale a eu et continuera d'avoir des conséquences significatives sur l'industrie marbrière. D'un côté, les contraintes environnementales sont prises en compte dans toutes les étapes du processus de production, de l'autre, la technicité des différentes étapes de la production s'est fortement accrue, surtout dans les pays occidentaux comme la France. Par contre, la Chine, en tant que le plus grand producteur et exportateur du monde, a un fort besoin de s'améliorer sur le plan technique de la marbrerie.

L'objet de ce mémoire est de diffuser la culture générale marbrière, tout en souhaitant d'être en mesure d'apporter des informations utiles aux traducteurs français et chinois dans ce domaine spécifique.

N. B. : Dans cet article, les termes faisant l'objet d'une fiche terminologique apparaissent en gras à leur première occurrence pertinente, suivis de leur numéro de fiche terminologique entre parenthèses, en exposant et en gras (ex. marbre(01)).

Bibliographie:

[1] Pierre Noël. *Technologie de la pierre de taille*[M]. Paris: SEBTP, 1994.

[2] Pascal Julien. *De carrière en palais: Du Midi à Versailles, du sang des dieux à la gloire des rois*[M]. Manosque: Le Bec en l'Air, 2006.

Annexe: fiches terminologiques exemplaires

Préambule terminologique

Dans la famille de roches ornementales, le marbre est doté de nombreuses vertus. Mais au niveau de techniques de travail, il est difficile de définir celles qui sont utilisées exclusivement pour cette matière. Dans la plupart des cas, ces techniques sont communément pratiquées pour plusieurs sortes de pierre de taille, le granit par exemple.

Les cinq fiches terminologiques que nous avons choisies de présenter ici couvrent les domaines suivants du marbre: la prospection des gisements, ls propriétés du marbre, l'extraction.

La difficulté principale que nous avons rencontrée au cours de la rédaction de ces fiches réside dans la recherche de documents synthétiques en deux langues. Même s'il existe des documents en français, ceux qui traitent exclusivement le marbre restent très peu nombreux, les documents sont souvent classés avec ceux traitant de la pierre de taille ou la pierre ornementale. De ce fait, nous avons dû nous renseigner auprès de spécialistes pour trouver les informations fiables et pertinentes sur le marbre. En ce qui concerne les documents chinois, nous avons eu également recours aux spécialistes et dû explorer des articles de revues professionnelles afin de trouver des informations utilisables. Cependant, le résultat des recherches a été satisfaisant.

La rédaction de ces fiches terminologiques nous a été fort enrichissante pour mieux éclairer le sujet et nous a été très utile pour connaître le domaine.

Fiches terminologiques

MODÈLE DE FICHE TYPE

Les fiches terminologiques ci-après sont conformes à la méthodologie adoptée par EURODICAUTOM, chacune contenant les champs suivants:

-CM: Code Matière(domaine):

AR6 = Art plastique

CH4 = Chimie théorique

CH9 = Minéralogie et cristallographie

INC = Industrie des pierres et des terres

MIJ = Carrières

MI5 = Travaux d'ouverture et d'exploitation des gîtes miniers

NO8 = Méthodes de mesure

-AU: AUteur de la fiche

YOU = Yu OU

-ZH: chinois

-FR: FRançais

-VE: VEdette(terme faisant l'objet de la fiche et ses synonymes)

-DF: DéFinition de la vedette

-PH: PHrase(contexte)

-NT: NoTe:

EXP = renseignements encyclopédiques qui ne font pas partie de la définition

GRM = indications GRaMmaticales

USG = indications relatives àl'USaGe, au niveau de la langue, au registre, etc.

REL = renvois associatifs à d'autres termes

-RF: RéFérences(sources bibliographiques)

CM		INC MIJ
AU		YOU
FR	VE	marbre

DF   Toute Roche, sédimentaire, métamorphique ou magmatique, susceptible d'être résistible, polissables et ornementales, le mot n'a pas de sens pétrographique précis, même s'il s'applique le plus souvent à des marbres calcaires.

PH   Le calcaire de nature métamorphique est connu comme étant un marbre dont la structure saccharoïde découle des processus de cristallisation de calcaire organogène.

NT   EXP1 : Toutefois, quand on emploie le mot "marbre", on continue presque toujours à indiquer un calcaire cristallin, tandis que, par "produit marmoréen" ou "activité marbrière", on entend normalement toutes les pierres ornementales.

EXP2 : Au point de vue naturaliste, on doit employer le mot "marbre" au sens le plus strict du terme, c'est-à-dire en ne parlant que des calcaires cristallins métamorphiques; mais étant donné l'affirmation dans le commerce et l'industrie d'utiliser le terme dans un sens large, c'est-à-dire en se référant à toute pierre ornementale en mesure de devenir polie et brillante, on se servira d'une classification qui comprend tous ces types de roches.

EPX3 : A l'expression "industrie marbrière", la loi italienne établit le liste suivante : marbre, granit, serpentine, syénite, diorite, quartzite, porphyre, albâtre, trachyte.

USG1 : Marbre signifie également un morceau, un objet ou un statut de marbre.

USG2 : En terme technique, le marbre signifie table, plaque métallique parfaitement plane, servant à divers usages.

USG3 : En typographie, le marbre signifie grande table sur laquelle on étale les formes pour les corriger et faire la mise en page.

	RF	VE, DF, PH: Luciana, Tiziano Mannoni, traduction de Josette Spitcheff, Le Marbre Matière et Culture, 1984, SAGEP éditrice, Gênes, ISBN 88 – 7058 – 104 – 7, p7; EXP1, EXP2, EXP3: souece VE, p7/10/38; USG1, USG2, USG3: Dictionnaire Hachette illustré, 2005, Hachette Livre, 2004, sous marbre
ZH	VE	大理石；点苍石；苍石；榆石；天竺石；文石；礎石；醒酒石；贡石。
	DF	变质岩、沉积岩和火成岩中，具有一定块度、硬度、可加工性、抛光性和装饰形的岩石。
	PH	装饰用石材分为天然石材和人造石材两种，其中天然石材主要又大理石和花岗石两种。
	NT	EXP1：大理石，过去专指岩石学中的大理岩而言，即指石灰岩、白云岩等碳酸盐岩景区与变质作用或热接触变质作用形成的变质岩石，苍山大理石即属此类。当今石材市场上所称的大理石，是一个广义的概念，凡是具有装饰效果的沉积岩、变质岩和火成岩，都统称为大理石，主要成分为碳酸盐矿物，一般质地较软，如白云岩、大理岩、灰岩、砂眼和板岩。洱海东岸大理石即属这种广义的大理石。 EXP2：大理石的主要组成成分是方解石和白云石。北京房山产的汉白玉，云南大理产的大理石，辽宁产的丹东绿均为著名品牌。 REL：饰面石材 USG：2），3）：因石出点苍山，人们称大理石为"点苍石"或"苍石"；4）：因大理古称榆城，人们称大理石为"榆石"；5）：因大理曾有"天竺妙香国"之说，人们称大理石为天竺石；6）：处于大理石案头文具的用途，如砚台、笔架、镇纸、笔同等，人们称之为"文石"；7）：用于房屋柱蹲、基础的，民间俗称"礎石"。"礎石"这个别称，大理至今还沿用；8）：夏日炎炎，大理石能给人一种清凉消暑、"凉生肘腋间"的感觉，因袭，让戴西川节度使李德裕由巴大理石成为"醒酒石"；9）：因大理石在历史上多作为贡品，故又称"贡石"。

RF　VE：杨祯祥，大理市重工业局，大理市大理石志，1991 年，第 2 页；DF，EXP1：SEC：同 VE；王福川，现代建筑装饰材料及其施工，1986 年，中国建筑工业出版社，第 4 页；PH，EXP2：SEC：王福川，中国建筑工业出版社，现代建筑装饰材料及其施工，1986 年，第 4 页；2），3），4），5），6），7），8），9），USG：王嘉杰，李兴任，王观远 主编，武汉工业大学出版社，大理石，1988 年，第 3 页。

FR　VE　veine

DF　M Marque longue et étroite qui va en serpent dans les roches marbrières capricieusement par rapport à la stratification, due à une variation de couleur ou à des filonnets de matières différentes.

PH　En effet, les lits de marbre noir ne forment que des veines plus ou moins importantes dans un ensemble de calcaires de couleur et de granulométrie variables.

NT　EXP：Les motifs ornementaux du marbre dépendent de la position des minéraux autour des veines.

RF　VE, DF：SEC：Henry Guédy, Encyclopédie-Roret I Marbrier, Chez Leonce Laget, Paris, 1981, p91；PH：Eric Groessens, Pierre Actual, avril 2005, L'industrie du marbre en Belgique, p28；EXP：source DF

ZH　VE　脉纹。

DF　特指大理石表面矿物成分和颜色区别于底色的细长条纹。

PH　蛇纹石大理石主要由蛇纹石（硅酸镁水合物）组成，绿色或深绿色，伴有由方解石、白云石或菱镁矿等组成的脉纹。

NT　EXP：大部分大理石都拥有脉纹，晶体粒度从隐晶度到 5mm 不等。

RF　VE, DF：王嘉杰，李兴任，王观远 主编，武汉工业大学出版社，大理石，武汉，1988 年出版，第 10 页；PH：同 DF；EXP：于俊清，张显志，石材，2001 年第 2 期，石材杂志社，北京，蛇纹岩石材的命名及其找矿方向，第 24 页。

FR   VE   Mohs

            DF   L'échelle relative ou comparative destinée à mesurer la dureté d'un minéral ou d'une roche.

            PH   Il s'agit d'une matière première de bonne qualité pour la taille, à la dureté égale à 6 sur l'échelle de Mohs.

                    n. : dureté, échelle de *

            NT   EXP: L'échelle de Mohs comporte dix degrés relatifs à dix minéraux index de dureté 1 à 10, dans l'ordre de dureté croissante: Talc, Gypse, Calcite, Fluorine, Apatite, Orthose, Quartz, Topaze, Corindon, Diamant. Pour classer les minéraux simplement, on utilise une autre échelle comparative composée d'outils facilement disponibles que l'on peut rayer en fonction de la dureté(d): ongle d > 2, cuivre d > 3, couteau d > 5, plaque de verre d > 6.

            RF   VD, DF: SEC: René-Michel Lambertie, Presses Universitaires de France, Que sais-je ? N° 977, L'industrie de la pierre et du marbre, Paris, 1965 p56; Dictionnaire thématique des mines et carrières, Société de l'industrie minérale, Paris, 2001, sous Mohs; PH, EXP: 1e source DF, p57

ZH   VE   摩氏硬度;莫氏硬度。

            DF   用来鉴定矿物和岩石相对硬度的标准,使矿物和岩石抵抗外来机械作用的能力。

            PH   测量岩石相对硬度一般采用摩氏硬度,把被测岩石与摩氏标准矿物相互刻划,依其软硬关系进行比较来确定岩石的相对硬度。

NT   EXP：摩氏硬度，是由德国矿物学家摩尔首先提出的。他根据矿物间相对强度大小，制定了一个标准矿物系列，由 10 种不同硬度的矿物组成。由低到高划分为 10 级，它们的排列顺序是：滑石—石膏—方解石—萤石—磷灰石—长石—石英—黄玉—刚玉—金刚玉，称为摩氏硬度计。

EXP2：矿物和岩石的硬度根据研究方法的不同，通常分为相对硬度和绝对硬度两种类型，其中相对硬度又分为摩氏硬底和工艺硬度两种类型。

EXP3：我国根据摩氏硬度，把石材划分为三大类。一大类：硬质石材(摩氏硬度 6 ~ 7)；二大类：中硬石材(摩氏硬度 3 ~ 5)；三大类：软质石材(摩氏硬度 2 ~ 3)。我国石材界，通常把花岗石称为硬质石材，大理石称为软质石材。

RF   1)，DF：于俊清，张显志，石材，2001 年第 10 期，石材杂志社，北京，论石材硬度分类及其找矿，第 40 页；2)：郝书魁主编，王庆、刘传惠 副主编，同济大学出版社，上海，建筑装饰材料基础，1996 年 1 月第一版，第 117 页；PH：同 DF，低 40 页；EXP1，EXP2，EXP3：同 DF，第 40/41/42 页。

FR   VE   découvert，découverte，morts-terrains

DF   Ensemble de la masse qu'il faut déblayer，dans une carrière à ciel ouvert，pour atteindre le premier banc exploitable.

PH   Les morts terrains sont déposés en dehors du site d'exploitation pour un gisement se poursuivant en profondeur (c'est-à-dire exploitation dans une fosse ou une cuvette)，en arrière de la zone d'extraction pour les exploitations d'une couche plus ou moins horizontale(c'est-à-dire exploitation à flanc de colline par exemple)，amorçant ainsi un début de réaménagement poursuivi ultérieurement.

	NT	EXP1: Le découvert, ou la découverte, s'entend de tout ce qui recouvre la pierre de taille, y compris les bancs pour moellon, pierre à chaux, matériaux d'empierrement, castine, etc. EXP2: Avant d'ouvrir une carrière à ciel, il faut savoir si le volume de stériles ou morts terrains à extraire n'est pas trop important par rapport au volume de matériaux. GRM: On utilise plutôt le pluriel de 3).
	RF	1), 2), 3), DF: Pierre Noël, Technologie de la pierre de taille, SEBTP, Paris, 1994, p127; PH: Mémento roches et minéraux industriels-les pierres ornementales, BRGM, Paris, 1987, p23; EXP1, EXP2: source PH; GRM: source VE
ZH	VE	废石层
	DF	指在露天采矿过程中需要剥离的围岩、夹石层。
	PH	在大多数石灰岩质大理石矿脉中,废石层和矿层往往交错出现,一层矿石覆盖一层废石,应以剥离先行为指导方针,尤其是在废石的量大而且比较集中的情况下,这样有利于矿山资源的综合利用。
	NT	EXP: 矿体圈定时,将废石夹层准确的圈出后,更能真实的反映矿体的形态及产状。
	RF	VE, DF: 吴道夫,石材,2003 年第 6 期,石材杂志社,北京,石材矿床地质条件与开采方法的选择,第 4 页;PH, EXP: 杨祯祥,大理市大理石志,大理市重工业局,大理,1991 年,第 49/50 页。
FR	VE	Bloc brut
	DF	Masse compacte et hexaédrique de grande taille de marbre non taillé.
	PH	Pour déterminer la base du bloc de marbre, il fait faire un lit sous la plinte du bloc, ce lit lui sert de base générale pour diriger toutes ses mesures et tirer toutes ses lignes.

NT　　EXP：Dans la technique d'explosif comme pour celle au coin éclateur, les blocs irréguliers doivent être écaris pour prendre une forme orthogonale. Ce retaillage ou écarissage (souvent dans le sens du lit pour avoir un découpe la plus droite possible) permet de transporte et de travailler plus facilement les blocs.

USG：Certaines carrières ne prononcent jamais le c, et disent blo. Par exemple un bloc de marre, dites：un blo de marbre；on prononce encore le c quand bloc est suivi d'une voyelle ou d'une h non aspirée：un bloc énorme, dites：un blo-k énoreme.

REL1：bloc

REL2：bloc d'échantillon

REL3：bloc decommande

RF　　VE, DF：Pierre Noël, Technologie de la pierre de taille, 1994, SEBTP, Paris, p65；PH, EXP：Encyclopédie ou dictionnaire raisonné des sciences, des arts et des métiers, 1993, Flammarion, p814/815, sous sculpture de marbre；USG：source VE

ZH　　VE　　荒料。

DF　　从矿体中分离出来的具有规则形状，用以加工饰面板材的石材。

PH　　按整形方法将大理石荒料分为两类：锯面荒料，即六个面都是锯切方法整形的荒料；劈面荒料，既有一面或数面是用劈凿方法整形的荒料。

NT　　EXP1：按荒料的尺寸允许级差、平面度允许极限公差、角度允许极限公差与外观质量，分为一等品(B)、合格品(C)两个等级。

EXP2：荒料命名顺序为：荒料产地地名、色调花纹特征名称、大理石。

EXP3：同一批荒料的色调花纹基本一致。

RF　　VE, DF, PH：天然大理石荒料起草小组，石材，2001 年第 5 期，石材杂志社，北京，天然大理石荒料标准，第 14 页；EXP1, EXP2, EXP3：同 VE，第 15 页。

L'acte de langage du désaccord dans le français oral contemporain

——Une analyse basée sur les données du corpus oral[*]
Yang Xiaoyan[**]

Résumé：Au cours des interactions verbales, le désaccord est un des actes de langage le plus fréquemment observé. Les locuteurs s'engagent à communiquer des informations, à construire leur identité, même à imposer leur puissance, en exprimant des points de vue différents. Dans une interaction, l'expression du désaccord est généralement considérée comme un FTA (Face-Threatening-Act, un acte de langage qui produit potentiellement une menace à la face de l'interlocuteur. (Kerbrat-Orecchioni 1992, 2005). Par conséquent, leur production demandera soit un «évitement» (Brown & Levinson 1978), soit une «réparation» ou un «adoucissement» (Kerbrat-Orecchioni 1992). Par ailleurs, le désaccord est censé être désavantageux pour le bon déroulement de la conversation ainsi que pour le maintien des relations interpersonnelles, en raison de sa nature intrinsèquement menaçante. De ce fait, il nous paraît convenable de passer en revue l'acte du désaccord et d'en dégager la procédure. Cela nous aidra à mieux connaître l'acte du désaccord, à mieux comprendre les productions langagières de l'interlocuteur et à aboutir à nos buts communicatifs spécifiques en exprimant des points de vue différents d'une manière appropriée.

Mots-Clés：désaccords en français oral；corpus du français parlé；amorces；clôture

---

　＊ 论文题目：现代法语口语中的异议表达——基于口语语料库的分析。

　＊＊ 作者简介：杨晓燕(YANG Xiaoyan)，云南大学外国语学院法语系讲师。研究方向：法语社会语言学，互动话语分析。

Introduction

Au cours des interactions verbales, la manifestation des points de vue différenciés du nôtre est l'un des actes de langage les plus fréquents. L'acte de langage du désaccord suscite pour autant un grand intérêt chez des linguistes en raison de sa nature intrinsèquement menaçante, du point de vue pragmatique, sociolinguistique ou interculturel. Mieux comprendre ce qui se passe et comment s'engagent les locuteurs dans un acte du désaccord nous aideront à mieux appréhender les productions langagières et les interprétations linguistiques de notre interlocuteur. De ce fait, nous voudrions expliciter dans le présent travail la procédure séquentielle idéale d'un désaccord, en nous appuyant sur des données du corpus CFPP 2000 (Branca-Rosoff, 2012: 12). Nous nous concentrons sur les amorces qui se trouvent en tête puisqu'elles traduisent de manière implicite ou explicite la prise de position du locuteur, sans oublier le rôle important que jouent la négociation et la clôture au cours du déroulement de la communication.

1. Définitions et notions clés

Partant d'un constat des théories de l'énonciation, selon lequel«les interlocuteurs laissent des traces de leur présence et de leurs activités au sein des messages échangés» (Vion 1996: 20), nous sommes en mesure de repérer la présence des locuteurs à travers des éléments d'un énoncé. Dans le cas étudié, les locuteurs véhiculent leur propre interprétation et leurs attentes au résultat d'un désaccord dans les amorces qu'ils choisissent. En ce sens, les amorces du désaccord jouent un rôle important de*girouette* dans le déroulement de la communication.

Nos analyses feront référence à des extraits du corpus CFPP 2000 et s'appuient de manière principale sur la méthode de l'analyse du discours en interaction, à savoir une description détaillée de l'interaction, en illustrant comment les locuteurs expriment leur désaccord, par le biais de diverses amorce et leur sens grammatical. Dans le présent article, nous nous concentrerons sur leurs fonctions grammaticale et sémantique lors de la réalisation du désaccord. À travers la référence complète attachée à chaque extrait, nous pourrons repérer où se trouve précisément l'extrait.

Les interactions verbales sont des activités sociales qui exigent des efforts d'au moins deux individus, ayant pour objectif de se transmettre des messages. Les partenaires en échange font usage de diverses ressources linguistiques et discursives, partagent leurs opinions et défendent leurs points de vue. Tout le monde se met d'accord sur le fait que les locuteurs, au cours d'une communication quelconque, font des efforts pour que la conversation se déroule dans une ambiance relativement «harmonieuse», en parlant et s'exprimant «correctement» (Márquez Reiter 2000: 5). Les locuteurs co-construisent des interactions verbales et il s'agit avant tout d'un processus collectif.

Cependant, l'expression des opinions contraires qui résulte des différences du système de valeurs et des expériences personnelles est un acte de langage récurrent dans les pragtiques langagières et met en enjeu les «faces» des locuteurs, la relation interpersonnelle ou même «la conversation elle-même» (Brown & Levinson 1987).

Au cours d'une communication, le désaccord est considéré comme «the expression ofa view that differs from that expressed by another speaker» (l'expression d'un point de vue différenct de celui exprimé par un autre locuteur, Sifianou 2012: 1554); ou «an oppositional stance verbal or non-verbal to an antecedent verbal ou non-verbal action» (la prise de positionnement antagoniste verbale ou non-verbale à une action antécédente verbale ou non-verbale. Kakavá 1993: 36); «la rupture et le bouleversement temporaires» des accords entre énonciateurs au cours de leur communication (Maydieu 1952: 10) et «the failure between interactants» (l'échec entre les interactants, Myers 2004: 112).

Dans le cadre de la théorie des actes de langage, les actes d'accord et de désaccord sont généralement mis en relation avec la notion de «préférence» (Sacks 1973, 1987: 65; Pomerantz 1984: 77; Levinson 1983: 307; Kerbrat-Orecchioni 2015: 1). Ils sont souvent donnés comme «exemples prototypiques d'enchaînements respectivement préféré et non préféré» (Kerbrat-Orecchioni 2015: 2). L'accord est naturellement un enchaînement préféré dans le sens où il se conforme bien au but de l'interaction qui est de poursuivre des points en commun. En conséquence, par rapport au désaccord, l'interlocuteur s'attend plus à l'apparition d'un accord qui se caractérise par la rapidité et l'économie de formulation.

Dans le cadre de la théorie de politesse, le désaccord est généralement considéré comme une action potentiellement menaçante qui nuit à la face négative de l'interlocuteur en indiquant qu'il a tort et que ses assertions ne sont pas prises en considération, il existe une évaluation négative de sa position, c'est un FTA qui «est largement destructif de la solidarité sociale» (Heritage 1984: 268) et qui devrait être «mitigé » ou «évité » (Pomerantz 1984 ; Brown & Levinson 1987 ; Leech 1983 ; Sifianou 1992).

Conformément au noyau de notre étude, nous nous contenterons de définir l'objet étudié plutôt au niveau linguistique : le désaccord comme acte de langage se produisant dans une interaction verbale et exprimant une attitude ou une position opposée ou/et négative en réponse à une assertion ou à une prise de position adoptées par l'énonciateur précédent. Au niveau de la formulation, le désaccord pourrait se réaliser sous «formes extrêmement diverses et différentes » (Angouri & Locher 2012 : 1550), à tout niveau linguistique. En tant qu'acte du désaccord verbal, il semble se caractériser par des traits suivants :

1) il apparaît comme acte en réponse au dicours précédent et «qui s'inscrit dans le cadre d'un échange» (Kerbrat-Orecchioni 2015 : 2). Cela implique qu'au moins deux participants ou énonciateurs se présentent dans le contexte où nous pouvons rencontrer ou entendre des désaccords, et l'existence d'un échange en interaction ;

2) il apparaît à la suite d'une opinion ou d'une position exprimée par l'un des locuteurs ; étant un écho réactif, le désaccord ne saurait généralement se présenter à l'endroit de préliminaire (même si dans le cas d'auto-correction) ;

3) il exprime une réaction, une attitude opposée ou/et négative dans le but de défendre ses propros points de vue ou position, il est donc intrinsèquement teinté de la négation et du refus.

Il nous paraît cependant nécessaire de signaler l'existence de certains désaccords particuliers, à savoir des auto-corrections, qui sont présentes dans notre corpus, ayant pour fonction d'opérer certaines modifications, rectifications, réparations ou compléments à ses idées ou aux faits qu'il a rapportés précédement. Malgré le caractère réflexif, les auto-corrections manifestent pareillement des traits mentionnés.

2. Procédure séquentielle d'un acte de désaccord

Ayant pour objectif de gérer des situations relativement harmonieuses ou plus ou moins délicates, dans lesquelles les sujets parlants partagent des conventions communicatives communes, les locuteurs suivront de manière inconsciente certains «processus rituels» pour assurer «le bon déroulement de la communication » (Gumperz 1982 ; Ducrot 1969). Les processus rituels constituent eux-mêmes une séquence des composantes discursives de l'interaction. De ce point de vue, nous considérons un acte de langage comme une interaction minimale telle que requête, invitation ainsi que désaccord étudié dans notre travail.

Selon le modèle de l'organisation séquentielle dite*structurale*, proposé par Kerbrat-Orecchioni, « tous les types d'interactions comportent en principe une séquence d'ouverture, une partie médiane, et une séquence de clôture mais il arrive que certaines de ces composantes ne soient pas réalisées » (1990: 269). Il s'agit d'un modèle idéal et typique de l'interaction. L'avènement des contingences et des facteurs imprévus rendront beaucoup plus complexe la situation réelle. Parfois il se peut que certaines parties soient absentes ou que certaines à distances plutôt que ponctuelles soient présentes.

Partant de la complexité et de la diversité de réalisation, une description minutieuse de l'interaction nous fait entrer dans les détails de l'évolution de l'interaction. Suite de notre observation, nous sommes en mesure de proposer qu'à partir du modèle de Kerbrat-Orecchioni une séquence complète d'un acte du désaccord en situation typique comporte: une ouverture qui se déclenche par des amorces, marqueurs de négation; une partie médiane qu'est une négociation dynamique entre partenaires de l'interaction; une clôture du désaccord qui se traduit soit par une nouvelle mise en accord, soit par un conflit. Nous allons nous référer à la figure ci-dessous pour appréhender le processus d'un désaccord:

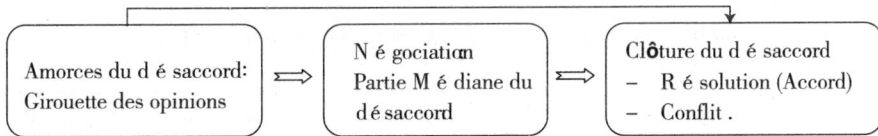

Figure 2. 1 **Processus idéal d'un acte du désaccord complet**

Toutefois, nous constatons que dans notre corpus, autant qu'au quotidien, le déroulement réel et le dénouement d'un désaccord varient en fonction du développement de l'interaction et sont déterminés par des éléments complexes. En fait il en résulte que le trio de ces séquences n'apparaît pas forcément simultanément ou séquentiellement dans un désaccord. La situation définie et le moment déterminé entraînent l'absence ou la réitération de certaines composantes. Par exemple, cela peut se traduire par la prise du tour de parole trop tôt de l'autre locuteur, ce qui provoque une interruption, ou le manque d'explication, de justification ou d'argumentation et finalement l'absence de clôture du désaccord. Cela indique que l'organisation du désaccord n'est pas constamment systématique et il nécessite une description plus détaillée d'un point de vue syntaxique. Nous allons mettre en lumière l'une après l'autre ces composantes dans la partie suivante, en nous appuyant sur des extraits du corpus.

2. 1   Ouverture du désaccord(Amorces)

Se trouvant en position initiale de l'enchaînement séquentiel du désaccord, l'amorce révèle d'emblée l'attitude conçue du locuteur par rapport à ce que lui a dit son interlocuteur. Notre observation des données nous permet de constater qu'une amorce joue le rôle de *girouette* dans toute évolution du désaccord. Cela rejoindrait éventuellement notre expérience personnelle et notre intuition.

Les amorces peuvent être réalisées au moyen de formes linguistiques multiples, telles que morphème isolé, locutions ou tournures. Notre observation implique que le morphème «non» ou «si», suivi d'une rectification, reste l'amorce privilégiée et routinière des locuteurs de notre corpus pour initier leurs désaccords. Dans notre corpus, les amorces se réalisent sous formes suivantes:

1) L'expression directe d'une assertion ou une position opposée, initiée par le morphème de négation«non» et«si».

Ce genre d'amorces a pour objectif de signaler d'emblée l'attitude du locuteur par rapport à l'énoncé précédemment tenu. Le trio «oui, non et si» fait l'objet de nombreuses études de grammaire(Grevisse 2011), ainsi que de l'analyse du discours en interaction(Plantin 1982; Diller 1984; Kerbrat-Orecchioni 2001).

	Accord	Désaccord
Assertion positive Question positive	Oui	Non
Assertion négative Question négative	Non	Si

Tableau 2. 1   **Le trio«oui, non et si», établie par Diller**(1984)

Le tableau ci-dessus établi par Diller nous montre bien que les morphèmes«non» et«si» servent à exprimer une prise de position ou une idée contraire et que le morphème«si» est employé exclusivement dans l'expression du désaccord.

Dans notre corpus, «non» ou «si» apparaît soit isolément, soit suivi d'une explication de son désaccord, qui s'incarne comme excuse, justification, argumentation ou proposition d'une alternative. Nous allons nous référer aux extraits suivants pour appuyer notre analyse. Comme par exemple dans cet épisode:

Extrait

spk5[2462. 468] : *moi j'suis j'suis j'suis assez loin des marchés en fait finalement euh*

spk3[2465. 164] : *t'es loin d'tout hein[rire collectif]*

spk5 [2467. 232] : *nan mais c'est vrai nan c'est v-nan mais XX carrément moi j'suis assez loin des commerçants donc euh les marchés euh non pas vraiment ou euh quand j'y passe quoi quand quand j'm'y retrouve j'me retrouve là par hasard oui j'y vais volontiers mais euh*

(CFPP2000[03 – 01]Ozgur_ Kilic_ H_ 32_ alii_ 3ᵉ)

Dans cette intervention, l'enquêtrice invite les enquêtés à lui dire les endroits où ils font des achats. Le locuteur 5 explicite le fait qu'il est loin du marché. Le locuteur 3 exprime son assertion en se moquant du locuteur 5, qui provoque «un rire collectif». Le locuteur 5 émet son désaccord par un morphème de négation «nan», pour introduire directement un énoncé.

Dans ce cas-là, le morphème «nan» est présent dans la réponse à une assertion affirmative, pour montrer de manière explicite le désaccord du locuteur. Par la suite, il donne une explication pour appuyer son point de vue.

En même temps, nous voudrions également signaler que l'usage de «ouais» et «nan», que le français écrit considère comme familier voire dans certains endroits vulgaire, est répandu dans le français oral contemporain.

Extrait

spk1[1314. 996] : *d'accord + + quatorzième vous ne + vous n'y allez pas du tout*

spk2 spk1[1318. 961] : [1]*mm*[2]*à Porte*

spk1[1319. 271] : *d'Orléans + tout ça c'est*

spk2 spk1[1320. 177] : [1]*si*[2]*pas*

spk2[1320. 94] : *mais si si mais*

(CFPP2000[07 – 04]Raphael_ Lariviere_ H_ 23_ 7ᵉ)

Dans cet extrait, les participants discutent de leurs endroits fréquentés. L'enquêtrice introduit le sujet abordé par une question interro-négative qui est, selon Heritage, «treated as accomplishing assertions of opinion rather than questioning» (Les interro-négatives sont considérées comme expression des points de vue plutôt que des interrogations. Heritage 2002）. Le locuteur 2 prend le tour de parole par la particule pragmatique «mm» comme un accord avec cette assertion dans le but d'encourager l'enquêtrice à continuer son discours.

Tout d'un coup, à la suite de la deuxième option, le locuteur 2 intervient en chevauchement avec l'interrogation de l'enquêtrice par le morphème «si», pour exprimer son désaccord sur le fait abordé. Ses interventions se caractérisent par le style succinct, sans aucune explication, parce qu'il s'agit d'une interaction concernant la description du fait. Dans notre corpus, l'expression de cette manière est présente plus chez les hommes que les femmes. Ce qui constitue un des caractères du parler des hommes de nos données.

Outre le désaccord *succinct* initié par le morphème isolé, la structure constituée d'un morphème suivi d'une composante explicative est aussi fréquemment observée dans notre corpus. Cette composante assume la gestion du désaccord, sous forme de justification, argumentation, remerciement, excuse et ainsi de suite.

2) Changement du sujet

Au lieu de lancer explicitement son désaccord avec l'interlocuteur, par «non» ou «si», certains locuteurs choisissent de camoufler leur attitude derrière une alternative optimale, dans le but d'éviter d'affronter catégoriquement l'interlocuteur à des points de vue différents. Ils expriment un désaccord de manière implicite, en contournant le sujet de la discussion de façon subtile et permettant à son interlocuteur de «déduire son point de vue réel» (Ducrot 1969). Différentes des morphèmes simples, les amorces qui servent à initier un changement du sujet renvoient à un ensemble de structures complexes.

Quand les locuteurs qui s'aperçoivent que le désaccord va conduire à un débat ou à une âpre dispute, ou qu'ils ont probablement du mal à exprimer leur désaccord directement, ils ont tendance à choisir de contourner le sujet abordé pour escamoter toute discussion désagréable.

Extrait

spk1[573. 255]: *et le la Pyramide ? +*

spk2[574. 853]: *euh alors la Pyramide + j'suis pas + j'ai jamais vu avant en fait donc j'peux pas vraiment*

spk2 spk1[580. 101]: [1]*juger*[2]*oui + +*

spk2[581. 413]: *euh + c'est assez + moi j'suis pas j'suis pas un grand fan de la Pyramide*

(CFPP2000[07 – 04]Raphael_ Lariviere_ H_ 23_ 7ᵉ)

Dans cet exemple, l'enquêtrice demande ce que le locuteur 2 pense de «la Pyramide», l'enquêté exprime son désaccord par un changement de sujet, en donnant une argumentation.

Dans son premier tour de parole, il s'exprime par une tournure de modalisateur «j'peux pas vraiment juger», dans le but d'éviter une appréciation dévalorisée, et de minimiser des dommages éventuellement produits. L'accent est donc mis ici sur le fait qu'il n'a jamais vu «la Pyramide», au lieu d'énoncer son évaluation. Dans l'enchaînement discursif prochain, il élucide la véritable raison pour laquelle il ne saurait juger«la Pyramide» : c'est qu'il n'est pas«un grand fan».

Finalement, nous arrivons à comprendre que l'enjeu majeur de son désaccord est plutôt une affaire de goût que de jugement. Le locuteur choisissant le changement du sujet prend soin de ne pas affronter le point risqué du désaccord lui-même, et cherche à introduire avant tout une explication raisonnable pour sa divergence de point de vue.

Extrait

spk1 spk3 [5451. 362] : [1] *est-ce que le monde est rentré dans la cuisine?* [2] *euh* spk3 [5454. 111] : *non ben c'est vrai quand j' fais des choses c'est plutôt un peu inspiré d' ma mère et c'est aussi une cuisine + méditerranéenne mais plutôt + turque en fait* (mm)

spk1 [5463. 931] : *d'accord*

spk3 [5465. 405] : *donc euh enfin*

(CFPP2000[12 – 04]Mathieu_ Rosier_ H_ 28_ Elisa_ Rysnik_ F_ 26_ 12ᵉ)

Dans cet exemple, l'enquêtrice interroge sur l'influence exercée par la mondialisation sur le plan alimentaire du locuteur. Le locuteur 3 explicite son désaccord par une description de son habitude alimentaire au lieu de réfuter directement la question posée.

Il semble que la mise en usage de«plutôt» joue un rôle délicat dans l'expression du désaccord du locuteur 3. Cela implique qu'il tient davantage à l'influence introduite par «plutôt», à savoir l'inspiration de sa mère, mais pas celle indiquée par l'enquêtrice. Le changement du sujet escamote le noeud de discussion qui constituerait potentiellement le point chaud d'une interaction. Les amorces de ce genre s'observent souvent dans notre corpus.

3) Un refus à une proposition ou une invitation qui se teinte de désaccord en représentant une attitude négative

Un acte du désaccod manifeste généralement une attitude ou une réponse négative à l'énoncé précédemment tenu, qui exprime parfois une proposition ou une invitation faite par le locuteur. Dans ce sens, le désaccord présente d'une certaine manière des caractéristiques de l'acte du *refus*.

Extrait

spk2[1885. 462]: *et alors maintenant c'est des cafés sans cigarettes au fait j'vous ai pas demandé si vous fumez tout à l'heure*

spk1[1889. 115]: *oui je fume mais j'attendrai*

spk2 spk1[1890. 642]: [1]*et bien + + + + +non non ?* [2]*tout à l'heure non non non non non + non non j' fumerai dehors*

(CFPP2000[11 − 01] Anita_ MUSSO_ F_ 46_ 11e)

Dans cet extrait, l'interaction ne touche pas aux sujets planifiés, il s'agit donc d'une conversation*hors du sujet.* À la suite de notre observation, toute la communication se déploie sous forme d'«acte de langage indirect» (Searle 1975), c'est-à-dire qu'un acte de langage est exprimé sous le couvert d'un autre acte.

Dans le premier tour de parole, l'enquêtrice(la locutrice 2) dit que«j'vous ai pas demandé si vous fumez tout à l'heure» sert d'une proposition à son interlocutrice, qui pourrait être glosée par«vous voulez une cigarette? ». Par la suite, la locutrice 1 émet son désaccord avec cette proposition par une assertion affirmative, à la place d'un refus direct. Ce désaccord initié par«mais j'attendrai» sous-entend que«non, merci, pas maintenant! ».

Dans notre corpus, les amorces exprimant un refus à une proposition ou à une invitation servent à manifester un acte du désaccord, d'une manière implicite ou explicite. Il s'agit d'une attitude négative ou d'une prise de position opposée à l'assertion de l'interlocuteur.

4) Désaccord exprimé par l'impératif

Dans notre corpus, les désaccords exprimés par l'impératif ne représentent que quatre occurrences dans nos données. Cependant, ils méritent d'être développés plus en détail dans la perspective sociolinguistique. La situation de communication et l'interconnaissance entre les locuteurs jouent un rôle important dans la mise en utilisation de la stratégie.

Il nous semble ainsi convenable de signaler d'une part, que ces quatre occurrences se limitent à l'impératif d'un verbe spécifique : «arrêter» ; et d'autre part que ces quatre présences à l'impératif ne s'utilisent qu'à la seconde personne du singulier«tu». Ce qui recèle déjà une certaine intimité ou du moins une relation relativement proche entre les locuteurs (un couple, des soeurs et des amis depuis l'enfance). Nous allons expliciter ces quatre extraits en détail dans le4. 3. 2.

Extrait

spk2 [2208. 715] : *moi j'le lis dans mon canapé*

spk5 [2211. 17] : *oh arrête de mentir*

(CFPP2000[03 − 01]Ozgur_ Kilic_ H_ 32_ alii_ 3e)

Dans cette partie, le locuteur 2 décrit la manière par laquelle il s'informe sur le quartier. L'intervention du locuteur 5 suggère qu' il n'y croit pas. À travers notre observation, l'impératif du verbe d'«arrêter» a pour objectif de manifester un désaccord avec le discours en cours et de l'empêcher de continuer.

2. 2 Médiane du désaccord(Négociation)

Le langage utilisé recèle l'orientation de convergence et l'orientation de divergence. C'est-à-dire que les locuteurs en interaction choisissent de converger vers un but communicatif en commun ou de se diverger, en fonction de leur certitude par rapport à l'énoncé, de leur style de communication et de l'interconnaissance. Au sein d'un acte du désaccord, nous arrivons à bien repérer ces deux orientations. Elles se traduisent manifestement au cours de l'évolution de la négociation du désaccord.

Au cours d'un échange séquentiel d'un désaccord, une amorce servira à entamer et annoncer d'emblée une prise de position, suivie ou non d'une précision qui sert d'explication, d'argumentation et de justification pour défendre son avis, ou pour s'excuser; ensuite, les deux partenaires de la conversation banale (des débats menés par des hommes politiques, comme par exemple les présidentielles d'entre-deux tours ne sont pas souvent le cas) s'engageront respectivement et conjointement dans la résolution du désaccord dont la procédure se caractérise par la persuasion et/ou la concession mutuelle.

De ce point de vue, la partie médiane sert à une négociation intermédiaire de va-et-vient, les locuteurs se dirigent dans la même direction qui est le maintient de la communication ; et finalement, les locuteurs auront toute chance d'aboutir à la clôture du désaccord au moyen de la concession d'un des locuteurs ou d'un changement de sujet, ce qui est considéré comme une résolution appropriée pour une interaction dans*l'impasse*.

Nous pouvons constater que la négociation conversationnelle est cruciale dans le sens qu'elle joue le rôle de démarcation, en déterminant la direction et le résultat d'un acte de désaccord. Les participants de l'interaction arriveront en compromis ou en conflit à l'issue d'une négociation, en fonction du déroulement de la négociation.

2.3 Clôture du désaccord(Résolution ou Conflit)

Tout désaccord n'a pas de clôture. Une clôture, si elle est susceptibled'exister, est toujours le résultat d'une négociation ou de plusieurs tours de négociation, ce qui suppose toujours une certaine concession d'au moins un des partenaires. La consession vise la résolution d'un désaccord, individuellement ou conjointement.

Notre observation suggère que la plupart des désaccords seclôturent généralement en *paix*, apparemment ou véritablement. L'autre forme de clôture, à savoir le conflit verbal ou physique, n'est pas présente dans notre corpus. Nous n'en parlerons donc pas bien que cela puisse se produire dans la vie quotidienne. Dans nos données, le désaccord se termine par :

1)la concession d'un locuteur ou un compromis entre deux partenaires ;

2)l'introduction d'un nouveau sujet, le désaccord censéêtre *stérile* ;

3)l'intervention d'une tiercepersonne ;

4) des procédés non-verbaux tels que le silence ou le rire qui empêche l'interaction d'entrer dans une impasse.

Conclusion

Pour conclure, nous signalons qu'en tant qu'acte de langage, un désaccord pourrait s'organiser comme une séquence conversationnelle structurale, qui comporte une ouverture réalisée par diverses amorces, une partie médiane qui rend possibles des va-et-vient discursifs entre les locuteurs et une clôture qui se dirige soit vers la résolution du désaccord, soit vers un conflit, soit vers un compromis entre les locuteurs. Compte tenu de l'importance de l'amorce dans l'expression du désaccord, nous voudrions mettre l'accent sur l'analyse descriptive des amorces du désaccord dans notre corpus. Un inventaire de ce genre a pour objectif de mieux comprendre les amorces disponibles que les locuteurs emploient, et l'effet sémantique ou grammatical.

Bibliographie

[1]Angouri, Jo. , and Miriam A. Locher. *Theorising Disagreement. Journal of Pragmatics.* [J]Vol. 44, No12, 2012: 1549 – 1553.

[2] Brown, Penelope. , and Stephen C. Levinson. *Politeness: Some Universals in Language Usage*[M]. Cambridge: Cambridge University Press, 1978.

[3] Diller, Anne-Marie. , and François Récanati. *La Pramatique: Présentation. Langue Française.* [J]No42, 1979: 3 –5.

[4]Ducrot, Oswald. *Présupposés et Sous-entendus. Langue Française.* [J]Vol. 4, No1, 1969: 33 –43.

[5]Ducrot, Oswald. *Dire et Ne Pas Dire: Principes de Sémantique Linguistique.* [J] Paris: Hermann, 1972.

[6] Ducrot, Oswald. *Les Lois de Discours. Langue Française.* [J] N° 42, 1979: 21 –33.

[7]Grevisse, Maurice. *Le Bon Usage*[M]. Paris: Éditions Duculot, 1980, 2011.

[8] Gumperz, John J. *Discourse Strategies* [M]. New York: Cambridge University Press, 1982.

[9]Gu, Yueguo. *Politeness Phenomena in Modern Chinese. Journal of pragmatics.* [J] Vol. 14, 1990: 237 –257.

[10] Heritage, John. *The Limits of Questioning: Negative Interrogatives and Hostile Question Content. Journal of Pragmatics.* [J]Vol. 34, 2002: 1427 –1446.

[11]Kakavá, Christina. *Discourse and Conflict. Handbook of Discourse Analysis.* [C] Eds. Schiffrin, Deborah. , Deborah Tannen, and Heidi E. Hamilton. Oxford: Blackwell, 2003: 650 –670.

[12] Kerbrat-Orecchioni, Catherine. *Les Interactions Verbales* [M]. *Tome. 1.* Paris: Armand Colin, 1990.

[13] Kerbrat-Orecchioni, Catherine. *Les Interactions Verbales* [M]. *Tome. 2.* Paris: Armand Colin, 1992.

[14] Kerbrat-Orecchioni, Catherine. *Les Interactions Verbales* [M]. *Tome. 3.* Paris: Armand Colin, 1994.

[15]Kerbrat-Orecchioni, Catherine. *Négocier dans les Petits Commerces. Négociations.* [J]N°2, 2004: 7 –22.

[16] Kerbrat-Orecchioni, Catherine. *L'Analyse du Discours en Interaction: Quelques Principes Méthodologiques. Limbaje si comunicare.* [C]NoIX, 2007: 13 –32.

[17] Kerbrat-Orecchioni, Catherine. (*Im*)*politesse et Gestion des Faces dans Deux Types de Situations Communicatives*: *Petits Commerces et Débats Électoraux. Soprag.* [C] Berlin: de Gruyter. Vol. 2, N°1, 2014: 293 – 326.

[18] Kerbrat-Orecchioni, Catherine. *Le Désaccord, Réaction* «*non préférée*»? *Le Cas des Débats Présidentiels. Praxiling* 2013: *Manifestation* (*s*) *du Désaccord*: *Approches Pluridisciplinaires.* [C] Université Paul Valéry Montpellier 3, 2015.

[19] Leech, Geoffrey. *Principles of Pragmatics* [M]. London: Longman, 1983.

[20] Márquez Reiter, Rosina., and María E. Placencia. *Spanish Pragmatics* [M]. New York: Palgrave Macmillan, 2005.

[21] Maydieu, André-Jean. *Le Désaccord* [M]. Paris: Presses Universitaires de France, 1952.

[22] Plantin, Christian. *Mots, les Arguments, le Texte.* [C] Paris: Centre National de Documentation Pédagogique, 1989.

[23] Pomerantz, Anita. *Agreeing and Disagreeing with Assessments*: *Some Features of Preferred / Dispreferred Turn Shapes. Structures of Social Actions.* Eds. Atkinson, J. Maxwell. And John Heritage. [C] Cambridge: Cambridge University Press, 1984: 57 – 101.

[24] Sacks, Harvey. *On the Preferences for Agreement and Contiguity in Sequences in Conversation. Talk and Social Organization.* Eds. Button, G., and R. W. Lee. [C] Clevedon: Multilingual Matters, 1987: 54 – 69.

[25] Searle, John Roger. *Indirect speech acts. Syntax and Semantics*: *Speech acts.* [J] Vol. 3, 1975: 59 – 82.

[26] Sifianou, Maria. *Disagreement, Face and Politeness. Journal of Pragmatics.* [J] Vol. 44, 2012: 1554 – 1564.

[27] Vion, Robert. *L'Analyse des Interactions Verbales. Les Carnets du Cediscor.* [J] N°1, 1996: 19 – 32.

Sites

[28] Branca-Rosoff, Sonia., Florence Lefeuvre, Serge Fleury., and Mat Pires: < http: //cfpp2000. univ-paris3. fr >.

[29] Branca-Rosoff, Sonia., Florence Lefeuvre, Serge Fleury., and Mat Pires. 2012: *Présentation du Corpus de Français Parlé Parisien des années* 2000. < http: //cfpp2000. univ-paris3. fr/Presentation. html >.

日本語受動文における視点の制約性*

張麗花　曹　曦**

摘　要：「内の視点」の日本語は、基本的に主語を変えずに記述を続ける傾向にあるので、頻繁に受動文の使用を要求される。能・受動態の選択過程には、単文・複文・テクストの三つのレベルでそれぞれ異なる条件が与えられている。単文レベルでは共感度の高い存在(一人称・[＋特定]・[＋有情])、複文レベルでは従属節が主節と同一の名詞(句)、テクストレベルではテクストによって指定された対象を主語に据える傾向が見られる。

キーワード：日本語受動文；内の視点；主語項視点；共感度視点

1　従来の研究

　最も早い段階で視点理論を用いて日本語受動文の説明を試みたのは久野(1978)である。受動文の用法について、久野は次のように説明している。受動文が内包する視点制約を「受身文のカメラ・アングルは、新しい主語の指示対象よりである」(久野，1978：130)、つまり「E(新しい主語) ＞ E(古い主語)」(久野，1978：169)のように規定している。

　そして、これらの視点制約は、次に挙げる共感度視点の原則(久野，1978：146 - 149)と、矛盾してはならない。即ち、発話当事者の視点ハイアラーキーの原則は「1 ＝ E(一人称) ＞ E(二、三人称)」で、談話主題の視点ハイアラーキーの原則は「E(談話主題) ≧ E(新登場人物)」を意味するのである。

　このような視点制約と共感度視点の原則から、下例 b 文が日本語として不自然である理由を説明することができる。

---

　*　論文題目：視点在日语被动句中的制约性。
　**　作者简介：张丽花，云南大学外国语学院日语系教授，研究方向：日语语言学。曹曦，文理学院副教授，研究方向：日语语言学。

例1 a 私は太郎に殴られた。

　　 b 田中は私に殴られた。

例2 a 鈴木は見知らぬ人に殴られた。

　　 b 見知らぬ人が鈴木に殴られた。

　共感度視点の原則に従えば、例1では発話当事者の視点ハイアラーキーが、例2では談話主題の視点ハイアラーキーが、それぞれE(私)とE(鈴木)に視点を寄せることになっている。しかし、例文bのような三人称の「田中」と新登場人物の「見知らぬ人」が主語になる受動文は、共感度視点の原則に違反しているゆえ、不自然な文と見なされる。

　久野(1978)のほか、奥津敬一郎(1983、1992)による一連の研究、特に非情物の受身は日本に固有のものか否かという問題をめぐる研究がよく知られている。奥津は、非情物の受身は古語にも多く存在するので、日本語固有のものであると主張している。その上、『枕草子』、『徒然草』、『万葉集』における受身文の使用状況から、直接受身文の話し手が視点を動作主と受動者のどちらに置くかという要素と視点の序列の仮説によって、なぜ受身文が使用されるのかという説明に力を入れている。例えば、次の用例では、[＋有情]と[-有情]で、前者の方が視点の序列が高い。

例3 a 神社の木は太郎になぎ倒された。

　　 b 神社の木はなぎ倒された。

　例文aのように、[-有情]の受動者が主語になる受身文は、視点の序列に違反するため、不自然な文になる。しかし、例文bは、非情物の受身であっても、動作主が文中に現れないため、自然な文と見られる。

　奥津は、受動文・能動文の別を問わず、「視点＝主語項」と捉えている。そして、この主語項における視点の理論を、立てた主語をできるだけ途中で変更しないように受身文が使われるという「視点固定の原則」に発展させていく。

2　本稿の立場

　従来の研究をまとめてみれば、日本語受動文の用法には共感度視点と主語項視点との二つの原則が関与していることがわかる。しかし、主語を一つしか持たない単文レベルと主語を二つ以上持つ複文やテクストレベルとでは、視点の関わり方が同様なものとは考えられない。単文では、主語項視点の原則が関与する余地がないのにに対して、複文では、受動文の使用動機となる。よって、受動文における視点の制約性については、少なくとも単文レベルで

の「共感度視点」と複文レベルでの「主語項視点」との二つに分けて考察してい
く必要があるし、更にテクストにおける制約状況を研究してみる価値がある
と思われる。そこで、本稿は関連理論に関する研究成果を踏まえ、単文・複
文・テクストと三つのレベルにおいて、日本語受動文における視点の制約性
を詳しく考察していくことにする。

　そのためには、まず本稿における視点の定義をはっきりさせる必要がある。
共感度という意味での視点、基準点・参照点という意味での視点、特定の項
（特に主語項）に視点を置くもの、事象の把握の仕方（眺め方）という意味での
視点等、さまざまな意味で使われている。そして、学者によってもその定義
が少しずつ異なっている。例えば、下地（2004）は「視座・注視点」、池上
（2003）は「客観的把握・主観的把握」、益岡（2009）は「事象に対する内の視点
・事象に対する外の視点」などと定義付けている。これほど、視点研究が注目
を集めているということであるが、本稿では、日本語受動文における視点の
制約性を考察していくために有効なものとして、「内の視点」の定義を重要視
する①。

　「内の視点」とは、話し手がある事象を言語化する際に、どのような把握の
仕方（眺め方）をするかという観点による分類である。これについて、下地早
智子（2011）が「視座」、木村英樹（1996）が「現場立脚当事者」という概念を以っ
て対照的に捉えている。例えば、道を尋ねられた時、日本人は「あの信号のと
ころを左に曲がって、まっすぐ行くと銀行があります。」というように、「右/
左・前/後」などの相対的な空間名詞を用いて答える。つまり、日本語では、
話し手が聞き手の身になって、仮想上の言動を共に行うという意味で、「現場
立脚当事者」型、「内の視点」である

　以上を踏まえて、「内の視点」を次のように定義することができよう。「内
の視点」とは話し手がある事象を事象の内側のどこから眺め、言語化するかと
いう意味での視点（すなわち「視座」が深く関わっている視点）である。「内の
視点」の場合は、話し手が事象の内側に位置して、視点を寄せやすい存在（一
人称、［＋特定］、［＋有情］、テクストによって指定された対象）に視点を寄
せ、それを「視座」と見なして主語の位置に据える。

---

　① 「内の視点」は、単に本研究における言い方に限っている。言葉を借りれば、下地
（2011）の「視座」、益岡（2009）の「事象に対する内の視点」、池上（2003）の「主観的把握・」
等の言い方にほぼ相当する。

3 日本語受動文の表現形式と認定

日本語の受動表現には二つの形式がある。一つは文法形式で、動詞の受動形「V 未然形＋れる/られる」を述語にし、受動者が主語に立って、動作主が補語になる構文である。その補語は「に、から、によって」によってマークされる。例えば、「直孝ハ祖母に育テラレタ」、「直孝ハ五歳ノトキ父母ニ死ナレタ」などのような表現はこの形式に分類できる。

もう一つは語彙形式で、動詞固有の意味によって「動作、作用を受ける」ということを表すものである。例えば、「被る、蒙る、浴びる、負う、もらう、預かる、授かる」などの動詞が挙げられる。これらの動詞は受動的意味を持つ動詞とは言えても、動詞の受動態ではないとされている①。

日本語の受動文は、「動作・作用の主体が、他の何ものかに働きかける場合に、動作主、つまり動きの発するところを主役とするのでなく、動きの受けるもの、動きの向こう先を主役として事態を描く表現」である。受動態が「格」の交替という特徴を持っている②。

寺村（1982）では、ある表現を受動態と言い得るためには、次のような一般的な形態・統語・意味的特徴が認められるということが必要となる③。

XガY ニ Vれる/られる

X：Vの動作、変化、出来事の主体

Y：「XがVする」ことによって影響を受ける主体

つまり、主格に立つ名詞 Xが述語動詞の動作を受けることを表し、動作主のYが補語になり、それに述語動詞 Vが受動の述語の一般的な形態的特徴「Vれる/られる」を備えているということは受動表現の認定条件とされる。例えば、日本語で「太田が田中を殺した/太田杀了田中。」という事件を表す方法としては、次の三種類が挙げられる。

例4 a 太田が田中を殺した。（能動文）/太田杀了田中。

　　 b 田中は太田が殺した。（目的語を主題化した「YはXがV」型構文）/
　　　 田中是太田杀的。

---

① 寺村秀夫（1982）『日本語のシンタクスと意味Ⅰ』くろしお出版、p212を参照。

② 同上、p212を参照。

③ 同上、p212 – 214を参照。

　　c　田中は太田に殺された。（受動文）/田中被太田杀了。

　aは能動文である。bは「太田が田中を殺した」のヲ格目的語である「田中」を主題化して、文頭に持ってきた文である。このような構文は目的語を主題化した「YはXがV」型構文（以下、「YはXがV」型構文）と言う。cは受動文である。[①] 日本語受動文の認定条件については異論がないゆえ、本研究では原則として文法形式の受動表現（受動文）、つまり日本語受動文の一般的な形態的特徴「Vれる／られる」を備えたものを研究対象とする。

4　単文レベルの場合

　単文の場合、主語述語の関係が一つしかないので、発話者と主語の関係において視点のおきかたを考えればよいのである。主語になるものは一人称、二人称、三人称のほかあり得ない。発話者は二、三人者より共感度の高い一人称者と一体に言動を共にしやすい。つまり、ほかより一人者を主語に置いて、視点を据える傾向が強いと考えられる。したがって、一人称を主語に据えた受動文は適格とされるが、一人称非主語の受動文（動作主の一人称を非主語に格下げする受動文）はコンテクストが単純な単文レベルでは一切不適格とされるのである。

　　例5　a　私は太郎に殴られた。　　　　　　　　　　（適格）
　　　　　b　田中は私に殴られた。　　　　　　　　　　（不適格）

　これはいわゆる発話当事者の視点ハイアラーキー［E（一人称）＞E（二、三人称）］の原則である（久野，1978：146）。しかし、次の用例はどうだろう。−bが不適格文とされたのはなぜなのか。

　　例6　a　鈴木は見知らぬ人に殴られた。　　　　　　（適格）
　　　　　b　見知らぬ人が鈴木に殴られた。　　　　　　（不適格）
　　例7　a　太郎は突然の苦しみに襲われた。　　　　　　（適格）
　　　　　b　紙が太郎に破られた。　　　　　　　　　　（不適格）

　いずれも一人称が使われてない受動文である。この場合、発話者は非特定の「見知らぬ人」や非情物の「紙」より、特定できる「鈴木」や「太郎」に対して共感と持ち、視点を共にしやすい。

　したがって、ある事象に参与する存在（いずれも三人称）のうち、発話者にとって熟知度のある［＋特定］の名詞（句）の方が［−特定］の名詞（句）より談話主題になりやすい。同じように、［＋有情］と［−有情］の場合では、［＋有

---

　　① 庵功雄、高梨信乃、中西久実子、山田敏弘（2001）『中上級を教える人のための日本語文法ハンドブック』東京スリーエーネットワーク、p110。

情]の名詞(句)の方が談話主題になる。つまり、単文レベルでは、談話主題になりやすいのは[＋特定]、あるいは[＋有情]の名詞(句)である。[＋特定]あるいは[＋有情]の名詞(句)を主語に据えた受動文は適格となる。一方、[－特定]や[－有情]の名詞(句)を主語に据えた受動文はほとんど不適格となる①。

5 複文レベル

複文レベルで、日本語の受動文の用法に関与しているのは「主語項視点」の原則(主語固定の原則)である。それがどのように、どの程度で受動文の用法に関与しているかについては、複文内の従属節の従属度②に関する野田尚史(1995)の観点が有効だと思う。

野田によれば、従属節の主節に対する従属度が高ければ高いほど、「主語項視点」の原則の遵守をより厳しく要求されている。このことの妥当性を証明するためには、主節に対する従属度に応じて従属節を分類する必要があるが、それについて、田窪行則が明確な分類付けを提示している。田窪は、従属節をA類からD類までの四つの階層に分類し、それぞれ次のような接続助詞を取りうるとしている。(1987：38–39)

A類：て(様態)、ながら(同時動作)、つつ、ために、まま、ように(目的)……

B類：て(理由、時間)、れば、たら、から(行動の理由)、ために(理由)、ように(比況)……

C類：から(判断の根拠)、ので、が、けれど、し、て(並列)……

D類：と(引用)、という

そこで、田窪(1987)の分類法に基づき、本研究では、次の通り、主・従属節が同一主語を要求するもの、主・従属節が同一主語を要求しないものに分類して考察してみたいと思う。

①主・従属節が同一主語を要求するもの

この分類は、田窪(1987)によるA類従属節とB類従属節の「―て(理由、時間)」節に相当するものである。それは、主節の述語を直接に修飾する働きを

---

① 潜在的受影者が想定される場合に限り適格となる。益岡(1991)では、文中に顕現する被動作主が[－有情]であっても、当該の事象そのものから影響を受ける[＋有情]の「潜在的受影者」が想定できる場合、[－有情]の受動文が成立するということを指摘している。そして、潜在的受影者が想定される場合の[－有情]の受動文は、潜在的受影者寄りの視点を要求する。

② 野田尚史(1995)による。

するものであるため、従属節と主節の主語は同一でなければならない。その
ため、「主語項視点」の原則を遵守しなければ必然的に文全体が不適格とな
る。つまり、主・従属節が同一主語を要求するものには、「主語項視点」の原
則が非常に強く関与しているということである。

例8　a　太郎は母親に連れられて、幼稚園に行った。　　　　（適格）

　　　b　母親が太郎を連れて、太郎は幼稚園に行った。　　　（不適格）

例9　a　太郎は宿題を忘れて、先生に叱られた。　　　　　　（適格）

　　　b　太郎は宿題を忘れて、先生は太郎を叱った。　　　　（不適格）

②主・従属節が同一主語を要求しないもの

　この分類は、田窪（1987）によるB類従属節の「れば、たら、から（行動の理
由）」などの「一て（理由、時間）」節以外のものと、C類従属節と、D類従属節
である。中には、B類従属節の「れば、たら、から（行動の理由）」従属節や、
C類従属節の順接を表すもの（「から」、「ので」）①などの場合は、必ずしも
「主語項視点」原則を適用しなければいけないが、従属節の主語に「は」がつく
場合は、「主語項視点」原則の遵守を強要する。反対に、従属節の主語に「が」
がつく場合は、この原則に従わなくても文は適格である。

例10　a　太郎は宿題を忘れば/たら、先生に叱られるだろう。　（適格）

　　　a′　太郎は宿題を忘れば/たら、先生は太郎を叱るだろう。　（不適格）

　　　b　太郎が宿題を忘れば/たら、先生に叱られるだろう。　（適格）

　　　b′　太郎が宿題を忘れば/たら、先生は太郎を叱るだろう。　（適格）

例11　a　私は大事なところで失敗したから、みんなに責められた。（適格）

　　　a′　私は大事なところで失敗したから、みんなは私を責めた。（不適格）

　　　b　私が大事なところで失敗したから、みんなに責められた。（適格）

　　　b′　私が大事なところで失敗したから、みんなは私を責めた。（適格）

　一方、C類従属節の逆接を表すもの（「が」、「けれど」）と並列を表すもの
（「し」、「て」）、またD類の接続助詞「と、という」を伴う「引用」の内容であ
る従属節の場合は、従属節の主節に対する従属度はほぼゼロに等しい。した
がって、「主語項視点」の原則の関与は非常に弱くなる。

例12　a　私は大事なところで失敗したが、みんなに責められなかった。
　　　　（適格）

　　　b　私は大事なところで失敗したが、みんなは私を責めなかった。
　　　　（適格）

---

　①　田窪（1987）により、C類従属節は、①順接を表すもの（「から」、「ので」）、②逆
接を表すもの（「が」、「けれど」）、③並列を表すもの（「し」、「て」）の三つに分けられる。

例13　a　太郎は次郎を非難し、次郎に非難された。（適格）

　　　　b　太郎は次郎を非難し、次郎は太郎を非難した。（適格）

例14　a　太郎は「いつも次郎にいじめられる」といった。（適格）

　　　　b　太郎は「次郎がいつも僕をいじめる」といった。（適格）

6　テクストレベル

　結論から言えば、テクストレベルにおいては、「結束性」の原則が「共感度視点」や「主語項視点」の原則よりも強く関与し、これに基づいて日本語の能・受動文の選択が行われる。結束性とは、「文に一貫性を持たせ、一連の文法的に独立した文を結びつけ、テクストにテクスト性を与える言語的な記号のこと」である①。本研究の立場で言えば、つまり、なるべく注視点を変えずに、同一の存在をできるだけ長く叙述しつづけるという原則なのである。

　ただし、テクストの種類によって、結束性を比較的強く要求すると思われるテクスト（小説、エッセイなど）と、そうではないテクスト（新聞、記事など）との区分がある。そして、結束性に対する要求の強弱により、視点の選択のされ方も異なっている。

　例15　（ⅰ）そのとき叫び声が聞こえた。振り向くと、滝のなかへ吸い込まれるアキの姿が見えた。激しい流れに揉まれて、彼女の身体はコマのようにくるくるまわっている。泣き叫びながら、両手で水面を叩いている。アキの声が遠く耳に届いた。ぼくは叫び返した。彼女の名前を呼びつづけた。（ⅱ）しかし手が、顔が、水面に広がる髪が、流れに呑み込まれていく。（ⅲ）恐怖と絶望に見開かれた目が、青い水とともに吸い込まれて見えなくなる。（S. P194）②

　以上のテクストでは、（ⅱ）のところで、（ⅱ）′しかし流れは彼女の手を、顔を、水面に広がる髪を呑み込んでいく。

　というような能動文の表現も文法的には適格であるが、原文は受動文になっている。そこで、考察の範囲をテクストレベルにまで拡大すると、原文の（ⅱ）のところではなにゆえ受動文が選ばれているのかという点が問題になる。

　もし例15のテクストを全体的見てみれば、（ⅰ）では主に「彼女（アキ）の姿・身体」を、（ⅲ）では「（彼女の）目」が主語に据えられて叙述をしていること

---

①　『外国語教育学大辞典』（1999）による。

②　「S」は日本語小説『世界の中心で、愛をさけぶ』（片山恭一［著］、小学館、2001 年）の略称。以下、『世界の中心で、愛をさけぶ』中の研究例を「例 S」と表記する。

が分かる。それで、（ ii ）のところで受動文が選ばれているのは、やはり「（彼女の）手、顔、髪」が主語に据えられて、（ i ）から（ iii ）までも同一の存在である「彼女の身体」について叙述しつづけられるためであると考えられる。

　以上の例によって、テクストレベルでは、「結束性」の原則が大きく関与し、これに基づいて能・受動文の選択が行われるということが明らかになってくる。

　上述のように、「内の視点」の日本語では、話し手は視点を寄せやすい存在として、一人称・［＋特定］・［＋有情］・テクストによって指定された対象を選定し、これを主語に据える傾向が強い。

7　おわりに

　本稿の出発点は、視点が具体的にどのように日本語受動文の用法にかかわっているかという問題意識を持ったことである。これに対して、本稿は視点に関する先行研究を幅広く参照し、視点概念を用いた受動文研究の理論的研究成果を十分に踏まえた上で、日本語には「内の視点」が受動文の用法に関与しているということをはっきりさせた。それから、日本語における「内の視点」の意味を明確した上で、日本語受動文における視点の制約性について考察した。具体的には、単文・複文・テクストレベルで見たときの、日本語受動文の採用における「内の視点」の制約状況を詳細に分析してみた。結論として、次のようにまとめることができると思う。

　日本語は「内の視点」言語であるゆえ、基本的に主語を変えずに記述を続ける傾向にある。したがって、頻繁に受動文の使用を要求されるのである。日本語で能・受動態の選択過程には、単文・複文・テクストの三つのレベルでそれぞれ異なる条件が与えられている。単文レベルでは共感度の高い存在（一人称・［＋特定］・［＋有情］）、複文レベルでは従属節が主節と同一の名詞（句）、テクストレベルではテクストによって指定された対象を主語に据える（同一の存在をできるだけ長く叙述し続ける）というような傾向が見られる。

参考文献

[1]池上嘉彦.言語における＜主観性＞と＜主観性＞の言語的指標(1)[J].
　　認知言語学論考, 2003(3).

[2]池上嘉彦.言語における＜主観性＞と＜主観性＞の言語的指標(2)[J].
　　認知言語学論考, 2004(4).

[3]奥津敬一郎.何故受身か――＜視点＞からのケース・スタディー[J].国
　　語学, 1983(132).

［4］奥津敬一郎．日本語の受身文と視点［J］．日本語学，1992（8月号）．

［5］亀井孝・河野六郎・千野栄一．「受動態」言語学大辞典：第6巻 述語編［M］．日本：三省堂，1996．

［6］木村英樹．中国語はじめの一歩［M］．日本：筑摩書房（ちくま新書），1996．

［7］久野暲．談話の文法［M］．日本：大修館書店，1978．

［8］久野暲．新日本文法研究［M］．日本：大修館書店，1983．

［9］久野暲．受身文の意味―黒田説の再批判―［J］．日本語学，1986（2月号）．

［10］古賀悠太郎．受動文の使用／不使用と日本語話者の視点――テクストレベルでの考察――［J］．神戸市外国語大学研究科論集，2013（16）．

［11］下地早智子．日中両言語における文法事象としての視点の差異――移動動詞・受身の表現・テンス／アスペクトの場合――［J］．神戸市外国語大学外国学研究，2004（58）．

［12］下地早智子．「視点」の違いから見るアスペクト形式選択の日中差――非限界動作動詞の場合――［J］．日中言語研究と日本語教育，2011（4）．

［13］田窪行則．統語構造と文脈情報［J］．日本語学，1987（5月号）．

［14］寺村秀夫．日本語のシンタクスと意味Ⅰ［M］．日本：くろしお出版，1982．

［15］日本語記述文法研究会（編）．現代日本語文法②［M］．日本：くろしお出版，2009．

［16］野田尚史．現場依存の視点と文脈依存の視点――日本語の複文・連文でボイス・テンス・ムード形式がとる視点――［A］．仁田義雄．複文の研究（下）［C］．日本：くろしお出版，1995．

［17］益岡隆志．モダリティの文法［M］．日本：くろしお出版，1991．

［18］益岡隆志．日本語の尊敬構文と内・外の視点［A］．坪本篤朗・朝瀬尚子・和田尚明．「内」と「外」の言語学［C］．日本：開拓社，2009．

［19］渡辺伸治．「視点」諸概念の分類とその本質［J］．大阪大学言語文化部大学院言語文化研究科「言語文化研究」，1999（25）．

［20］M. A. K. ハリディ・ルカイヤ・ハサン（著）、安藤貞雄等（訳）．テクストはどのように構成されるか［M］．日本：ひつじ書房，1997．

日本語配慮表現に関する一考察

——中国人日本語学習者の視点から[*]

饒瓊珍[**]

要　旨：周知のように言語は文化の伝達手段である。日本語の配慮表現は日本語の表現上における特徴の一つであり、日本文化の特徴の一つでもあるといえる。人間関係に気にしている日本人の日常生活のコミュニケーションの中に配慮表現がよく使われている。配慮表現は曖昧表現とのけじめがはっきりしていないので、曖昧表現ともいわれている。このような表現は日本人にとっては馴染み深くて、当たり前に使っているが、中国人日本語学習者にとっては、その表現の中に隠れている文化や発想などが異なるので、なかなか身に付けられないし、間違いやすく、実際の言語実践や日本人とコミュニケーションするとき、よくぶつかりやすいところでもある。筆者は日本語教師として、普段の仕事に深くかかわる中国人日本語学習者という視点から、日本語の配慮表現を学習したり、応用したりするときに最も間違いやすいところを例にして、日本語配慮表現の特徴やその中に隠れている日本文化現象を明らかにし、中国人日本語学習者に有益な提言をしてみようと思う。

キーワード：配慮表現；コミュニケーション；文化現象

始めに

「言語は文化の伝達手段の働きがあるといわれているが、実は言葉は言語行為としての運用にその本質が現れ、話し手である人間のフィルターによって、さまざまに色付けがなされていく。使用している人間を抜きにしては、言葉

　＊　论文题目：日语配慮表达考察——以中国日语学习者为视点。

＊＊　作者简介：饶琼珍，云南大学外国语学院日语系副教授，研究方向：日语语言学。

の問題は語れない。談話・文章はいうに及ばず、文法や意味の問題も使い手である人間の視点に焦点を合わせて眺めていくと、意外な事実に気づかれるものである」①。今度、本研究課題を取り上げるのは日本語の配慮表現を通して日本人の人間関係やその言葉の裏に隠れている日本文化の現象、及び日本人の対人関係における表現上の特徴などに発見し、それを中国人日本語学習者向きの日本語教育に生かして、より良い日本語教育結果を得るため、学習者の日本語勉強の意欲を引き立てるためにもなると思う。

　人間関係を重視する日本人は他人とコミュニケーションをするとき配慮表現を談話の中に良く使われ、配慮表現を通して、他人との関係や和を保たれるばかりではなく、より良い人間関係が維持できる。それは日本語表現における特徴の一つであり、日本文化の現象でもある。「配慮表現」の研究を抜きにしては日本人の人間関係における「待遇表現」の本質の把握は有り得ない。「配慮表現」は言語生活で見過ごすことのできない言語事象という点には異論を挟む余地はないが、それを「待遇表現」の体系の中でいかに位置づけるか大きな課題である②。この話しとおりに「配慮表現」は日本語待遇表現の中に含まれ、抜きにしてはいけない重要な役割を果たしていると思われる。配慮表現と言っても様々な種類がある。普通は大きく二種類を分けられている。即ち形式からみた配慮表現の種類と機能から見た配慮表現の種類である③。配慮表現は研究範囲や研究の方法において多様性という特徴があるゆえにいろんな視点から研究できるが、本論文は主に中国人日本語学習者という視点から学習者が日本語の配慮表現を勉強したり使ったりするときに間違いやすいところを例にして日本語の配慮表現の特徴を考察してみる。考察を通してその中に隠れて日本文化や日本人の発想などを明らかにし、中国人日本語学習者の配慮表現におけるミスやぶつかりやすいところの要因をも分析し、まとめてみたいと思う。

1. 配慮表現の定義

　配慮表現の定義について学者によって、文字的な説明が多少異なっているが、そのポイントは同じであると言っても過言ではない。この面においての

---

　① 森田良行『話者の視点が作る日本語』株式会社ひつじ書房 2006 年 12 月 5 日初版 1 刷 p236.

　② 彭飛『日本語の「配慮表現」に関する研究』研究所シリーズ第一巻和泉書院 2005 年 10 月 10 日 p29.

　③ 野田尚史・高山善行・小林隆著『日本語の配慮表現の多様性』くろしお出版 2014 年 6 月 16 日 p8.

学者の本定義をいくつ次のように挙げる。

　配慮表現とは対人的コミュニケーションにおいて、相手との関係をなるべく良好にたもつことに配慮して用いられる言語表現である①。

　話し手は聞き手と円滑なコミュニケーションを行うため、人は伝えたいことをそのまま言語化して伝えるわけではない。話し手の尊厳やその人らしさなどを意志や意向が過不足なく伝わるよう、かつ聞き手との関係を望ましい形で維持できるように、敬意や改まり、親しさや距離感の設定など様々な配慮をし、それを言語表現にこめている。このような配慮を反映した言語表現を配慮表現と呼ぶ。(守屋三千代)

　配慮表現というのは、聞き手や読み手に悪い感情を持たないようにするために使う表現である②。

　配慮表現とは、人間が言語でコミュニケーション活動をなす場合に、緩和表現、受益表現、プラス価値付加表現、心地よい気分表現(気分をよくさせる表現)などの表現を用いて、相手の心が傷つかないように、また自分が相手に好ましい印象を与えるように配慮する対人関係の表現を指すものである③。

　以上は日本語の配慮表現における代表的な学者の定義を挙げてみた。文字的な叙述がそれぞれ個性的で、異なっているが、どれも聞き手視点を中心に、コミュニケーションの中で聞き手との関係を維持するために、聞き手の感情や気持ちを損なう言葉を避けて、心地よい気分表現を使うように配慮する。このような表現は言うまでもなく、裏に隠れているのが日本文化の特徴であり、日本人の人間関係の反映であり、日本語の表現上の特徴でもある。以心伝心でコミュニケーションに慣れている日本人同士は問題ないが、文化背景が違う中国人日本語学習者にとっては難点の一つであり、実際、日本人とコミュニケーションするとき、もっとも間違いやすく、ぶつかりやすいところだといえる。

2. 配慮表現の先行研究

　筆者の調査によると、日本では配慮表現に関する研究は20世紀90年代から始まり、今日まで数多くの学者がそれについて様々な視点から研究し、喜

---

　①　山岡政紀・牧原功・小野正樹著『コミュニケーションと配慮表現』明治書院平成22年2月22日初版発行 p143.

　②　野田尚史・高山善行き・小林隆著『日本語配慮表現の多様性』くろしお出版 2014年6月15日第1刷発行 p3.

　③　彭飛『日本語の配慮表現に関する研究』和泉書院 2005年10月10日初版第1刷発行 p3.

ばしい成果が収まった。本論文の中で年代に追ってその中の一部の代表的な成果を挙げてみる。『日本語の配慮——文法構造からのアプローチ——』(J)(2003 年 11 月北京日本学研究センター);『配慮表現からみた日本語』(J)(姫野伴子月刊日本語 2004 年 2 月);『日本語の「配慮表現」に関する研究』(M)(彭飛 2005 年 10 月和泉書院);『コミュニケーションと配慮表現』(M)(山岡政紀・牧原功・小野正樹明治書院 2010 年);『現代人の言語行動における"配慮表現"——「言語行動に関する調査」から』(J)(塩田雄大放送研究と調査 2012年 7 月);『日本語の配慮表現に関する文法カテゴリー』(牧原功群馬大学国際教育・研究センター論集第 11 号 2012);『日本語の配慮表現の多様性』(M)(野田尚史、高山善行、小林隆編 2014 年 6 月くろしお出版社)など。

中国国内の日本語学学界でも日本語の配慮表現において研究する学者がいるが、研究が始まる時間が遅く、研究成果も日本と比べると数が限られる。この面の研究成果は主に雑誌に載られる論文と学位論文に集中し、この面に関する著作はまだ一冊も見つからなかった。文章としては多少見つけたが、例えば:『日本語助言行為において文末に出る「配慮表現」』(楊慧科教文匯(中旬刊)2016 – 04 – 20);『語用論視点の下の「配慮表現」教学研究——プライドネス原則の応用を例に』(邢黎黒龍江教育(高等教育研究と評価 2014 – 04 –22);『日本語の依頼の中の「配慮」表現』(禹永愛沈陽工程学院学報 2013 – 07– 15);『「緩和語」の使用から日本語の「配慮」表現を見る』(厳莉延安職業技術学院学報 2013 – 10 – 15);『「配慮表現」原則に基づく日本語の丁寧語の習得』(金伊花語文学刊(外国語教育教学)2013 – 07 – 25);『「配慮表現」原則に基づく日本語ガイドの丁寧語の習得』(金伊花・馬安東長春理工大学学報 2012– 05 – 15);『日本語の会話の中の「配慮表現」』(谷恒勤・戦建麗菏沢学院学報報 2010 – 01 – 25)など。

以上のとおりに日本語の配慮表現において代表的な研究成果を挙げた。それらの成果の中で日本側の学者は主に応用言語学の視点や文法の角度から、配慮表現の種類、使用する背景、意義などポライトネスの原則に基づいて深く研究してきた。その中に中国語と比較しながら研究するのもある(彭飛)。中国側の研究は主に配慮表現がコミュニケーションの中のポライトネスの原則の学習と応用などである。本論文は前人たちの先行研究を土台に中国人日本語学習者の視点から日本語配慮表現の勉強と使用においてぶつかりやすいところや間違いやすいなどの原因を明らかにしてみようと思う。

3. 配慮表現の研究の枠組み

日本語の配慮表現は対人的な行動の柱の一つとしてその研究の枠組みは幅

広いといえる。彭飛の書かれた『日本語の「配慮表現」に関する研究』という本によると、配慮表現の研究は日本語・日本文化の本質に迫る重要性を持つ。その枠組みは次のような四つの領域(枠組み)が分けられる①。

 A. 緩和表現(表現形式や用語の変更(場面的表現変更)、場面的添加、場面的省略(客観的な表現、明示回避など)

 B. 受益表現(直接受益、期待型受益(期待、期待実現など)

 C.プラス価値付加表現

 D. 心地よい気分表現(気分をよくさせる表現)

以上、挙げた配慮表現の研究の枠組みを彭飛先生が『日本語の「配慮表現」に関する研究』の中に次のように解釈する。

「緩和表現」は「配慮表現の四領域」の中で日常の言語生活においてもっともよく用いれらる表現である。「緩和表現」とは聞き手に対して発話する場合、露骨、断定的、単刀直入などの表現を用いず、遠まわしに仄めかしたり、種種の「和らげる」手法をとって、判断、評価、拒絶、否定などの話者の叙述内容や意志、感情が聞き手に柔らかく伝わるように工夫する表現を指す②。

「受益表現」は相手から何らかの恩恵や利益を蒙った表現を指す。これは自分にプラスになったことを明確にした形で表す表現である。例えば、「ありがとうございました」が直接的な感謝表現であるのに対して、「よく来てくれました」は間接的な感謝表現である③。

「プラス価値付加表現」は用語変更・表現の変化によって、よりよいイメージや語感を帯びるようにして、好感、好印象を相手に抱かせる表現を指す④。

「心地よい気分表現」は、積極的に相手に快・喜などの感情をもたらすように表現し、相手を心地よい気分にさせる表現である。「配慮表現」における直接的な表現と言ってもよく、「賞賛表現」「祝福表現」「同情表現」などが相手の心情、利益、立場などに配慮する直接的な表現となる。敵意のないことを示す表現、親しみを感じさせる表現、自分が相手に歓迎されたいという心理が

 ① 彭飛『日本語の「配慮表現」に関する研究』和泉書院 2005 年 10 月 10 日初版第 1 刷発行 p6.

 ② 彭飛『日本語の「配慮表現」に関する研究』和泉書院 2005 年 10 月 10 日初版第 1 刷発行 p7.

 ③ 彭飛『日本語の「配慮表現」に関する研究』和泉書院 2005 年 10 月 10 日初版第 1 刷発行 p9.

 ④ 彭飛『日本語の「配慮表現」に関する研究』和泉書院 2005 年 10 月 10 日初版第 1 刷発行 p9.

働く表現も考察対象とする①。

　日本語の「配慮表現」の研究は名詞、動詞、副詞、助詞、カタカナ語（外来語）、方言など、様々な角度から研究・分析ができる。また文法論、語彙論、統語論（構文論）、修辞学、音声学、文字学、語用論、モダリティ、敬語、待遇表現、談話分析、言語行動と非言語行動、表現行動、縄張り理論、コミュニケーション論、発話行為、対照言語学、メタ言語など、日本語の研究の多くの領域とも深く関係している②。

4. 配慮表現とポライトネス

　現代日本語の研究は配慮表現はポライトネス理論と共通の原理に基づく言語現象であると言われている。ポライトネス理論はフェイス侵害を極力避けるための、言語行動の選択のストラテジーを理論化したものである。それに対して、日本語の配慮表現はフェイスを侵害してしまうことへの配慮を表現する言語現象が主である。日本語の中に配慮表現という用語がはじめて用いられたのは『言語』（1997年）特集「ポライトネスの言語学」に収められた生田（1997）だったと考えられる。ポライトネス理論と配慮表現との間に明確な区別があることを論じているのは川村よし子、姫野伴子である。川村（1991）によると、

　日本語の文化においては、利益を受けることを精神的負担と受け止める傾向があり、そのため、相手に利益を与えながらも相手の心の負担を軽くしようとする配慮が働くとしている。姫野（1992）では、利益を得ることによって負う精神的負担を「負債」と呼んで負担と区別し、新たに「思いやりの原則」（他者の負債を最小限にせよ、自己の負債を最大限にせよ）を立てている③。

　ポライトネスの原理とは反比例的な原理としての「配慮表現の原理」④を次のように挙げる。

---

① 彭飛『日本語の「配慮表現」に関する研究』和泉書院 2005 年 10 月 10 日初版第 1 刷発行 p9.

② 彭飛『日本語の「配慮表現」に関する研究』和泉書院 2005 年 10 月 10 日初版第 1 刷発行 p10.

③ 山岡政紀・牧原功・小野正樹著『コミュニケーションと配慮表現』明治書院平成 22 年 2 月 22 日初版発行 p140.

④ 山岡政紀・牧原功・小野正樹著『コミュニケーションと配慮表現』明治書院平成 22 年 2 月 22 日初版発行 p140.

	①ポライトネスの原理	②配慮表現の原理
（A）配慮表現の原則	（a）他者の負担を最小限にせよ	（a）他者の負担が大きいと述べよ
	（b）他者の利益を最大限にせよ	（b）他者の利益が小さいと述べよ
（B）寛大性の原則	（a）自己の利益を最小限にせよ	（a）自己の利益が大きいと述べよ
	（b）自己の負担を最大限にせよ	（b）自己の負担が小さいと述べよ
（C）緩和の原則		（a）他者への非難を最小限にせよ
（D）謙遜の原則		（a）自己への賞賛を最小限にせよ

5. 配慮表現の働き

　日本語の言語学の研究は欧米の言語学理論の影響を深く受けている。日本語語用論研究は配慮表現が主流となっている。リーチ（leech）ポライトネス原理と「配慮表現」とが明確に区別されて用いられたのは生田（1997）である。生田は「言葉のポライトネス」に対して「配慮表現」という名称を与えた①。

　リーチのポライトネス原理のうち、気配りの原則である「他者の負担を最小限にせよ」「他者の利益を最大限にせよ」に照らして次の例文を見てみよう。

　（1）このじゃがいもの皮をむいてください。

　（2）このじゃがいもの皮をむいてほしいのですが。

　（3）このじゃがいもの皮をむいていただけませんか。

　（4）ご面倒で恐縮ですが、このじゃがいもの皮をむいていただけないでしょうか。

　（5）誠に失礼ですが、もしお時間が許せば、このじゃがいものをむいていただけると大変ありがたいのですが。

　例（1）から（5）まで順番に配慮表現の度合いが高くなっている。例（5）のように表現したからと言って相手に負担が減るわけではないのだが、配慮が相手に伝わることによって相手の負担感が相対的に緩和される。このようにし

---

　① 　山岡政紀・牧原功・小野正樹著『コミュニケーションと配慮表現』明治書院平成22年2月22日初版発行 p138.

て選択された表現が配慮表現である。

（6）つまらないものですが。（「他者の利益が小さいと述べよ」という配慮表現の原理に沿うものである）

（7）お忙しいところ、わざわざありがとうございます。（「他者の負担が大きいと述べよ」という配慮表現の原理に沿うものである）

（8）君の文章はちょっと荒いな。

（9）わたし、英語がそこそこできるんです。

（10）その金額はちょっと無理かと思いますが。

（11）東京育ちの君にはちょっと分からないかもしれないけれど。

（12）今年の夏は例年よりちょっと暑い。

例（8）から（12）までの例文の中の程度副詞「ちょっと」はこれらの文の配慮表現としての働きは主に相手との摩擦を避けて、相手の消極的なフェイスを脅かし、同時に相手との良好な人間関係を築こうとする話し手自身の積極的なフェイスを脅かすということである。それらを緩和するための方略として、話し手は無意識に使用される。①

（13）来週、テニスの親善大会があるんですが、Bさんもいかがですか。

いいですね。ぜひ参加させてください。

（14）わざわざお越しいただきまして、ありがとうございます。

例（13）は発話の機能から分析すると、話し手の「勧誘」に対する聞き手の「参加」する意思の表明であり、配慮表現の働きから分析すると、聞き手の受諾は自分にとって負担ではなく、むしろ利益であるとして、相手を安心させようとする配慮である。例（14）は発話の機能は相手に対する「感謝」の気持を示し、配慮の働きは相手が自分のためにかけた負担に対する認識を示すことである。

5.1　間接的な表現→相手を追い詰めない配慮②

（1）ぐらい、ほど、ばかり

例（15）すみません、千円ばかり貸していただけませんか。

この例文の発話機能と配慮の働きは主に話し手は聞き手の立場に立って、もし千円貸せと言って相手が九百九十円しか持っていなかったら、相手は恥ずかしい思いをするという考えで、相手を追い詰めないように、千円でなく

---

①　山岡政紀・牧原功・小野正樹著『コミュニケーションと配慮表現』明治書院平成22年2月22日初版発行 p193.

②　水谷信子『心を伝える日本語講座』研究者出版株式会社 1999年12月24日初版発行 pp. 36 – 39.

てもいいのだと幅を示すことによって相手が気楽になるようにするのが話し手の聞き手に対する配慮である。

　例(16)三日ほど拝借します。

　例(17)あと三日ぐらい待ってくれないかな。

　例(16)、(17)の話し手の発話機能と配慮の働きは例(15)と同じで、聞き手を追い詰めないように、時間を表す数詞の後にそれぞれ副助詞「ほど」と「ぐらい」を付けた。

　(2)お茶でも飲みませんか

　人を誘うときによく「でも」が使われる。仕事が一段落したり、昔の知人に会ったりしたとき、お茶に人を誘うが、その時は

　例(18)お茶でも飲みませんか。

　例(19)ちょっと軽くお食事でもいかがですか。

　例(18)、(19)それぞれ「お茶」と「お食事」のあとに「でも」を付けることを通して話し手の聞き手に対する幅のある発話機能を示し、相手に対する配慮も示した。これらの例文から日本人の「人を誘うときには幅のある表現が好まれるということが大切になる。」[1]が現れると思う。

5.2　相手を受け入れる態度→「はい」と「けど」[2]

　(1)はい、おりますけど

　あるアメリカ人Bさんは山田さんの家に電話したとき、電話に出た奥さんとの会話場面：

例(20)

山田さん、いらっしゃいますか。

　──はい、おりますけど……

　──あの、呼んでまいりましょうか。

　──はい、お願いします。

　この場合の「けど」は逆接ではなく、相手の依頼や指示を待っているという、いわば受け入れの意思表示に使われているのである。

　中国から来たある留学の陳さんが田中といううちへ電話するときの会話場面：

---

　①　水谷信子『心を伝える日本語講座』研究者出版株式会社 1999 年 12 月 24 日初版発行 pp. 39 – 40.

　②　水谷信子『心を伝える日本語講座』研究者出版株式会社 1999 年 12 月 24 日初版発行 pp. 41 – 42.

例(21)

——陳です、田中さんのお宅ですか。

——田中ですけど。

——高橋さんとおっしゃる方、おられますか。

——私ですが/けど。

この場合の「が」や「けど」も同じように、相手が次に行動に出やすいように、受け入れの態度を表明するものである。

——社長さん、いらっしゃいますか。

——はい、おりません。

この場合の「はい」は英語の「yes」の意味だけでなく、「お話、うけたまわりました」という一種の受け入れの意味がありますので、あとの文は否定文でも関係ない。

例(22)

——やっていただけますか。

——はい。まあ、考えてみます。

と言うときの「はい」は「やるつもり」という意味表示とは限らないわけである。

(2)いつでもけっこうです①

この話は相手の誘いや要求を受け入れる場合に使われる。例えば、ある外国人のMさんが日本人の知人のYさんと会社訪問の日時を決めようとした時の会話場面:

例(23)

——いつがよろしいでしょうか。

——いつでもけっこうです。

——じゃ、来週の火曜日

——火曜日は会社におりませんので。

——それでは水曜日

——その日は健康診断に行きますので。

——じゃ、木曜日か金曜日

——よろしかったら、金曜日のほうがありがたいのですが。

こんなことならはじめから「金曜日にしてください」と言ってくれれば、余計な時間を使わなくてよかったのに、なぜ「いつでもいいです」というのかと

---

① 水谷信子『心を伝える日本語講座』研究者出版株式会社 1999 年 12 月 24 日初版発行 p44.

Mさんが不満だということになった。たしかに日本人全部がYさんのような話し方をするとは限らない。もっとも能率的な場合もある。しかし、この場合は

　Yさんが相手のMさんに対する遠慮、相手を受け入れなくてはいけないという一種の強迫観念にとらわれ、反射的に「いつでもいいです」と言ってしまう場面であろう。つまり、話し手としてのYさんは聞き手としてのMさんに対する「受け入れ」という配慮表現であるといえる。

　（3）ちょっとむずかしい①

　こんなやり取りの例があるという。中国から来たSさんという女性があるとき、友達になった日本人女性にその人の属している研究会に入れてほしいと頼んだが。

　例（24）

　──ちょっとむずかしいと思う。

　と答えた。Sさんは「非常にむずかしいのではなく、ちょっとむずかしいだけなのだから、頼んでくれるだろう」と思って、しばらく待ったが、どうも頼んでくれる様子がない。そこで、催促すると、話し手側の日本人の友達がびっくりした様子で。

　──むずかしいと言ったと思うけど。

　──ちょっとむずかしいと言ったけど、ちょっとむずかしいだけならできると思ったので、待っていた。と聞き手側のSさんが答えると、聞き手側の友達は困った顔で。

　──ちょっとむずかしいというのは、たいへんむずかしいということよ。

　と言ったそうだ。この論理でいくと「ちょっと」イコール「たいへん」ということになって、非論理的な話になる。しかし、その話し手の言うとおり、「ちょっとむずかしい」と言った時は「むずかしいから、だめだと思ってほしい」という断りであって、この場合の「ちょっと」は「少し」という程度を示すものではなくて、「言いにくいが」ということを伝えるためだったのですが、中国人学習者は母語の影響で「ちょっと」の意味を文字とおりに「困難の程度が少ない」と理解したために、話し手の話の裏に隠れいている本当の意味を誤解したのだと思う。実は言葉には現象面を客観的に述べるという機能のほかに、話し手の気持ちを表す機能もある。言うまでもなく、ここの話し手の気持は聞き手に対する配慮である。

---

　①　水谷信子『心を伝える日本語講座』研究者出版株式会社 1999 年 12 月 24 日初版発行 pp. 45 – 46.

（3）ちょっと用事がありますので

それは話し手としての客が辞去するときなど、よく使う言葉の一つだといえる。普通は以下のような話しを切り出して。

例（25）

——ちょっと用事がありますので

例（26）

——これからまわるところがありまして

とかという理由を述べると、その先に「もう帰ります」という辞去のことばは言わなくても、主人として聞き手側は理解する。こうした黙然の理解があると「もう帰ります」という言いにくいことを言わずにすむ。この「言わずにすむ」ように仕向けるのは、聞き手側の「受け入れ態度」だといえる。他の表現でいえば、相手の言いたいことを「察する」コミュニケーションのやり方ともいえよう。この場合の話し手の発話の機能は例（25）、（26）のような話しを言って、自分の事情を遠慮がちに聞き手に告げ、聞き手がその先を察する余地を残すほうが適切である。話し手が聞き手に共通の理解を期待する配慮表現のストラテジーである。

終りに

以上のように日本語配慮表現の先行研究、配慮表現の研究の枠組み、配慮表現とポライトネス、中国人日本語学習者の視点から日本語配慮表現が日常コミュニケーションにおける配慮表現の働きをめぐって、副詞が配慮表現としての働き、間接的表現としての配慮表現の発話機能及びその表現の裏に隠れている意義と話し手が聞き手に伝達する気持ちなどを述べ、例を挙げながらそれらの例文を使う場面と文の中に含まれている話し手が聞き手に対する配慮の意図を分析してみた。本文に挙げられた例文は日本人が日常生活の中に当たり前に使っているが、中国人日本語学習者は字面的な意味を捉え、日本語と中国語両言語の裏に隠れている差違、違う発想による発話の方法の違いなどを意識しなかったり、母語の影響を受けたりする原因で、日本語の配慮表現を身に付けられなくて、言語対象国の日本人とコミュニケーションするとき、相手の話の意味を誤解したり、相手との談話がスムーズに進まなくなかったりするあげくになってしまう場合がよくある。

参考文献:

[1]堀口純子．日本語教育と会話分析[M]．くろしお出版，1997.

[2]山岡政紀・牧原功・小野正樹．コミュニケーションと配慮表現[M]．明治書院，2010.

[3]彭飞．日本語の「配慮表現」教育と会話分析[M]．和泉書院，2005 年.

[4]水谷信子．心を伝える日本語講座[M]．研究社出版，1999.

[5]祝大鸣．强调"以心传心"的暧昧语言文化——日语语言文化特点续探．日本语言文化论集(第二辑)[C]．北京：北京大学出版社，2000.

[6]森田良行．話者の視点がつくる日本語[M]．株式会社ひつじ書房，2006.

[7]滝浦真人・大橋理枝．日本語とコミュニケーション[M]．一般財団法人放送大学教育振興会，2015 年.

[8]笹川洋子．日本語のポライト再考——発話行為・発語媒介行為・相互行為．春風社，2016 年.

[9]東森勲．シリーズ〈言語表現とコミュニケーション2〉対話表現はなぜ必要なのか—最新の理論で考える—[M]．朝倉書店，2017 年.

相対自動詞と相対他動詞の受け身について[*]

李月婷^{**}

要　旨：日本語の場合は動詞の未然形＋「れる、られる」で受身になるが、すべての動詞に受身があるわけではない。相対他動詞とペアになる相対自動詞に受身はないが、受身の意味が表せるものはある。本文では、動作の受け手を有情物と非情物に分け、受身の意味を持っている相対自動詞を整理し、それに対する相対他動詞の受身と比較してみる。

キーワード：相対自動詞　受け手 動作主

1. はじめに

　　日本語の受身は動詞の未然形に「れる、られる」をつけて、主語が他人の動作や働きを受ける文である。中国の日本語学科で使用される『総合日本語』『現代日本語』という教科書に、受身は6 種類と5 種類に分けられるが、相対自動詞に受身の意味が表せるものがあるという説明はない。教科書にその説明が載っていない状況で、日本語学習者は相対自動詞の使い方が習得できるかどうかを調べるために、31 名の中級日本語学習者に「樹枝被台風刮断了」という文の日本語訳を選んでもらった結果、相対自動詞「折れる」を選んだのはただ6 人だけであった。相対他動詞の受身と相対自動詞が同じ問題の選択肢として出た場合、日本語学習者が正しい答えを選択するのが難しいことだとわかった。野村（1982）は「非情物が主語になる場合には、自動詞による表現が好まれ、有情物が主語になる場合には受身の表現が好まる」と指摘した。本文は野村の分析によって、主語すなわち動作の受け手を有情物と非情物に分

---

　　*　论文题目：关于日语成对自动词和他动词被动形式的研究。
　**　作者简介：李月婷，云南大学外国语学院日语系讲师。研究方向：语言学。

け、受身の意味を持っている相対自動詞の意味を分析したうえで、相対他動詞の受身との相違を分析しようと思う。

2. 受け手が有情物の場合

　日本語の動詞はその前に目的語が来ることができるかどうかによって、自動詞と他動詞に分けられる。寺村(1982)は「割れる－割る」の「war-」、「建つ－建てる」の「tat-」ように、語幹を共有する形態的ペアを持つ自動詞、他動詞を相対自動詞、相対他動詞と呼ぶとの定義を下した。本文は寺村が下した定義を基準に、研究対象になる相対自動詞と相対他動詞を選出した後、受身の意味を持っている相対自動詞とそれに対応する相対他動詞の受身と比べ、両者の違いを明らかにしようと思う。

　では、受け手が有情物である場合の文を見てみよう。

　(1)お喋りな奥さんに捕まって、ついつい長時間立ち話をしてしまった。(被爱聊天的太太逮住，不知不自觉站着说了很长时间话)

　(2)行方不明になっていた少年が北海道で見つかった。(去向不明的年轻人在北海道被发现了)

　(3)奇跡的に助かった。(奇迹般地获救了)

　(4)今日、英語の授業でまた3回当たった。(今天的英语课上又被点了3次)

　(5)彼は無罪と決まった。(他被认为无罪)

　(6)肌の白い人は日に焼けやすい。(皮肤白的人容易被晒黑)

　(7)校則にとらわれて、自由に行動できない。(被校规所管制，不能自由活动)

　以上の例文は動作の受け手がすべて有情物の例文であるが、(1)－(4)の動作主は有情物で、(5)－(7)は非情物である。庵功雄(2001)は「自他の対応がある場合の自動詞は事態が非意志的に起ることを表す。主体は通常「もの」。自他の対応を持つ自動詞は通常非意志的自動詞」と指摘した。

　例(1)－(4)の中で、動作の受け手も動作主も有情物なので、受身を表すには二つの方法がある。一つは受身の意味が表せる有対自動詞を利用すること、もう一つは有対他動詞の受身を利用することである。森田良行(1989)が「つかまる/つかまえる」を比較し、「AハBニつかまる/BハAヲつかまえるの文型転換ができ、能動・受動の文型転換と共通する」と指摘した。例えば、「泥棒が警察につかまった」を「つかまえる」の受身で言い換えると、「泥棒が警察に捕まえられた」になる。つまり、受身の意味を表す相対自動詞「つかまる」の文と相対他動詞「つかまえる」の受身の文の構造が同じである。文の構造が同

じであっても、意味がまったく同じというわけではない。庵功雄（2001）は自動詞文と他動詞の受身文を比べ、「受動文には動作主の存在が含意されているのに対して自動詞にはそうした含意がない」という結論を出した。「泥棒が警察につかまった／泥棒が警察に捕まえられた」この二つの文を中国語に訳すと、二つとも"小偷被警察抓住了"になる。「泥棒が警察に捕まえられた」は動作主の存在を強調しているが、「泥棒が警察につかまった」は動作主が何をしたかよりも、「泥棒がつかまった」という結果に焦点を絞っている。例文（1）－（4）に、（1）以外の文に、動作主が出ていないのは文の焦点が動作主の存在ではなく、結果にあるためである。「なる」型言語と言われる日本語では、相対自動詞も相対他動詞の受身も使用できる場合に、動作主の存在を強調して言いたい場合を除いたら、相対自動詞を優先的に選ぶ傾向が見られる。

　例文（5）－（7）のように、動作の受け手は有情物であるが、動作主は非情物である場合は、相対他動詞の受身はあまり使用されない。その理由は次節で明らかにする。

3. 受け手が非情物の場合

　多くの相対自動詞は物事が非意識的に発生する場合によく使われるため、おおかたの主語が物になる。

　　（8）台風で枝が折れた。（树枝被台风刮断了。）

　　（9）煙で汚れた空気だ。（被烟雾污染的空气）

　　（10）水をかぶって髪がぬれてしまった。（头发被水冲湿了）

　　（11）嘘がばれても平気だった。（谎言被揭穿也满不在乎）

　　（12）木が雷で真っ二つに裂けてしまった。（树被雷劈成了两半）

　例文（8）－（12）を中国語に訳すと、いずれも中国語の受身のしるしである「被」がついている。相対自動詞と相対他動詞の受身に関する日本語学習者の習得状況を考察するため、日本語学習者に「树枝被台风刮断了」の日本語訳を選ばせた結果、大多数の学習者が「枝が台風に折られた」という訳を選んだのがわかった。しかし、「枝が台風に折られた」という文は日本語にない、正しくない文である。日本語学習者が間違った訳を選ぶ理由として、母国語の干渉を受けたと考えられる。中国語では、動作主が「台風、煙、水、雷」等動作や意識と関係のない名詞でも、受身を表す「被」を使うことができる。中国語の受身における動作主について、木村（1997）は動作や意識に関係のない物事でも、結果と関係性があれば、受身の動作主として使えるが、日本語は受身の動作主に厳しい条件が設けられ、動作主が動作や意識のない物事なら、文

は成立しないと述べた。例文(5)(6)に相対他動詞の受身が存在しないのは動作主に相当する「日」、「校則」は動作や意識のない物事であるためである。

　以上、相対自動詞の多くは人間の意志に左右されず、自主的に発生することを表すため、相対自動詞の主語、つまり動作の受け手になるおおかたは「もの」である。したがって、受け手が有情物である相対自動詞の文はそれほど多くない。また、中国語と違い、受身の動作主になる名詞に条件が設けられ、動作主が「もの」の場合、相対他動詞の受身よりは相対自動詞のほうが使用される。

　2, 3では、相対自動詞と相対他動詞の動作の受け手を有情物、非情物に分けて、その違いを分析してみた。4では、日本語学習者がそれを習得できない理由を考えていようと思う。

4. 習得困難の理由

　日本語の相対自動詞に関する習得の難しさには二つの理由が考えられる。①母国語の干渉。中国語の受身の主語、つまり動作の受け手は、意志を持つ人間だけでなく、結果と直接関連しているなら、「もの」もよく受け手になる。その一方、日本語の受身は複雑である。受け手が人間か、ものかによって、相対他動詞の受身が使えるかどうかが決まる。しかし、日本語学習者が中国語の知識をもとに、日本語を勉強しているため、「被」が付いている文を日本語に訳す時、受け手のことを考えずに、日本語の受身で対応することがわかった。②教材、教師の説明不足。筆者が働く大学で使用する北京大学出版の『総合日本語』で、その中に自動詞、他動詞についての説明はほんの数行しかない。「日语的动词可以分为自动词(不及物动词)和他动词(及物动词)两种。自动词一般不能带「を」格补足语(表示移动动作的自动词除外),他动词一般可以带「を」格补足语,表示动作涉及的客体。当然,也有的动词兼有自他两种动词的性质。」というように説明してあるが、有対自動詞と有対他動詞の説明は一切載っていない。教材に載っていない内容を教師がわざわざ説明する可能性はないわけではないが、詳しく説明する可能性は低いと思う。教材、教師による説明不足で、日本語学習者が中国語にない使い方をマスターするのは極めて困難なことであろう。

5. 結　論

　日本語の受身は日本語学習者にとって、もともと習得しにくい文法の一つである。受身の意味が表せる相対自動詞は余計習得しにくい文法だと思うが、

動作の受け手を有情物と非情物に分けることで、相対自動詞と相対他動詞の受身の違いが分かりやすくなる。動作の受け手が有情物の場合、相対自動詞と相対他動詞の受身は構造が同じであるが、相対自動詞は結果に、相対他動詞の受身は動作主の存在に焦点を絞っている。受け手が非情物の場合、相対他動詞の受身より相対自動詞のほうがたくさん使われる。

参考文献：

［1］庵功雄．新しい日本語学入門－言葉のしくみを考える［M］．東京：スリーエーネットワーク，2001.

［2］野村剛史．自動・他動・受身動詞について［J］．日本語・日本文化第11号，1982.

［3］木村英树．汉语被动句的意义特征及其结构上反映［J］.《Cahier de Linguistique_ Aise Orientale》26，1997.

［4］寺村秀夫．日本語のシンタクスと意味［M］．東京：くろしお出版，1982.

［5］森田良行．基礎日本語辞典［M］．東京：角川学芸出版，1989.

［6］胡振平．现代日本语［M］．上海：上海外语教育出版社，2003.

［7］彭广陆等．综合日语［M］．北京：北京大学出版社，2010.

テレビドラマから見た日本語の「ほめ」表現*

刘　一　　高明瑜**

要旨：「ほめ」はコミュニケーションの潤滑油として、その社会的役割が無視できないと言える。「ほめ」とは、いい人間関係を築くために、相手あるいは相手に関する人や物事の良さに関心を表し、肯定的表現を使い、相手を心地よくさせる言語行動である。

　本研究はこの三年間日本で放送された三本の家庭生活に関するテレビドラマを素材にし、「ほめ」とその応答の場面を収集し、観察を行った。素材を観察することを通じ、日本語母語話者の「ほめ」とその応答に関する言語の使用や行動の規律を総括し、日本語学習者の順調な異文化コミュニケーションに信頼できる参考を提供することを試みた。

キーワード：日本語の「ほめ」　「ほめ」への返答　スタイル

一、先行研究と研究目的

　「ほめ」について、小玉安恵(1996)と大野敬代(2003)の「ほめ」への定義を考察すると、小玉(1996)は「ほめ」の前提を「聞き手を心地よくさせること」と、そして大野(2003)は「ほめ」を「相手への好感情を表す言語行動」と定義しているが、誰でも明確的に「ほめ」の根本的目的、即ちいい人間関係を築くことを指摘しないと言える。以上をまとめてみると、「ほめ」に関するポイントは以下の通りである。①「ほめ」の対象は聞き手、あるいは聞き手に関わる

*　论文题目：从日本电视剧中看"表扬"的应用。

**　【作者简介】刘一，云南大学外国语学院日语系副教授，研究方向：日语语言、日本文化和社会。高明瑜，西安交通大学外国语学院外国语言文学专业硕士研究生，研究方向：日语语言学。

人/物/ことである。②「ほめ」の手段は聞き手、あるいは聞き手に関わる人/物/ことの良さを認め、明示的あるいは暗示的に高く評価すること。③「ほめ」の目的は自分の好感情を相手に伝わることによって、いい人間関係を維持すること。その他、金庚芬(2012)は「ほめ」のスタイルを「肯定的評価語のみ使用」、「肯定的評価語＋他の情報」、「肯定的評価語の不使用」に分類している。

　「ほめ」への返答スタイルについて、平田真美(1999)は「ほめ」の返答の仕方を分類している、その上、年齢、地位、性別による返答の相違を分析している。寺尾留美(1996)は褒め言葉の返答スタイルを「受け入れ」、「打消し」、「その他」の三つに分け、さらにそれを13種類に分類している。大野(2005b)は寺尾(1996)の分類に基づき、「ほめ」の返答を受け入れ、否定、回避に分け、その上寺尾(1996)に修正を加える。そして、どんな人間関係にでも回避型が圧倒的に多いと述べている。

　では、「ほめ」はいい人間関係を築く手段として、一般的にどんなスタイルがあるのか。その中で、実生活で一番頻繁的に日本語母語話者に使われているのはどれなのか。そして、日本語母語話者は他人の「ほめ」に対してどう返答するのか。本稿は日本語学習者の理解を深め、誤解を避けていい人間関係を築くには、どうやって相手を褒めるのか、さらに相手の「ほめ」にどう対応するのか、その的確なスタイルと参考になれる実例を研究していきたい。

二、研究方法

　本稿は近年日本で放送された三本の家庭生活に関するテレビドラマを対象に、その映像を繰り返し再生し、「ほめ」(計547例)と「ほめ」への返答(計485例)に関する場面を抽出し、そのセリフを文字化して収集することにした。さらにそのデータを分類し、整理したものに基づいて文化背景や語用論の知識で分析していきたい。

　選ばれたテレビドラマは以下の通りである。

表1　研究対象一覧

テレビドラマ	放送年月	合計(回)
過保護のカホコ	2017年7~9月	10
家族ノカタチ	2016年1~3月	10
デート－恋とはどんなものかしら－	2015年1~3月	10

　以下、『過保護のカホコ』が『カホコ』と、『家族ノカタチ』が『家族』と、『デート－恋とはどんなものかしら－』が『デート』と略称する。引用したセリフについて、『　』内にドラマ名を記す。なお、セリフ引用の際には、褒め言葉に「<u>いいなあ、立派な息子がいて</u>」のような下線を、返答の言葉(非言語表現も含む)に「<u>本当。本当だよ。</u>」のような波線を付す。

三、研究結果

(一)「ほめ」のスタイル

　金庚芬(2012)の理論を基に、「ほめ」の三つのスタイルをテレビドラマから抽出した実例で検証して分析する。

　1. 肯定的評価語のみ使用

　「肯定的評価語のみ使用」というスタイルは、形容詞、形容詞＋形容詞、形容詞＋動詞、動詞、副詞、副詞＋動詞、名詞などを使い、直接に聞き手あるいは聞き手に関する人、物、ことの良さを褒める明示的ものである。このような褒め方は非常に分かりやすいため、会話の流れを見なくてもその文だけが褒め言葉だということも明らかである。

　例1　加穂子：<u>やっぱりママのオムライス最高!</u>

　　　　　　　　　　　　　　　　　　　　　　　　　　　　　『カホコ』

　例2　鷲尾：<u>依子さん、めちゃくちゃ美味しいです!</u>
　例3　宗太郎：<u>こいつなりに一生懸命踊ったんだしさ。</u>

　　　　　　　　　　　　　　　　　　　　　　　　　　　　　『デート』

　例1　では形容詞だけを使い、例2~3では「形容詞＋形容詞」「形容詞＋動詞」の形で「ほめ」を表している。このスタイルは一番簡潔に「ほめ」の気持ちを表している表現だと言え、「良い」、「凄い」、「美しい」、「可愛い」、「面白い」、「綺麗」、「偉い」、「かっこいい」、「素晴らしい」、「優しい」、「楽しい」、「珍しい」、「強い」、「心強い」、「旨い」、「爽やか」、「幸せ」、「半端ない」、「おしゃれ」、「ロマンチック」、「立派」、「元気」、「健気」、「陽気」、「完璧」、「貴重」、「上手」、「賢明」、「完全無欠」、「有意義」、「効率的」、「圧倒的」などの形容詞がよく見られる。

　例4　陽三：<u>大介頑張ったんだよ。</u>

　　　　　　　　　　　　　　　　　　　　　　　　　　　　　『家族』

　例4　は「頑張る」という動詞で「ほめ」を伝えている。他には「きっちりする」「効く」、「似合う」、「モテる」、「感動する」、「やる」、「しっかりする」、「癒される」、「助かる」などの動詞もよく見られる。

例5　みんな：よかったね、<u>さすがだねぇ</u>。

『カホコ』

例6　葉菜子：<u>「今の若者は」とか散々言われてきたけど、私たちって堅実に生きてますよね</u>。

『家族』

例5~6　では、「さすが」という副詞、また「堅実に生きる」という「副詞＋動詞」のスタイルで褒めを伝えている。その他、「よく」、「なかなか」、「よく似合う」、「よくできた」、「よく言った」、「よく撮れた」、「すごく頑張った」、「上手にできた」などもよく見られる。

例7　宗太郎：<u>写真で見る限りなかなかの美人じゃねえかよ</u>！

『デート』

例7　では、「美人」という名詞で「ほめ」を表している。他には「日本一」「天才」、「幸せ者」、「イケメン」、「勉強家」、「世界一」、「できた人」、「奇跡」、「ヒーロー」、「人気者」、「お似合い」、「大したもの」、「楽しみ」などの名詞がよく使われる。

2. 肯定的評価語＋他の情報

「肯定的評価語＋他の情報」というのは、ただ肯定的意味を表す言葉を使用するだけではなく、その上、「ほめ」に関する詳しい理由や説明もある明示的褒め方である。

例8　葉菜子：<u>あの成長っぷりには驚くわ。田中さん、今日は絶対仕事が手につかないんじゃないかと思ってたけど。プロポーズの答え気にしながら健気に仕事もこなしてた</u>。

『家族』

例8　では、葉菜子は大介に莉奈の成長を褒め、その具体的様子ついて詳しく説明している。

3. 肯定的評価語の不使用

「肯定的評価語の不使用」とは、「良い」、「素敵」などの肯定的評価語とその評価語を説明する文のように直接に聞き手あるいは聞き手に関する人、物、ことの良さを褒めるのではなく、間接的に「ほめ」を行うスタイルである。会話の流れを見ないとその文が褒め言葉だということが分かりにくい暗示的褒め方である。

例9　佐々木：<u>あれから師匠と相談してさ、デートコース考えてもらって、おかげでこれ</u>。

『家族』

例9　では、佐々木は大介に大介のお父さんへの感謝の意を伝える。このパターンでは、話し手は聞き手が自分のためにしたことを高く評価し、相手の恩恵に浴することによって「ほめ」の意を伝える。

　　例10　浩太：俺は…誰かに褒められたことなんてなかったから、羨ましくて。

『家族』

例10　では、浩太は大介に対する羨ましさを通じ、大介を間接的に褒める。このスタイルでは、「…が大好き」、「羨ましい」、「理想だな」、「…できたらいいな」、「…なら大丈夫」、「…がそばにいるだけで安心する」、「応援する」などの話し手の感想や気持ちを表す表現がよく見られる。

　　例11　教子：今は就職浪人なんて当たり前だし。加穂子は私と違って恵まれてるんだから。

『カホコ』

例11　では、教子は自分と姪っ子の加穂子との比較を通じ、今の新しい時代を生きている加穂子の方が就職しやすいということを褒める。このスタイルでは、話し手は自分に不利な情報あるいは相手に有利な情報を提供することで、自分と相手の差異、特に相手の優勢を明らかにすることによって、相手を褒める目的を達成する。

　　例12　おばあさん：初くんみたいな人に簡単に会えるとは思えないし。

『カホコ』

例12　では、おばあさんは直接に「初くんはいい人だ」と初を褒めるのではなく、初を例として、初のようないい人がどこにもいるわけではないという実際の状況を提示し、もっと慎重に決断を下した方がいいと加穂子を暗示的に説得する。このパターンでは、褒められる対象は滅多にいないほどのいい人と高く評価するのがよく見られる。

　　要するに、本章の研究結果は以下の通りである。

表2　「ほめ」のスタイルと使用の状況

	使用例（例）	使用率（％）
肯定的評価語のみ使用	290	53.02
肯定的評価語＋他の情報	142	25.96
肯定的評価語の不使用	115	21.02
合計	547	100

（二）「ほめ」への返答スタイル

寺尾（1996）の分類に基づき、テレビドラマから抽出した実例を分析し、一番使われている返答スタイルを確認していきたい。

1. 受け入れ型

1.1　賛同の発言

例13　男：お強いですね。依子：アルコール類には酔ったことがありません。

『デート』

例13　では、婚活パーティーで、男の人の「ほめ」に対して、依子はそれを気さくに認める。

1.2　感謝・喜び

例14　陽三：合格した? いやすげえな恵ちゃん。恵：うん、ありがとうね陽ちゃん。これでようやく第一歩が踏み出せる。

『家族』

例14　では、陽三の「ほめ」に対して、恵は陽三への感謝の意を伝える。

1.3　控えめな同意・微笑

例15　おばあさん：いい人ね~初くん。加穂子：あっ、うん。

『カホコ』

例15　では、おばあさんの「ほめ」に対して、加穂子は少々ためらってそれを認める。

1.4　ほめ返し

例16　陽三：大介、そこのな、妙齢なご婦人はな、上の507の葉菜子さんのお母さん、律子さん。律子：陽三さん、素敵な息子さんじゃない。

『家族』

例16　では、自分への「ほめ」に対し、律子は陽三の息子の大介を高く評価して褒め返す。

2. 打消し型

2.1　不賛成の発言、しぐさ及び自分に不利な情報の提示

例17　俊雄：美味しい。依子：気休めは止めて。

『デート』

例18　重富：腕上げたなあ。浩太：（首を振った）

『家族』

例19　環：でもほら、結構男の子にモテたじゃん、あんた。泉：うん、そ

うそう…節：<u>モテたっつったって、うちの旦那みたいな情けないのばっかりだ</u>
<u>もん。</u>

『カホコ』

例17　では、依子は自分の料理に失望したため、俊雄の「ほめ」を否認する。例18では、浩太はしぐさで「ほめ」を否認する。例19では、節は夫の悪口を言い、自分に不利な情報を提示することで「ほめ」を否認する。

2.2　的確さへの疑問

例20　美佳：<u>誰でもよかったと思う？ 大介だから、大介じゃなきゃダメだ</u><u>から、話したんじゃん。</u>大介：<u>そりゃどうかな？</u>

『家族』

例20　では、褒められる人は疑った気持ちで「どうかな」、「そうかな」のような疑問で応答する。このパターンでは、他には「そうでしょうか」、「そう」などの言い方がよく見られる。

2.3　意図への疑い

例21　初：あの、そのかわり、ひとつだけお願いしてもいいですか？

正高：あぁ、もちろん、なんでも言って。

初：<u>お父さんって結構素敵なんですね。</u>正高：<u>えっ…いや…そ…そうかな？</u>

『カホコ』

例21　では、会話の流れを見ると、初が正高に自分の絵のモデルになってもらうために正高を褒めるが、その本当の意図を知らない正高は少々疑う。

3. その他

3.1　シフト

「シフト」とは、他人のおかげとすることである。

例22　部長：<u>分かってきたね、莉奈ちゃん。</u>莉奈：<u>葉菜子さんのおかげで</u><u>す。ねッ？</u>

『家族』

例22　では、莉奈は部長からの「ほめ」を直属の上司の葉菜子のおかげとする。

3.2　情報的コメント

このスタイルでは、褒められる人はその「ほめ」に関する詳しい状況を説明し、自主的に「ほめ」のレベルを下げるのがよく見られる。

例23　おばさん：<u>本当に美味しい。何でも出来ちゃうのねえ。</u>鷲尾：<u>一人</u>
<u>暮らし長いんで。</u>

『デート』

例 23　では、鷲尾は自分の料理が美味しいのは一人暮らしが長いからだと説明する。

3.3　無視・話を逸らす

例 24　初：<u>お～やっぱ成長してるね、お前。</u>加穂子：<u>ねぇ、パパが出てた時神様は加穂子に独り立ちしろって言ってるって初くんは言ってたけど、今回は神様加穂子に何て言ってると思う？</u>

『カホコ』

例 24　では、初は加穂子の成長に感心する。だがその時期、加穂子のお母さんは家出をしている。加穂子はお母さんを帰らせる方法を急いで考えるため、話を逸らして初にアドバイスを求める。

3.4　会話の流れに沿って話が逸れる

例 25　佳織：<u>いいですね。ダスティン・ホフマンとキャサリン・ロス。</u>留美：<u>宗太郎くんは今日何してんの？奥さんと初詣とか？</u>

『デート』

例 25　では、佳織が映画を褒めるのに対し、留美は佳織のお兄さんの状況を聞く。

3.5　ほめ言葉の内容の確認

例 26　佳織：<u>優しい子よのう。女の子にもモテたしね。</u>依子：<u>本当にモテたんですか？</u>

『デート』

例 26　では、「ほめ」に対して、褒められる人の関係者は信じられない気持ちでそれをもう一度確認する。

3.6　冗談・おどけ・照れ

例 27　葉菜子：<u>楽しみだね。</u>入江：<u>（照れた）</u>

『家族』

例 28　初：ねぇねぇ、もしかしてこちらがお母さん？
加穂子：あっ、うん。
初：うっそ！あんまりお若いから、お姉さんかと思った！泉：やだ…

『カホコ』

冗談、おどけの用例は資料では見つからなかった。照れを表す仕方には、例 27 のような表情で伝えるものもあるが、例 28 のような「やだ」などの言い方で伝えるものもある。

要するに、本章の研究結果は以下の通りである。

表3 「ほめ」への返答スタイルと使用の状況

	使用例(例)	使用率(％)
受け入れ	224	46. 19
打消し	96	19. 79
その他	165	34. 02
合計	485	100

四、おわりに

　本稿の研究によると、「ほめ」とその返答の使用傾向は以下の通りである。

　日本語母語話者の「ほめ」に関する会話で、肯定的評価語だけを使用する場合は圧倒的に多いと言える。肯定的評価語の上に詳しい情報を追加する場合と間接的に「ほめ」を伝える場合は、使用率でそれぞれ第二位と第三位である。そして、日本語母語話者は「ほめ」を否認することより受け入れることが明らかに多く、それを無視することや会話を続行することなどの回避のような応答も少なくないと言える。

　以上の日本語母語話者の行動様式は、農耕生活や昔から形成された文化からの影響を強く受けていると言える。米は昔から日本人の主食だったため、それを栽培するには労力や用水施設の共有などが必要となった。その結果、家と家の関係が深まり、共同生活を保証するには集団で自ずから上下関係が生まれた。仲間はずれされないよう、日本人は人間関係を大切にする。個人の意見を強く主張することが少ないため、謙遜も遠慮も美徳として認識されると言える。その他、飛鳥時代から日本人の特徴の一つとなった「和」の精神も、日本人の行動様式に大きく影響を及ぼしている。周囲との協調性を維持するには相手を配慮することが多いため、相手との摩擦や食い違い、相手を傷つけることをできるだけ避けようとする意識が非常に強いと言える。

　本稿の研究は以上の文化背景と一致している。「ほめ」を否認することは相手を傷つける失礼なことだと思われ、日常生活の中で一番少なく使われている。そして、相手との摩擦を避けるために、「ほめ」を素直に受け入れる日本人は明らかに多いと見られる。だが、「和」を保つには謙遜の品格も必要不可欠だと思われるため、多くの日本人は他人の反感を買わないよう、会話を続行することなどの自主的に「ほめ」のレベルを下げる仕方で応答すると見られる。

　また、本稿の研究は語用論からも解釈できる。大野(2005a)によると、受け入れ型が一番多く現れるのは相手の意見をなるべく同意するという原則があるからだという。そして、大野(2005b)によると、回避型(本稿の「その他」というスタイルに相当するもの)が多い理由の一つは、相手の意見を否定したくないと同時に謙遜したいという状況で、FTA¹をできるだけ軽減するには過大評価を避けるのが一番適切のではないかということである。つまり、自主的に「ほめ」のレベルを下げる仕方で応答するということである。

　今後、より多量で広範囲の会話資料で研究を深めていきたい。

注釈:

1　FTA：Face　Threatening　Act(面目を脅かす行為)。

参考文献目録:

[1]小玉安恵．対談インタビューにおけるほめの機能(1)—会話者の役割とほめの談話における位置という観点から—[J]．日本語学，1996年．

[2]大野敬代．「形式ほめ」の条件について—シナリオ談話における先行要素の調査から[J]．早稲田大学大学院教育学研究科紀要別冊，2003．

[3]金庚芬．日本語と韓国語の「ほめ」に関する対照研究[M]．東京：ひつじ書房，2012．

[4]平田真美．ほめ言葉への返答[J]．横浜国立大学留学生センター紀要，1999年．

[5]寺尾留美．ほめ言葉への返答スタイル[J]．日本語学，1996年．

[6]大野敬代．「ほめ」の意図と目上への応答について—シナリオ談話における待遇コミュニケーションとしての調査から—[J]．社会言語科学，2005b7(2)．

[7]小玉安恵．Conversation openerとしてのほめ言葉—日米の文化的背景をめぐって[R]．第五回日本言語文化学研究会発表要旨1992年．

[8]大野敬代．日本語における謙遜表現とその機能[J]．早稲田大学教育学部学術研究(国語・国文学編)，2005a第53号．

[9]金庚芬、関崎博紀、塔娜、陳臻渝．東アジアの言語使用からみた対人関係調整上の志向性—日・中・韓・モンゴルの「ほめ/けなし」場面を中心に[J]．社会言語科学，2011．

[10]大野敬代．「ほめ意図表現」の枠組みと機能[J]．早稲田日本語研究，2007　16：109－120．

［11］大森和夫、大森弘子．新日本概况：日文［M］．北京：外语教学与研究出版社，2015 年．

［12］刘笑明．日本国家概况(第三版)［M］．天津南开大学出版社2015.

［13］董玲燕．日本語の「ほめ」表現の研究「D」院生論文2014.

［14］張婷婷．日本語の「ほめ言葉への返答」に関する一考察—テレビドラマのセリフを資料として.「D」院生論文2010.

［15］崔暁．「ほめ」とその返答の中日対照研究「D」院生論文2014.

［16］甘能清．日语称赞表达的文化视角研究［J］．日语学习与研究，2003 总第113 期．

［17］刘红艳、李悦娥．话语分析诸方法对比分析(上)［J］．教育理论与实践，2009 29(4).

［18］刘红艳、李悦娥．话语分析诸方法对比分析(下)［J］．教育理论与实践，2009 29(5).

［19］张玉论．日语称赞语应答方式的变化［J］．陕西教育·高教，2014.

［20］杨磊．日语称赞表达研究「D」研究生论文2016.

Chuyển loại của từ trong tiếng Việt và cách dịch sang tiếng Hán *

Zhang Shaoju**

Tóm tắt: Hiện tượng chuyển loại của từ là hiện tượng một từ khi thì được dùng với ý nghĩa và đặc điểm ngữ pháp của từ loại này, khi thì được dùng với ý nghĩa và đặc điểm ngữ pháp của từ loại khác. Từ trong tiếng Việt không có hình thức ngữ âm riêng cho từng từ loại, cũng không biến đổi hình thức ngữ âm để biểu hiện các ý nghĩa ngữ pháp khác nhau và quan hệ ngữ pháp khác nhau. Do đó có nhiều trường hợp vẫn cùng một hình thức ngữ âm nhưng khi thì mang những đặc điểm ngữ pháp của từ loại (tiểu loại) này, khi thì mang các đặc điểm ngữ pháp của từ loại (tiểu loại) khác. Hiện tượng đó được gọi là sự chuyển loại của từ. Tiếng Việt cũng như là tiếng Hán đều là ngôn ngữ đơn lập không biến hình, hiện tượng chuyển loại của từ rất phổ biến và dễ dàng, những hiện tượng chuyển loại của từ trong hai thứ tiếng lại không hoàn toàn giống nhau, cho nên khi thực hiện chuyển dịch lại luôn luôn gặp rất nhiều khó khăn, người dịch phải khắc phục những khó khăn trong hiện tượng chuyển loại của từ mới dịch cho đúng được.

Từ khóa: Chuyển loại của từ; tiếng Việt; cách dịch; tiếng Hán

---

  * 论文题目：越南语的词类活用及其汉译。

  ** 作者简介：张绍菊(Zhang Shaoju)，云南大学外国语学院越南语系讲师，研究方向：对比语言学、越南文学。

I. Dẫn nhập

Chuyển di từ loại là hiện tượng phổ biến trong nhiều ngôn ngữ và đặc biệt là trong các ngôn ngữ thuộc loại hình ngôn ngữ đơn lập. Đó là hiện tượng một từ khi thì được dùng với ý nghĩa và đặc điểm ngữ pháp của từ loại này, khi thì được dùng với ý nghĩa và đặc điểm ngữ pháp của từ loại khác. Chuyển loại là một hiện tượng tích cực trong ngôn ngữ, là một biểu hiện của quá trình tự điều chỉnh hệ thống ngôn ngữ, là một trong các phương thức cấu tạo từ. Hiện tượng chuyển loại là một quá trình cần được xem xét trên quan điểm đồng đại động. Việc phân biệt chuyển loại với đồng âm và với đa nghĩa; việc chỉ ra các mức độ khác nhau của quá trình chuyển loại; phân biệt chuyển loại đã ổn định với kiêm nhiệm từ loại và với chuyển loại lâm thời là một việc làm cần thiết trong quá trình nghiên cứu từ loại tiếng Việt.

1.1 Từ loại là gì?

Từ loại là những lớp từ có cùng bản chất ngữ pháp, được phân chia theo ý nghĩa, theo khả năng kết hợp với các từ ngữ khác trong ngữ lưu và thực hiện những chức năng ngữ pháp nhất định ở trong câu. Hệ thống từ loại có tính chất là cơ sở của cơ cấu ngữ pháp một ngôn ngữ nhất định.

1.2 Các tiêu chuẩn phân định từ loại trong tiếng Việt

Xu hướng hiện nay được nhiều nhà nghiên cứu chấp nhận là từ loại trong tiếng Việt bao gồm các đặc trưng cơ bản dùng làm tiêu chuẩn phân loại sau đây: a. Ý nghĩa khái quát (còn được gọi là ý nghĩa phạm trù) b. Khả năng kết hợp c. Chức năng cú pháp (Theo giáo sư Diệp Quang Ban, tiêu chuẩn này chỉ nên xét như một tiêu chuẩn tham khảo.)

Theo ba tiêu chuẩn trên đây có thể phân định từ loại tiếng Việt thành danh từ, động từ, tính từ, số từ, đại từ, phụ từ (phụ từ đi kèm theo danh từ được gọi là định từ, đi kèm theo động từ và tính từ được gọi là phó từ), kết từ và tiểu từ (trợ từ và tình thái từ). (Diệp Quang Ban, Hoàng Văn Thung, *Ngữ pháp tiếng Việt*, 2012)

II. Hiện tượng chuyển di từ loại trong tiếng Việt và cách chuyển dịch sang tiếng Hán

Trong cuốn *Vấn đề cấu tạo từ trong tiếng Việt hiện đại*, tác giả đã nhận xét rằng : "Ngôn ngữ càng có tính tổng hợp chừng bào thì càng ít có điều kiện cho sự chuyển loại chừng ấy. Bởi vì trong ngôn ngữ đó, có những phụ tố có tác dụng phân biệt từ loại rất rõ ràng. Trái lại, ngôn ngữ càng có tính phân tích chừng nào thì càng có điều kiện cho sự chuyển loại chừng nấy. Như tiếng Anh chẳng hạn. Những hiện tượng chuyển loại trong tiếng Việt còn nhiều hơn, và trong không ít trương hợp còn có tính chất "triệt để" hơn so với tiêng Anh. Bởi vì tiếng Việt là ngôn ngữ đơn lập nên tính phân tích của nó rất cao."(Hồ Lê 2002: tr.11)

Ở các ngôn ngữ biến hình như tiếng Anh, tiếng Pháp, sự chuyển loại chưa ở dạng triệt để nhất, thuần túy nhất của nó. Trong các ngôn ngữ biến hình thường có một số dấu hiệu tiêu chí cho mọi từ loại. Ví dụ từ "light" khi đứng một mình có thể là một tính từ có nghĩa là "sáng", khi kết với "the" thành *the light* thì trở thành danh từ có nghĩa là "ánh sáng". Khi đi sau "to" thành *to light* lại trở thành động từ có nghĩa là *chiếu sáng*. Trong trường hợp này, "the" và "to" là những dấu hiệu hình thức của danh từ và động từ. Nhưng bên cạnh đó, trong tiếng Việt có nhiều trường hợp chuyển loại mang tính chất "triệt để". Ví dụ:

Mẹ ra mua *đá1* về làm trà đá cho chúng con uống.

Hôm nay lớp mình *đá2* bóng với lớp bạn.

Hạt *mưa1* đá rơi thật mau, đau thật đau em có biết/trong lòng anh bây giờ đây như hạt *mưa1* kia vỡ nát/anh lặng im buốt giá mi cay nhìn *mưa2* xót xa.

Những từ được in nghiên có mang số 1 là danh từ và mang số 2 là động từ.

Trong các trường hợp trên, từ chuyển loại không cần mang theo một "phụ phẩm" hình thức nào của nó như trong tiếng Anh là "the", "to" v.v… Chỉ có vị trí của nó trong cụm từ hay trong câu là đặc điểm "hình thức" duy nhất của nó mà thôi.

Sự chuyển loại trong tiếng Việt có thể dẫn ra hoặc giữa thực từ và hư từ. Như trường hợp các loại nguyên vị trung gian, hoặc trong phạm vi thực từ, như trường hợp *đề nghị* trong "Tôi xin đề nghị lớp ta đi liên hoan tối nay." Và trong "Đề nghị của anh hợp lý đấy!", *cưa* trong "cưa cây" và "kéo cưa" v.v…Hoặc trong phạm vi từng từ loại như trường hợp *cánh con chim*(danh từ biệt loại)-*cánh buồm* (danh từ chỉ cá thể); *tôi lắc đầu* (động từ nội động)-*đầu lắc* (động từ ngoại động).

Như chúng ta đã biết, tiếng Hán cũng như tiếng Việt là thuộc loại hình đơn lập, từ không biến đổi hình thái trong câu, hiện tượng chuyển loại từ rất phổ biến. Trong tiếng Việt, thường gặp một số trường hợp chuyển loại như sau:

2.1 Hiện tượng chuyển di từ loại giữa thực từ và thực từ

2.1.1 Chuyển loại từ danh từ sang động từ

Trong trường hợp này, thường hay gặp nhất là một số danh từ chỉ dụng cụ chuyển loại sang một số động từ chỉ hoạt động cơ bản khi sử dụng dụng cụ ấy. Ví dụ: *cuốc* trong *cái cuốc* là danh từ chỉ dụng cụ, còn *cuốc* trong *cuốc đất* chỉ động từ hoạt động cơ bản khi người ta sử dụng cái cuốc. Nói là hoạt động cở bản, vì hoạt động ấy phản ánh chức năng cơ bản của dụng cụ là cái cuốc. Dĩ nhiên, cái cuốc còn có thể làm những việc khác như đập con rắn, đánh con lợn hay chống cái liếp chẳng hạn. Nhưng đó đều không phải là chức năng cơ bản của cai cuốc. Đối với một số dụng cụ có thể xác định được chức năng cơ bản của nó, nhưng đối với nhiều dụng cụ, không thể xác định được chức năng cơ bản của chúng. Ví dụ *cái gậy* có thể dùng để đánh, để đập, để chống đỡ, để quật, để phang v.v… và trong số chức năng ấy, không thể nói chắc chức năng nào là cơ bản. *Con dao* cũng vậy, có thể dụng nó để đẵn, để chặt, để chém, để chẻ, để băm, để xắt... và không phân biệt được chức năng nào là cơ bản hơn chức năng nào. Cái bàn, cái chiếu, con thuyền v.v...đều là những dụng cụ như vậy. Có thể nói rằng: dụng cụ nào mà chức năng cơ bản của nó là chức năng dễ được xác định thì danh từ biểu thị dụng cụ ấy có khả năng chuyển loại thành động từ biểu thị hoạt động, phản ánh chức năng cơ bản ấy. Những từ như cuốc, cày, cưa, đục, bào, bơm, dũa, hái, bừa, cáng v.v... đều là danh từ có thể chuyển loại sang động từ.

Trường hợp hay gặp thứ hai là chủ yếu là các danh từ có khả năng thường xuyên đi đôi trong những ngữ cảnh nhất định với một vài động từ nào đó và làm bổ ngữ cho nó. Mà mức độ thường xuyên đi đôi này mạnh đến nỗi nếu có lược bỏ động từ thì chỉ riêng danh từ còn lại cũng đủ thay thế cho cả tổ hợp "động + danh" ấy.

Ví dụ: Nó giết(làm) thịt một con lợn. Trong loại ngữ cảnh này, thịt chỉ thường xuyên kết hợp với vài động từ như giết, làm và những tổ hợp "giết thịt", "làm thịt" về cơ bản là đồng nghĩa với nhau. Do khả năng đồng hóa giữa những dấu hiệu ngôn ngữ đứng gần nhau và do sự tác động của qui luật tiết kiệm trong ngôn ngữ, từ "thịt" trong "giết thịt" và "làm thịt" qua một quá trình sử dụng, dần dần có nghĩa là giết thịt hay làm thịt và vì vậy có thể thay những cụm động từ ấy. Đây là hiện tượng "gộp" (bao gòm gộp nghĩa và gộp chức năng) thường thấy trong tiếng Việt.

2.1.2 Chuyển loại từ động từ sang danh từ không biệt loại

Trường hợp này thường được gặp trong các động từ sai khiến là từ hai âm tiết: *yêu cầu, quyết định, chỉ thị, đòi hỏi, thông tri, quy định, thách thức* v.v...và động từ cảm nghĩ hai âm tiết như *thắc mắc, băn khăn, nhận thức, nhận xét, suy nghĩ, lo buồn, thu hoạch, tưởng tượng* v.v... Các động từ biểu thị những động tác có khả năng làm cho đối tượng bị tác động từ hình thức rời rạc, không cố định trở thành hình thức khối, dễ dàng cho sự di chuyển từ nơi này sang nơi khác. Ví dụ *gói, bọc, nắm, bao, cuộc, bước, m, với, gang, sải* v.v...

2.1.3. Chuyển loại từ danh từ sang tính từ

Những danh từ chỉ những đối tượng tiêu chuẩn biểu cho tínhc cách xấu xa như *khỉ, gấu, dê, cáo, tào tháo, tư sản, chó* v.v…luôn có khả năng chuyển loại. Ví dụ:

Nhà bác Thanh có sau con *dê*.   (danh từ)

Ông ấy *dê* lắm!(tính từ)

Những danh từ chỉ những đối tượng tiêu biểu cho những tính cách hoặc phong cách tốt đẹp như *văn nghệ, thơ, anh hùng, đồng chí, hữu nghi, lịch sự* v.v… cũng luôn có khả năng chuyển loại. Ví dụ:

Chúc *hữu nghị* giữa chúng ta mãi mãi xanh tươi. (danh từ)

Đây là giá *hữu nghị* rồi em ạ. (tính từ)

2.1.4. Chuyển loại từ danh từ biệt loại sang danh từ chỉ cá thể

Sự chuyển loại này đi đôi với sự hoán dụ và ẩn dụ. Hoặc là dungd một đối tượng do danh từ A biểu thị để ví một đối tượng do danh , từ B biểu thị. Và trong điều kiện đó, danh từ A có khả năng chuyển từ danh từ biệt loại sang danh từ chỉ cá thể. Chẳng hạn:

lá rụng từ cây (danh từ biệt loại)

một *lá* thư (danh từ chỉ cá thể)

2.1.5. Chuyển loại từ danh từ chỉ cá thể sang danh từ không biệt loại

Danh từ chỉ cá thể ở đây, về ý nghĩa là danh từ chỉ đơn vị đo lượng như *cân, thước, tạ, tấn* v.v…

2.1.6. Chuyển loại từ danh từ biệt loại sang danh từ không biệt loại

Tất cả những danh từ biệt loại nào có khả năng biểu thị một thể tích hay một diện tích nhất định đều có thể chuyển thành danh tự không biệt loại. Ví dụ: một cái *nhà* (danh từ biệt loại)=>một *nhà* đầy sách vở (danh từ không biệt loại).

2.1.7. Chuyển loại từ động từ ngoại động sang động từ nội động

Những động từ có khả năng biểu thị hoạt động điều khiển một số bộ phận trong cơ thể. Ví dụ: *lắc, rụt, há, di, đưa, co, múa, liếc, vểnh, cúi, gập, uốn, phổng, chun, gác, gục, đút, tra* v.v…

Trên đây là các trường hợp chuyển di từ loại giữa từ thực với từ thực. Trong tiếng Việt, sự chuyển di từ loại còn diễn ra giữa từ thực và từ hư.

2.2. Sự chuyển di từ loại giữa thực từ và hư từ

2.2.1 Chuyển loại từ danh từ sang kết từ

Những danh từ chỉ vị trí như: trên, dưới, trong, ngoại v.v…chuyển thành kết từ : ngồi *trên* nghế, đi *dưới* nước, học *trong* lớp, chơi *ngoài* sân v.v…

2.2.2. Chuyển loại từ động từ sang kết từ

Một số kết từ có nguồn gốc động từ như lấy *cho* tôi, đi *bằng* xe ô-tô, đi *vào* xã hội, học *để* dùng v.v…

2.2.3. Chuyển loại từ danh từ sang đại từ

Nhiều danh từ chỉ người trong quan hệ thận thuộc như *ông, bà, anh, chị, em, cô, chú, bác, dì, dượng* v.v… chuyển thanh đại từ xưng hô lâm thời.

2.3. Chuyển loại trong nội bộ hư từ

Một số phụ từ có thể thực hiện chức năng liên kết của kết từ: *còn, rồi, vẫn* v.v… hoặc dùng phối hợp hai phụ từ để kiêm chức năng liên kết: *vừa…vừa, đã… lại, mới…đã* v.v… hoặc dùng phối hợp một kết từ với một phụ từ: *vừa mới… nên…* v.v…

Qua phần tích trên, chúng ta có thể thấy rằng, sự chuyển di từ loại trong tiếng Việt có mấy đặc điểm sau đây:

a) Từ chuyển loại có hình thức đồng âm. Một từ thuộc từ loại này khi chuyển thành từ loại khác vẫn giữ nguyên võ ngữ âm.

b) Từ chuyển loại có yếu tố nghĩa từ vựng chung. Yếu tố nghĩa từ vựng chung đó là cơ sở của ý nghĩa từ loại, là phần trong ý nghĩa khía quát của từ. Khi một từ chuyển loại, yếu tố nghĩa từ vựng chung sẽ được giữ lại trong cả hai từ, do đối tượng phản ánh trong từ không thay đổi.

c) Từ ban đầu có khả năng kết hợp và chức năng ngữ pháp khác với từ chuyển loại, mặc dầu không phải lúc nào cũng xác định hoặc phân biệt được một cách dứt khóat. Do đó, hiện tượng chuyển loại phần nào giống như hiện tượng "nhất từ đa loại". Tình hình này dẫn đến phủ nhận từ loại trong tiếng Việt, hoặc ngược lại mở rộng phạm vi chuyển loại, không phân biệt dạng thức cấu tạo từ và tổ hợp tự do với từ chuyển loại.

III. Cách chuyển dịch sự biến đổi từ trong tiếng Việt sang tiếng Hán

Tiếng Việt và tiếng Hán thuộc cùng một loại hình ngôn ngữ, phạm trù từ loại không được rõ ràng như các ngôn ngữ Ấn-Âu, hiện tượng chuyển di từ loại trong tiếng Việt Hán cũng như trong tiếng Việt khá phổ biến và đã hình thành một đặc điểm ngữ pháp. Tiếng Việt và tiếng Hán lại được tiếp xúc trong qua trình lâu đời, vì vậy cho nên hiện tượng chuyển di từ loại trong hai thứ tiếng Việt và tiếng Hán có sự giống nhau phổ biến, nhưng theo thói quen sử dụng từ vựng và đặc điểm riêng của hai ngôn ngữ khác nhau, dẫn đến sự khác nhau về chuyển loại từ của từng từ loại cũng như ý nghĩa của từ trong câu. Sâu đây chúng tôi xin nêu một sô ví dụ thường gặp trong sự khác nhau về chuyển loại từ của các từ loại cũng như ý nghĩa của những từ này trong câu.

3.1 Cách chuyển dịch sự biến đổi thực từ trong tiếng Việt sang tiếng Hán

Hiện tượng chuyển di từ loại của thực từ trong tiếng Việt khá phổ biến và nhờ phương thức tạo từ này mà đã làm cho từ vựng tiếng Việt phong phú hơn và tăng thêm khả năng biểu đạt của từ. Nhưng trong quá trình sử dụng phương thức chuyển loại từ nhiều khi các từ từ loại này chuyển sang loại khác chỉ có mang tính lâm thời trong một ngữ cảnh nhất định, như vậy mà đã và sẽ gây rắc rỗi cho người học cũng như người dịch từ tiếng Việt sang tiếng khác như là tiếng Hán chẳng hạn.

1) Tôi không *vợ con* gì với nó.

Trong câu này, từ *vợ con* đã từ danh từ chuyển loại sang động từ, trong tiếng Hán không có hiện tượng này. Cho nên khi dịch sang tiếng Hán phải dịch theo nghĩa là："我跟他一点关系没有。"

2）Thôi chú đừng *lý thuyết* nữa...

Trong câu này, từ *lý thuyết* từ danh từ chuyển loại thành động từ, chúng ta có thể dịch câu này thành "行了，您不要再跟我讲什么理论啦。"

3）Nón rất *Huế* nhưng đời không phải thế.

Huế vốn là một danh từ chỉ tên riêng, nhưng trong câu này người nói đã dùng từ này như là tính từ, cho nên khi dịch sang tiếng Hán cũng phải dịch theo nghĩa của nó trong câu hoặc nói cách khác là phải dịch theo ngữ cảnh là："斗笠倒是很有顺化味了，但生活却远非如此。"

4）…anh chỉ kết bạn với những ai ai, … hôm thì *rượu chè* linh đinh, hôm thì *cờ bạc* tấp nập.

Hai dânh từ *rượu chè* và *cờ bạc* trong câu trên đều được tính từ hóa để miêu tả cách sống của kẻ lang thang, cho nên khi dịch không nên dịch thẳng nghĩa gốc của nhưng từ này. Chúng tôi tạm dịch câu này thành "他尽结交些什么人呐，今天吃喝，明天嫖赌的。"

5) Bà *quê* lắm! Danh từ *quê* chuyển loại thành tính từ: 你太土了！

3.2 Cách chuyển dịch sự biến đổi từ loại của hệ thống hư từ trong tiếng Việt sang tiếng Hán

Ngoài hiện tượng chuyển di từ loại trong hệ thống thực từ ra, trong hệ thống hư từ cũng xuất hiện những hiện tượng chuyển di.

1) Lý trưởng *dạ* một tiếng dài. 里长长长的应了一声。

2) …ông quay lại *à* một tiếng rất thiếu tự nhiên.

他转过身，极不自然的"啊"了一声。

Trong câu hai câu đây, hai từ *dạ* và *à* từ trợ từ chuyển loại thành động từ, khi phiên dịch sang tiếng Hán, câu 1) chúng tôi dùng từ "应" để dịch từ *dạ*, và trong câu tiếng Hán không thể hiện được sự chuyển loại như từ *dạ* trong tiếng Việt, trong câu 2) chúng ta dùng từ tiếng Hán "啊" dịch từ tiếng Việt *à*, hai thứ tiếng đều có sự chuyển di từ loại.

3.3 Cách chuyển dịch sự biến đổi từ loại giữa hệ thống hư từ và thực từ trong tiếng Việt sang tiếng Hán

1) Bảy năm *về* trước, em mười bảy tuổi.

Trong câu này, từ *về* từ trợ từ chuyển sang đồng từ, nhưng trong tiếng Hán không có hiện tượng chuyển loại này, khi dịch chỉ dịch nghĩa của trước là có thể thể hiện được ý của câu là: "7年前，我17岁。"

2）Chúng đốt nhà cướp *của của* chúng tôi.

Trong câu này, từ *của* trước là danh từ, *của* sau là quan hệ từ. Câu dịch tiếng Hán là "他们烧我们的房子，抢我们的财物。"

3）*Trời*! Sao lại thế này!

Từ *trời* từ danh từ chuyển loại thành thán từ. Trong tiếng Hán cũng có sự tương tự như vậy, cho nên kiểu câu như vậy không phải là chuyện khó khăn trong chuyển dịch. Câu có thể dịch là "天哪！怎么又这样！"

4) Em cứ *để* sách của em ở đây *để* chị đọc cho em nghe.

Hai từ *để* trong câu *để* thứ nhất là động từ và *để* thứ hai là giới từ. Chúng tôi sẽ dịch câu này là "你把你的书放这儿让我读给你听。"

IV. Nhận xét

Các nhà Đông phương học Xô-viết đã khẳng định rằng việc chuyển di "*các từ từ loại này sang loại khác mà không thay đổi vỏ âm thanh của chúng (tức là hiện tượng chuyển loại) là một trong những đặc điểm quan trọng nhất của các ngôn ngữ này (ngôn ngữ đơn lập)*" [Hà Quang Năng 1998: tr.144]. Loại của từ trong tiếng Việt không phải là bất di bất dịch. Giữa các loại của từ có một bộ phận chuyển hoá lẫn nhau. Chuyển loại là một phương thức cấu tạo từ trong tiếng Việt, hiện tượng chuyển loại là một phương thức tạo từ trên cơ sở là sự chuyển biến ý nghĩa. Nhưng không phải hiện tượng chuyển nghĩa nào cũng tạo ra được từ mới. Chỉ trường hợp chuyển nghĩa nào làm cho từ có đặc điểm và chức năng ngữ pháp của từ loại khác mới được coi là hiện tượng chuyển loại. Chuyển loại là một hiện tượng tích cực trong ngôn ngữ, là một biểu hiện của quá trình tự điều chỉnh hệ thống ngôn ngữ.

Tiếng Việt và tiếng Hán thuộc cùng một loại hình ngôn ngữ, phạm trụ từ loại không được rõ ràng như các ngôn ngữ Ấn-Âu, hiện tượng chuyển di từ loại trong tiếng Hán cũng như trong tiếng Việt khá phổ biến và đã hình thành một đặc điểm ngữ pháp. Tiếng Việt và tiếng Hán lại được tiếp xúc với nhau trong lịch sử lâu đời, vì vậy cho nên hiện tượng chuyển di từ loại trong hai thứ tiếng Việt và tiếng Hán có sự giống nhau phổ biến, nhưng theo thói quen sử dụng từ vựng và đặc điểm riêng của hai ngôn ngữ khác nhau, dẫn đến sự khác nhau về chuyển loại từ của từng từ loại cũng như ý nghĩa của từ trong câu.

Tài liệu tham khảo:

[1] Diệp Quang Ban,Hoàng Văn Thung. Ngữ pháp tiếng Việt [M] NXB giáo dục Việt Nam, Hà Nôi: 2012.

[2] Hồ Lê. Vấn đề cấu tạo từ trong tiếng Việt hiện đại [M]. NXB khoa học xã hôi, Hà Nội: 2002

[3] Trung tâm khoa học xã hội và nhân văn. Ngữ pháp tiếng Việt [M]. NXB khoa học xã hôi, Hà Nội:2000.

[4] Lê Biên. Từ loại tiếng Việt hiện đại [M]. Nxb Giáo dục, Hà Nội:1999.

[5] Nguyễn Tài Cẩn. Từ loại danh từ trong tiếng Việt hiện đại, Nxb Khoa học xã hội, Hà Nội: 1975.

[6] Nguyễn Tài Cẩn. Ngữ pháp tiếng Việt, Tiếng-Từ ghép- Đoạn ngữ[M]. Nxb Khoa học xã hội, Hà Nội: 1975.

[7] Hà Quang Năng. Đặc trưng ngữ nghĩa của hiện tượng chuyển loại các đơn vị từ vựng tiếng Việt [J]. Tiếng Việt và các ngôn ngữ Đông Nam Á, Nxb KHXH, Hà Nội: 1998.

[8] Diệp Quang Ban. Ngữ pháp Việt Nam[M]. NXB giáo dục Việt Nam, Hà Nôi: 2013.

การศึกษาการออกเสียงสระภาษาไทยของนักศึกษาจีน*

Chen Yu**

บทคัดย่อ

ปัจจุบันนี้ การเปิดสอนหลักสูตรภาษาไทยของสถาบันการศึกษาต่างๆในมณฑลยูนนานเพิ่มมากขึ้นเรื่อยๆ ทำให้ครูบาอา
จารย์ต้องคำนึงถึงคุณภาพการเรียนการสอนให้ดียิ่งขึ้น ในกระบวนการการเรียนการสอนของภาษาไทย การออกเสียงภาษาไทยเป็น
เรื่องพื้นฐานและสำคัญมากที่สุด บทความบทนี้จึงมุ่งศึกษาปัญหาที่เกิดในการเรียนการสอนการออกเสียงภาษาไทยของนักศึกษา
จีน เพื่อที่แก้ไขปัญหาที่เกิดมาและพัฒนาคุณภาพการเรียนการสอนภาษาไทย จากผลการศึกษา เราสามารถเห็นได้อย่างชัดเจนว่า
ปัญหาที่เกิดขึ้นในการอ่านสระภาษาไทยของนักศึกษาจีนมีอยู่มากมาย ข้อผิดพลาดในการเรียนการออกเสียงภาษาไทยไม่ได้เกิดจาก
ความแตกต่างระหว่างทั้งสองภาษาแต่อย่างเดียว ความเหมือนก็กลายเป็นปัจจัยที่ทำให้เกิดข้อผิดพลาดได้เหมือนกัน ปัญหาเหล่านี้ที่
เกิดขึ้นต่างก็มองข้ามไม่ได้ ยังต้องให้ความสำคัญกับเสียงจริงที่นักศึกษาผลิตออกมาอีกด้วย

คำสำคัญ การออกเสียง; สระภาษาไทย; นักศึกษาจีน

๑. เบื้องหลังการวิจัยและความสำคัญของปัญหา

มณฑลยูนนานเป็นมณฑลทางภาคตะวันตกเฉียงใต้ของจีนที่ตั้งอยู่ใกล้ไทยมากที่สุด รวมทั้งมีวัฒนธรรมไตลื้อที่มีรากฐาน
ภาษาคล้ายคลึงกับภาษาไทย และมีอาณาเขตติดต่อกับหลายประเทศในอนุภูมิภาคลุ่มน้ำโขง ขณะนี้ มณฑลยูนนานก็ตระหนักถึง
ความสำคัญในความร่วมมือกับประเทศไทย และกำลังเตรียมการที่จะรับการติดต่อ ค้าขายและการลงทุนที่มีเพิ่มขึ้นไปอย่างมาก
ในอนาคตอันใกล้ ทั้งนี้ ทำให้รัฐบาลจีนมีนโยบายให้มณฑลยูนนานเปิดทางเรียนการสอนภาษาประเทศเพื่อนบ้าน สำหรับมณฑลยูน
นานแล้ว ภาษาไทยและภาษาอื่นๆของประเทศเอเชียอาคเนย์จึงเป็นภาษาที่มีความสำคัญเทียบเท่ากับภาษาอังกฤษ ภาษาไทยเป็นภาษา
ที่นักศึกษาจีนเลือกเรียนมากที่สุดในบรรดาภาษาประเทศเพื่อนบ้านจำนวน 5 ภาษา (ไทย ลาว พม่า กัมพูชา และเวียดนาม) เนื่องจาก
ไทยเป็นประเทศที่มีศักยภาพทางเศรษฐกิจสูงและมีการลงทุนจำนวนมากในมณฑลยูนนานทำให้นักศึกษาและผู้ปกครองเล็งเห็นถึง
โอกาสในการหางานได้ง่ายภายหลังสำเร็จการศึกษา

๑.๑ สภาพการเปิดหลักสูตรภาษาไทยในมณฑลยูนนาน

ในนครคุนหมิง ซึ่งเป็นเมืองเอกของมณฑลยูนนาน นักเรียนจีนมีแนวโน้มที่จะเรียนภาษาไทยมากขึ้นเรื่อยๆ โดยเฉพาะขณะนี้

---

* 论文题目：语音学视域下中国学生的泰语元音发音偏误分析。

**【作者简介】陈宇 (Chen Yu)，云南大学外国语学院泰语系讲师，研究方向：泰汉翻
译、语用学、话语分析。

เส้นทางบกกรุงเทพฯ-คุนหมิง ได้เปิดใช้อย่างเป็นทางการแล้ว ทำให้การเดินทางไปมาระหว่างกันมีความสะดวกยิ่งขึ้น ผู้ปกครองชาวจีนจึงยิ่งให้ความสนใจ ในการส่งบุตรหลานของตนไปศึกษาต่อในประเทศไทย เฉพาะในมณฑลยูนนาน สถานการศึกษาที่เปิดสอนวิชาภาษาไทยในระดับต่างๆ(ระดับประกาศนียบัตร และระดับปริญญา)มีถึง๒๘แห่ง ทุกปีมีจำนวนผู้เรียนภาษาไทยมากกว่า๔๐๐๐คน

๑.๒ ปัญหาที่เกิดขึ้นในกระบวนการจัดการเรียนการสอนภาษาไทย

ถึงแม้ว่าการเรียนภาษาไทยในประเทศจีนกำลังฟื้นฟู แต่ในกระบวนการจัดการ

เรียนการสอนภาษาไทยยังมีปัญหาอยู่มากมาย เช่น สื่อการเรียนการสอนไม่พอกับการสอน ขาดครูบาอาจารย์ผู้เชี่ยวชาญ พื้นฐานของนักศึกษาแต่ละคนไม่เท่ากัน เป็นต้น ทั้งๆที่นักศึกษาได้เรียนรู้ภาษาไทยอย่างเป็นระบบ แต่ก็เกิดปัญหามากมายในทางด้านการพูด การฟัง การอ่านและการเขียน

โดยเฉพาะการพูด ซึ่งต้องมีการออกเสียงที่ชัดเป็นพื้นฐาน ภาษาไทยเป็นภาษาที่ใช้ตัวอักษรแทนเสียง ถ้าหากออกเสียงผิดออกเสียงไม่ชัด ก็จะทำให้ความหมายของคำเปลี่ยนไปหรือทำให้ผู้ฟังไม่เข้าใจ อีกทั้งเนื่องจากว่าระบบเสียงภาษาจีนกับภาษาไทยมีความแตกต่างกัน จึงทำให้นักศึกษาจีนเกิดความผิดพลาดมากมายในการออกเสียงภาษาไทย เช่น แยกพยัญชนะต้นเสียงโฆษะ ไม่ออกแยกสระสั้นยาวไม่ชัดและอ่านพยัญชนะท้ายไม่ชัด

๑.๓ การพัฒนาคุณภาพการจัดการเรียนการสอนในการออกเสียง

เนื่องจากการออกเสียงภาษาไทยเป็นพื้นฐานที่สำคัญที่สุดในการเรียนการสอนภาษาไทย จึงจำเป็นต้องสำรวจและพิจารณาว่าสภาพจริงและปัญหาที่เกิดขึ้นในการออกเสียงภาษาไทยของนักศึกษาจีนเป็นอย่างไร จะได้นำผลการศึกษาไปประยุกต์ใช้ในการจัดการเรียนการสอน และปรับแก้กลวิธีการสอนของผู้สอน เพื่อที่จะพัฒนาคุณภาพได้ในการจัดการเรียนการสอนของการออกเสียง

๒.ขอบเขตการศึกษาและวัตถุประสงค์งานวิจัย
๒.๑ ขอบเขตการศึกษา

ระบบเสียงภาษาไทยมีความสมบูรณ์และความซับซ้อน พยัญชนะประกอบด้วย อักษรกลาง อักษรสูงและอักษรต่ำ พยัญชนะทำหน้าที่ทั้งต้นและท้าย สระมีเสียงสั้นกับยาว พยัญนะแต่ละชนิดสะกดกับสระสั้นยาวจะมีโทนที่แตกต่างกัน เสียงวรรณยุกต์มีถึง๕เสียง นองจากนี้ยังมีอักษรนำและอักษรควบกล้ำ ซึ่งทำหน้าที่เป็นพยัญชนะต้น ทั้งนี้มีความแตกต่างกันมากไปจากระบบเสียงภาษาจีนกลาง

ในงายวิจัยชิ้นนี้ ศึกษาเฉพาะสภาพการออกเสียงสระภาษาไทยของนักศึกษาจีนเท่านั้น

๒.๒ วัตถุประสงค์งานวิจัย

เพื่อสำรวจสภาพจริงในการออกเสียงสระภาษาไทยของนักศึกษาจีน และวิเคราะห์ปัญหาที่เกิดขึ้นในการออกเสียง รวมทั้งนำผลวิเคราะห์ไปประยุกต์ใช้ในวิธีการสอนของผู้สอน ตลอดจนพัฒนาและปรับปรุงกลวิธีในการจัดการเรียนการสอนการออกเสียงภาษาไทยสำหรับนักศึกษาจีน

๓. งานวิจัยเกี่ยวข้องที่มีคนทำไว้

งานเกี่ยวข้องที่ทำมาเป็นงานวิจัยวิเคราะห์การออกเสียงภาษาจีนของชาวไทย หรือการอภิปรายกลวิธีการจัดการเรียนการสอนภาษาจีนให้นักเรียนชาวไทย ในงานเหล่านี้มีมีส่วนที่เกี่ยวข้องจะเป็นการเปรียบเทียบระบบเสียงภาษาไทยกับภาษาจีนอยู่บ้าง แต่งานที่ทำมาซึ่งเป็นงานวิจัยวิเคราะห์การออกเสียงภาษาไทยของนักศึกษาจีนนั้นไม่ได้พบเจอ ส่วนที่เกี่ยวข้องกับการเปรียบเทียบระบบเสียงภาษาไทยกับภาษาจีนรวบรวมไว้ดังต่อไปนี้

1. CaiYiwen,HugoYu-Hsiu Lee(2015) ความไม่เหมือนในการออกเสียงสระระหว่างภาษาจีนกับไทย มี [y] [ei] [ou] [ie] [yɛ] [uei][iou]

2. He Shanyan(2010) หน่วยเสียงสระภาษาจีนที่เหมือนกับหน่วยเสียงสระภาษาไทยมี[a] [o] [i] [u] [ai] [ei] [au] [ou] [ua] [in] [aŋ] [iŋ] [uŋ] หน่วยเสียงสระภาษาจีนที่แตกต่างจากหน่วยเสียงสระภาษาไทยมี [y] [ə] [ŋ] [l] [iɛ] [yɛ] [yan] [yn]

3. LiHongyin(1995) ความผิดพลาดที่สำคัญในการออกเสียงสระภาษาจีนของคนไทยคือ แยกสระประสม[ua] [uo] [ia] [iɛ] [ɤi] [au]ไม่ได้

4. Zhengying,CaoWen(2002) สำหรับนักเรียนคนไทยวิธีการออกเสียงสระภาษาจีนต้องหลีกเลี่ยงการใช้เสียงที่ใกล้เคียงมาแทน

๔. แนวคิดทฤษฎีปและวิธีการวิเคราะห์ที่ใช้ในการศึกษา

๔.๑ การวิเคราะห์เชิงการเปรียบเทียบ (Contrastive Analysis หรือเรียกย่อว่าCA)

๔.๒ สมมุติฐานในการวิเคราะห์เชิงเปรียบเทียบ(Contrastive Analysis Hypothesis)

Lado(1957): เห็นว่า อุปสรรคและความยากลำบากในการเรียนภาษาที่สองอันเกิดจากความไม่เหมือนระหว่างภาษาที่หนึ่งกับภาษาที่สอง จึงต้องวิเคราะห์ความแตกต่างของทั้งสองภาษา

๔.๓ การวิเคราะห์ระบบเสียงทางกลสัทศาสตร์

๔.๓ การวิเคราะห์เสียงบันทึกเชิงคุณภาพ

๕. สมมุติฐาน

จากประสบการณ์การสอนภาษาไทยมาและตามแนวคิด Contrastive Analysis Hypothesis ซึ่งเป็นทฤษฎีที่ Ladoนำเสนอเมื่อปีคศ.1957 ตั้งสมมุติฐานไว้ว่า

๕.๑ แยกสระเสียงสั้นกับเสียงยาวไม่ออก

๕.๒ แยก [e] [e:] กับ [ɛ] [ɛ:] ไม่ออก

๕.๓ แยก [ɯ] [ɯ:] กับ [ɤ] [ɤ:] ไม่ออก

๖. วิธีการเก็บข้อมูล

๖.๑ กลุ่มเป้าหมายในงานวิจัย(Patter n)

กลุ่มตัวอย่างเป็นนักศึกษาจีนปริญญาตรีชั้นปีที่2ที่เรียนวิชาเอกภาษาไทยจำนวน 23 คน ซึ่งเคยเรียนการออกเสียงภาษาไทยอย่างเป็นระบบและระยะเวลาเรียนการออกเสียง ไม่น้อยกว่า 1ภาคเรียน

๖.๒ ข้อมูลอ่านและการบันทึกเสียง

ข้อมูลที่ให้อ่านประกอบด้วย 3 ส่วน คือ ๑.สระเดี่ยว ๒.สระประสม(Diphthongs กับ Triphthongs) ๓.ประโยคสั้นๆ ให้นักศึกษาทั้ง 23 คน อ่านตามลำดับที่ให้ไว้ บันทึกเสียงของแต่ละคนและทำเป็นไฟล์เสียง 23 ไฟล์

ข้อมูลที่ให้อ่านมีดังนี้

——สระเดี่ยว๑๘ตัว

อะ อา อิ อี อึ อือ อุ อู

เอะ เอ แอะ แอ โอะ โอ เอาะ ออ เออะ เออ

——สระประสม๒๗ตัว

ไอ เอา เอียะ เอีย เอือะ เอือ อัวะ อัว

อัย อาย อาว อิว อีว อุย อูย เอ็ว เอว แอ็ว แอว เอย โอย โอว อ็อย ออย

เอียว เอือย อวย

——ประโยค๒๒ประโยค

ภาษาไทยของเรานี้	มีสิ่งดีอยู่มากมาย
ภาษาไทยของเรานี้	มีสิ่งดีอยู่มากมาย
สระมีหลายตัว	ไม่มีมั่วเรียงตัวกัน
เริ่มที่ อะ อา นั้น	เรียงตามกัน อิ อี มา
อึ อื ก็มาด้วย	อุ อู ชาว เอะ เอ นา
แอะ แอ เอียะ เอีย มา	เอือะ เอือ นา อัวะ อัว มี
โอะ โอ เอาะ ออ พร้อม	เออะ เออ อำ ไอ ก็มี
นี่คือเสียงสระ	รวมกันแล้วมีหลายเสียง
มีตั้งสามสิบสองเสียง	อย่ามั่วเถียงจริงจริงหนอ
เสียงสระมีแค่นี้	ให้โชคดีนะเพื่อนหนา
วันนี้ฉันขอลา	ขอเวลาจบก่อนเอย

๓. วิธีการวิเคราะห์ การวิเคราะห์เชิงคุณภาพ

1.วิธีการวิเคราะห์เชิงการเปรียบเทียบ(Contrastive Analysis) วิเคราะห์เปรียบเทียบระบบเสียงสระของภาษาจีนกับภาษาไทย

ตาราง 1 ระบบเสียงสระหลักภาษาจีน(อ้างจากจากอ. LinTao—A course in phonetics 2013)

	Front		Central	Back
	Unrounded	Rounded	Unrounded	Rounded
Close	[i]	[y]		[u]
Close-mid			[ɤ]	[o]
Open-mid				
Open			[a]	

ในภาษาจีนมาตรฐาน มีสัทอักษร๓ตัวที่แตกต่างจากThe Secondary Cardinal Vowels

[ɤ] จะเป็นสระระหว่างสระกึ่งสูงกับสระกึ่งต่ำ ลิ้นส่วนกลาง ปากไม่ห่อ

[o] จะเป็นสระระหว่างสระกึ่งสูงกับสระกึ่งต่ำ ลิ้นส่วนหลัง ปากห่อ

[a] จะเป็นสระต่ำ ลิ้นส่วนกลาง ปากไม่ห่อ

ตาราง 2 ระบบเสียงสระหลักภาษาไทย(อ้างจากอ.อมร ทวีศักดิ—สัทศาสตร์2542)

	Short vowels/Long vowels		
	Unrounded		Rounded
	Front	Central	Back
Close	[i] [i:]	[ɯ] [ɯ:]	[u] [u:]
Close-mid	[e] [e:]	[ɤ] [ɤ:]	[o] [o:]
Open-mid	[ɛ] [ɛ:]		[ɔ] [ɔ:]
Open		[a] [a:]	

ในภาษาไทยมาตรฐาน มีสัทอักษร๒ชุดที่แตกต่างจากThe Secondary Cardinal Vowels

[ɤ] [ɤ:] จะเป็นสระกึ่งสูง ลิ้นส่วนกลาง ปากไม่ห่อ

[a] [a:] จะเป็นสระต่ำ ลิ้นส่วนกลาง ปากไม่ห่อ

ตาราง3 เสียงสระภาษาไทยที่ไม่มีในภาษาจีน

	Short vowels/Long vowels			
	Front		Back	
	Unrounded	Rounded	Unrounded	Rounded
Close			อี[ɯ] อือ[ɯː]	
Close-mid	เอะ[e] เอ[eː]			
Open-mid	แอะ[ɛ] แอ[ɛː]			เอาะ[ɔ] ออ[ɔː]

2. การวิเคราะห์เชิงคุณภาพโดยใช้วิธีการเช็คเสียง

เชิญอาจารย์คนไทยที่สอนภาษาไทยช่วยฟังเสียงบันทึกมาพร้อมเช็คเสียง ว่าเสียงไหนอ่านผิด และวิเคราะห์ว่าผิดที่ส่วนของลิ้นหรือความสูงต่ำของลิ้นหรือลักษณะของริมฝีปาก และปัญหาอื่น

๘. ผลการวิเคราะห์ข้อมูล

๘.๑ สภาพของสัดส่วน(เปอร์เซนต์)ความผิดพลาดในการอ่านสระภาษาไทย

ในตารางนี้ สระเดี่ยวกับสระประสมที่อ่านผิดพลาดจะคิดเป็นเปอร์เซนต์จากนักศึกษาทั้งหมด23คน

สระ	สัดส่วนความผิดพลาด(%)	สระ	สัดส่วนความผิดพลาด(%)	สระ	สัดส่วนความผิดพลาด(%)
อะ	9	อา	30	อิ	0
อี	22	อี	35	อือ	52
อุ	0	อู	22	เอะ	30
เอ	52	แอะ	48	แอ	30
โอะ	70	โอ	87	เอาะ	17
ออ	39	เออะ	13	เออ	35
ไอ	43	เอา	35	เอียะ	0
เอีย	21	เอือะ	35	เอือ	52
อัวะ	9	อัว	30	อัย	9
อาย	13	อาว	13	อิว	0
อีว	0	อุย	17	อูย	17
เอ็ว	30	เอว	30	แอ็ว	22
แอว	22	เอย	26	โอย	52
โอว	22	อ็อย	4	ออย	4
เอียว	0	เอือย	43	อวย	78

๘.๒ จากการเช็คเสียงบันทึก และตารางเปอร์เซนต์ข้างต้น พบว่าข้อสัดส่วนความผิดพลาดใน
การอ่านสระภาษาไทยของนักศึกษาจีนที่สูงมากว่า50%มี [ɤ] [e:] [o] [o:] [oi:] [uai:]

และปัญหาที่เกิดขึ้นในการอ่านมีดังนี้

1. อ่านสระลิ้นส่วนหลัง ปากห่อ [o][o：] เป็น [ɔ][ɔ：] ระดับลิ้นจะไม่สูงพอ มีถึง70%

2. แยกเสียงสั้นกับเสียงยาวไม่ชัด ถึง48%

3. แยก[e] [e:]กับ [ɛ][ɛ:] ไม่ชัด เวลาอ่าน [e][e:] จะอยู่ระหว่าง สระกึ่งสูงกับสระกึ่งต่ำ ถึง48%

4. อ่าน[ɰ][ɯ:] ไม่ชัด จะอ่านเหมือน[ɤ][ɤ:] หรือ[ʊ] ลิ้นสูง ไม่พอ มีถึง40%

5. เวลาอ่านเสียงสระยาวมี Glottal Stop อยู่ตอนท้ายถึง22%

6. อ่านสระประสม [ai] [au] ไม่มี Glottal Stop อยู่ตอนท้าย มักจะอ่านเป็นสระเสียงยาวถึง35%

7. อ่านสระ Triphthongs มักจะอ่านเป็น Diphthongs ที่ละ[a]ไป ก็คือ [u:ai]อ่านเป็น[ui]มีถึง78% และ[ɯ:ai] อ่านเป็น [ɤ:i]
มีถึง43%

๘.๓ ข้อสรุป

จากผลการศึกษา เราสามารถเห็นได้อย่างชัดเจนว่าปัญหาที่เกิดขึ้นในการอ่านสระภาษาไทยของนักศึกษาจีนมีอยู่มากมาย ข้อผิดพลาดในการเรียนการออกเสียงภาษาไทยไม่ได้เกิดจากความแตกต่างระหว่างทั้งสองภาษาแต่อย่างเดียว ความเหมือนก็กลายเป็นปัจจัยที่ทำให้เกิดข้อผิดพลาดได้เหมือนกัน ปัญหาเหล่านี้ที่เกิดขึ้นต่างก็มองข้ามไม่ได้ ยังต้องให้ความสำคัญกับเสียงจริงที่นักศึกษาผลิตออกมาอีกด้วย

๙. การอภิปรายและข้อเสนอแนะ
๙.๑ ด้านการวิเคราะห์

1. ข้อมูลอ่านที่ใช้ในการอัดเสียงยังไม่ค่อยสมบูรณ์ ควรมีข้อความที่ยาวกว่าประโยค และควรมีการพูดแบบธรรมชาติ จึงจะทำให้ผลการวิเคราะห์แม่นยำยิ่งขึ้น

2. เสียงบางเสียงถ้าใส่ลงในโปรแกรม Praat จะเห็นผลได้ชัดเจนยิ่งขึ้น งานต่อไปควรลองทำการวิจัยทางกลสัทศาสตร์

3. เนื่องจากว่านักศึกษาที่เรียนเอกภาษาไทยมากจากที่ต่างกัน จึงมีภาษาแม่ที่ต่างกัน เวลาเรียนการออกเสียงมักจะได้รับอิทธิพลมาจากการออกเสียงภาษาแม่ ถ้าวิเคราะห์อิทธิพลที่มาจากภาษาแม่ที่มีต่อการเรียนการออกเสียงภาษาไทย (ทั้ง Positive Transfer และ Negative Transfer) น่าจะต่อยอดได้จากรายงานชิ้นนี้

๙.๒ ด้านการจัดการเรียนการสอน

1. มหาวิทยาลัยที่เปิดหลักสูตรวิชาเอกภาษาไทย ควรเปิดวิชาที่แนะนำความรู้พื้นฐานด้านสัทศาสตร์ จะได้ทำให้นักศึกษาได้เรียนรู้อวัยวะที่ใช้ในการออกเสียง ความแตกต่างระหว่างพยัญชนะกับสระ และสภาพรวมระบบเสียงภาษาไทย ถ้านักศึกษามีความรู้ด้านสัทศาสตร์พอสมควร จะช่วยเขาเรียนการออกเสียงภาษาไทยได้ง่ายขึ้น

2. ครูอาจารย์คนจีนที่สอนภาษาไทยต้องพยายามปรับแก้การออกเสียงของตนให้ชัดมากขึ้น และต้องรู้ว่าปัญหาการออกเสียงภาษาไทยของนักศึกษาคืออะไร ต้องแก้ไขอย่างไร ถึงจะช่วยนักศึกษาอย่างมีประสิทธิภาพ

บรรณานุกรม

[1] อมร ทวีศักดิ์. [M]. สัทศาสตร์. กรุงเทพฯ. บริษัทสหธรรมิก จำกัด. 2542

[2] นันทนา รณเกียรติ. สัทศาสตร์(ภาคทฤษฎีและภาคปฏิบัติ). [M]. สำนักพิมพ์มหาวิทยาลัยธรรมศาสตร์. 2548

[3] พิณทิพย์ ทวยเจริญ. ภาพรวมของการศึกษาสัทศาสตร์และภาษาศาสตร์ [M]. สำนักพิมพ์มหาวิทยาลัยธรรมศาสตร์. 2547

[4] 彼得．赖福吉.张维佳（译）.语音学教程[M].北京：北京大学出版社，2013.

[5] 林焘.语音学教程 [M].北京：北京大学出版社，2013.

การศึกษาหน่วยคำ "นัก" และ "ผู้" ในภาษาไทย*

Zhang Shengnan**

บทคัดย่อ หน่วยคำ "นัก" และ "ผู้" ในภาษาไทยต่างก็มีความหมายอ้างถึงมนุษย์หรือผู้คน แต่ยังพบว่ามีความซับซ้อนอยู่ไม่น้อย บทความเรื่องนี้ได้นำแนวคิดทฤษฎีโครงสร้าง Item-and-Process Morphology กับ Item-and-Arrangement Morphology มาวิเคราะห์หน่วยคำเหล่านี้ จากการเปรียบเทียบสองแนวคิดนี้ พบว่าแนวคิด Item-and-Arrangement Morphology เป็นแนวคิดที่สามารถควบคุมปัญหาต่างๆและช่วยแยกแยะหน่วยคำเหล่านี้ได้ง่ายขึ้น

คำสำคัญ "นัก"; "ผู้"; Item-and-Process Morphology; Item-and-Arrangement Morphology

บทนำ

การใช้หน่วยคำ "นัก" และ "ผู้" ในภาษาไทยได้พบสองแบบ แบบแรกคือ "นัก" และ "ผู้" สามารถเกิดในตำแหน่งเดียวกันได้ เช่นคำว่า "นักเขียน" กับ "ผู้เขียน" มีคำตามหลังเหมือนกันและแสดงความเป็นมนุษย์เหมือนกัน แต่มีความหมายบางอย่างแฝงอยู่หรือต่างกัน แบบที่สองคือ "นัก" และ "ผู้" ไม่สามารถนำหน้าคำเดียวกันได้ เช่น "นักบิน *ผู้บิน ผู้หญิง *นักหญิง" จึงให้เห็นว่ามีความซับซ้อนเป็นอย่างมาก เมื่อมีการสร้างคำใหม่ที่สื่อความหมายเป็นมนุษย์ จะพบนักเรียนต่างชาติใช้หน่วยคำเหล่านี้ผิดบ่อยๆ จึงเกิดข้อสงสัยขึ้นมาว่า อันที่จริงหน่วยคำ "นัก" และ "ผู้" ควรเป็นอะไร มีสถานะอะไร ควรจะใช้อย่างไรถึงถูกต้อง ดังนั้นผู้เขียนจึงสนใจศึกษาเรื่องลักษณะการสร้างคำด้วยหน่วยคำ "นัก" และ "ผู้"ในภาษาไทย โดยใช้วิธีการเปรียบเทียบแนวคิดต่างๆในการศึกษาโครงสร้างของคำ ให้เห็นว่าแต่ละทฤษฎีหรือแนวคิดมีลักษณะอย่างไรในการวิเคราะห์เรื่องหน่วยคำและจะพบปัญหาอะไรบ้างในการแยกหน่วยคำที่กล่าวถึง

โดยจะยกทฤษฎีโครงสร้าง (หน่วยทางไวยากรณ์) มาอธิบายเรื่องนี้เป็นส่วนหลักๆ เพราะว่าทฤษฎียุคหลังๆไม่ได้ให้ความสำคัญเรื่องหน่วยคำเท่าทฤษฎีโครงสร้าง บางทฤษฎีมองว่าไม่ควรมีเรื่องหน่วยคำด้วยซ้ำ เห็นว่ามนุษย์คนเราจำคำเป็นก้อนๆไม่ได้แยกออกมาเป็นส่วนๆ (วิโรจน์ อรุณมานะกุล2559:11) เช่นภาษาศาสตร์ปริชานมองว่า ภาษาเป็นส่วนหนึ่งของสมอง มโนทัศน์ขึ้นอยู่กับเราเห็นภาพอะไร ความหมายไม่ได้จำกัดแค่คำคำและยังอยู่ในภาพที่เราเห็น คำจะเป็นตัวกระตุ้นให้เราเห็นภาพรวมและการทำความเข้าใจเกิดจากมโนทัศน์ จะไม่ได้แยกแต่ละส่วนแทนความหมายด้วยยะอะไร เราจำเป็นต้องอาศัยความรู้ทางโลกและประสบการณ์ต่างๆ ดังนั้นจึงนำทฤษฎีโครงสร้างแบ่งเป็นสองส่วน ส่วนแรกจะใช้ทฤษฎีโครงสร้างโดยตามแนวคิด Sapir ส่วนที่สองจะยึดตามแนวคิด Bloomfield จากการเปรียบเทียบสองแนวคิดนี้ได้พบผลสรุปที่ต่างกันและหวังว่าสามารถนำผลเหล่านี้ไปศึกษาในอนาคตต่อไป

งานวิจัยที่เกี่ยวข้องเรื่อง "นัก" และ "ผู้"

โครงสร้างเป็นมโนทัศน์ที่สำคัญในการวิเคราะห์ทางไวยากรณ์ ได้แสดงความสัมพันธ์ของส่วนต่างๆที่ประกอบกันเป็น

---

* 泰语语素 "nak" 与 "phuu" 的分析研究。

** 作者简介: 张胜男（Zhang Shengnan）, 云南大学外国语学院泰语系讲师, 研究方向: 语言学。

คำ หน่วยคำวลีและประโยค ในหนังสือ A Reference Grammar of Thai (Shoichi Iwasaki & Preeya Ingkaphirom2005:25)ได้ศึกษา
โครงสร้างการสร้างคำ โดยแบ่งเป็นคำไม่ซับซ้อนและคำซับซ้อน คำไม่ซับซ้อนคือประกอบด้วยหน่วยคำอิสระ เช่นม้า แม่ ส่วน
คำซับซ้อนคือประกอบด้วยหน่วยคำอย่างน้อยสองหน่วยคำ อาจจะใช้วิธีการเติมวิภัตติปัจจัย การซ้ำคำหรือการผสมคำ อย่างหน่วย
คำ "นัก" ถูกมองว่าเป็นการเติมอุปสรรคที่สื่อความหมายเป็นคนและสังกัดอยู่ภายใต้การแยกลักษณะประเภทของบุคคล(Classifying
prefixes): นักเรียน นักบิน นักร้อง นักการเมือง ส่วน "ผู้" จะถูกมองว่าเป็นหน่วยคำอิสระที่สามารถอยู่เป็นลำพังและเติมข้างหน้าคำ
อื่นได้ ทำหน้าที่คล้ายๆการเติมอุปสรรค (Quasi-prefixes) เป็นวิธีการสร้างคำประสมวิธีหนึ่ง เช่นผู้หญิง ผู้แทน

อย่างไรก็ตาม ไม่ว่าจะเป็นวิธีแบบใดต่างก็ให้เห็นว่า "นัก" และ "ผู้" ได้จัดเป็นส่วนหนึ่งของคำ ซึ่งต้องประกอบอะไรบาง
อย่างเพื่อสื่อความหมายเป็นมนุษย์ แต่สองหน่วยคำนี้ยังมีลักษณะที่ต่างกัน โดยมองจากสถานะว่าเป็นหน่วยคำอิสระหรือไม่อิสระ
ส่วนความหมายที่สื่อไม่ได้พูดถึงมากนัก จึงแสดงให้เห็นว่าการมองแบบอิสระไม่เพียงพอที่จะอธิบายหน่วยคำเหล่านี้ได้ชัดเจน

การวิเคราะห์การสร้างคำด้วยหน่วยคำ "นัก" และ "ผู้" ในภาษาไทยเชิงทฤษฎีโครงสร้าง

การศึกษาเรื่องวิทยาหน่วยคำเป็นเรื่องที่สำคัญในทฤษฎีโครงสร้าง โดยเฉพาะในช่วงแรกนักภาษาศาสตร์ให้ความสนใจต่อ
เรื่องวิทยาศาสตร์หน่วยคำเป็นอย่างมาก เช่น Sapir กับ Bloomfield สองคนได้ใช้มุมมองการศึกษาที่ต่างกัน ตามแนวคิด Sapir มอง
ว่าการสร้างคำต้องเกิดจากกระบวนการการเติม ส่วน Bloomfield มองว่าการสร้างคำเกิดจากการเรียงหน่วยคำต่างๆเข้าด้วยกัน
โดยแต่ละหน่วยคำมีมโนทัศน์ของตัวเองประกอบภายในเสมอ ดังนั้นจึงได้แยกเป็น Item-and-Process Morphology กับ Item-and-
Arrangement Morphology ซึ่งมีการนำวิธีอธิบายต่างกัน

Item-and-Process Morphology

Sapir มองว่ากระบวนการทางไวยากรณ์ทำหน้าที่เป็นสัญญาณ เพื่อสื่อมโนทัศน์บางอย่าง โดยผ่านกระบวนการการเติมปัจจัย
(Affixation) ต่างๆเข้าไป (Edward 1921:99) ตามแนวคิดนี้การสร้างคำที่มีมโนทัศน์ใหม่จะเกิดจากกระบวนการการเติมปัจจัย ไม่ใช่
การเชื่อมโยงมโนทัศน์กับหน่วยคำต่างๆอย่างโดยตรง รากคำจะเป็นตัวหลักที่บรรจุลักษณ์ (feature) ต่างๆอยู่ในตัว ส่วนการเติมอะไร
เข้าไปก็ขึ้นอยู่กับความต้องการของรากคำ ตัวอย่างเช่น การเติมพหูพจน์ในภาษาอังกฤษ / X /$_{[+N,+PL]}$ $\longrightarrow$ / Xz // Xs / และ / Xiz / ส่วน / z
//s/และ/iz/ที่เติมเข้าไป ไม่มีการแสดงพหูพจน์อยู่ในตัวมันเอง การเติมอะไรขึ้นอยู่กับความต้องการและเงื่อนไขทางเสียงของรากคำ
ตามแนวคิดนี้ การสร้างคำโดย "นัก" และ "ผู้" ก็จะมีลักษณะคล้ายๆกัน ถือว่าเป็นการเติมอุปสรรค (Prefix)ของคำและ ไม่สามารถอยู่
เป็นลำพังได้ ต้องเกาะกับหน่วยคำอื่นๆและอยู่หน้าของหน่วยคำอื่นเสมอ เมื่ออยู่หน้าคำกริยาแล้ว มีการทำหน้าที่ให้คำกริยากลาย
เป็นคำนาม (Nominalization) ด้วย เช่น

นัก-	ผู้-	นัก-	ผู้-
นักหวด	ผู้หวด	นักร้อง	ผู้ร้อง
นักเล่นกล	ผู้เล่นกล	นักพูด	ผู้พูด
นักดำน้ำ	ผู้ดำน้ำ	นักเรียน	ผู้เรียน
นักปักษี	ผู้ปักษี	นักศึกษา	ผู้ศึกษา
นักเขียน	ผู้เขียน	นักวิจารณ์	ผู้วิจารณ์
นักวิพากษ์	ผู้วิพากษ์	นักขาย	ผู้ขาย

คำเหล่านี้ได้เติมหน้าคำกริยาที่เหมือนกันและมีการสื่อความหมายที่เกี่ยวข้องกันหรือมีส่วนคล้ายคลึงกัน ถ้าหน่วยคำข้างหน้า

ถูกมองเป็นอุปสรรค คำที่ตามหลังก็จะกลายเป็นรากคำ ซึ่งเป็นคำกริยา เมื่อรากคำต้องการแสดงหรือสื่อความหมายเป็นมนุษย์ จะ
เลือกนัก- หรือ ผู้- ตัวใดตัวหนึ่งเข้าไปก็ได้ ผ่านกระบวนการการเติมปัจจัยให้กลายเป็นคำนามและสื่อมโนทัศน์ใหม่ ความหมายใหม่
นี้ไม่ได้เกิดจากหรือติดมาจากนัก- หรือ ผู้- แต่เกิดจากการผ่านกระบวนการการเติมเท่านั้น เช่น

$[X]_v \rightarrow [$นัก-$X]_{N[+animate]}$

$\rightarrow [$ผู้-$X]_{N[+animate]}$

อันที่จริงคำที่ประกอบด้วยนัก- หรือ ผู้- จะมีความหมายบางอย่างที่ต่างกันอยู่เสมอ ซึ่งอาจจะดูจากกระบวนการการเติมปัจจัย
อย่างเดียวไม่เพียงพอ เช่นคำที่ขึ้นหน้าด้วยนัก- จะสื่อความหมายว่ามีความสามารถเฉพาะด้าน เป็นคนที่มีความเชี่ยวชาญทางด้านใด
ส่วนคำที่ขึ้นหน้าด้วยผู้- จะสื่อความหมายว่าเป็นคนที่มีสภาพแบบใด จะไม่มีเรื่องความชำนาญแฝงอยู่ เช่น "นักร้อง" กับ "ผู้ร้อง" "นัก
ร้อง" มองเป็นคนที่เก่งด้านการร้องเพลง สามารถทำเป็นอาชีพได้ แต่ "ผู้ร้อง" แค่สื่อความหมายว่าเป็นคนที่ร้องเพลง จะร้องเพราะ
หรือไม่เพราะก็ได้ นอกจากนี้ ในบางกรณีหน่วยคำ "นัก" และ "ผู้" ไม่สามารถนำหน้าคำที่เหมือนกันได้ เช่น

นัก-	ผู้-	นัก-	ผู้-
นักภาษาศาสตร์	*ผู้ภาษาศาสตร์	*นักด้อยโอกาส	ผู้ด้อยโอกาส
นักบิน	*ผู้บิน	*นักหญิง	ผู้หญิง
นักเทนนิส	* ผู้เทนนิส	*นักอาวุโส	ผู้อาวุโส
นักข่าว	*ผู้ข่าว	*นักโดยสาร	ผู้โดยสาร
นักดนตรี	*ผู้ดนตรี	*นักแต่ง	ผู้แต่ง
นักปราชญา	*ผู้ปราชญา	*นักสูงศักดิ์	ผู้สูงศักดิ์

ในกรณีนี้ก็จะเห็นได้ว่า "นัก" และ "ผู้" ไม่ใช่เติมหน้าทุกคำได้เสมอ   การมองโครงสร้างแบบผ่านกระบวนการของ Sapir
จะพบปัญหามาก ถ้าตามกระบวนการการเติม บางทีคำออกมาจะผิด พบว่าคนไทยไม่มีการใช้แบบนี้ การมอง "นัก" และ "ผู้" เป็น
อุปสรรค (Prefix) ซึ่งไม่ได้โยงความหมายหรือมโนทัศน์เข้าไปในอุปสรรค ดังนั้นจากกระบวนการอย่างเดียวไม่สามารถอธิบายได้ว่า
ทำไมบางคำออกมาแล้วใช้ได้ บางคำ ออกมาแล้วใช้ไม่ได้

เพราะฉะนั้น ดิฉันคิดว่าการจัดสถานะหน่วยคำให้ "นัก" และ "ผู้" เป็นอุปสรรค (Prefix)ไม่ค่อยเหมาะสม และกระบวนการ
การเติมปัจจัย (Affixation) อาจไม่ใช่แนวคิดที่ดีที่จะวิเคราะห์การสร้างคำในกรณีนี้

Item-and-Arrangement Morphology

Bloomfield มองว่าหน่วยคำเป็นรูปทางภาษา ซึ่งหน่วยคำคำหนึ่งจะประกอบเสียงและความหมายที่ต่างกับหน่วยคำอื่นๆ และ
ต้องการให้เสียงกับความหมายตรงกับหน่วยคำที่อ้างถึง (Bloomfield 1933:161) การสร้างคำเกิดจากการเรียงหน่วยคำต่างๆต่อกัน
แต่ละหน่วยคำก็จะโยงกับมโนทัศน์อันหนึ่ง มีความสัมพันธ์แบบหนึ่งต่อหนึ่ง (One-to-one relation) และยังได้นำเรื่องหน่วยศัพท์
(Lexical unite) เข้ามาอธิบายเรื่องหน่วยคำในภาษาด้วย เช่น Root [+PL]
                                                              | |
                                                            dog   s

ถ้าตามแนวคิดนี้หน่วยคำ "นัก" และ "ผู้" มีการแจกความหมายตั้งแต่แรก "นัก" สื่อความหมายเป็นคนที่มีความเชี่ยวชาญ
เฉพาะด้านหรือมีหน้าที่เจาะจง ส่วน "ผู้" มีความหมายอ้างถึงบุคคลทั่วไปหรือสภาพบางอย่าง แล้วค่อยนำไปต่อกับคำอื่นๆอีกทีรวม
เป็นคำใหม่ที่สื่อมโนทัศน์ใหม่

ในกรณีที่มีคำเหมือนกันตามหลัง "นัก" และ "ผู้" ได้

นัก $\begin{bmatrix} +\text{animate} \\ +\text{skill} \end{bmatrix}$ +เขียน:คนที่มีความถนัดเรื่องการเขียน มีผลงานของตัวเอง

+ ศึกษา:คนที่มีหน้าที่ด้านการเรียน อายุไม่มาก เรียนอยู่ที่มหาวิทยาลัย

+ วิจารณ์ :คนที่มีหน้าที่หรือมีความเชี่ยวชาญในการให้คำตัดสิน มีความรู้
เชื่อถือได้

ผู้ $[+\text{animate}]$ +เขียน:คนที่เขียนเรื่องอะไรก็ได้ ไม่ต้องมีความชำนาญด้านนี้

+ ศึกษา:คนที่ทำการศึกษา ไม่ได้มีเงื่อนไขทางด้านหน้าที่หรืออายุ ไม่เก่งก็ได้

+ นักวิจารณ์:คนที่ให้คำตัดสิน ไม่ต้องมีความชำนาญด้านนี้ อาจจะพูดตาม
ใจตัวเอง ไม่น่าเชื่อถือก็ได้

ในกรณีที่มีคำเหมือนกันตามหลัง "นัก" และ "ผู้" ไม่ได้

นัก $\begin{bmatrix} +\text{animate} \\ +\text{skill} \end{bmatrix}$ + บิน:คนที่มีความเชี่ยวชาญด้านการขับเครื่องบิน ทำเป็นอาชีพ

+ เทนนิส:คนที่มีความเชี่ยวชาญในการเล่นกีฬาประเภทนี้ ทำเป็นอาชีพ

ผู้ $[+\text{animate}]$ + หญิง:อ้างถึงคนที่มีสภาพความเป็นหญิง

+ ด้อยโอกาส:คนที่ขาดโอกาสในด้านต่างๆ ไม่ได้เปรียบในด้านต่างๆ

คำ "*ผู้บิน *ผู้เทนนิส" ที่ใช้ไม่ได้ เพราะว่าในตัว "ผู้" ไม่มีความหมายสื่อถึงเรื่องความชำนาญหรือความถนัด ดังนั้นใช้คู่กับ "ผู้" ไม่ได้ ส่วน "*นักหญิง *นักด้อยโอกาส" อ้างถึงสภาพหรือลักษณะบุคคล ซึ่ง"นัก"ไม่มีการอ้างถึงสภาพของผู้คน จึงใช้คู่กันไม่ได้

จากคำที่พบในฐานข้อมูล "นัก" และ "ผู้" มีตำแหน่งการเกิดต่างกัน แต่บางกรณีมีการทับซ้อนกัน เช่น "นัก" อยู่หน้าคำนาม กับคำกริยา "ผู้" ส่วนมากอยู่หน้าคำกริยา รองมาเป็นคำวิเศษ ไม่ค่อยอยู่หน้าคำนาม เมื่อผสมกับคำนามหรือคำวิเศษ "นัก" และ "ผู้" แทนที่กันไม่ได้ ต้องเลือกตามความหมาย เป็นความสัมพันธ์แบบสับหลีก(Complementary distribution) เมื่อผสมกับคำกริยาส่วน มากแทนที่กันได้ แต่ความหมายต่างกัน

จากนี้ให้เห็นว่า ไม่ว่าในกรณีหนึ่งหรือสอง แนวคิด IAM สามารถอธิบายและควบคุมสถานการณ์ต่างๆได้ ทั้งในเรื่องการสื่อ ความหม ยและความถูกผิดการใช้ภาษาก็ตาม การใส่มในทัศน์ให้กับหน่วยต่างๆได้ช่วยการวิเคราะห์หน่วยคำเหล่านี้อย่างชัดเจน

จากการเปรียบเทียบสองแนวทางนี้ แสดงให้เห็นว่าตามแนวของ Sapir หน่วยคำ "นัก" และ "ผู้" จะถูกมองเป็นอุปสรรค ต้องผ่านกระบวนการการเติม (Affixation) เพื่อสร้างคำใหม่และแสดงความหมายใหม่ แต่การมองกระบวนการการเติมอย่างเดียว ไม่สามารถอธิบายด้วยว่าความหมายต่างกันอย่างไร ทำไมบางโครงสร้างใช้ได้ แต่บางโครงสร้างใช้แล้วผิด ส่วน Bloomfield จะจัด หน่วยคำ "นัก" และ "ผู้" เป็นหน่วยที่มีความหมายอยู่ในตัวตน เอาความหมายและหน่วยต่างๆต่อกัน เพื่อสร้างคำใหม่และมโนทัศน์ ใหม่ ตามแนวคิด Bloomfield การสร้างคำด้วยหน่วยคำ "นัก" และ "ผู้" มีความคล้ายคึงกับวิธีการสร้างคำประสม (Compound) ซึ่ง มีหน้าตาคล้ายกับหน่วยสร้างเข้าศูนย์ (Endocentric construction) โดย "นัก" และ "ผู้" ทำหน้าที่คล้ายกับส่วนหลัก (Head) ของคำและ มีส่วนตามเป็นส่วนเติมเต็ม (Complement) แต่เหตุผลที่ไม่ใช่คำประสม เพราะว่าในการสร้างคำประสม แต่ละส่วนที่รวมกันต้องเป็น หน่วยคำอิสระหรือคำที่สามารถอยู่เดี่ยวได้ และค่อยรวมเป็นคำใหม่ ซึ่งความหมายที่เกิดใหม่ไม่สามารถตีความจากส่วนใดส่วนหนึ่ง อย่างโดยตรง

การศึกษาหน่วยคำโดยเปรียบเทียบสองแนวคิด ให้เห็นว่าในการวิเคราะห์การสร้างคำด้วย "นัก" และ "ผู้" ในภาษาไทย ยึด ตามแนวคิด Item-and-Arrangement Morphology ของ Bloomfield เหมาะสมกว่า ถึงแม้ว่ามีหนังสือและนักภาษาศาสตร์มองว่าแนวคิด

Bloomfield มีข้อค้อยอยู่ เช่นบางกรณีหน่วยหนึ่งอาจจะสื่อมโนทัศน์หรือทำหน้าที่มากว่าหนึ่ง หรือบางที่ต้องการหลายๆหน่วยรวม กันเพื่อสื่อมโนทัศน์เดียว หรือบางครั้งไม่สามารถแยกแต่ละหน่วยอย่างชัดเจนว่าหน่วยใดทำหน้าที่หรือสื่อความหมายอะไร การมอง ความสัมพันธ์แบบหนึ่งต่อหนึ่งก็จะเจอปัญหาอย่างมาก อย่างไรก็ตาม ตามการแบ่งประเภทของภาษา ภาษาไทยจัดอยู่ในประเภท ภาษาคำโดด ซึ่งไม่มีการใช้หน่วยคำเติมหรือการเปลี่ยนรากคำ โดยปกติหนึ่งหน่วยคำก็เท่ากับหนึ่งคำและได้แทนความหมายอย่างหนึ่ง ดังนั้นเมื่อนำแนวคิด IAM มาวิเคราะห์ภาษาคำโดด ความสัมพันธ์แบบหนึ่งต่อหนึ่งก็ไม่เจอปัญหาที่กล่าวถึง กลับมายังช่วยในการ แยกความหมายของแต่ละหน่วยได้ดีและเมื่อผสมคำขึ้นมาก็แบ่งส่วนได้อย่างชัดเจน จึงได้แก้ไขปัญหาที่พบในแนวคิดของ Sapir

ในการวิเคราะห์เรื่องโครงสร้างคำในภาษาไทย ปัจจุบันพบว่า "นัก" ไม่สามารถอยู่เดี่ยวได้ แต่ "ผู้" อยู่เดี่ยวได้ในบางกรณี จากตรงนี้ยังบอกไม่ได้ว่า เดิมทีสองหน่วยคำนี้เป็นคำมาก่อนหรือไม่ อย่างเช่น มีใช้กับคำอื่นบ่อยๆ จึงเกิดการหลอมรวม (Fusion) ทำให้ความเป็นอิสระ (Autonomy) ของตัวเองลดลงไปจนกลายเป็นคำเดียวกัน (Lexicalization) ในที่สุดไม่สามารถแยกจากกันได้อีก ตรงนี้เราจะต้องย้อนกลับไปดูประวัติความเป็นมาหรือวิวัฒนาการของหน่วยคำเหล่านี้ ว่าจากอดีตจนถึงปัจจุบันมีอะไรเกิดขึ้นบ้าง และยังมีวิธีอื่นๆที่สามารถนำมาอธิบายได้ด้วย อย่างเช่น คลังข้อมูลร่วมสมัยและข้ามสมัย ซึ่งมีการขยายส่วนประกอบให้หัววิเคราะห์ จากคำไปสู่วลีหรือประโยค ให้เห็นว่ามีกระบวนการกลายเป็นรูปไวยากรณ์ (Grammaticalization) เกิดขึ้นในหน่วยคำ "นัก" และ "ผู้" หรือไม่ ส่วนสมมุติฐานเหล่านี้อาจนำไปศึกษาเพิ่มเติมในเวลาต่อไป

บรรณานุกรม

[1] Bloomfield, Leonard. Language [M]. New York: Holt, 1933.

[2] Eulalia Bonet. Item-and-Arrangement or Item-and-Process [J]. Cuademos de Linguistica XV, 2008.

[3] Shoichi Iwasaki & Preeya Ingkaphirom. A Reference Grammar of Thai [M]. Cambridge University Press, 2005.

[4] Sapir, Edward. Language [M]. New York: Harcout, Brace& World, 1921.

[5] Stephen R. Anderson. A short History of Morphological Theory [J]. Dept of Linguistics, YaleUniveiseity. [DB/OL].
https://cowgill.ling.yale.edu/sra/short-history.pdf

[6] วิโรจน์ อรุณมานะกุล. ทฤษฎีภาษาศาสตร์ [M]. ภาควิชาภาษาศาสตร์ จุฬาลงกรณ์มหาวิทยาลัย, 2559.

[7] คลังข้อมูลภาษาไทยแห่งชาติ [DB/OL]. http://www.arts.chula.ac.th/~ling/TNCII/

မြန်မာစာရေးသားရာ၌ စာလုံးပေါင်းမှားခြင်း အကြောင်းများလေ့လာချက် *

Li Tangying, Dr. Soe Moe Moe**

စာတမ်းအကျဉ်း

မြန်မာစာရေးသားရာ၌ စာလုံးပေါင်းမှားရခြင်းအကြောင်းများကို အချက်(၅)ချက်ဖြင့် လေ့လာတင်ပြထားပါသည်။ (၁)အသံထွက်ကိုလိုက်၍မှားခြင်းအကြောင်း၌ တစ်ချို့စကားလုံးများသည် အရေးနှင့်အသံတူညီမှုရှိသောကြောင့် အသံထွက်ကိုလိုက်၍ရေးမိသဖြင့် စာလုံးပေါင်း မှားရခြင်းကိုလေ့လာ တင်ပြထားပါသည်။ (၂) အသံပိုခြင်းလျော့၍မှားခြင်း၌ ဟထိုးသံပို၍ မှားခြင်း၊ ဟထိုးသံလျော့၍မှားခြင်းတို့ကို တင်ပြထားပါသည်။ (၃) အသံတူအရေးကွဲ၍ မှားခြင်း၌ အရစ်မှားခြင်း၊ အသတ်မှားခြင်းတို့ကို တင်ပြထားပါသည်။ (၄) ရေးချပိုခြင်းလျော့၍ မှားခြင်း၌ ရေးချလိုသော စကားလုံးတို့၌ ရေးချထည့်မိခြင်း၊ ရေးချလိုသော စကားလုံးများ၌ ရေးချမထည့်မိခြင်းတို့ကြောင့် မှားရခြင်းတို့ကို တင်ပြထားပါသည်။ (၅) အသုံးမှားခြင်းဟူ၍ စကားလုံးများ၏ အနက်အဓိပ္ပါယ်နှင့် အသုံးများကို လေ့လာတင်ပြထားပါသည်။

သော့ချက်ဝေါဟာရများ–အသံထွက်၊ အသံပိုခြင်းလျော့ခြင်း၊ အသံတူအရေးကွဲ၊ အသုံးမှားခြင်း

နိဒါန်း

ဘာသာစကားတွင် အပြောဘာသာစကား(Spoken Language)နှင့်အရေးဘာသာစကား (Written language)ဟူ၍ နှစ်မျိုးရှိပါသည်။ ဘာသာစကားပြောဆို ရေးသားရာ၌ ဝါကျ (Sentence) တစ်ခုဖြစ်ရန် စကားလုံးများ (words)၊ ပုဒ်စုများ(phrases)၊ ဝါကျခွဲများ (clauses)စသည်တို့ ပါဝင်ရမည်ဖြစ်ပါသည်။ ၎င်းတို့တွင်

* 论文题目: 缅语书写中的易错字研究。本文系云南大学人文社会科学青年研究基金项目 "云南大学缅语专业学生专业素质培养实践与探索"（16YNUHSS013）项目的阶段性成果。

**【作者简介】李堂英（Li Tangying）: 云南大学外国语学院缅甸语系讲师。研究方向: 缅甸语言文化。梭莫莫（Dr. Soe Moe Moe）: 缅甸曼德勒外国语大学缅甸语系教授。研究方向: 缅甸语言文化

အခြေခံအကျဆုံးအပိုင်းမှာ စကားလုံးဖြစ်ပါသည်။ စကားလုံး အဆင့်တွင် စာလုံးပေါင်း(spelling)သတ်ပုံမှန်ကန်မှု ရှိမှသာ ဆိုလိုသည့်အနက်အဓိပ္ပာယ်ကို ဖော်ဆောင်နိုင်မည်ဖြစ်သောကြောင့် ဤစာတမ်းကို ရေးသားရခြင်းဖြစ်ပါသည်။

၁။ အသံထွက်ကိုလိုက်၍မှားခြင်း

မြန်မာစာတွင် "ရေးတော့အမှန်၊ ဖတ်တော့အသံ"ဟူသော ဆိုရိုးရှိသောကြောင့် အသံထွက်ကိုလိုက်၍ စာလုံးပေါင်းမှားတတ်ကြပါသည်။ လေ့လာတွေ့ရှိရသော စကားလုံး များတွင် "ကတိကဝတ်"စကားလုံးကို အသံထွက်ရာ၌ "ဂတိဝဝတ်"ဟူ၍အသံထွက်ရပါသည်။ ထို့ကြောင့် "က"နေရာများ၌ "ဂ" ဖြင့်အသံထွက်ရသောကြောင့် "ဂတိဝဝတ်"ဟူ၍ မှားယွင်းစွာ ရေးမိကြသည်။ "ချင်း" စကားလုံးကို အသံထွက်ရာ၌လည်း "ဂျင်း"ဟုထွက်ရပါသည်။ ထို့ကြောင့် "ချင်း"ကို "ဂျင်း"ဟူ၍မှားယွင်းစွာရေးမိကြပါသည်။ "ဖြည်းဖြည်း"စကားလုံးကိုလည်း အမှန်တကယ်အသံထွက်မည်ဆိုပါက "ဖြီးဖြီး"ဟူ၍ အသံထွက်မည်ဖြစ်ပါသည်။ သို့သော် မြန်မာဘာသာစကား၌ "ဖြီးဖြီး"ဟုမထွက်ဘဲ "ဖြေးဖြေး"ဟူ၍ အသံထွက်ရ သောကြောင့် အသံထွက်အတိုင်း "ဖြေးဖြေး"ဟူ၍ရေးမိကြသဖြင့် စာလုံးပေါင်း မှားရခြင်းဖြစ်ပါသည်။

သာဓက–

စာလုံးပေါင်းအမှား	စာလုံးပေါင်းအမှန်
ဂတိဝဝတ်	ကတိကဝတ်
ဂျင်း	ချင်း
ဖြေးဖြေး	ဖြည်းဖြည်း

၂။ အသံပို၍လျော့၍မှားခြင်း

ဤ၌အမှားမျိုး၌ အထူးသဖြင့် ဟထိုး(ှ)သံ ပို၍လျော့၍ရွတ်ဆိုမိရာမှ စာလုံးပေါင်း မှားခြင်း မျိုးဖြစ်သည်။

၂.၁။ ဟထိုးသံပို၍မှားခြင်း

ဟထိုးသံ(ှ)မပါသောစကားလုံးများတွင် ဟထိုးသံများထည့်၍ ရေးမိသောကြောင့် စာလုံးပေါင်း မှားရခြင်းဖြစ်သည်။ လေ့လာတွေ့ရှိရသော စကားလုံးများတွင် "ကောက်နုတ်ချက်"စကားလုံးကို အဘိဓာန်တွင် "ကောက်နှုတ်ချက်"ဟုပင်အသံထွက် သော်လည်း ခွင်း၊ ပါးစပ်ဟု အဓိပ္ပာယ်ရသော "နှုတ်"နှင့်မှားယွင်းကာ "ကောက်နှုတ်ချက်" ဟု ထွက်တတ်ကြသဖြင့် စာလုံးပေါင်းမှားရခြင်းဖြစ်သည်။ "မြှား"စကားလုံးကို အသံထွက် ရာ၌ "မျှား"ဟုအသံထွက်ရသောကြောင့်၊ "မြှား"

ဟူ၍အသံထွက်အတိုင်း ရေးမိကြသဖြင့် စာလုံးပေါင်းမှားတတ်ကြသည်။ "ခေတ်မီ" စကားလုံးကို အဘိဓာန်တွင် "ခေတ်မီ" ဟူ၍ပင်ထွက်သော်လည်း ခေတ်ကို အမီလိုက်သည်ဟူသောသဘောဖြင့် "ခေတ်မှီ"ဟူ၍ အသံထွက်ရေးသားကြရမှ စာလုံးပေါင်းမှားရခြင်းဖြစ်ကြောင်း တွေ့ရှိရပါသည်။

သာဓက–

စာလုံးပေါင်းအမှား	စာလုံးပေါင်းအမှန်
ကောက်နုတ်ချက်	ကောက်နုတ်ချက်
ခေတ်မှီ	ခေတ်မီ
မြှား	မြှား

၂။၂။ ဟထိုးသံလျော့၍မှားခြင်း

ဟထိုးသံ(ှ)ပါသော စကားလုံးများကို ဟထိုးသံလျော့၍ ရေးမိသောကြောင့်စာလုံးပေါင်းမှားရခြင်း ဖြစ်သည်။ လေ့လာတွေ့ရှိရသောစကားလုံးများတွင် "ကိုယ်စားလှယ်"ကို "ကိုယ်စားလည်" ဟူ၍ပင် ပြောဆိုလေ့ရှိကြသောကြောင့်၊ ဟထိုးသံဖြုတ်၍ "ကိုယ်စားလည်" ဟုရေးသားမိသောကြောင့်၊ စာလုံးပေါင်းမှားရခြင်း ဖြစ်သည်။ "လျော့"ကို အသံထွက်ရာ၌ "ယော့" ဟူ၍ အသံထွက်ရသောကြောင့် "လျော့ဈေး" ဟုရေးသားရာ၌ ဟထိုးသံဖြုတ်၍ "လျော့ဈေး" ဟူ၍ ရေးမိကြသောကြောင့်၊ စာလုံးပေါင်းမှားရခြင်း ဖြစ်သည်။ "လျှမ်း" စကားလုံးကို အသံထွက်ရာ၌လည်း "ယှုန်း" ဟူ၍ အသံထွက်ရပါသည်။ ထို့ကြောင့်၊ "လျှမ်းလျှမ်းတောက်" စကားလုံးကို ရေးသားရာ၌ ဟထိုးသံမပါဘဲ"လျှမ်းလျှမ်းတောက်" ဟူ၍ ရေးလေ့ရှိသောကြောင့်၊ စာလုံးပေါင်းမှားရခြင်း ဖြစ်ပါသည်။

သာဓက–

စာလုံးပေါင်းအမှား	စာလုံးပေါင်းအမှန်
ကိုယ်စားလည်	ကိုယ်စားလှယ်
လျော့ဈေး	လျှော့ဈေး
လျမ်းလျမ်းတောက်	လျှမ်းလျှမ်းတောက်

၃။ အသံတူအရေးကွဲ၍မှားခြင်း

မြန်မာစာတွင် အသံထွက်တူသော်လည်း စာလုံးပေါင်းမတူသဖြင့် အနက်အဓိပ္ပာယ် ကွဲပြားသောစကားလုံးများ

ရှိပါသည်။ အသံတစ်သံတည်းကို စာလုံးပေါင်းနှစ်မျိုးဖြင့် ရေးနိုင်သောကြောင့် စာလုံးပေါင်းမှားရခြင်းဖြစ်သည်။

၃၊၁။ အရစ်မှားခြင်း

မြန်မာစာအရေးအသား၌ ယပင့်(ျ)နှင့် ရရစ်(ြ)ဟူ၍ အရစ်နှစ်မျိုးရှိသည်။ ထိုအရစ်များနှင့် ရေးသော စကားလုံးတို့သည် အသံတစ်သံတည်းထွက်ရသောကြောင့် စာလုံးပေါင်း မှားရခြင်းဖြစ်သည်။

၃၊၁၊၁။ ယပင့်(ျ)နှင့်ရေး၍မှားခြင်း

စာလုံးပေါင်း၌ ယရစ် (ြ)နှင့်ရေးရမည်ကို ယပင့် (ျ)ဖြင့် ရေးမိ၍မှားရခြင်း ဖြစ်သည်။ မြန်မာစာ၌ စာလုံးပေါင်းကိုယပင့်နှင့်ရေးသည်ဖြစ်စေ၊ ရရစ်နှင့်ရေးသည်ဖြစ်စေ အသံထွက်တူသော်လည်း အဓိပ္ပာယ်မှာကွဲပြားမှုရှိသည်ကို သတိမမူမိသောကြောင့်၊ အရစ် မှား၍ ရေးမိကြခြင်းဖြစ်သည်။ လှပတင့်တယ်သော၊ အချိုးအစားကျသောဟု အဓိပ္ပာယ်ရသော "ကြော့" ကို "ကျော့" ဟူ၍ အရစ်မှားရေးမိပါက နောက်ထပ်တစ်ကြိမ် ထပ်၍လုပ်သည်။ တိရစ္ဆာန်များကို ထောင်ဖမ်းသော ကျော့ကွင်းဟူသော အဓိပ္ပာယ်ကို သက်ရောက်စေသောကြောင့်၊ ဂရုစိုက်ရမည်အချက်ဖြစ်သည်။ ထို့အတူ နေရာအနှံ့ရောက်အောင်ပို့သည်ဟု အနက်ရသော "ဖြန့်ဖြူး" ကို "ဖြန့်ဖျူး" ဟု အရစ်မှားရေးမိပါက မြန်မာစကား၌ အသုံးမရှိ သောကြောင့်၊ စာလုံးပေါင်းမှားယွင်းသည်အထိဖြစ်နိုင်ပါသည်။ ထို့အတူ ကြွင်းကျန်စေသည်။ ချန်စေသည်ဟု အဓိပ္ပာယ်ရသော "ခြွင်းချက်" ကို အရစ်မှား၍ "ချွင်းချက်" ဟု ရေးမိပါက မြန်မာစာ၌ အသုံးမရှိသောကြောင့် စာလုံးပေါင်းမှားယွင်းသည်အထိ ဖြစ်ရသည်။

သာဓက–

စာလုံးပေါင်းအမှား	စာလုံးပေါင်းအမှန်
ကျော့ရှင်း	ကြော့ရှင်း
ဖြန့်ဖျူး	ဖြန့်ဖြူး
ချွင်းချက်	ခြွင်းချက်

၃၊၁၊၂။ ယရစ် (ြ)နှင့်ရေး၍မှားခြင်း

စာလုံးပေါင်း၌ ယပင့် (ျ)နှင့်ရေးရမည်ကို ယရစ် (ြ)ဖြင့် ရေးမိ၍မှားရခြင်း ဖြစ်သည်။ လေ့လာတွေ့ရှိချက်အနေဖြင့်၊ ယပင့်နှင့်ရေးရသည့်စကားလုံးဖြစ်သော တာဝန်ဝတ္တရားများ ပြီးမြောက်အောင်လုပ်သည်ဟု အနက်ရသော "ကျေပွန်" မှ

"ကျေ"ကို ယရစ်နှင့် "ကြေ"ဟု ရေးမိပါက မြန်မာစာ၌ အသုံးမရှိသောစကားလုံးအဖြစ် စာလုံးပေါင်းမှားနိုင်ပါသည်။ ထို့အတူ "ချက်ချင်း"ဟူသောစကားလုံး၌လည်း "ချက်ခြင်း"ဟု ရေးမိပါက မဆိုင်းမင့်ဟူသော အဓိပ္ပာယ် အစား အချက်တစ်ခုခြင်းဟူသောအကြောင်းအရာ အဖြစ်အပျက်များကို ပြဆိုသော နောက်ဆက်"ခြင်း"ဖြင့် ရေးမိသောကြောင့် စာလုံးပေါင်း မှားနိုင်ပါသည်။ ထို့ပြင် ကြည်ရှုစောင့်ရှောက်သည်ဟု အဓိပ္ပာယ်ရသော "ထိန်းကျောင်း" စကားလုံးမှ "ကျောင်း"ကို ယရစ်ဖြင့် "ကြောင်း"ဟုရေးမိပါက စာလုံးပေါင်းမှားသဖြင့် အနက်လည်း ပြောင်းသွားမည်ဖြစ်ပါသည်။

သာဓက–

စာလုံးပေါင်းအမှား	စာလုံးပေါင်းအမှန်
ကြေပွန်	ကျေပွန်
ချက်ခြင်း	ချက်ချင်း
ထိန်းကြောင်း	ထိန်းကျောင်း

၃၊၂။ အသတ်မှားခြင်း

မြန်မာစာရေးသားရာ၌ ဗျည်းအားလုံးကို အသတ်(်)စကားလုံးများအဖြစ် အသုံးပြုနိုင်သည်။ အသတ်စကားလုံးတစ်ချို့တွင် အသတ်မတူသော်လည်း အသံထွက်တူသောစကားလုံးများရှိသောကြောင့် စာလုံးပေါင်း မှားရခြင်းဖြစ်သည်။

၃၊၂၊၁။ "ပ"သတ် (−ပ်)နှင့် "တ"သတ် (−တ်)မှားခြင်း

အသတ်စကားလုံးတို့၌ ပသတ်(−ပ်)နှင့် တသတ်(−တ်)တို့သည်အသံထွက် တူသောအသတ်များဖြစ်၍ မှားရခြင်းဖြစ်သည်။ လေ့လာတွေ့ရှိရသောစကားလုံးများတွင် ပြုလုပ်နေဆဲပစ္စည်းတစ်ခုခုကို ပြီးဆုံးစေသည်ဟု အနက်ရသော "အစသတ်"စကားလုံးကို "သပ်"ဖြင့် "အစသပ်" ဟုရေးမိပါက စာလုံးပေါင်းမှား၍ ဆိုလိုသည့်အဓိပ္ပာယ်ကို ရောက်ရှိနိုင်မည်မဟုတ်ပေ။ ထို့အတူ နောက်ဆုံးအဆင့်ချောအောင် ပြုလုပ်သည်ဟု အဓိပ္ပာယ်ရသော "အချောသပ်" စကားလုံးကို "သတ်"ဖြင့် "အချောသတ်" ဟုရေးမိပါက စာလုံးပေါင်းမှားပြီး အဓိပ္ပာယ်လည်းလွဲနိုင်ပါသည်။ "အစိပ်အကျဲ" စကားလုံးကိုလည်း "အစိတ်အကျဲ"ဟု ရေးမိပါက စာလုံးပေါင်းမှားယွင်းပြီး ဆိုလိုသည့် အဓိပ္ပာယ်လည်း လွဲနိုင်ပါသည်။

သာဓက–

စာလုံးပေါင်းအမှား   စာလုံးပေါင်းအမှန်

အစသပ်   အစသတ်

————   ————

အချောသတ်   အချောသပ်

အစိတ်အကျ   အစိပ်အကျဲ

၃၊၂၊၂။ "န"သတ် (–န်)နှင့် "မ"သတ် (–မ်)မှားခြင်း

အသတ်စကားလုံးတို့၌ နသတ် (–န်)နှင့် မသတ်(–မ်)တို့.သည် အသံထွက်တူသော အသတ်များဖြစ်၍ မှားရခြင်းဖြစ်သည်။ လေ့လာတွေ့ရှိရသောစကားလုံးများတွင် မဆင်မခြင် ထင်ရာပြုသည်ဟု အဓိပ္ပာယ်ရသော "ရမ်းကား"စကားလုံးကို "ရန်းကား"ဟု စာလုံးပေါင်း မှား၍ ရေးတတ်ကြသည်။ စည်းကားသိုက်မြှိုက်စွာ ကျင်းပသည့်ပွဲလမ်းဟု အဓိပ္ပာယ်ရသော "အခမ်းအနား"ကို "အခန်းအနား"ဟု စာလုံးပေါင်းမှား၍ ရေးမိတတ်ကြသည်ကိုလည်း တွေ့ရပါသည်။ ထို့အတူ အခန်းကြီးဟု အဓိပ္ပာယ်ရသော "ခန်းမ"ကို "ခမ်းမ"ဟူ၍ စာလုံးပေါင်းမှား၍ ရေးမိတတ်ကြသည်ကိုလည်း တွေ့ရပါသည်။

သာဓက–

စာလုံးပေါင်းအမှား   စာလုံးပေါင်းအမှန်

ရန်းကား   ရမ်းကား

အခန်းအနား   အခမ်းအနား

————   ————

ခမ်းမ   ခန်းမ

၃၊၂၊၃။ "င"သတ် (–င်)နှင့် "ညကလေး"သတ် (–ဉ်)မှားခြင်း

အသတ်စကားလုံးတို့၌ ငသတ်(–င်)နှင့် ညကလေးသတ် (–ဉ်)တို့.သည် အသံထွက် တူသော အသတ်များဖြစ်၍ မှားရခြင်းဖြစ်သည်။ လေ့လာတွေ့.ရှိရသော စကားလုံးများတွင် ကျဉ်းကျပ်သောဟု အဓိပ္ပာယ်ရသည် "ကျဉ်းကျပ်"စကားလုံးကို "ကျင်းကျပ်"ဟူ၍ စာလုံးပေါင်းမှားယွင်းပြီး ရေးတတ်ကြပါသည်။ ထို့ပြင် ခွဲထားသော

ခြေတစ်ချောင်းပေါ်သို့ အခြားခြေတစ်ချောင်းကို ခွေ၍ထပ်တင်သည်ဟု အဓိပ္ပာယ်ရသော "တင်ပျဉ်ခွေ" စကားလုံးကိုလည်း "တင်ပျင်ခွေ"ဟု၍ စာလုံးပေါင်းများယွင်းပြီး ရေးတတ်ကြသည်ကို တွေ့ရပါသည်။ ထို့ပြင် အကောင်းဆုံး၊ အတော်ဆုံးအဖြစ် သီးသန့်ရွေးချယ်ထားသော အနက်ရသည် "လက်ရွေးစဉ်"စကားလုံးကိုလည်း "လက်ရွေးစဉ်"ဟူ၍ စာလုံးပေါင်းများပြီး ရေးတတ်ကြသည်ကိုတွေ့ရပါသည်။

သာဓက–

စာလုံးပေါင်းအမှား	စာလုံးပေါင်းအမှန်
ကျင်းကျွတ်	ကျဉ်းကျွတ်
တင်ပျင်ခွေ	တင်ပျဉ်ခွေ
———————	———————
လက်ရွေးစဉ်	လက်ရွေးစင်

၃၊၂၊၄။ "န"သတ် (–န်)နှင့် "သေးသေးတင်" (–ံ)များခြင်း

အသတ်စကားလုံးနသတ်(–န်)နှင့် သေးသေးတင်(–ံ)တို့၏ အသံထွက်မှာတူသောကြောင့် များရှိခြင်း ဖြစ်သည်။ လေ့လာတွေ့ရှိရသော စကားလုံးများတွင် မပျက်စီးလွယ်သော၊ မလှုပ်မရှား၊ မယိုင်မနဲ့ဖြစ်သော "ခိုင်ခံ့"ဟူသောစကားလုံးကိုလည်း "ခိုင်ခန့်"ဟူ၍ စာလုံးပေါင်းများယွင်းစွာ ရေးသားတတ်ကြသည်ကိုတွေ့ရပါသည်။ ထို့ပြင် အကျိုးမဲ့သုံးသည်ဟု အနက်ရသော "သုံးဖြုန်း" စကားလုံးကိုလည်း "သုံးဖြုး" ဟူ၍ စာလုံးပေါင်းများယွင်းစွာ ရေးသားတတ်ကြသည်ကို တွေ့ရပါသည်။ ထို့ပြင် အသင်းအဖွဲ့ စသည်တို့၌ လိုအပ်သည်အခါသုံးရန် စုစောင်းထားသည့် ငွေဖြစ်သော"ရန်ပုံငွေ" စကားလုံးကိုလည်း "ရပုံငွေ"ဟုစာလုံးပေါင်းများကာ ရေးတတ်ကြသည်ကို တွေ့ရပါသည်။

သာဓက–

စာလုံးပေါင်းအမှား	စာလုံးပေါင်းအမှန်
ခိုင်ခန့်.	ခိုင်ခံ့
———————	———————
သုံးဖြုး	သုံးဖြုန်း
ရပုံငွေ	ရန်ပုံငွေ

၃၊၂၊၅။ လုံးကြီးတင်ဆန်ခတ် (–ုံ)နှင့် ညသတ်(–ည်)များခြင်း

သရစကားလုံးဖြစ်သော လုံးကြီးတင်ဆန်ခတ်နှင့် အသတ်စကားလုံးဖြစ်သော ညသတ်(-ည်) တို့၏ အသံထွက်မှာ တူနေသောကြောင့် စာလုံးပေါင်းမှားရခြင်းဖြစ်သည်။ လေ့လာတွေ့ရှိရသောစကားလုံးများတွင် ညီညွတ်သည်၊ပူးပေါင်းသည်ဟု အဓိပ္ပါယ်ရသော "စည်းလုံး"စကားလုံးကို"စီးလုံး" ဟူ၍ စာလုံးပေါင်းမှားယွင်းကာ ရေးတတ်ကြသည်ကို တွေ့ရပါသည်။ ထို့အပြင် တစ်ဦးနှင့်တစ်ဦး ကြင်ဖော်အဖြစ် အထူးရည်မှန်းထားသူဟု အဓိပ္ပါယ် ရသည့် "ရည်းစား"စကားလုံးကိုလည်း "ရီးစား"ဟူ၍ စာလုံးပေါင်းမှားယွင်းကာ ရေးတတ်ကြ သည်ကို တွေ့ရပါသည်။ ထိုအတူ ဆင်၊ မြင်းစီး၍တစ်ယောက်ချင်း တိုက်သည်ဟု အဓိပ္ပါယ် ရသော"စီးချင်းထိုး"စကားလုံးက"စည်းချင်းထိုး" ဟူ၍ စာလုံးပေါင်းမှားယွင်းကာ ရေးတတ်ကြ သည်ကို လေ့လာတွေ့ရှိရပါတယ်။

သာဓက-

စာလုံးပေါင်းအမှား	စာလုံးပေါင်းအမှန်
စီးလုံး	စည်းလုံး
ရီးစား	ရည်းစား
———————	———————
စည်းချင်းထိုး	စီးချင်းထိုး

၃၊၂၊၆။ ဒရရစ် (ြ)နှင့် ညမှားခြင်း

ဒရရစ်(ြ)နှင့် ရေးသော စကားလုံးနှင့် ညဖြင့်ရေးသော စကားလုံးတို့သည် အသံတူတတ်သောကြောင့် စာလုံးပေါင်းမှားရခြင်းဖြစ်သည်။ လေ့လာတွေ့ရှိရသော စကားလုံးများတွင် လူအများသိအောင်လုပ်သည်ဟု အဓိပ္ပါယ်ရသော "ကြော်ငြာ"စကားလုံးကို "ကြော်ညာ"ဟူ၍ စာလုံးပေါင်းမှားယွင်းကာ ရေးတတ်သည်ကိုတွေ့ရပါသည်။ ထိုအတူ ဟစ်အော်ကြွေးကြော်၍ ပတ်ဝန်းကျင်ကို လှုံ့ဆော်သည်ဟု အဓိပ္ပါယ်ရသော "ငြာသံပေး" စကားလုံးကိုလည်း "ညာသံပေး" ဟူ၍ စာလုံးပေါင်းမှားကာရေးတတ်ကြပါသည်။ ထိုပြင် ကိုယ်စိတ်ဆင်းရဲကြောင်း ထုတ်ဖော်မြည်တမ်းသည်ဟု အဓိပ္ပါယ်ရသော "ညည်းည။" စကားလုံးကို "ဦးည။"ဟူ၍စာလုံးပေါင်းမှားယွင်းကာ ရေးမိတတ်သည်ကို လေ့လာတွေ့ရှိ ရပါသည်။

သာဓက

စာလုံးပေါင်းအမှား	စာလုံးပေါင်းအမှန်
ကြော်ညာ	ကြော်ငြာ
ညာသံပေး	ငြာသံပေး
———————	———————
ငြီးညူ	ညည်းညူ

၃၊၂၊၇။ ယ နှင့် ရမှားခြင်း

မြန်မာဗျည်းများဖြစ်သည့် ယပက်လက်(ယ)နှင့်ရကောက်(ရ)တို့ကိုအသံထွက်ရာ၌ ယ/ရ ဟူ၍ပင်ထွက်သောကြောင့် စာလုံးပေါင်းမှားရခြင်းဖြစ်သည်။ လေ့လာတွေ့ရှိရသော စကားလုံးများတွင် တန်းတူအပြိုင်လိုက်လျက်ဟု အဓိပ္ပာယ်ရသော "ရင်ပေါင်တန်း" စကားလုံးကို "ယဉ်ဘောင်တန်း"ဟူ၍ စာလုံးပေါင်းမှားယွင်းကာ ရေးတတ်သည်ကို တွေ့ရပါသည်။ ထို့အပြင် အဝတ်အထည်ရက်လုပ်သော အတတ်ပညာဟု အဓိပ္ပာယ်ရသည့် "ရက်ကန်း"စကားလုံးကို "ယက်ကန်း"ဟူ၍ စာလုံးပေါင်းမှားယွင်းကာ ရေးတတ်သည်ကို တွေ့ရပါသည်။ ထို့အတူ မှန်ကန်ညီညွတ်ခြင်း၊အမှန်အတိုင်းဖြစ်ခြင်းဟု အဓိပ္ပာယ်ရသော "ယထာဘူတ"စကားလုံးကို "ရထာဘူတ"ဟူ၍ စာလုံးပေါင်းမှားယွင်းကာ ရေးတတ်သည်ကို တွေ့ရှိရပါသည်။

သာဓက–

စာလုံးပေါင်းအမှား	စာလုံးပေါင်းအမှန်
ယဉ်ဘောင်တန်း	ရင်ပေါင်တန်း
ယက်ကန်း	ရက်ကန်း
———————	———————
ရထာဘူတ	ယထာဘူတ

၄။ ရေးချ (–ာ)ပို၍လျော့၍မှားခြင်း

မြန်မာဘာသာစကား၌ အသုံးပြုလျက်ရှိသည့် တစ်ချို့သော (ပါဠိ၊ သက္ကတ)ဘာသာ စကားလုံးတို့ကို အသံထွက်ရာတွင် ရေးချ(–ာ)သံများပါဝင်နေတတ်သည်။ ထို့ကြောင့်ရေးချ ပိုခြင်းလျော့ခြင်းဖြစ်ကာ စာလုံးပေါင်းမှားရခြင်းဖြစ်သည်။

၄၊၁။ ရေးချပို၍မှားခြင်း

ရေးချ(—၁)မပါသော စကားလုံးများကို ရေးချ(—၁)ထည့်၍ ရေးမိသောကြောင့် စာလုံးပေါင်း မှားရခြင်း ဖြစ်သည်။ လေ့လာတွေ့ရှိသော စကားလုံးများတွင် သြကာသလောကကြီးတစ်ခုလုံးဟု အဓိပ္ပာယ်ရသော "စကြဝဠာ"စကားလုံးကို "စကြာဝဠာ" ဟူ၍ စာလုံးပေါင်းမှားသွင်းကာ ရေးတတ်ကြသည်ကို တွေ့ရပါသည်။ ထို့အပြင် စိတ်နှလုံးဟု အဓိပ္ပာယ်ရသော "ဟဒယ" စကားလုံးကိုလည်း "ဟာဒယ" ဟူ၍စာလုံးပေါင်းမှားသွင်းကာ ရေးတတ်ကြသည်ကို တွေ့ရပါသည်။ ထို့အတူ အနောင့်အယှက်ပေးရန်ဟု အဓိပ္ပာယ်ရသော "အန္တရာယ်"စကားလုံးကိုလည်း "အန္တာရာယ်" ဟူ၍ စာလုံးပေါင်းမှားသွင်းကာ ရေးတတ်ကြသည်ကို လေ့လာတွေ့ရှိရပါသည်။

သာဓက–

စာလုံးပေါင်းအမှား	စာလုံးပေါင်းအမှန်
စကြာဝဠာ	စကြဝဠာ
ဟာဒယ	ဟဒယ
အန္တာရာယ်	အန္တရာယ်

၄၊၂။ ရေးချလျော့၍မှားခြင်း

ရေးချ(—၁)ပါသော စကားလုံးများကို ရေးချ(—၁)မထည့်ဘဲရေးမိသောကြောင့် စာလုံးပေါင်း မှားရခြင်းဖြစ်သည်။ လေ့လာတွေ့ရှိရသော စကားလုံးများတွင် ဇာတ်လမ်း ဇာတ်ကွက်ဖြင့် ကပြသောပွဲဟု အဓိပ္ပာယ်ရသော"ဇာတ်"စကားလုံးကို "ဇတ်" ဟူ၍ စာလုံးပေါင်း မှားသွင်းကာ ရေးတတ်ကြသည်ကိုတွေ့ရပါသည်။ ထို့အပြင် အပြန်အလှန် ဖွယ်ဖွယ်ရာရာ ပြောသောစကားဟု အဓိပ္ပာယ်ရသော "အာလပသလ္လာပ" စကားလုံးကိုလည်း "အလပသလ္လာပ" ဟူ၍ စာလုံးပေါင်း မှားသွင်းကာ ရေးတတ်ကြသည်ကိုတွေ့ရပါသည်။ ထို့အတူ သစ်ပင်ပန်းမန် စိုက်ပျိုးထားရာနေရာဟု အဓိပ္ပာယ်ရသော "ဥယျာဉ်"ကိုလည်း "ဥယျဉ်" ဟူ၍စာလုံးပေါင်း မှားသွင်းကာ ရေးတတ်ကြသည်ကို လေ့လာတွေ့ရှိရပါသည်။

သာဓက–

စာလုံးပေါင်းအမှား	စာလုံးပေါင်းအမှန်
ဇတ်	ဇာတ်
အလပသလ္လာပ	အာလပသလ္လာပ

ဥယျဉ်   ဥယျာဉ်

၅။ အသုံးမှားခြင်း

မြန်မာဘာသာစကားသည်   ဧကဝဏ္ဏဘာသာစကား   (Monosyllabic   language)   ဖြစ်သောကြောင့်
စကားလုံးတစ်လုံး၊ အသံတစ်ချက်၊ အနက်တစ်ခုရှိသည်။ စကားလုံး တစ်လုံးစီ၏အနက်အဓိပ္ပာယ်နှင့် သတ်မှတ်ထားသော
အသုံးတို့ကို ဂရုမပြုမိ၍ စာလုံးပေါင်း မှားရခြင်းဖြစ်သည်။

၅၊၁။ "ပဲ"နှင့်"ဘဲ" အသုံးမှားခြင်း

"ပဲ"မှာ အနက်စွဲ အရေးဖြစ်သည်။ ပဲကို-

(၁) "ပဲ"ရည်ညွှန်းသောပုဒ်အား လေးနက်သောစကားလုံးအဖြစ်

သာဓက– လူပဲ၊ နတ်ပဲ၊ ကျွန်တော်ပဲ ဟုလည်းကောင်း

(၂) ကြိယာ၊ နာမ်တို့၏အနက်ကို ကန့်သတ်လိုရာ၌ သုံးသောစကားလုံးအဖြစ်

သာဓက– စားပဲစား၊ အိပ်ပဲအိပ်၊ သွားပဲသွား ဟုလည်းကောင်း သုံးလေ့ရှိပါသည်။

"ဘဲ"မှာ   အသံစွဲအရေးဖြစ်သည်။   ဘဲကိုအငြင်းပြုစွဉ်း   "မ"နှင့်   တွဲဖက်၍   ဆန့်ကျင်ခြင်းအနက်ဖြင့်
ဝါကျအချင်းချင်းဆက်ပေးသောစကားလုံးအဖြစ်သုံးသည်။

သာဓက– မသိဘဲ၊ မတတ်ဘဲ၊ မလေ့လာဘဲ ဟူ၍သုံးသည်။

၅၊၂။ "ဖက်"နှင့်"ဘက်"အသုံးမှားခြင်း

"ဖက်"အသုံးကို မှတ်သားရာ၌–

(၁) ကြိယာဖက်အဖြစ် (သာဓက–လိုက်ဖက်၊ ယှဉ်ဖက်၊ တွဲဖက်)ဟုလည်းကောင်း

(၂) အဖော်အဖက်အဓိပ္ပာယ်ဖြင့်(သာဓက– ကြင်ဖော်ကြင်ဖက်၊ လုပ်ဖော်ကိုင်ဖက်၊ ကူဖော်လောင်ဖက်) ဟုလည်းကောင်း

(၃)သင်္ချာနှင့်တွဲသော ဖက်အဖြစ်(သာဓက– တစ်ဖက်တစ်ချက်၊ နှစ်ဦးနှစ်ဖက်၊ သုံးဖက်မြင်)ဟူ၍လည်းကောင်း
သုံးလေ့ရှိပါသည်။

"ဘက်"အသုံးကို မှတ်သားရာ၌–

(၁)အရပ်မျက်နှာနှင့်တွဲလျှင်ဘက်(သာဓက၊ အရှေ့ဘက်၊ အနောက်ဘက်၊တောင်ဘက်) ဟုလည်းကောင်း

(၂)တည်နေရာနှင့်တွဲလျှင်ဘက် (သာဓက–အိမ်ဘက်၊ ကျောင်းဘက်၊ ဈေးဘက်)ဟု လည်းကောင်း

(၃)သူ၊ ငါ၊ ကျား၊ မ စသည့်တို့နှင့်တွဲလျှင် ဘက် (သာဓက–သူ့ဘက်၊ ငါ့ဘက်၊ မိန်းမဘက်) ဟုလည်းကောင်း

(၄)အာဒိ(အစ) စကားလုံးဖြစ်လျှင်ဘက် (သာဓက–ဘက်ကန်၊ ဘက်စုံ၊ ဘက်လိုက်) ဟူ၍လည်းကောင်း သုံးလေ့ရှိသည်ကို မှတ်သားထားရမည်ဖြစ်ပါသည်။

၅၊၃။ "ဖူး" နှင့် "ဘူး" အသုံးမှားခြင်း

"ဖူး"ကို ထိတွေ့ကြုံကြိုက်ရသည့်အခါမျိုးတွင် သုံးသည်။(သာဓက–တွေ့ဖူး၊ စားဖူး၊ သွားဖူး)

"ဘူး"ကို ငြင်းပယ်သောအနက်ဖြင့် ကြိယာကိုထောက်ကူသော စကားလုံး အဖြစ်သုံးသည်။(သာဓက–မမြင်ဘူး၊ မလုပ်ဘူး၊ မစားဘူး)

၅၊၄။ "တ" နှင့် "တစ်" အသုံးမှားခြင်း

"တ"ကို စကားအဆက်အစပ်အနေဖြင့် စကားလုံးဖြစ်အောင်သုံးသည်။ အထူးသဖြင့် ကြိယာဝိသေသန သဘောသက်ရောက်သော ရှေ့ဆက်အဖြစ်သုံးလေ့ရှိသည်။(သာဓက–တငိုငို၊ တရယ်ရယ်၊ တထစ်ချ)

"တစ်"ကို တစ်၊ နှစ်စသောအရေအတွက် အဓိပ္ပာယ်ဆောင်လျှင် သုံးလေ့ရှိသည်။ (သာဓက–တစ်ကိုယ်ကောင်း၊ တစ်ခါတစ်ရံ၊ တစ်စုံတစ်ရာ)

၅၊၅။ "မှ" နှင့် "က" အသုံးမှားခြင်း

"မှ"နှင့် "က"သည် သဒ္ဒါသဘောအရ ထွက်ခွာရာပြပုဒ်များဖြစ်သောကြောင့် အသုံးတူသည်ဟု ယူဆ၍ မှားကြသည်။

"မှ"ကို အရေးတွင်သုံးပြီး ပြုလုပ်သူ၏နေရာတွင်မသုံးရပါ။

သာဓက – အိမ်မှ သွားသည်။ လေဆိပ်မှထွက်ခွာသည်။

– ဆရာကြီးမှ အမှာစကားပြောသည်။ (မှား)

"က"ကို အရေးအပြောနှစ်ခုလုံးတွင် အသုံးပြုနိုင်သည်။ ပြုလုပ်သူ၏နေရာတွင် သုံးသောစကားလုံးဖြစ်သည်။

သာဓက – ဆရာမကြီးအိမ်ကထွက်လာပြီတဲ့။

– ဆရာကြီးက အမှာစကားပြောကြားပါမည်။

၅၊၆။ ဝိုက်ချ(–၁)နှင့်မောက်ချ (–၁)အသုံးမှားခြင်း

ရေးချတွင် ဝိုက်ချ(–၁)နှင့် မောက်ချ (–၁)ဟူ၍နှစ်မျိုးရှိပါသည်။ "ခါ၊ ဂါ၊ င၊ ဒါ၊ ပါ၊ ဝ" ဗျည်း (၆)လုံးတို့ကို ဝိုက်ချမသုံးရပါ။ "ခင်ဦးငါ၊ ဒေါ်ပုံဝ၊ ဝိုက်ချမသုံးရ"ဟု မှတ်သားထား ရပါမည်။ သို့သော် ထိုအက္ခရာ(၆)လုံးတွင် (ျ၊ ြ၊ ့၊ ္)များယှဉ်လာမည်ဆိုပါက ဝိုက်ချနှင့်တွဲသုံးနိုင်ပါသည်။

ခြုံငုံသုံးသပ်ချက်

မြန်မာစာပေရေးသားရာ၌ စာလုံးပေါင်းမှားရခြင်းအကြောင်းများအနက် အသံထွက်ကို လိုက်ရေးမိ၍မှားခြင်း၊ အသံတူအရေးကွဲ၍မှားခြင်း၊ အသံပို၍လျော့၍မှားခြင်း ဟူသော အသံနှင့်ပတ်သက်၍ အမှားများသည်ကိုတွေ့ရှိရပါသည်။ ပါဠိ၊ သက္ကတဘာသာတို့က ဆင်းသက်လာသော စာလုံးပေါင်းများ၌ ရေးပို၍လျော့၍ စာလုံးပေါင်းမှားခြင်းကို တွေ့ရှိ ရပါသည်။ အရေး၊ အပြော အသုံးခွဲခြားထားမှု သန္ဒါအသုံးနှင့်အရာဌာနအလိုက် သတ်မှတ် ထားသောအသုံးများကို မှန်ကန်စွာမသုံးနိုင်ခြင်းကြောင့် စာလုံးပေါင်းမှားရခြင်း ဖြစ်ကြောင်းကိုလည်း တွေ့ရှိရပါသည်။

နိဂုံး

မြန်မာစာတွင် စာလုံးပေါင်းမှားလျှင် အနက်အဓိပ္ပာယ်ကိုပါ ပြောင်းလဲစေနိုင်သောကြောင့် အထက်ပါ လေ့လာတွေ့ရှိချက်များကို မှတ်သားလိုက်နာ၍ရပြုမည်ဆိုပါက စာလုံးပေါင်းသတ်ပုံ အမှားအယွင်းမရှိ မှန်ကန်လာနိုင်မည်ဖြစ်ကြောင်း တင်ပြအပ်ပါသည်။

ကျမ်းကိုးစာရင်း

[1] ခင်မင်၊မောင်၊ခနေဖြူ။ မြန်မာစကား၊ မြန်မာရုပ်ပုံလွှာ[M]။ ရန်ကုန်၊ စာပေဗိမာန်ပုံနှိပ်တိုက်၊ ၁၉၉၈။

[2] မြန်မာစာအဖွဲ့။ မြန်မာ–အင်္ဂလိပ်အဘိဓာန်[M]။ ရန်ကုန်၊ တက္ကသိုလ်များပုံနှိပ်တိုက်၊ ၁၉၉၃။

[3] မြန်မာစာအဖွဲ့။ မြန်မာစာ၊ မြန်မာစကား[M]။ ရန်ကုန်၊ တက္ကသိုလ်များပုံနှိပ်တိုက်၊ ၂၀၀၃။

[4] မြန်မာစာအဖွဲ့။ မြန်မာသဒ္ဒါ[M]။ ရန်ကုန်။ တက္ကသိုလ်များပုံနှိပ်တိုက် ၂၀၀၃။

[5] မြန်မာစာအဖွဲ့။ မြန်မာအဘိဓာန်[M]။ နေပြည်တော်။ ပညာရေးဝန်ကြီးဌာန၊၂၀၁၃။

[6] ဟုတ်စိန်၊ ဦး။ ပါဠိ မြန်မာအဘိဓာန်[M]။ ရန်ကုန်။ ပြည်ထောင်စုမြန်မာနိုင်ငံတော် အစိုးရပုံနှိပ်ရေးနှင့် စာအုပ် ကိရိယာဌာန၊ မ–၁၃၁၃။

Studies on Language Teaching

Role of Reading Aloud in Big Data Aid English Learning Environment[*]

Ma Ling   Xia Aimilun[**]

School of Foreign Languages, Yunnan University,

Kunming Yunnan

Department of College English, Yunnan Univeristy,

Kunming Yunnan

Abstract: This paper reviews the important role that reading aloud plays in college English teaching. Readingaloud is the prerequisite for the realization of EFL listening and speaking. Readingaloud input is optimal language input. It improves students' language proficiency in the long run. In addition, it builds up students' motivation for autonomous learning. It also suggests that reading aloud becomes viable for teaching and learning in big data aid learning environment.

Key words: reading aloud; input; memory; big data

Background of the Study

Reading aloud has been neglected at college English class in the last decade. In the course of college English teaching, teachers pay much attention to the knowledge of grammar, listening, reading and writing (Zhu 2013; Xiang 2010; Huang, 2010). In addition, long-term neglect of English reading aloud training, resulting in a serious lack of language input which leads to inability in speaking and writing. Although students in learning English for many years, even if with a large number of accumulated rich vocabulary, grammar knowledge, have passed through

---

 * 论文题目：朗读在大数据辅助英语学习环境中的作用。

 ** 作者简介：马玲(MaLing)，云南大学外国语学院英语系教授；研究方向：应用语言学；学术英语写作；夏艾米伦(Xia Aimilun)，云南大学大学外语教学部助教；研究方向：应用语言学；语篇分析。

the practical English test or university English four, six levels of tests, the majority of them in the specific communicative environment speak English or write in English in Chinese thinking, consequently their English communicative abilities are comparatively weak. Ai Yi(2007)points out that neglecting reading aloud can lead to poor hearing; ignoring reading aloud can lead to poor oral expression; ignoring reading can lead to poor reading ability. Moreover, since most of the students are influenced by their own dialects, they have shown many problems in pronunciations and tunes(Suzanne, 1992; Zhong 2009). The reason why some students make lots of mistakes during speaking practice and use a large number of Chinglish sentences is that they read aloud less and lack a good sense of English. Reading aloud is a kind of comprehensive practice of pronunciation.

Besides, reading aloud teaching was originally applied in the Chinese language learning, which is a kind of teaching mode for improving learners' language ability. In ancient China, people had paid attention to the reading. Children in the private schools always read the Three-word Confucian classics. So, up to present, reading aloud is one of the efficacious and traditional methods to the mother language teaching (Gao, 2006; Xiang, 2010; Huang 2010).

The Role of Reading Aloud in English Learning

Reading aloud is indispensable to learning English. For many English learners, they spend a lot of time in training their sense of language, speaking like a native speaker is like a distant goal that they can never achieve(Zhu 2013). Reading aloud is a language behavior which requires the reader to speak and listen simultaneously. This is a process of increasing sensibility of characteristic of sound, which is necessary in developing English speaking ability. English is a kind of intonation in language which stress, intonation and rhythm play an important role in their vocal structure (Catherine, 1991; Gao, 2006; Zhong 2009; Zhu 2014). Reading aloud helps to improve proper intonation and pronunciation. When reading the materials aloud, the students actually consider them as language materials, which help to practice their speaking abilities. Reading aloud furnishes second language learners with meaningful contact with the written from of language without causing them to experience frustrations associated with traditional reading instruction content. It increases vocabulary. It improves language and speaking skills (Catherine, 1991; Suzanne1992; Zhu 2014; Lee & Heinz, 2016). Wang (2002) points out that reading aloud can not only enhance memory, but also stimulate and improve the ability of thinking. It is a good way to acquire two languages.

Reading aloud is an understandable input of information and is the key to effective input. Enough comprehensible language input is the precondition of the output (Krachen, 1998). Renandya (2018) indicates that by increasing the amount of interesting and understandable written input without increasing class time, learners had almost doubled the language proficiency gains of those who followed a program involving the same amount of class time but with much less input. Gao (2006) in her empirical research points out that reading aloud is a good comprehensive test tool for English ability. If the students read repeatedly, they can repeatedly deepen the impression of the language input form in the brain. Through reading aloud, the students can store substantial English phrases and sentences in their minds. So when they are using English, these phrases and sentences will pop out and turn into the language for their own use.

In addition, researches suggest reading aloud promotes the memory of brain unconsciously after continuous practices (Zhu 2014). In his empirical study shows that vocabulary, sense of language and application ability of language can be accumulated and improved through reading aloud unconsciously due to the effects of implicit memory. It can be confirmed by a recent research releasing that "Reading out loudly proved to be the best way to remember the information" (UCLA, 2017). Reading aloud, involving speaking and listening activities, can not only help learners improve their English intonation, language sense and conversational skills, but also help them develop their listening skills, increase the power of memory, foster thinking in English way, and improve their language proficiency.

Listening and speaking improvements via reading aloud

Reading aloud is actually a potential practice process for listening (Jiang, 2011). It is helpful to improve both the students' listening and speaking competences. For some students who don't have the confidence to practice spoken English, reading aloud can help them overcome the errors of speech, repeat, improper pause, and develop natural and good pronunciation habit. Reading aloud can not only help them open their mouths, but also improve our oral English evidently. Further, one important benefit of reading aloud as opposed to silent is that reading aloud develops an awareness of sound-symbol texts which expands learners' auditory with the target language by exposing them to words that are not ordinarily heard in spoken. Most feel that ESL students at all levels benefit from reading aloud although they emphasize that reading aloud is always a voluntary activity for individuals in their classes (Huang, 2010; Jiang, 2011; Zhu, 2013).

In the long run, students are no longer strange to a large number of complex sentence patterns by reading aloud, so the quality of hearing will be greatly improved. Reading much and listening much is not only good for memory, but also the level of language sense and fluency will go up step by step. When accumulating to a certain amount, it will come to a successful conclusion. It also can be seen that there is a chain of relationships between reading aloud and listening comprehension. The key element of reading aloud is likely to lead to corresponding changes in other links, which ultimately affect the development of listening ability (Suzanne, 1992; Zhu, 2013).

As far as a learner's oral proficiency is concerned, we pay more attention to accuracy and fluency which lead to the learner's success of communication. "Accuracy refers to the ability to produce language correctly in terms of pronunciation and grammar. We score high on this indicator if our speech or writing is free of language errors. Fluency refers to the ability to express ideas smoothly and to use language resources to sustain the flow of our communication and avoid communication breakdowns" (Renandya, 2018: 2) Accordingly, reading aloud training promotes the development of oral ability in accuracy and fluency. We know that the formation of the sense of language can not be separated from a large number of listening and speaking exercises. In foreign language learning, because of the lack of a large amount of natural contact and the use of foreign languages, conscious listening and speaking exercises are particularly important. Reading aloud has some features of "listening" and "speaking", which are "quasi listening" and "quasi speaking" (Xiang, 2010; Jiang, 2011).

Autonomous Learning in big data aid learning environment

The widely used multimedia and network recently provide a favorable teaching and learning environment. Information Communication Technology (ICT) breakthroughs have brought new opportunities to restructure the language learning/teaching settings. ICT has opened new avenues and brought new challenges to language learners as well as teachers (Ghasemi& Hashemi, 2011). Learning has evolved from traditional methods and has incorporated new tools designed to best fit learners' needs. The traditional learning paradigm involving face-to-face interaction with students is shifting to highly data-intensive electronic learning with the advances in Information and Communication Technology(Teodorescu, 2015; Wu&Chen, 2017). Martins defines E-learning as "intentional use of networked information and communications technology in teaching and learning. E-Learning can be defined in this way too: the application of electronic systems such as internet, computers, multimedia CDs which their aim is to reduce the amount of expenses and goings and comings"(2015: 77).

An important component of the e-learning process is the delivery of the learning contents to their intended audience over a network technology, with distinctive features such as mobility, reachability, personalization, spontaneity, and ubiquity, is widely used to facilitate language teaching and learning(Wu & Chén, 2017). The main advantage of e-learning is that it increases the engagement; attendance and motivation of students which are requisite for learning. Further, it provides convenience for students to access any time, any place(Mohammadia et al. 2011; Martins, 2015).

In the last decades, there has been a steady increase in reported cases of successful high level acquisition by out-of-classroom, informal learners through the affordances of the E-learning. According to cole and Vanderplank(2016), the results reveal how the new affordances for naturalistic learning have transformed informal language learning, enabling significant numbers of independent, informal learners in foreign language contexts to achieve very high levels of proficiency. "With the emergence of the Internet and the concomitant rise of English as a lingua franca, the language has come to have a new functional role in the everyday lives of non-native English users all over the world". (Cole & Vanderplank, 2016: 31).

From CALL (computer assisted language learning) to ICT (information and communicationtechnology), teachers and researchers have long been interested in uses of new technologies in foreign/second language teaching and learning, and not without reason. Marins(2015)classifies different stages of call as follows:

Stage	Technology	Pedagogical approach	Computer use	Teacher role
Behaviourist Structural	Mainframe	Grammar translation andaudiovisual	Translation exercises Drill-and-practice	Only source of information Instructor
Communicative	Personal computer	Communicative approach	Role-plays Textual reconstruction Simulations	Activator Facilitator
Integrative	Multimedia and Web-based apps.	Content-based learning	Authentic social Contexts Exercises combining Reading, Reading, listening and writing	Supervisor Mentor

(Martins, 2015: 78)

From the table we can particularly see that the teacher's role has evolved from instructor to mentor which suggests that learning autonomy becomesthe core in CALL environment. Teachers face challenges of shifting teaching ideology, teaching methods, and teaching content to meet the new needs of learners in the process. Moreover, in the last decade, ICT has become more influential in teaching and learning in terms of:

—Increasing the quality of learning and taught students and students

—Ease of access to a very high volume of information and knowledge available in the world.

—Rapid and timely access to information in very little time

—Reduction of some educational expenses

—Improving the quality, accuracy and scientific texts for academic disciplines

—Indirect creation of learning experiences

—Creating an exact relationship

—Creating an interest in learning

—Increasing learning opportunities

Educators can evaluate students, they have collected the necessary information and appropriate feedback to students presented(Ghasemi & Hashemi, 2011: 3099)

Further, mobile learning has gaining its popularity among young people. Mobile learning, or M-learning, has recently emerged as a new type of learning model which allows learners to obtain learning materials anywhere and anytime using mobile technologies and the internet. The most popular mobile devices consist of smartphones, tablets, laptops, media players, designed as small portable electronic devices, and meant to facilitate sophisticated ways of interacting and communicating (Teodorescu, 2015: 1536). M-learning provides students with the opportunity of transcending the limited space of the classroom, while enhancing learning effectiveness and developing greater autonomy. (Teodorescu, 2015; Wu&Chen2017). M-learning seems to be fit for autonomy because it is claimed to provide greater freedom and flexibility to learn at one's own pace and convenience, whether within the context of a language course or beyond. Educators were particularly interested in technology's interactive capabilities, such as providing immediate feedback and increasing learner autonomy (Ghasemi& Hashemi, 2011). M-learning is incorporated into the teaching/learning process supplements and enriches long-established learning methods, makes learning more accessible and flexible, and enhances learners' autonomy (Cole&Vanderplank, 2016).

Testimonies of advanced English language learners in an English as a Foreign Language (EFL) context suggest that learner autonomy manifested in self-regulated learning activities may be crucial for successful foreign language learning. In the EFL context, learners with a strong sense of autonomy may engage in self-regulated learning activities, and taking control of their learning(Lee&Heinz, 2016: 67).

In order to be a good autonomous one, the learner should make decisions about his/her own learning, he/she should be able to set realistic goals, plan program of work, develop strategies for coping with new and unforeseen situations, evaluate and assess his/her own work and generally to learn how to learn from his/her own successes and failures in ways which will help his/her to be more efficient learners in the future (Haddad, 2016; Lee& Heinz, 2016; Cole&Vanderplank, 2016;). It has been argued that new technologies, in particular computer networks, have the potential to increase learner autonomy when used appropriately. It is the teacher responsibility to foster the student's ability of autonomous learning by designing class activities and create positive atmosphere, a language context and make students want to learn and know how to learn(Haddad, 2016). Zhu(2013)suggests that a good habit of reading aloud can promote the initiation of autonomous learning and thus improve the efficiency of learning English input for the students, but also arouse their initiation for self-practice, self-control and self-adjustment. Multimedia and network can provide vivid audio and visual materials and language environment for students, and let students feel and imitate English, and some phonetic phenomena such as tone, assimilation, loss of blasting can appear in the colloquial language characterized materials. Familiarity with these phenomena and understanding of their changes can make students' pronunciation more authentic. The language environment can deepen the students' understanding of language(Mohammadia, et al 2011; Teodorescu, 2015; Wu&Chen2017).

Feasibility of Reading aloud via online AES System

Automated essay assessment (AEA) systems can provide immediate computer-generated quantitative assessments and qualitative diagnostic feedback on an enormous number of submitted essays (Lu&Li, 2016; Bai&Hu, 2017). The AEA system contributes greatly to improving EFL graduate students' writing, and enhancing their motivation and autonomy in learning English as long as they put enough efforts and time in using it(Ma 2013; Lu&Li, 2016; Bai&Hu, 2017)

Reading aloud is not a learning burden, but a step by step review and consolidation of knowledge method. To accomplish this task, we should first cultivate students' interest of reading, reading aloud and arouse their awareness, to provide some opportunities to improve students' reading ability to read aloud. Traditionally, it is time consuming for the teacher to assign reading aloud tasks. Particularly, it is painstaking to offer feedback objectively and effectively on the tasks. Aiding in big data technology, it becomes an easy access for the teacher to assign the task in a systematic and interesting way. Ma (2013) suggests that E-assessment is becoming increasingly widely used due to its many advantages over traditional paper-based assessment by markers. The advantages mainly comprise instant feedback to students, lower long-term costs, "ensured impartiality, improved reliability, greater storage efficiency, greater flexibility with respect to location" (Ma, 2013: 158). AEA system (*http: www. pigai. org.*)which provides learners plenty of corpus in case of reading aloud, a number of reading materials are offered online by tagging a batch of data, according to the 0 ~ 8 points, two points for each grade, and the scoring machine combines three dimensions(integrity, standard and fluency) and five aspects (right and wrong, missing words, multi word, repeat)to evaluate reading and give the final score.

Therefore, it is easy for teachers to assign 5 to 10 minutes reading passage aloud to the students on *Pigai* learning website each week, the students are required to read as many times as possible on their own without the teachers interference, then they send back their sound recording to the web for evaluation, and feedback is offered instantly. In this way, the feedback affirms their merits, and praises their progresses, so as to enhance their interest in learning. Consequently, students may find it is fun to do it and willing to do it. That means they are stimulated to learn by themselves as well. As a practice, reading aloud can make up with the lack of oral English and listening, for its material has wide range in topic, vocabulary and grammar. In the long run, it may contribute to the improvement of EFL learners' oral and listening proficiency.

Conclusion

In EFL context, a serious lack of language input which leads to inability in speaking and writing. Reading aloud is an understandable input of information and is the key to effective input. Enough comprehensible language input is the precondition of the output. Reading aloud is indispensable to English learning. It is a language behavior which requires the reader to speak and listen simultaneously. This is a process of increasing sensibility of characteristic of sound, which is necessary in developing English speaking ability. English is kind of intonation language which stress, intonation and rhythm play an important role in their vocal structure to improve proper intonation and pronunciation.

Reading aloud is not a learning burden, but a step by step review and consolidation of knowledge. To accomplish this task, we should first cultivate students' interest of reading, reading aloud and arouse their awareness, to provide some opportunities to improve students' reading ability to read aloud. E-learning makes it feasible to cultivate students' autonomy in learning and it is efficient and convenient to have access to plenty of effective input. In a long run, students' language proficiency improves.

参考文献

[1] Bai & Hu, *In the face of fallible AWE feedback: how do students respond?*. Educational Psychology, 2016, 37(1, 67 – 81), DOI: 10. 1080/01443410. 2016. 1223275.

[2] Catherine, *A. Motivating Students through Reading Aloud*[J] The English Journal, 1991(6).

[3] Cole, J & Vanderplank, R. *Evidence for the present-day advantages of informal*,

out-of-class learning[M]. System, 2016(61).

[4] Ghasemi, B. & Hashemi, M. *ICT: Newwave in English language learning/ teaching*[J]. Social and Behavioral Sciences, 2011(15).

[5] Haddad, R. H. *Developing Learner Autonomy in Vocabulary Learning in classroom: How and Why can it be Fostered?* [J]. Procedia-Social and Behavioral Sciences, 2016(232).

[6] Huang, L. *Reading Aloud in the Foreign Language Teaching*[J]. Asian Social science, 2010(6).

[7] HealthDay. University of Waterloo, news release[EB/OL], http://uwaterloo. ca, 2017.

[8] Krashen, S. *Second Language Acquisition*[M]. London: Pengoman Press, 1998.

[9] Lee, J & Heinz, M. *English Language Learning Strategies Reported By Advanced Language Learners* [J]. Journal of International Education Research-Second Quarter 2016(12).

[10] Lu & Li, *Exploring EFL learners' lexical application in AWE-based writing*. In S. Papadima-Sophocleous, L. Bradley & S. Thouësny(Eds), CALL communities and culture-short papers from EUROCALL.

[11] Martins, M. L. *How to effectively integrate technology in the foreign language classroom for learning and collaboration*[J]. Social and Behavioral Sciences, 174(2015).

[12] Ma, K. *Improving EFL Graduate Students' Proficiency in Writing through an Online Automated Essay Assessing System* [J]. English Language Teaching; 2013, 6(7).

[13] Mohammadia. N., Ghorbanib. V. & Hamidiab, V. *Effects of e-learning on Language Learning*[J]Procedia Computer Science, 3(2011).

[14] Renandya, W. A. *WHAT KIND OF ENGLISH PROFICIENCY IS NEEDED FOR EFFECTIVE TEACHING?* (C) paper presented at the Indonesian TESOL Summit, 2018.

[15] Suzanne, M. *Reading Aloud. An Educator Comments*[J]TESOL Quarterly, 1992, 26(4).

[16] Zhu H. X. *Renovating the Traditional Reading Aloud Approach for ESL Autonomous* [C]. Learning Proceedings of the 7th International Conference on Innovation & Management 1913 – 1915, 2013.

[17] Zimmerman, B. J. (2011). *Motivational sources and outcomes of self-regulated*

learning and performance[C]. In Schunk, D. H. & Zimmerman, B. J. (Eds.). Handbook of self-regulation of learning and performance. Routledge Taylor & Francis Group: New York and London.

[18]Teodorescu, A. *Mobile learning and its impact on business English learning*[J]. Procedia-Social and Behavioral Sciences, 2015(180).

[19]Wu, W. C. V., Chen Hsieh, J. S., & Yang J. C. *Creating an Online Learning Community in a Flipped Classroom to Enhance EFL Learners' Oral Proficiency.* [J]Educational Technology & Society, 2017(20).

[20]王宗炎. 朗读与英语学习[J]. 外语与外语学习, 2002(8).

[21]高霞. 朗读与外语能力测量[J]. 现代外语, 2006(4).

[22]艾懿. 新教学环境下对大学英语朗读问题的探讨[J]. 吉林工程技术师范学院学报, 2007(9).

[23]向银华. 试析朗读对外语学习的促进作用[J]. 重庆交通大学学报(社科版), 2010(9).

[24]江宝庭. 大学英语听力教学中的朗读输入研究[J]. 琼州学院学报 2011(1).

[25]朱子奇. *The Effect of Reading Aloud on English Speaking Ability*[J]. 海外英语 2014(3).

[26]钟文天. 用朗读与默读进行英语阅读的对比研究[J]. 西安外国语学报, 2009(2).

Chinese Style VS American Style

——Research about Curriculum Design in $1-2-1$ Program
at Troy University [*]

Meng Na [**]

School of Foreign Languages, Yunnan University,

Kunming Yunnan

Abstract: As the first university to collaborate with Chinese universities for a $1-2-1$ double degree exchange program, and an American university that has been cooperating with Yunnan University for more than 15 years, Troy University's international exchange program has become an object worthy of research by educators. This article takes students and faculties who participated in the $1-2-1$ program at Troy University as samples, with interviews and questionnaires to reveal existing problems in the curriculum design of exchange program, hoping to provide feasible solutions for these problems. Meanwhile, except for the comparative study between Chinese education style and American education style, this article also compares the traditional education pattern in China with the brand-new education pattern in new era. At the end, the author points out advantages of Chinese new education pattern as well as the necessity of international exchange program and international education cooperation.

Keywords: curriculum design; exchange program; education pattern; overseas students; language acquisition.

1. Introduction

With the development of globalization, more and more students are willing to

---

  * 论文题目：中国式 VS 美国式——特洛伊大学 121 项目课程设计研究。

  ** 作者简介：孟娜（Meng Na），云南大学外国语学院英语系讲师；研究方向：语言学。

study abroad, to learn from other countries and other cultures. The United States, due to its advanced education system and concept, has long been considered as the top choice for Chinese students who'd like to further their study abroad. According to the latest data of the Ministry of Education in China, in 2013, China had in all 413, 900 oversea students. It was an increase of 3.58% over 2012. This number has reached over 500, 000 in 2015. In 2013, there were 103, 427 oversea students in the U. S. studying for their master degree, and 93, 768 oversea students studying for their bachelor degree (http://www. eol. cn/html/lx/2014baogao/content. html). In the 2014 – 2015 academic year, Chinese students enrolled in the U. S. undergraduate and graduate schools increased nearly 10.8% to 304, 040 from the prior academic year (Wei 2016: 153). Students from China have become the most primary source for overseas students in the U. S.

In accordance with the data from Report on Chinese Students' Oversea Study 2017 released by New Oriental Education and Technology Group (NYSEEDU), the U. S. has been Chinese students' top choice since 2014—50% of all the overseas students tend to continue their education in the United States. Big events like American Presidential Election happened, but 51% Chinese students expressed that their choice won't be changed by the transformation of international situation(http://edu. cnr. cn/ list/20170523/t20170523_ 523767613. shtml).

Table 1. Main destination countries for Chinese overseas students
(https://www. iie. org/, Project Atlas, 2017)

Countries	Numbers of Chinese students in the country	Proportion of Chinese students of all foreign students	Ranking of Chinese students number in the country
The United States	328, 547	31. 50	1
United Kingdom	94, 995	19. 1	1
France	28, 043	9. 1	2
Australia	97, 984	27. 3	1
Russia	20, 209	13. 4	4
Canada	83, 990	31. 8	1
Germany	30, 259	10. 1	1
Japan	74, 921	41. 6	1

续 表

Countries	Numbers of Chinese students in the country	Proportion of Chinese students of all foreign students	Ranking of Chinese students number in the country
South Korea	66, 672	62	1
New Zealand	16, 520	32. 7	1

Figure 1. The numbers of oversea students in the U. S. from China in 2008 – 2017

Ten Year Trend of Chinese Students in the U.S.

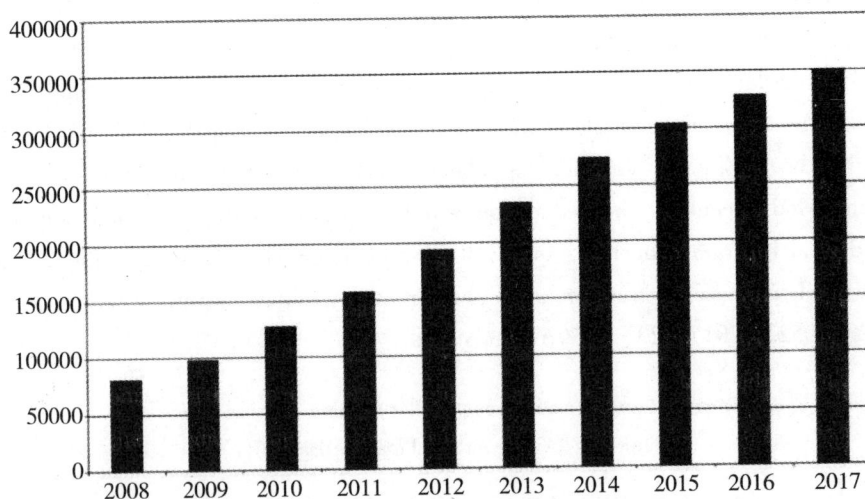

Source: 2017 Open Doors Report, Institute of International Education

Under this trend of overseas study, colleges and universities in the U. S. have been trying their best to provide all kinds of study programs to attract more international students as well as to facilitate foreign students study. As a result, international exchange programs between universities and countries make great progress in recent years. This makes internalization of curriculum become a general trend of higher education research.

2. 1 – 2 – 1 exchange program

Based on this background, a large number of international exchange programs were born at the right moment for Chinese students who'd like to study abroad. Almost every Chinese university has cooperation with the U. S. or other foreign universities to provide international exchange programs, such 3 + 1, 2 + 2, etc.

Just as its name implies, 1 – 2 – 1 exchange program allows Chinese sophomore students to continue their second and third grade study in the U. S. universities. With two-year study in the U. S. and senior year study back to Chinese universities, students will graduate with diplomas from both universities in China and in the U. S.. During four years process, many students choose different majors in both Chinese and the U. S. universities. This gives them experience and diplomas of more than one research field. 1 – 2 – 1 exchange program was initiated by American Association of State Colleges and Universities (AASCU) and China Center for International Education Exchange(CCIEE) in 2001. After more than a decade development, now there are altogether 114 Chinese universities and 31 American universities joined in this program. This program is a good example of putting two countries' education styles and cultures together. Because of the author's exchange scholar experience at Troy, this research will take Troy University as an example, to compare and contrast the similarities as well as differences between Chinese and American teaching styles. Troy University, which locates in Alabama and has more than 130-year history, has been the first university took part in the 1 – 2 – 1 program since 2001. Till 2015, with the help of 1 – 2 – 1 exchange program, there were more than 500 Chinese students went to study at Troy University. Among them 380 Chinese students obtained their bachelor or master degrees from Troy. Most 1 – 2 – 1 graduates continue their study for master or doctorate degree at other universities in the U. S..

Exchange or international programs are noticed because they connect two countries' students, educations, knowledge and cultures together. The Chinese and U. S. studying experiences of these exchange students and scholars provide living examples for educators to do comparative study about Chinese and American education patterns. This article is going to focus on different teaching styles and curriculum design in both countries' education systems. To analyze the curriculum of an exchange program, we do not only study the program itself, to research about the connection of curricula and exchange of cultures is also significant.

3. Historical and cultural background of curriculum design in two countries

At the beginning, let us take a look at the historical and cultural background of education system's development in both Chinese and American universities, as well as the differences and similarities between Chinese and American curriculum design.

From 1949 to 1977, in the period between the foundation of People's Republic of China and the recovery of university entrance examination, higher education in China was under unified and strict control of the central government. Consulting the educational pattern of the former Soviet Union, all schools were public schools which followed the same teaching schedule, used unified curriculum, and applied assigned text books. Under such circumstances, students' creativity and individualities were almost ignored (Xiong 1983: 135). Under the historical condition, the goal of education was to cultivate specialists for industrial construction and science development to enhance national strength of a newly-established country, curriculum design focused more on subjects of natural science and technology rather than subjects of literary and social science. There were obvious disadvantages of this kind of educational pattern: comprehensive universities and subjects of liberal arts were weakened. Because curriculum in higher education was excessively specialized and narrowed, students' ability of adaptation and creation could not be fully developed. In 1980s, the rapid increasing of students' enrollment in higher education and their incompetence after graduation made educators and government realize the necessity to implement higher education reform (Zheng 1994). From 1990s to now, positive changes and improvements have happened to China's higher education. Local government and educational institutions have become more independent in organizing and managing local education. Support and development of comprehensive universities and colleges were taken seriously by government and educational institutions. Besides support from the central government, educational institutions could also be supported by social organizations and individuals. Comprehensive development of students' competence is considered as a main goal of modern education. Students now have more choices of majors, optional courses and curriculum schedules. Though during these past years education reform has received pleasant outcome, there is still a long way for the modernization and globalization of Chinese higher education. A more flexible and comprehensive curriculum is expected. A more open and stimulative learning environment is required.

Compared with the Chinese rigid higher educational pattern, the higher education style in the United States may be somewhat "laissez-faire". As early as 1897, the elective system which provided students different choices of courses was promoted by President Elliot at Harvard. This kind of "laissez-faire" in academic field was the basis for the modern American University. At that time, the general or liberal education played the leading role. Besides the knowledge on literal arts, vocational technique was another concern in education. When educators refer to the term"vocational", it means that college or university curricula should focus on professional preparation. The discussion on how to develop specialization in curriculum design while saving general education had continued till the middle of twentieth century. From then on, American students were required"to widen their intellectual horizon at the same time they are specializing"(Bisesi 1982: 199 – 203). From this perspective, we can tell that students' professional knowledge and comprehensive knowledge in all walks of life are both taken seriously in American education system at all levels.

After World War II, developing marketable skills was considered the primary task facing American undergraduate education. Nowadays, reviewing their undergraduate curriculum, American educators follow what was reported in Harvard's *The Chronicle of Higher Education* about an educated person: An educated person"... must be able to think and write clearly and effectively... should have a critical appreciation of... literature and the art... history... social sciences... philosophical analysis... and the mathematical and experimental of the physical and biological sciences... can not... be ignorant of other cultures and other times... should have some understanding of moral and ethical problems... should have achieved depth in some field of knowledge"(Bisesi 1982: 204 – 212). Base on this teaching philosophy, there comes the so-called"general education"of American.

In accordance with the above definitions, China and the U.S. possess two different education concepts and that definitely will lead to two different teaching patterns. Comparing two countries' curriculum designs and teaching styles becomes meaningful for educators. Modernized world and globalized communication require our students' to experience different countries. International exchange program can perfectly meet the need of experiencing different cultures, histories and educations.

4. Differences between Chinese and American education styles

After describing a brief background of Chinese and American curriculum development, several differences can be clearly viewed.

First of all, American universities have more autonomy than Chinese universities do. The educational system in the United States allows colleges and universities to design curriculum and choose textbooks according to their special needs and typical situations. The design of curriculum is more elastic and flexible in American universities. Courses include major courses, interdisciplinary courses, professional preparation courses and courses in accordance with students' individual interests. Textbooks are changed with the development of times and social requirements. Therefore the design of curriculum can keep pace with the world's development and advancement of culture, technology, economy, etc. In China, for the past several decades, government decides which textbook and what general courses students will take, especially for elementary and secondary education. For higher education, making a decision of textbook changing or curriculum amending takes a long period of discussion and complicated procedures. This leads to the process of education development and curriculum reform drag on for years and can not catch up with the fast variation of national economy and technology. The lack of novel subjects and interdisciplinary courses impedes students' competence in their future work and study. Because of the lagging of curriculum reform, the need for graduates of all specialized field can not be satisfied.

Secondly, the curriculum design in Chinese university seldom provides a tight relation between what students learn from class and their future career. To build a modern education system, Chinese university should offer students more autonomous right in choosing curriculum, changing majors, arranging post-class activities, etc. Because the decision of curriculum and textbooks are under education institutions and university academic offices' control, students' choice of majors or optional courses, even the choice of instructors and professors, as well as the arrangement of each semester's compulsory or optional courses are very narrow. The responsibility of advisers in American universities is realizing students' potential and interest, guiding their study and even occupational planning in the future, helping them choose the most suitable curriculum to finish their academic study. However, in Chinese university, students do not have an adviser with whom they can discuss what they would like to do in the future, how they can make a reasonable plan for future, what courses and practical programs are helpful for their career goal. Usually when students start their study, they don't have chance to change their majors and major courses. With alike and unified curriculum, students' individuality and professional ability may not be cultivated enough. In accordance with the empowerment evaluation of David M. Fetterman: "people response best when they play an active and substantive role in making decision about issues that affect their lives" (Armstrong 2003: 274).

Therefore, with the support from advisers and professors, granting students the right to make their own decision about what to learn and when to learn is worth learning for Chinese education reform. Being excluded in the designing process of curriculum, students' enthusiasm for study won't be stimulated. Moreover, because of the difference of two countries' curriculum design, American students may not be as good as Chinese students in taking a standardized theoretical exam, but they are more capable and competent in practical job applications. International program can help exchange students gain both of these abilities.

Last but not least, there are obvious differences about two countries' teaching methodology. Compared with Chinese teacher-centered classroom, American classroom encourages the interaction between students and professors. Direct and immediate communication with professors is considered as an encouraged virtue. A lot of courses are taught during the process of discussion between students and instructors. Chinese traditional culture places a high value on respect for teachers. In the Warring States period, there is the saying "one-day teacher, life-long father". Due to traditional culture, Chinese students may be reluctant to express oneself, to discuss or debate with professors. Participating in exchange programs let students experience two different cultures and learn useful things from each other. Many Chinese students learn to express their personal thoughts while showing respect to their teachers' advise and inculcation. Besides communication between students and professors, communication between students and their international peers are also very valuable and meaningful. The world now is growing into a "global village". Nobody and no country are isolated. Further development needs communication and exchanging. International experience is significant for students, universities and countries. International exchange programs have great significance in cultivating students' international horizon.

5. Significance of 1 – 2 – 1 exchange program

As we mentioned, the Sino-American 1 – 2 – 1 Joint Degree Program is established by AASCU (the American Association of State Colleges and Universities) and CCIEE (the China Center for International Education Exchange). AASCU represents more than 430 public colleges, universities and systems of higher education in the U. S. and promotes support for higher education, conducts analysis and advocates for change in public policy and provide professional development for higher education leaders. CCIEE is affiliated with the Ministry of Education of China and supports international educational exchange programs throughout the world. It works to meet the needs of students for high-quality education opportunities and the needs of China for a well educated work force(Hurst 2005). At Troy University, now there are about 300 exchange students from China. 86 of them are 1 - 2 - 1 students who currently study in Troy campus. The 1 - 2 - 1 exchange program is a dual degree program which allows Chinese students to spend their first year in Chinese university and then study at Troy University for two years, and then return to China for their senior year. After four-year study in both Chinese university and Troy, they can receive degrees from both universities.

1 - 2 - 1 program provides opportunity for Chinese students to study American language and culture, to experience a more free and independent learning style. Their higher education experience in the United States can make them more competent and employable when they return to China. To obtain two degrees from both universities, students must meet the graduation requirements for both universities. English proficiency, of course, is quite important and necessary. With the development of globalization, especially after China entered WTO, basic knowledge of using English becomes an important standard of competency. Features and benefits of this kind of exchange program can be fully demonstrated by the connection and interaction between Chinese and American curriculum styles.

According to Dr. Futao Huang, about 273 new programs with international subjects or contents were introduced into China from 1990 to 2002. Among the newly-introduced programs, the number of programs in foreign languages or linguistics and interdisciplinary programs such as regional and areas studies covering more than one country has increased most fast, rising by 166 and 85 respectively. What is especially worth noting is that there are some programs leading to joint or double degrees(Huang 2006: 521 - 539). Besides American education pattern, original English textbooks and teaching bilingually or in English are meaningful learning experience for exchange students. "The driving force behind the development of English language programs lies... in... an important way to internationalize the curricula in one's own institution and upgrade quality and standards, and as a mechanism for facilitating the internationalization of the higher education system" (Huang 2006: 537).

There are three important principles that serve as the basis for curriculum: "1. learners should be active participants in the learning program; 2. the learning experience should be meaningful to the learner; 3. learning should have a critical focus" (Fraser 2006: 269 – 284). What are the advantages and disadvantages of curriculum designing in both Chinese university and American university? What benefits can students get from the connection and contradiction of two countries' different curriculum designing? How can we find the most suitable curriculum while providing higher education to Chinese exchange students who study in both China and the United States? How can the curriculum design effectively connect two countries' cultures and education together? What more can universities and faculties do to serve the goal of cultural and educational exchange? All of these questions make the research meaningful.

This research is about students' perceptions of curriculum design in 1 – 2 – 1 program. It mainly focuses on 168 Chinese exchange students at Troy University from 2010 – 2016. Data are collected from 100 1 – 2 – 1 students, exchange scholars and related faculties. These 100 participants are chosen according to their studying or working experience at Troy University, such as different majors, different degrees, different learning terms spent at Troy. The research is about students' perceptions of the curriculum of their academic courses rather than their language courses such as ESL (English as Second Language) courses. Participants are students who have already finished their ESL courses, passed TOEFL test, and already started their academic study. The questionnaire is in both English and Chinese, thus it is easier for participants to understand. This ensures the reliability and precision of their answers and conclusion. Besides exchange students and scholars, some faculties and teachers about this program also participated in this research, for example Troy faculties in charge of 1 – 2 – 1 students, teachers of 1 – 2 – 1 students at Troy University, faculty of CCIEE(the China Center for International Education Exchange) in China. Records and archives of 1 – 2 – 1 program are also important resource for data collection. Those participants, interviewees and archives are all relevant to the research problem.

Understanding students' viewpoints about the curriculum design of 1 – 2 – 1 program is the main purpose of this research. On the one hand, in qualitative study, the following can be clearly described and analyzed: the setting of exchange program, situation of curriculum, process of designing curriculum, relationships between Chinese and American education systems, and the description of 1 – 2 – 1 students and their learning situation.

On the other hand, 1 – 2 – 1 program is a joint degree program which started in 2001 but only gets fully development in recent years. There are only few new reports about it. There is no professional research paper especially dealing with this issue. Troy University pays a lot of attention to the improvement of this program. Studying about students' perceptions of this program's curriculum design can help providing useful information about this program, as well as students' and faculties' perceptions of this program. To make the research feasible and valid, research mainly focuses on the aspect of curriculum design. Qualitative study enables researchers to gain observation data of a particular phenomenon, of people's different conceptions about the phenomenon, and develop new perspectives about this phenomenon and discover problems that exist within this phenomenon.

A generalization of those different assumptions or perceptions needs to be made within real-world context. Qualitative study is most helpful in this aspect. Evaluation in qualitative study enables researchers to judge the effectiveness of existing policies or practices. Testing the effectiveness, advantages and disadvantages of curriculum in 1 – 2 – 1 program, and deciding what possible improvements need to be made is the ultimate goal of this research.

6. Questionnaire survey data analysis

Questions in the survey are developed concentrating on the effectiveness of curriculum design in 1 – 2 – 1 program. Those questions are about flexibility and accessibility of curriculum, instructors' ability and proficiency and students' learning experience and achievements at Troy University. Students' perceptions of curriculum in this program can be identified according to their answers, because their answers reflect their thoughts, satisfaction and expectation of curriculum design. Universities and faculties can know what improvement they can make in the future according to students' responses. Questions in this survey are open-ended questions, because this survey deals with students' conception about curriculum design of 1 – 2 – 1 program. Researcher does not provide certain answers for participants to choose, but give them enough room to freely express their thoughts about this program. Conclusion can be made after analyzing, coding and generalizing students and interviewees' answers.

Except for 9 faculties and teachers in 1 – 2 – 1 program, there are altogether 9 of 1 – 2 – 1 exchange students participated in this research. They are all undergraduate students who come from Chinese universities and study for or obtain their bachelor degree at Troy University. Students of different majors are includ: Computer Science, Accounting, Finance, English, Education, etc. They all study at Troy more than one semester. According to students' answers, features, benefits and problems of Troy University are revealed.

As the first impression of American education exposed in front of those Chinese students, Troy University can be considered as a representative of American universities and education pattern. Most participants agree that compared with their Chinese universities, Troy has several advantages in education that we can learn from:

(1) Latest textbooks are used. Unlike Chinese universities, Troy changes textbooks frequently in accordance with the fast development of times and situations. Cases and examples used in textbooks are not only new, but also impressive and interesting. Students can get authentic firsthand materials of all fields. 55% students said that their universities were still using textbooks published from 1999 – 2004. The reasons include: a. Schools and education institutions usually need years to discuss, decide and then replace the old textbooks; b. Teachers are reluctant to change a new textbook. That means they need to prepare whole new teaching plans. In terms of this issue, education reform in China now strongly encourage the publication of excellent teaching materials and textbooks that contain not only basic theory knowledge but also add a lot of practical activities for the students to use specialty knowledge and skills in practical application. Textbooks published more than 10 years can not be used anymore.

(2) Professors at Troy University are more humorous; classroom climate is easy and relaxing. With a very vivid and relaxing atmosphere, professors teach knowledge in their typical methods and plans, while most Chinese professors follow the same and rigid teaching plan which is designed according to the university's requirement. Moreover, 67% students feel more respected in American classroom. Students and professors are at the equal position. They can freely ask questions, discuss or even debate with professors. According to several participants, American professors are more amiable and approachable. Besides discussion in classroom, professors provide office hours, which do not exist in most Chinese university, to communicate with students. After years development, it is undeniable that most Chinese teachers are also wise, amiable and humorous. Chinese teachers and universities have been trying to improve the work environment. In some universities, office hours are limited simply because the numbers of teachers and the numbers of offices are out of proportion. This, I believe, can be completely solved in the near future. It is also true that most Chinese teachers need systematic training with pedagogy. Some professors are excellent in their area of

expertise, however, the lack of suitable teaching methodology hinders them from passing on their knowledge to students.

(3) Chinese universities give students more homework but fewer tests. However, Troy University gives students more tests and fewer assignments. 45% students prefer Chinese testing style: only twice exams in each semester——the mid-term and the final test. Surprisingly, there are 38% participants prefer more quizzes and tests——this makes them keep on studying and reviewing frequently. Knowledge is accumulated through daily review. Exchange students said that tests are not as difficult as that in Chinese university, but Chinese students must be self-motivated enough to make a high score. Some students prefer more tests or quizzes because in American universities, several tests are open-book examinations. Testing forms are different including paper writing, field study, presentations, discussion contributions, etc. Various testing forms make students feel relaxed. They believe they can have better performance and scores with different testing forms.

(4) Team work are strongly advocated in their learning process. Students like to have more chances to work together. Group study and group meeting are important way of learning. 89% Chinese students declared that their team spirit is cultivated well at Troy and they believe cooperating with other people is an important skill for learning and future career. In American classroom, teachers set aside more time for group discussion. Students' contribution and performance in discussion are considered as very important criterion for final evaluation. Of course, with the education reformation, now almost every Chinese university have the standard of evaluation that contains not only the final test score, but also students' classroom performance that includes their speech, presentation, discussion in the classroom and cooperation with their peers. And free study rooms in American university libraries with chairs, desks even blackboards are convenience for team work, which should be advocated in Chinese university libraries.

(5) In addition to major courses, optional courses at Troy University are more interesting and diversified. In addition to their major courses, Troy provides students more choices for optional courses. Students can participate in various courses, have access to different domains of knowledge. For example, students who major in finance or accounting can take criminal justice course (one of Troy's popular majors) or music education. For professional elective courses, students have more choices. Take education major students as an example, in addition to their compulsory courses, they

can also choose to take professional elective courses such as educational psychology, preschool education, etc. Thus they can learn more about their professional fields. Education reform offers more choices for Chinese students in Chinese universities. There are all kinds of optional courses called "quality education elective courses" in China. These courses expand students' vision as well as promote their all-round development. Optional courses like Southeast Asian Languages, movie appreciation, handcraft or marital psychology are very popular. Many Chinese universities even have some Chinese featured courses, such as tea art, flower arrangement, Tai Ji, Chinese traditional instruments, and so on. In a sense, Chinese universities are now providing more opportunities and possibilities for students' all-round development.

7. Advantages of 1 – 2 – 1 exchange program

Generally speaking, 1 – 2 – 1 exchange program connects Chinese education with American education. Each country can learn a lot from a different education pattern. According to our interviews, it is undoubtedly that international exchange program can benefit students in many ways:

(1) It provides an opportunity of experiencing different educations and cultures. Studying abroad giues them a different life experience in several aspects. The exchange program is the first chance for these students to live independently in a foreign country for years. With the nationwide English learning trend in China, having an opportunity to deeply understand the culture, history and people of an English speaking country is very precious experience for Chinese students.

(2) Besides their merits of diligence and industriousness, Chinese students can not only improve their language proficiency, but also learn good qualities from American students, such as Americans' independence and confidence. Original English textbooks and authentic teaching materials are really helpful for Chinese students' language acquisition. Being exposed to the language everyday is a great challenge as well as a great opportunity for exchange students. Every interviewee said that their abilities of English(including ability in speaking, listening, reading and writing) had been greatly improved since they came to study at Troy.

(3) The program is an excellent chance for Chinese students to learn knowledge in various fields, major knowledge as well as historical and cultural knowledge. It is also a good way to internalize their major knowledge. It is typically helpful for students

majoring in International Business and English. More than 85% students expressed their thought of continuing their study in the U. S. , therefore they can better serve their country when they go back to China with knowledge learned from the most developed country in the world.

(4) Besides the improvement of English ability and major knowledge, students can get two degrees from both universities in 4 ~ 5 years. This makes them highly competitive in future job hunting. Among all the participants, 67% of them chose a different major at Troy, so they can get diplomas from both universities with two majors. This is one of the most attractive benefits of dual-degree international exchange program.

8. Problems and solutions

However, there are still some problems existing in the curriculum design of $1 - 2 - 1$ program. Chinese students feel confined in choosing courses, even though they have more autonomy at Troy University. Most of their courses are decided by their American advisers who may not have enough knowledge about Chinese universities' curriculum. Some courses are overlapped in both Chinese and American universities.

On one hand, at Troy University, several courses have to be taken step by step. Taking Business major for instance, students can not take Finance if they did not take Accounting; before they take International Management, they must finish Management. Therefore, sometimes they have to take the same courses again at Troy, even if they had already finished those basic courses in Chinese universities. Students complain that it is a waste of time and money. Also, there are problems in the process of credit transfer. Some courses they take in China have no equivalent courses at Troy. Another problem is that the names of some courses are same in both Chinese universities and Troy University, but the learning contents are different. For example, students who took Business Statistics I in China can directly take Business Statistics II at Troy, but actually Business Statistics I at Troy is different from what they took in China. Those students often feel the courses they take at Troy are so difficult, because they did not take the basic courses there. The main problem in $1 - 2 - 1$ program's curriculum design is the connection and communication between two countries' universities about credit transfer. Students are often confused about how many credits they can transfer from Chinese universities to Troy, or from Troy to Chinese university. As consequence, they are puzzled about what courses they should take at

Troy University and which way of choosing courses is most beneficial for their studying and graduation.

On the other hand, some courses require students' strong ability of understanding in English. Those courses are hard for international students, especially students from non-English speaking countries. Besides curriculum of major courses, students are not so satisfied with several basic English courses. Some courses, for instance composition, have strict criteria in grammar details. According to 1 – 2 – 1 students, this kind of courses can not effectively improve their practical English ability. What they need is the ability of understanding and expressing in English, especially the ability of speaking and listening. One of the interviewees in Business major said that the nitpicking in grammar was not necessary and it did not help for the practical use of English in their major field. "My goal in major study is not writing beautiful composition but use major knowledge in this field. Detailed grammar is not as significant as vocabulary and spoken-English. Of course, grammar is indispensable, but getting an 'F' only because I did not put a comma after 'and then' is somewhat nitpicking", said the student. Any course offered in curriculum should be stimulator rather than barrier for students' future study.

Last but not least, one aim of 1 – 2 – 1 program is improving students' English. However, Chinese students' narrow social world impedes the development of their language competence. They need more contacts with a different culture. Under this situation, activities that can enhance communication between Chinese students and American students should be considered in curriculum design.

9. Conclusion

This research mainly focuses on exchange students who attended Troy University between 2010 – 2016. Many participants went to study at Troy university six or seven years ago, some of them spent 3 ~ 5 years or longer at Troy, so their opinions about Chinese universities curriculum and teaching style are inevitably limited. With China's development in all fields, especially after the 18th and the 19th National Congress of the Communist Party of China, education reform has long been a key topic of China's social development. The globalization and internationalization of education are top priority for China. In past few years, traditional education pattern in Chinese universities have been experiencing huge improvement. Colleges and universities now have more power in decision-making about curriculum arrangement, textbook choosing and admission standards. Students have more autonomous right in choosing or changing their majors, selecting a second even a third major, taking optional courses and choosing their favorite professors. The traditional teachers-evaluate-students pattern has been changed. Students' evaluation for each teacher and professor becomes a very important part of their teaching performance. Furthermore, overseas study experiences are becoming a necessary requirement for university teachers. The numbers of teachers who have overseas study experience and have obtained foreign country degrees are increasing and this has become an evaluation criterion of universities' competence. Learning experience in Chinese universities are becoming better. However, as a vivid and direct way to experience a foreign country, international exchange program always has its advantages.

To conclude, all interviewees are almost satisfied with the way of instructing and learning during the exchange program. 82% of them are not satisfied with the transfer credit system between Chinese universities and Troy University. Every interviewee learned useful things and knowledge from study experience at Troy. To improve 1 − 2 − 1 program and better serve exchange students, it is necessary to design a more flexible curriculum from which students can learn solid major knowledge, meanwhile, their language competence can be cultivated. It is also necessary to provide a stable and unified system of credit transfer in which students can learn what they want to learn and need to learn, with their money and time worthwhile. Besides the problems and solutions mentioned in this research, there are still a lot to do for Chinese education reform in new era. This is a momentous mission for all Chinese educators in this new age.

References

［1］魏华颖. 我国在美留学生回国意愿和就业意向特征分析［J］. 中国行政管理, 2016, 09.

［2］王蔚. 中美教育教学比较［M］. 上海: 上海大学出版社, 2014.

［3］熊明安. 中国高等教育史［M］. 重庆: 重庆出版社, 1983.

［4］郑登云. 中国高等教育史［M］. 上海: 华东师范大学出版社, 1994.

［5］中国青年报. 2017 中国留学白皮书［DB/OL］. http: //edu. cnr. cn/list/ 20170523/t20170523_ 523767613. shtml, 2017 − 05 − 16/ 2018 − 01 − 23.

［6］Armstrong, David G. *Curriculum Today*, *Upper Saddle River*［M］. New Jersey: Prentice Hall, 2003.

［7］Bisesi, Michael. *Historical Developments in American Undergraduate Education*:

General Education and the Core Curriculum [J]. British Journal of Educational Studies, 1982(7).

[8] Brown, Jonathan N. *Consensus and Divergence in International Studies: Survey Evidence from* 140 *International Studies Curriculum Programs* [J]. International Studies Perspectives, 2006(11).

[9] Ellis, Andy. *Troy University International*, [EB/OL]. http: //www. troy. edu, 2005 – 01 – 28/ 2016 – 04 – 15: 34 – 38.

[10] Fraser, Sharon P. , Bosanquet, Agnes M. *The curriculum? That's just a unit outline, isn't it?* [J]. Studies in Higher Education, 2006.

[11] Huang, Futao. *Internationalization of Curricula in Higher Education Institutions in Comparative Perspectives: Case Studies of China, Japan and The Netherlands* [J]. Higher Education, 2006.

[12] Hurst, Fred. *Sino-American* 1 – 2 – 1 *Joint Degree Program* [M]. Arizona: North Arizona University, 2005.

[13] *Troy University beefs up cooperative programs with China.* [EB/OL]. http: // www. dothaneagle. com/gulfcoast/dea/local_ news. apx. , 2007 – 11 – 29/ 2018 – 01 – 23.

[14] Johnson, James A. *Foundations of American education: perspectives on education in a changing world* [M]. Boston, Mass: Pearson A&B, 2008.

Zum Einsatz von Bildern zur Schulung der interkulturellen Kompetenz im DaF-Unterricht[*]

Wang Jie[**]

Abstrakte：In diesem Beitrag handelt es sich hauptsächlich darum，wie man mit Bildern die interkulturelle Kompetenz im DaF-Unterricht fördern kann und didaktische Vorschläge werden ausgearbeitet，die zu Gestaltung des DaF-Unterrichts mit Bildern zur Förderung der interkulturellen Kompetenz beitragen können. Im ersten zwei Teilen wird die Grundlage der Theorien：das Verarbeiten von Bildern und interkulturelles Lernen eingegangen und im zweiten Teil sind die zu diesem Thema vorhandenen didaktischen Implikationen gewidmet. Anschließend werden die methodologischen Überlegungen ausführlich dargestellt.

Stichwörter：Bilder；interkulturelle Kompetenz；DaF-Unterricht

Der Einsatz von Bildern in FU ist schon lange ein Thema. 1658 wurde das erste fremdsprachliche Lehrwerk mit Bildern veröffentlicht，seitdem kommen Bilder immer häufiger im FU zum Einsatz. Gemäß den pädagogischen，lernpsychologischen，fremdsprachlichdidaktischen，medienspezifischen und landeskundlichen Argumenten wird der Einsatz von Bildern im FU bevorzugt und übernehmen Bilder immer mehr Funktionen und Wirkungen zum Wissenserwerb beim (Fremd-) Sprachenlernen (z. B. Weidenmann 1988；Hog & Müller 1990；Sturm 1991；Weidenmann 1991；Peeck 1994；Scherling & Schuckall 1994；Sturm 1994；Weidenmann 1994；1994a；Ballstaedt 1995；Weidenmann 1995；Biechele 1996；Hellwig 1996；Macaire &

　＊　论文题目：德语课堂中以跨文化能力培养为目标的图片运用方法论。
　＊＊　作者简介：王洁(Wang Jie)，云南大学外国语学院德语讲师，研究方向：德语教学法。

Hosch 1996; Bachmann 1997; Biechele 1997; 1998; Weidenmann 2004; Huber 2005; Biechele 2006; Badstübner-Kizik 2007). Bilder weisen Potenzen auf, die durch andere Medien nicht ersetzt werden können. All diese Vorzüge und Funktionen von Bildern im FU sind damit verbunden, dass durch Bilder das Ziel des FU effektiv erreicht werden kann, den Erwerb einer weit gefassten interkulturellen Kompetenz.

1. Zum Verarbeiten von Bildern

Seit der kognitiven Wende rückt die Informationsverarbeitung ins Zentrum des Forschungsinteresses, somit also die Frage, wie menschliches Wahrnehmen und Verarbeiten von Sinneseindrücken verläuft und Lernen bewirkt.

1. 1   Bildwahrnehmung

Unter dem Einfluss der Philosophie wurde Wahrnehmung lange Zeit von der Kognition (der gedanklichen Verarbeitung des Wahrgenommenen) unterschieden und als das sinnliche Abbild der Außenwelt im Zentralnervensystem von Lebewesen bezeichnet (vgl. Wiesing 2002, S. 242ff.). Mit der Entwicklung von Neurophysiologie, Psychologie und Kognitionswissenschaft besteht aber in zahlreichen Theorieentwürfen Übereinstimmung darin, dass die Wahrnehmung kein Abbild der Welt liefert, sondern als ein Konstruktionsprozess der Wirklichkeit, in der man sich bewegt (vgl. Bering 2002, S. 95). In Psychologie und Physiologie bezeichnet Wahrnehmung die Summe der Schritte von Aufnahme, Auswahl, Verarbeitung (z. B. Abgleich mit Vorwissen) und Interpretation sensorischer Informationen – und zwar nur jener Informationen, die der Anpassung (Adaptation) des Wahrnehmenden an die Umwelt dienen oder die ihm eine Rückmeldung über Auswirkungen seines Verhaltens geben. Gemäß dieser Definition sind also nicht alle Sinnesreize Wahrnehmungen, sondern nur diejenigen, die kognitiv verarbeitet werden und der Orientierung eines Subjekts dienen. Wahrnehmung ist eine Grundlage von Lernprozessen (vgl. Goldstein 2008, S. 4ff.). Wegen der engen Zusammenhänge zwischen Wahrnehmung und Kognition setzt die heutige Wahrnehmungsforschung bei ihren Untersuchungen nicht mehr ausschließlich bei den einzelnen Sinnesorganen an, sondern im Zentrum, bei den konstruierenden Prozessen im Gehirn. Bering (2002, S. 94) hat den Wahrnehmungsprozess nach den Forschungsergebnissen von Wahrnehmungspsychologie so beschrieben: „ ... Wahrneh mung kein passiver, gleichsam abbildender Vorgang, sondern vielmehr eine Strukturierungsleistung des Gehirns ist. Innere Zustände ordnen und definieren die Reizempfindungen, die das Subjekt aufnimmt. Diese innere Struktur, bestehend aus früheren Erfahrungen, stellt die Ordnungsmuster und - kategorien bereit, nach denen die von außen kommenden Reize einer Hierarchisierung und Strukturierung unterworfen werden. Auch hier ist der kulturelle Horizont für den Aufbau von Ordnungskategorien des Wahrgenommenen entscheidend. Im Gehirn liegt also bereits eine - zerebrale - Repräsentation vor. Dabei ist zu berücksichtigen, dass diese innere Struktur nicht der Außenwelt übergestülpt wird, sondern diese bildet in einem wechselseitigen Prozess zugleich die Voraussetzung für die Entstehung einer, Internen Repräsentation' der Welt. "

Zusammengefasst lässt sich Wahrnehmung so charakterisieren (vgl. Bering 2002, S. 94f. ; Biechele 2006, S. 20): aktiv, subjektiv, selektiv, konstruktiv, vorwissensbasiert, interpretativ, kontext-und kulturabhängig, sie ist abhängig vom jeweiligen „ Perceptual Set ", nämlich dem Zusammenwirken von Einstellung, Erwartung, Aufmerksamkeit, Instruktion, kulturellem Orientierungssystem, Emotionen und Lernbiografie. Der Akzent der Bildwahrnehmung liegt vor allem auf dem wahrnehmenden Subjekt selbst, seiner kognitiven und emotionalen Dispositionen sowie kulturbestimmten Erfahrungen.

1. 2　Bildverstehen

Verstehen ist ein Kernbestandteil von Wahrnehmung. Weidenmann (1991, S. 47ff.) definiert Verstehen als den Verarbeitungsprozess, in dem die aufgenommenen Sinnesdaten mit bestehenden Wissensstrukturen abgeglichen werden, wobei versucht wird, die vorhandenen Wissensstrukturen in den neuen Daten zu bestätigen. Im Verlauf des Verarbeitungsprozesses wird ein möglichst kohärentes und strukturiertes mentales Produkt konstruiert.

Ich trete für Weidenmann (1994a, S. 12) ein, wenn er schreibt, dass Bildverstehen eine kognitive Leistung ist und ebenso wissens- und erfahrungsabhängig wie das Verstehen anderer Informationen. Zu den Komponenten dieser Wissensstrukturen beim Bildverstehen gehört nicht nur deklaratives Wissen, sondern auch prozedurales Wissen. Notwendige Vorwissen für das Verstehen von Bildern umfasst z. B. :

	Allgemeines Wissen um Bildcode	Soziokulturelles Wissen
Deklaratives Wissen	Arten von Bildern und deren Darstellungskonventionen	Soziokulturelle Zusammenhänge und deren visuelle Darbietungsmuster sowietraditionen (Welche Themen und Situationen werden warum, wie und in welchen Quellen festgehalten? Welche Interpretationsschemata für Mimik, Gestik, Persönlichkeitseigenschaften, Raum sind anwendbar...)
	Spezifika des ikonischen Zeichensystems (zweidimensionale Darstellungen, die Raum, Perspektive, Entfernung wiedergegeben; Hell-Dunkel-Werte, Kontraste, Farben, Arten von Linien...)	
		piktorale Symbole, Metaphern...
		Bildhandschriften (subjektive, landesspezifische, historische...)
Prozedurales Wissen	Wissen um Verfahren, Bilder, lesen " zu können, dabei deklaratives Wissen im Prozess des Bildverstehens und – verarbeitens umzusetzen sowie Bildverstehen für rezeptives und produktives Handeln mit Texten einzusetzen.	

Nach Biechele (1996, S. 750f. ; 1998, S. 23; 2006, S. 22f.) und Scholz (2004, S. 108 – 116) referieren die deklarativen Wissenskomponenten zum einen auf universelle Eigenschaften des Bildcodes; zum anderen auf soziokulturelle Erkenntnisse, die beim Lerner des Deutschen als Fremdsprache in Bezug auf das Zeichensystem oft berücksichtigt werden müssen. Prozedurales Wissen gehört zum Konzept der Bildkompetenz oder „ Visual Literacy". Um prozedurales Wissen für das Lernen mit Bildern ausbilden zu können, sind Einsichten in den Prozessverlauf des Bildverstehens unabdingbare Voraussetzung. Hier sei verwiesen auf einige Aufsätze über den Bildverstehensprozess aus verschiedenen Perspektiven (z. B. Weidenmann 1988; 1994a; Ballstaedt 1995; Doelker 1997; Scholz 2004;). In dem Beitrag wird Weidenmanns Modell (1988, S. 97f.) des Bildverstehensprozesses vorgestellt, weil es sich im Paradigma der kognitiven Informationsverarbeitung verankern lässt:

● Vorphase: Sie beginnt mit dem ersten Blickkontakt und kennzeichnet, dass der Betrachter in einer bestimmten Verfassung dem Bild begegnet (kognitiv, motivational, emotional).

● Initialphase：Hier fängt die erste Auseinandersetzung mit dem Bild an. Kennzeichen dieser zweiten Phase sind Normalisierungsversuche der Betrachter. Als Normalisierungsversuche bezeichnet Weidenmann Verstehens versuche der Betrachter. Für den Betrachter bekannte und einfache Bilder führen schnell zu dem Eindruck, ein Bild verstanden zu haben. Damit verbunden ist, dass er keinen Normalisierungsbedarf mehr wahrnimmt und den Blickkontakt abbricht. Um eine tiefere Auseinandersetzung zu erreichen, sollte der Betrachter nach der ersten Verarbeitung eines Bildes, den Eindruck gewinnen, noch nicht alles verstanden zu haben (z. B. durch unbekannte oder unerwartete Bildaspekte). Dadurch bleibt ein Normalisierungsbedarf erhalten und die Beschäftigung mit dem Bild wird intensiviert.

● Progressionsphase：Die Aufrechterhaltung der Auseinandersetzung mit einem Bild führt in die Progressionsphase. Kennzeichen dieser Phase ist die intensivere Verarbeitung der Bildinformationen. Ziel dieser Phase sind zwei Formen des Bildverstehens：Zum einen versucht der Betrachter zu erkennen, welche Objekte oder Sachverhalte im Bild dargestellt sind (ökologisches oder natürliches Bildverstehen), zum anderen versucht er die Intention der Darstellung zu erfassen(indikatorisches Bildverstehen).

● Stabilisierungsphase：Als letzte Phase der Auseinandersetzung bezeichnet Weidenmann die Stabilisierungsphase. Als Kennzeichen gilt, dass der Betrachter keine neuen Informationen mehr wahrnimmt und deshalb der Normalisierungsbedarf bis zum Abbruch des Bildkontaktes abnimmt.

● Speicherungsphase：In der Stabilisierungsphase ist der Prozess des Bildverstehens noch nicht abgeschlossen. Nach dem Abbruch des Bildkontaktes werden die piktoralen(bildlichen)Informationen im Gedächtnis gespeichert. Die Qualität der Speicherungsphase hängt von der Intensität der Bildverarbeitung ab. Je intensiver die Progressionsphase verlaufen ist, desto differenzierter und adäquater fällt das vom Lernenden aufgebaute geistige Modell aus. Dies wiederum führt zu besserer Vernetzung des neuen Modells mit bereits vorhandenem Wissen. Ergebnis eines solchen Prozesses sind bessere Erinnerungsleistungen.

Weidenmann (1988, S. 138) versteht Bilder als Kommunikate mit spezifischem Informationspotenzial und Bildverstehen als einen „ Normalisierungsprozess", in dem durch aktive Verarbeitung der Botschaft Ambiguität reduziert und ein kohärentes mentales Modell konstruiert wird. Er entwickelte weitere Theorien zum Bildverstehen, die auf empirischen Arbeiten basieren. So geht er von zwei qualitativ verschiedenen Verstehensmodi aus (vgl. Weidenmann 1994, S. 46f. ; 1994a, S. 26):

●Ökologisches／natürliches Bildverstehen： Es wird als Wahrnehmung „ auf einen Blick " realisiert. Das heißt, ein Bild wird auf Grund unseres erworbenen Wissens mühelos und entsprechend schnell verstanden. Dieser Prozess verläuft in der Regel automatisch ab und deshalb ohne bewusste Anstrengung. Charakteristisch für das natürliche Bildverstehen ist, dass nicht die Details zuerst erfasst werden, die nach und nach zu einem Gesamteindruck führen, sondern sich dieser schon vorher gebildet hat.

●Indikatorisches Bildverstehen： Es führt den Rezipierenden zu tieferer Verarbeitung, wobei beim Konstruieren von Kohärenz mehr Stimuli des visuellen Informationsträgers durch Berücksichtigung von mehr Bildaspekten, von mehr eigenem Welt-und Bildwissen einbezogen werden. Das Symbolsystem Bild mit seinem spezifischen Code wird in Interaktion mit speziellen Wissensbeständen elaboriert.

Der zweite Verstehensmodus beim indikatorischen Bildverstehen ist nach Weidenmann (1994, S. 48ff. ; 1994a, S. 28) besonders für die Verwendung von Bildern in Lehr - Lernsituationen von Bedeutung, denn er geht über das Erkennen des Abgebildeten hinaus und richtet sich auf das Erfassen von Mitteilungsabsichten. Die Bezeichnung „ indikatorisch "wählte er, weil der Betrachter bei diesem Prozess die Merkmale des Bildes als Indikatoren für die Mitteilungsabsicht interpretiert. Es entwickelt sich entlang der Suchrichtung des Betrachters und verlangt einen größeren Aufwand an Zeit und geistigem Einsatz. Voraussetzung für diese beiden Modus sind Kenntnisse über das bildliche Symbolsystem und seine Verwendung, womit ein leichteres Verstehen verbunden ist. Im Gegensatz zum natürlichen Bildverstehen verlangt das indikatorische aber eine tiefere Verarbeitung, die die Veränderung kognitiver Strukturen erst bewirkt und damit Lernen.

In der Praxis wird der Verstehensprozess von Bildern häufig nach der automatischen natürlichen Bildverarbeitung abgebrochen (vgl. Weidenmann 1994, S. 51), weil das Wahrnehmen selektiv ist, das heißt, man nimmt etwas wahr, was man erwartet. Um ein mit den Erwartungen übereinstimmendes Bild zu bekommen, ist man bereit, Details zu übersehen, übermäßig zu betonen bzw. unvollständig Wahrgenommenes zu vervollständigen. Macaire und Hosch (1996, S. 104) beschrieben die Gefahr, dass sich Lernende schnell vom Bild abwenden, weil sie glauben, dass sie das Bild schon verstanden haben, ohne es näher und genauer anzuschauen und damit wird nicht nur die Chance vertan, die Bilder bieten, sondern es entstehen evtl. auch Missverständnisse. Um diesen Gefahren zu entkommen, wird m. E. eine verlangsamte, bewusste und intensive Wahrnehmung gefordert, was auch Beitrag für interkulturelle Kompetenzentwicklung im FU leistet.

2. Interkulturelles Lernen

Clapeyron(2004, S. 5f.)stellt fest, dass man schon lange in einer Gesellschaft lebt, die von Ein-und Auswanderung geprägt ist, und in einer Arbeitswelt, die sich stets internationalisiert. Deshalb steht man vor der Situation, mit Menschen verschiedener Herkunft und anderer Kulturen in unmittelbarer Nähe wohnen und arbeiten zu müssen. Die Konfrontation mit „ Fremden " ist für den Menschen schon immer eine unbequeme Situation gewesen, die zunächst Unsicherheit, Unverständnis und ein gewisses Unwohlsein auslösen. In diesem Sinne werden pädagogische Einrichtungen beauftragt, Lernende zu befähigen, in interkulturellen Kontexten zu leben und zu arbeiten.

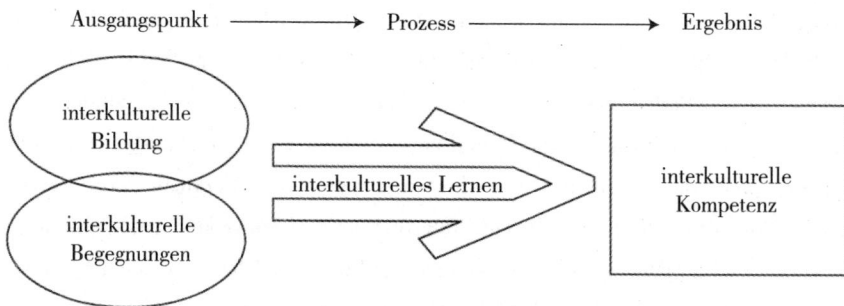

Abb. 1(aus: Clapeyron, 2004, S. 6)

Barkowski und Eβer(2005) erwähnten in ihrem Aufsatz „ wie buchstabiert man K-U-L-T-U-R? ", dass der FU ein Ort interkultureller Begegnung ist. Nach Abb. 1 erfüllt deshalb der FU die zwei Ausgangspunkte des kulturellen Lernens. Fragen sind dabei: Wie läuft eigentlich der Prozess des interkulturellen Lernens ab? Welche interkulturelle Kompetenz kann man durch welche didaktischen Mittel und welche Prozessgestaltung im FU trainiert werden? Welche Probleme gibt es bei der interkulturellen Kompetenzentwicklung? Zur Beschäftigung mit interkulturellem Lernen sollte man vor allem den Begriff „ Kultur"klären.

2.1 Kultur

Vor über 50 Jahre erwähnten Kroeber und Kluckhohn (1952, S. 149f. zit. nach Oksaar 2003, S. 18) 164 überwiegend ethnologische Kulturbegriffe. Seitdem erscheinen zahlreiche neue Definitionen über Kultur aus unterschiedlichen Betrachtungsperspektiven. Steinbacher (1976, S. 7 zit. nach ebd. S. 19) registrierte 1976 schon 300 Begriffe von Kultur.

In diesem Beitrag sollen aber nur Definitionen auf das kulturelle Handlungsorientierungssystem begrenzt werden, das sich auf Bildwahrnehmung auswirken könnte.

Alexander Thomas (1996, S. 112) definiert Kultur als:

> „ ... ein universelles, für eine Gesellschaft, Organisation und Gruppe aber sehr typisches Orientierungssystem. Dieses Orientierungssystem wird aus spezifischen Symbolen gebildet und in der jeweiligen Gesellschaft usw. tradiert. Es beeinflusst das Wahrnehmen, Denken, Werten und Handeln aller ihrer Mitglieder und definiert somit deren Zugehörigkeit zur Gesellschaft. Kultur als Orientierungssystem strukturiert ein für die sich der Gesellschaftzugehörig fühlenden Individuen spezifisches Handlungsfeld und schafft damit die Voraussetzungen zur Entwicklung eigenständiger Formen der Umweltbewältigung. "

Meine Kritik an dieser Definition wäre, dass sie keine „ Einzelkulturen " bzw. „ Subkulturen " berücksichtigt und Abgrenzung zwischen Kulturen überbetont. Als Ergänzungen würde ich folgende Bemerkungen machen:

● Altmayer (1997, S. 9) meint, dass der Kulturbegriff zwar einerseits der überindividuellen „ Standardisierung " von Verhaltens-, Denk-, Empfindungsweisen sowie Wertorientierungen gerecht werden muss, „ er muss aber andererseits auch hinreichend Spielräume lassen für die je individuelle Ausgestaltung solcher Standardisierungen. Gerade im Hinblick auf Lern-und Unterrichtsprozesse, wie sie im Zentrum des Faches Deutsch als Fremdsprache stehen, muss der Kulturbegriff so gefasst werden, dass er auch den Individuen in ihrer Subjektivität und Emotionalität gerecht wird... ", nämlich sollen Lernende sich bewusst sein: Einerseits ist Kultur zwar Orientierungssystem einer gesellschaftlichen Gruppe, es bedeutet aber nicht, dass alle Mitglieder in dieser Gruppe absolut gleich handeln und absolut gleiche Denkweisen besitzen, sondern jedes Individuum ist Geschöpf einer spezifischen Kultur (vgl. Eβer 2006, S. 5). Im FU ist Kultur deshalb vor allem als ein

Orientierungssystem ansehbar, das Einfluss auf deren Mitglieder ausübt. Anschließend muss aber Einzelkultur berücksichtigt werden, um Stereotypen zu vermeiden.

●Bolten(2007 S. 16)konstatiert, dass Kulturen keine Container sind, sie sind weder homogen noch mit dem Zirkel voneinander abgrenzbar, sondern an den Rändern mehr oder weniger stark „ ausgefranst " zu denken. Unterschiedliche Kulturen beeinflussen sich einander und haben bestimmte Gemeinsamkeiten. Transkulturelle Konzepte versuchen Phänomene mit kulturübergreifenden, d. h. nicht an einen bestimmten Kulturraum gebundenen Gemeinsamkeiten zu beschreiben. Sie gehen davon aus, dass es sich bei der Beschäftigung mit der Kultur von Menschen immer um folgende Aspekte handelt(vgl. Biechele 2006, S. 27):

- ❖ Natur des Menschen
- ❖ Beziehung von Menschen und Natur
- ❖ Zeitgefühl
- ❖ Aktivitäten
- ❖ Soziale Beziehungen

Um darstellen zu können, in welchen allgemeinen, übergreifenden Kategorien sich Kulturen grundsätzlich unterscheiden und in ihrer strukturierten Gesamtheit das spezifische Profil einer Kultur bilden, beschrieb Maletzke(1996, zit. nach ebd.) „ kulturelle Strukturmerkmale", wie

- ❖ Nationalcharakter, Basispersönlichkeit
- ❖ Wahrnehmung, Denken, Wertorientierung
- ❖ Zeit-und Raumerleben
- ❖ Verhaltensmuster: Sitten, Normen, Rollen
- ❖ Soziale Beziehungen
- ❖ Kommunikationsweise

Diese transkulturellen Konzepte und kulturellen Strukturmerkmale sind ein wichtiges Themenauswahlkriterium des interkulturellen Lernens im FU. Genauer gesagt betrifft es in diesem Beitrag die Bildauswahlkriterien.

2. 2　Interkultur

Wie der Kulturbegriff ist „ Interkultur"auch uneinheitlich definiert. Mit Blick auf das Lernen mit Bildern ist es wichtig, dass die Lernenden in Vorbereitung auf spätere interkulturelle Situationen ihre Wahrnehmung schärfen. Daher wird versucht, den

Begriff „ Interkultur " mit Bezug auf den Einfluss von Kultur auf Wahrnehmung zu beschreiben. Nach Bolten(2007, S. 22) hat das lateinische „ inter" eine Bedeutung im Sinne von „ zwischen ". Interkultur kann sich zu Zwischenkultur verwandeln, hierbei handelt es sich aber weniger um einen Raum als um einen Prozessbegriff: Interkulturen entstehen dann, wenn Beteiligte aus den unterschiedlichen Kulturen miteinander agieren bzw. kommunizieren. Dieser Prozess wird nach Losche (1995, S. 65) nicht nur von unterschiedlichen Kommunikationssignalen, sondern auch von unterschiedlicher Wahrnehmung und Interpretation dessen, was die anderen mitteilen und wie sie es tun, beeinflusst. Um zu einer situationsadäquaten Einschätzung zu gelangen, greift dabei jeder der Beteiligten auf den jeweiligen soziokulturell geprägten Erfahrungshintergrund zurück. Tritt dann die vorausberechnete Reaktion nicht ein, entsteht Verunsicherung.

Eine Interaktion kann nur zu allseitiger Zufriedenheit gelingen, wenn die Interpretationsschemata übereinstimmen. Interpretation heißt Verleihen einer Bedeutung dem Wahrgenommenen. Aus dieser Interpretation entsteht ein Gefühl oder ein Urteil, das die Handlung in der Kommunikation direkt bewirkt (ebd.). Somit spielt Wahrnehmen eine große Rolle dabei, zugleich ist es oft problematisch:

● Wahrnehmen wird unbewusst von der eigenen Kultur gesteuert, und deshalb nimmt man oft die fremdkulturellen Phänomene auf der Folie der eigenen Kultur wahr. Es kann zu schwerwiegenden Missverständnissen führen, wenn man ein in der eigenen Kultur übliches Deutungsmuster unreflektiert auf Erscheinungen anderer Kulturen anwendet.

● Unsere Wahrnehmung ist subjektiv und erfahrungsabhängig. Das heißt, sie bleibt nicht frei von Emotionen, Voreinstellungen, Motivationen. Je näher das Andere auf „ Eigenes " zukommt, desto akzeptabler und vertrauter wird es. Wie „ fern " und fremd etwas Fremdes ist, kommt nicht auf die objektiven Kriterien an, wie geografische Entfernungen, sondern wird von Subjekt entschieden.

● Unsere Wahrnehmung ist selektiv und konstruiert. Um ein mit unseren Erwartungen übereinstimmendes Bild zu bekommen, sind wir bereit, Details zu übersehen oder übermäßig zu betonen, spezifische Einzelmerkmale als repräsentativ für das Ganze anzusehen, unvollständig Wahrgenommenes zu vervollständigen. Durch dieses Umdeuten der Umwelt entstehen oft Missverständnisse.

● Unsere Wahrnehmung wird häufig nach der automatischen natürlichen Verarbeitung der Anderen abgebrochen. Nach Badstübner-Kizik(2007, S. 20) kommen schnelle Wahrnehmung, schnelle Interpretation, schnelles Urteil und dann schnelle Abhandlung oft beim Umgang mit Anderen vor. Durch diese schnelle Wahrnehmung ohne Reflexion, Analyse und Differenz entstehen oft Stereotypen und Vorurteile, die die individuellen Unterschiede übersehen.

Zusammengefasst wird Wahrnehmung von der eigenen Kultur stark und unbewusst beeinflusst, was bei interkultureller Begegnung oft zu Missverständnissen und Konflikten führen. Um sie möglichst zu vermeiden, wird eine bewusste mit Eigenkulturreflexion und Fremdkulturanalyse verbundene Wahrnehmung gefordert.

2.3 Interkulturelle Kompetenz

Nach Abb. 1 wird deutlich, dass die Zielsetzung des interkulturellen Lernens die Vermittlung und Schulung der interkulturellen Kompetenz ist. Definitionen von interkultureller Kompetenz kommen in unterschiedlichen Bereichen vor wegen der unterschiedlichen Schwerpunkten sind sie nicht übereinstimmend. Barkowski (2001, S. 299) fasst interkulturelle Kompetenz als Handlungsfähigkeit bei der interkulturellen Begegnung zusammen. Genauer definiert Bolten (2007, S. 87f.) sie „ als das erfolgreiche ganzheitliche Zusammenspiel von individuellem, sozialem, fachlichem und strategischem Handeln in interkulturellen Kontexten" und „ Jemand ist interkulturell kompetent, wenn er in der Lage ist, dieses synergetische Zusammenspiel von individuellem, sozialem, fachlichem und strategischem Handeln ausgewogen zu gestalten. "

In Bezug auf den DaF-Unterricht wird sie konkret in Profile Deutsch dargestellt:

Interkulturelles Bewusstsein	Interkulturelle Fertigkeiten
Kenntnisse, Bewusstsein und Verständnis von Ähnlichkeiten und Unterschieden verschiedener Welten und Kulturen. Bewusstsein über die eigenkulturell geprägte Wahrnehmung (Vorurteile und Stereotypen).	Die Fähigkeit, die Ausgangskultur und die fremde Kultur miteinander in Beziehung zu setzen. Die Fähigkeit, Strategien für den Kontakt mit Angehörigen anderer Kulturen zu identifizieren und anzuwenden. Die Fähigkeit, als kultureller Mittler zu agieren und wirksam mit interkulturellen Missverständnissen und Konfliktsituationen umzugehen. Die Fähigkeit, stereotype Beziehungen zu überwinden.

kulturelle Kompetenz in Profile Deutsch(*aus Glaboniat* 2002, *S.* 36)

Zusammengefasst werden m. E. die folgenden Schwerpunkte betont:

● Fähigkeit zum Kulturvergleich

● Bewusste Reflexion der eigenen Wahrnehmung, zwecks Explizieren von Stereotypen und Vorurteile

● Umgang mit Missverständnissen und Konflikten in der interkulturellen Kommunikation.

Der letzte Punkt wird auf der Basis der anderen zwei Punkte aufgebaut. Ohne die Fähigkeit zum Kulturvergleich sowie Bewusstwerden von Stereotypen und Vorurteilen kann man Missverständnisse und Konflikte nicht vermeiden.

2.4 Interkulturelles Lernen im DaF-Unterricht

Der FU ist per se ein Ort der interkulturellen Begegnung. Er soll und kann „ tatsächlich auf interkulturelles Handeln in einer (veränderten) mehrsprachigen Welt vorbereiten. " (Krumm 1995; zit. nach Badstübner-Kizik 2007, S. 18). Vor diesem Hintergrund kommt der interkulturelle Ansatz im FU immer mehr ins Spiel. Sein Erkenntnis-und Forschungsgegenstand sind Ausschnitte aus der eigenen Kultur in ihren Beziehungen und Wechselwirkungen zu Ausschnitten aus einer anderen Kultur (vgl. Li 2007, S. 42). Durch die dargestellte Begrifflichkeit von Kultur, Interkultur und interkulturelle Kompetenz wird verdeutlicht, oberflächliche Vermittlung über fremde Verhaltensweise, Sitten und Gebräuche nicht erreichen können, Lernende in der interkulturellen Begegnung richtig handeln zu lassen. In einem interkulturellen FU sollen Lernende nicht nur Fremdsprachenerkenntnisse und faktische Landeskunde erwerben, sondern auch interkulturelles Bewusstsein und interkulturelle Fertigkeiten entwickeln.

Nach Badstübner-Kizik (2007, S. 18) und Li (2007, S. 42) weist der interkulturelle Ansatz zwar auch noch einen starken Handlungsbezug auf, aber es geht hier nicht um Vermittlung von angemessener Verhaltensweise in der Zielsprache, sondern er versucht, den potenziellen kulturellen Konflikt produktiv zu nutzen, indem ein systematisches Wahrnehmungstraining durchgeführt wird, das kulturgebundene Deutungsmuster in der Mutter-und Fremdsprache aufsucht und Prozesse des Selbst-und Fremdverstehens in den Mittelpunkt rückt, somit wird der Kulturvergleich nicht nur als Nebenprodukt des Unterrichts hingenommen, sondern absichtlich angeregt. Ziel dabei ist, sowohl das Fremde auf der Folie des Eigenen besser zu verstehen als auch das Eigene durch das Fremde in Frage stellen zu lassen und differenzierter einschätzen zu können. Kurz in zwei Stichwörtern zusammengefasst: Wahrnehmungstraining und/ mit Kulturvergleich:

●Wahrnehmungstraining kann die interkulturellen Schwierigkeiten auf einerseits schnelle oberflächliche Wahrnehmung eines Fremden, andererseits unbewusste Übertragung eigener Wahrnehmung auf den Anderen zurückführen. Deshalb sollte es beim interkulturellen Lernen im FU zwei Seiten berücksichtigen:

❖ Bewusste Wahrnehmung eines fremden Objektes bzw. einer fremden Situation, das schrittweise, langsame Aufnehmen seiner bzw. ihrer Botschaft (vgl. Badstübner-Kizik 2007, S. 20). Durch entsprechende Aufgabenstellungen, die zur Genauigkeit zwingen, gelingt die verlangsamte und sensible Wahrnehmung, die als Voraussetzung des Kulturkennens gilt. Kultur ist abstrakt und die wahrnehmbaren kulturellen Phänomene sind nur ein kleiner Oberflächenteil von Kultur, aber sie sind der erste Anhaltspunkt (vgl. Eβer 2006, S. 6). Das heißt, die Lernenden können durch Wahrnehmen und dann Analysieren der Oberflächenphänomene die verdeckte nicht wahrnehmbare, aber wesentlich als Grundlage dieser Phänomene dienende Kultur konstituieren.

❖ Bewusste Reflexion der eigenen Wahrnehmung im Verhältnis zu anderen und ihre schrittweise sprachliche Umsetzung. Wichtig werden neben Fragen, wie „ *Wie finde ich das?* ", auch andere, wie „ *Warum gefällt es mir(nicht)* "? (vgl. Badstübner-Kizik 2007, S. 20). Dadurch kann man sich auch den eigenen Standpunkt und die eigene Kultur bewusst machen und daraus schließend entsteht Rollendistanz und weiterhin „ Bewusstsein über die eigenkulturell geprägte Wahrnehmung(Vorurteile und Stereotypen) ".

●Kulturvergleich: Barkowski(1992, S. 187. zitiert nach Merten 1995, S. 216) präzisiert, dass interkulturelles Lernen „ Lernen von Menschen, die einander in einigem oder vielem gleichen und sich zur gleichen Zeit in vielem oder einigem voneinander unterscheiden " ist. Nämlich ist Kulturkontrast nicht nur eine bedeutende Methode, sondern auch die Wesenheit des interkulturellen Lernens. Durch Vergleich und Analyse der Unterschiede und Gemeinsamkeiten zwischen zwei Kulturen wird nicht nur Zielkultur vermittelt, sondern macht auch scheinbar selbstverständliche „ Eigenkultur " explizit(vgl. Kiel 1997). Durch Kulturvergleich kann man Kenntnisse, Bewusstsein und Verständnis von Ähnlichkeiten und Unterschieden verschiedener Welten und Kulturen erwerben. Sie sind Voraussetzung der Fertigkeiten, die Ausgangskultur und die fremde Kultur miteinander in Beziehung zu setzen und Missverständnisse sowie Konflikte zu vermeiden oder zu umgehen.

In der Praxis werden sie oft zusammengebunden. Kulturvergleich integriert sich in Wahrnehmungstraining. Mit einer intensiven, bewussten und verlangsamten Wahrnehmung von Fremdem sowie einer reflektierenden Wahrnehmung von Eigenem lässt sich ein stereotyp- und vorurteilsfreier Kulturvergleich realisieren. Kulturvergleich ist ein wichtiger Teil des Wahrnehmungstrainings. Durch den Vergleich lässt sich erst „ das Fremde " in vorhandene Schemata integrieren und dies dient als Voraussetzung der Interpretation, nämlich der Rekonstruktion der Schemata.

3. Bilder zum Ziel der Beförderung interkultureller Kompetenz im DaF-Unterricht

„ Mein Bild von Deutschland, Erlebte Landeskunde mit Bildern, so stelle ich mir den typischen Deutschen vor, Mimik und Gestik in Bildern, Werbebilder mit Stereotypen, Landeskundebilder u. v. a. evozieren die Auseinandersetzung mit der Frage, welche Potenzen Bilder für den Ansatz interkulturellen Lernens besitzen. " (Biechele 1998, S. 26)

●Bilder sind kulturelle Produkte und repräsentieren die Perspektive der jeweiligen Kultur. Sie sind ein Anhaltpunkt einer Kultur. Durch Interpretation kann man die tiefe Kulturstruktur erreichen.

●Für den Einsatz von Bildern ergibt sich nach Biechele (2006, S. 34) eine doppelte Offenheit, eine, die auf der Polyvalenz von Bildern beruht, und eine, die der fremdkulturell geprägte Betrachter in seine Interpretation einbringt. Bilder zeigen stets Menschen in bestimmten soziokulturellen Kontexten, Personen in definierten Raum-Zeit-Verhältnissen, Menschen, die in bestimmten Tätigkeitssituationen Aussagen über die spezielle Alltagskultur anregen, und dabei werden diese Informationen komplex und vollständig vermittelt. Die Deutungen, die Lernende in Bezug auf Bilder vornehmen, sind kulturspezifisch.

●Andersartigkeit und Gemeinsamkeiten sind leicht in Bildern zu erkennen, was für den Kulturvergleich sehr bedeutungsvoll ist (vgl. Badstübner-Kizik 2007, S. 19). In der Regel müssen während des Rezeptionsprozesses nur geringe sprachliche Barrieren überwunden werden. Somit können sich Lernende mehr auf den Inhalt konzentrieren, ohne Berücksichtigung der komplizierten (Fremd-) sprachestrukturen.

● Beim Wahrnehmungstraining durch Bilder können die Betrachtungsvorgänge problemlos beliebig oft und unter immer neuen Gesichtspunkten wiederholt werden. Lehrende können zum Beispiel die Bilder zerschneiden, um ein Detail zu betonen, oder sie umdrehen, um einen neuen Betrachtungsstandpunkt zu bekommen.

●Lernende einer Fremdsprache haben Bilder im Kopf, mentale Bilder oder internale Wissensformen, Bilder der eigenen Kultur und solche der Ziel- oder Fremdkultur. Bilder können diese impliziten Bilder(vgl. Bolten 2007, S. 90), inkl. Stereotypen und Vorurteile darstellen. Zum Beispiel durch Bildanalyse einer „ typischen"Personen- oder Situationsdarstellungen können sich Lernende diese Stereotypen und Vorurteile bewusst machen.

● Bilderkommen beim Wissenserwerb ins Spiel, wobei Wissen nicht nur deklaratives, sondern auch prozedurales Wissen bedeutet. Bilder entweder aus der eigenen oder der fremden Kultur können nicht nur kulturelles Faktenwissen vermitteln, sondern initiieren auch das kulturelle prozedurale Wissen, das sich der interkulturellen Kompetenz widmet.

Bilder werden zwar oft im FU und in fremdsprachlichen Lehrwerken eingesetzt, aber in Bezug auf den interkulturellen Ansatz im FU mangelt es noch an Arbeiten und Forschungen(vgl. Biechele 2006, S. 17). Die Schwerpunkte liegen darin, dass einerseits in Bezug auf die Bildauswahl unter fremdkulturellem und interkulturellem Aspekt noch bis heute Fragen existieren(ebd. , S. 36)und andererseits interkulturelles Bildverstehen einer der großen„ weißen Flecken" in der Bildforschung ist(vgl. Sturm 1991, S. 7). Denn Bildwahrnehmung ist subjektiv und kulturgeprägt. Ein gleiches Bild wird von den Bildrezipienten aus verschieden Kulturkreisen unterschiedlich wahrgenommen und interpretiert. Es besteht sogar die Gefahr, dass es in bestimmten Kulturen durchaus in den Bereich von Bildtabus einzuordnen ist, da durch die Art der Darstellung Maximen kulturellen Handelns verletzt werden könnten(vgl. Biechele 2006, S. 39). Deshalb ist es unmöglich, ohne die Bilderrezipienten zu berücksichtigen, allgemein und überall geltende Bilder zur interkulturellen Kompetenzschulung auszuwählen und einzusetzen. Aus diesen Gründen wäre es dann vernünftig, dass die Arbeit zu diesem Thema sich auf bestimmte Bildrezipientenbezieht, bei Auswahl der Bilder und Prozessgestaltung sollen Lehrende neben der Zielkultur auch die Ausgangskultur der Lernenden berücksichtigen. Bilder sollten sich auf„ kulturelle Strukturmerkmale"bzw. auf„ transkulturelle Konzepte"beziehen, zum Beispiel Menschen, Persönlichkeiten, Verhaltensmuster, soziale Beziehungen, kommunikative Dimension.

Zusammengefasst ergeben sich für interkulturell orientiertes Lernen mit Bildern folgende Handlungsfelder:

●sensibles, differenziertes Wahrnehmen des Abgebildeten, reflektierende Klärung, Verstehen des Fremden, Anerkennung des Anderen

●wesentliche Merkmale, Grundmuster und Entwicklungen der eigenen und der fremden Kultur erkennen, Fremdverstehen und Selbsterkenntnis

- ●Fokus auf Gleiches und Unterschiedliches richten
- ● Bilder aus Ausgangskultur verwenden und mit denen aus Zielkultur oder verschiedenen Kulturen vergleichen
- ●eigene Bilder der Lerner verwenden

Bilder spielen beim interkulturellen Lernen nicht nur die Rolle als visuelle fremdkulturelle Informationsträger, sondern übernehmen auch Aufgaben zur Schulung der interkulturellen Kompetenz. Durch das Lernen mit Bildern sollen sich Lernende eigene Wahrnehmungen bewusst machen und trainieren, bewusst langsam und sorgfältig das Fremde wahrzunehmen. Auf dieser Basis fügt Kulturvergleich erst hinzu, um zu vermeiden, dass Lernende zwei Kulturen mit eigenen Stereotypen und Vorurteilen ungerecht vergleichen, interpretieren und beurteilen. Deshalb soll der Schwerpunkt beim Bildeinsatz nicht nur auf der Andersartigkeit in Bildern liegen, sondern mehr auf dem bewussten Wahrnehmungsprozess. Nach obigen Theorien werden folgenden Kriterien zur Auswahl von Bildern und zur Prozessgestaltung im DaF-Unterricht herangezogen:

3.1 Auswahlkriterien

Bilder, die für Lerner zu einfach oder zu komplex sind, die viele fremde Informationen enthalten, die uninteressant sind, oder für deren Verarbeitungsprozess der Lernende die notwendigen Strategien indikatorischen Verarbeitens nicht zur Verfügung hat oder nicht erhält, bewirken keine Veränderung kognitiver Strukturen. Nach der Charakterisierung der Wahrnehmung des indikatorischen Bildverstehens im Kontext interkulturellen Lernens soll der Lehrende bei der Bildauswahl im FU folgende Kriterien berücksichtigen (vgl. Sturm 1991, S. 6; Scherling & Schuckall 1994, S. 32 – 40; Biechele 1998, S. 25; 2006, 40f. ; Li 2007, S. 202):

❖Bilder sollen an die Erfahrungswelt des Lerners anknüpfen, dadurch Emotionen bewirken, Assoziationen ermöglichen und vermeiden, dass Lerner aus Mangel an Vorwissen die gezeigten Bilder nicht verstehen können.

❖Bilder sollten neben vertrauten Abbildungselementen und-techniken auch solche der Fremdheit, des Ungewohnten, des nicht Erwarteten enthalten, d. h. , sie sollten die Neugier von Lernenden wecken, um zu vermeiden, dass Lernende die Bilder nur überfliegen.

❖Bilder sollten „ unvollständig " in mehrfacher Hinsicht sein: Sie sollten inhaltlich Leerstellen wie auch gestalterische Lücken bzw. Fremdheiten aufweisen und damit eine tiefere Auseinandersetzung und ein Handeln als Elaborieren,

Ergänzen, Vervollständigen bewirken.

❖ Bilder sollten funktionsgerecht, wie offen, anregend, informativ, mehrdeutig sein, damit Lernende sie interpretieren können.

❖ Es sollten Bilder zum Entdecken sein. Der Anreiz dazu kann sich auf den Bildautor/ Künstler, die Geschichte, die Kultur, die Intention usw. richten, aber auch auf die Details, die abgebildet sind, bzw. auf die Geschichte, die „ erzählt " wird, damit Lernende Interesse für die tiefere Bildverarbeitung behalten können.

❖ Bilder sollten authentisch sein, nicht für Lehrzwecke produziert, damit eine authentische Kommunikationssituation im FU entsteht, sonst verlieren Lernende auch schnell das Interesse an Bildern.

❖ Es sollten verschiedenste Bildarten, Bildgenres, Handschriften, Quellen sein, eingeschlossen Bilder aus verschiedenen Kulturen, Zeitepochen usw.

❖ Bilder sollten aufgabenfähig sein, d. h. angezielte Lernhandlungen müssen bildangemessen und sinnvoll sein.

❖ Bilder in Lehrbüchern für DaF oder im DaF-Unterricht sollen sich auf Kulturmerkmale und transkulturelle Konzepte beziehen und sie in hohem Maße veranschaulichen sowie Möglichkeiten einräumen, fremdkulturelles Wissen akzentuiert oder immanent zu erwerben.

❖ Bilder dürfen Themen, Inhalte und Darstellungsformen nicht aufgreifen, die Tabuthemen in der Kultur der Lernenden ansprechen.

❖ Last, not least soll die inhaltliche Qualität und auch die Darstellungsqualität von Bildern berücksichtigt werden. Weil Wahrnehmung subjektiv und selektiv ist, sehen wir, was wir sehen möchten. Wenn die dargestellten Bilder schlechte Qualität haben, z. B. eine chaotische Struktur oder Unerkennbarkeit, möchten sich Lernende auch nicht damit beschäftigen.

3.2 Didaktische Prozessgestaltung

Der Vorgang der Bildwahrnehmung erfolgt oft unbewusst: In weniger als einer Sekunde entsteht bereits ein Globalverständnis, mit dem die Bildwahrnehmung normalerweise abgeschlossen ist. Im FU kommt es wesentlich darauf an, diesen Vorgang zu verlangsamen, genau hinzuschauen, um das Spezifische einer fremden Kultur sehen zu lernen. Das Grundprinzip ist Verbalisierung(vgl. Weidenmann, 1991, S. 16):

❖ Legenden, die die Wahrnehmung explizit steuern. Direkte Hinweise für das Bildlese-Verhalten des Betrachters scheinen besonders sinnvoll bei der Schulung des Bildverstehens.

❖ Aufgaben, für deren Bearbeitung das Bild zutreffend untersucht und befragt werden muss. Zum Beispiel ein Bild beschriften, den Inhalt zusammenfassen, Bilder vergleichen, Bilder ergänzen.

❖ Gemeinsames Reden über das Bild/ Interpretation des Bildes in der Klasse. Hier dienen Bilder nicht nur als Redeanlass/Sprechanlass, sondern tragen auch zur tieferen Verarbeitung von Bildern und zur Schulung des Bildverstehens bei. Denn Bildverstehen geschieht subjektiv, selektiv, erfahrungsabhängig, deshalb ist das Verstehensergebnis sehr unterschiedlich. Durch gemeinsames Reden interpretiert jeder sein eigenes Verstehensergebnis, dann haben die Lernenden mehr Chancen, aus unterschiedlichen Aspekten dasselbe Bild zu betrachten und zu verstehen.

Das methodische Vorgehen beim Wahrnehmungstraining sollte in Phasen verlaufen, die den Lernenden vom Bekannten zur Interpretation des Fremden führen. Konkret, verbunden mit Weidenmanns „ 5-Stufe-Modell" sind die folgenden didaktischen Vorschläge vorzubringen (vgl. Weidenmann 1994, S. 53ff. ; Macaire & Hosch 1996, S. 107f. ; Biechele 1998, S. 26f. ; Scholz 2004, S. 112; Weidenmann 2004, S. 247ff. ; Biechele 2006, S. 38;) :

❖ Bevor man einem Bild begegnet, ist bereits eine bestimmte Erwartungshaltung aufgebaut, denn im Alltag findet die Begegnung mit einem Bild nicht in einem luftleeren Raum statt, sondern sie ist eingebettet in eine bestimmte Situation. Im FU soll der Lehrende durch bestimmte Aufgabenstellungen den Lernenden helfen, einen Kontext bzw. eine Erwartungshaltung aufzubauen.

❖ Wenn der Lernende ein Bild ansieht, aktiviert er schnell und unbewusst sein Vorwissen. Im Unterricht orientiert sich der Blick der Lernende an Bekanntem, um zu einem Globalverständnis zu kommen. Zu diesem Zeitpunkt soll der Lehrende Lernende steuern, Vorwissen und Erfahrungswelt der Lernende ansprechen, um Bekanntes zu identifizieren. In der Regel wird der Bildkontakt abgebrochen, wenn man das Gefühl hat, das Bild verstanden zu haben-wenn das Bild nicht zuviel Unbekanntes enthält. Um dies zu vermeiden, soll der Lehrende durch Hinweise, wie „

Achten Sie besonders auf...", oder durch Hinzeigen bzw. optische Mittel, wie Abdecken der anderen Bildteile, Ausschnittsvergrößerung, farbliche Markierung, die Lernenden auffordern, Details in diesem Bild zu beachten, dabei sollen etliche Aufgabenstellung angeboten werden, damit Lernende aktiv etwas mit dem Bild tun müssen, z. B. es beschriften, abzeichnen, ergänzen usw., um das Fremde zu erkennen und zu benennen.

❖ Wenn die dargestellten Elemente unter einem fremden Schema liegen, z. B. fremde Darstellungskonvention, fremde Kultursymbole, kann es zu Fehlinterpretationen und Missverständnissen kommen. Lernende neigen dazu, Unbekanntes/Fremdes in einem Bild zu überspringen. Es ist dann nötig, dass Interesse für ein genaues Bildverstehen zu wecken, d. h. Details im Bild und auch Unbekanntes/Fremdes sehen zu wollen. Dazu muss der Lehrende das Vorwissen systematisch ergänzen-durch die Einführung von Zusatzkenntnissen über Darstellungskonventionen (z. B. unterschiedliche Leserichtung, Perspektive im Bild, die Bedeutungen der Farben), über Phänomene, Sachverhalte oder Prozesse aus der fremden Kultur. Diese Kenntnisse können mündlich von Lehrenden ergänzt oder von Lernenden mit Hilfe von Wörterbüchern und Nachschlagewerken, weiteren Bildern und Zusatztexten selbst erschlossen werden.

❖ Um die neuen Informationen in die vorhandenen Schemata besser zu integrieren, kann man die neuen Informationen mit eigenem Vorwissen vergleichen(*Was ist gleich/ähnlich/anders als Ihre Vorstellung/ Erwartung/ Kultur/Erfahrung...?*), dadurch werden die neu wahrgenommenen Informationen stabilisiert.

❖ Aus der Zusammensetzung der Einzelwahrnehmungen entsteht dann ein genaueres Bild, erst daraus ergibt sich eine genauere Bedeutung. Durch Interpretation und gemeinsames Reden über dieses rekonstruierte Bild und die Beurteilung(*Wie gefällt Ihnen das? Wie finden Sie das? Was fällt Ihnen auf? ...*)wird eine kognitive und emotionale Reaktion initiiert, damit diese besser im Gedächtnis gespeichert und auch nach einer längeren Zeit abgerufen werden kann.

4. Zusammenfassung

Der(Bild-) Wahrnehmungsprozess ist subjektiv, konstruktiv und abhängig vom jeweiligen kulturellen Orientierungssystem. Zu den Erklärungen über die Begriffe „ Kultur" und „ Interkultur" bin ich von einem weit gefassten und nicht ausgrenzenden Orientierungssystem ausgegangen, das oft unbewusst Wahrnehmung und Handlungen des Mitgliedes in der jeweiligen Kultur steuert, deshalb bestehen eventuell Missverständnisse in der interkulturellen Kommunikation. Um interkulturellen Konflikte zu lösen oder gar zu vermeiden, soll die interkulturelle Kompetenz gefördert werden, was das Ziel des interkulturellen Lernens ist. Gemäß der Beschreibung der Anforderungen der interkulturellen Kompetenz in „ Profile Deutsch " werden die folgenden Teilziele in meiner Arbeit betont:

● Fähigkeit zum Kulturvergleich

● Bewusste Reflexion der eigenen Wahrnehmung, um Stereotypen und Vorurteile zu explizieren bzw. zu überwinden

● Fähigkeit zum Umgang mit Missverständnissen und Konflikten in der interkulturellen Kommunikation.

Durch Wahrnehmungstraining und Kulturvergleich könnten diese Teilziele durchgesetzt werden. Dabei bieten Bilder vielfältige Potenziale. Trotzdem können nicht alle Bilder eingesetzt werden, nach der Wahrnehmungsforschung von Weidenmann und der interkulturellen Trainingsforschung entwickeln sich die Auswahlkriterien und die didaktischen Prozessgestaltungsimplikationen, die die theoretische Grundlage anbieten, wie man ein Curriculum mit Bildern didaktisiert, um interkulturelle Kompetenz im DaF-Unterricht zu fördern.

Das institutionelle Lernen bzw. die konkrete Unterrichtssituationwerden „ von einer Fülle von – offen zutage tretenden oder verdeckt wirksamen – Faktoren beeinflusst" (Neuner 2001, S. 37). Das Gelingen eines Konzeptes ist folglich „ das Ergebnis des Zusammenwirkens zahlreicher Faktoren [...], die sich sowohl auf die Lehr-und Lernbedingungen im Klassenzimmer als auch auf psychologische und soziale Komponenten außerhalb des Klassenzimmers beziehen und die selbstverständlich in engem Bezug zum Lerngegenstand zu sehen sind" (Bausch & Krumm 1995, S. 9) Aus diesem Grund muss man bei der didaktischen Forschung immer das komplexe Geschehen im Blick behalten und den speziellen Kontext, in dem das Ergebnis erzielte wird, ausführlich erläutern. Man müsste nach den unterschiedlichen praktischen Rahmenbedingungen das Curriculum bearbeiten und verändern.

Literaturverzeichnis

[1] Altmayer, C. *Zum Kulturbegriff des Faches Deutsch als Fremdsprache* [J]. In:

Zeitschrift für Interkulturellen Fremdsprachenunterricht[DB/OL]2(2). http：// zif. spz. tu-darmstadt. de/jg－02－2/beitrag/almayer3. htm，1997.

[2]Badstübner-Kizik，C. *Bild-und Musikkunst im Fremdsprachenunterricht：Zwischenbilanz und Handreichungen für die Praxis*[M]. Frankfurt/M：Langenscheidt，2007.

[3]Ballstaedt，S. P. *Bildverstehen und Sprache.* In：Spillner，Bernd（Hrsg. ）（1995）：*Sprache：Verstehen und Verständlichkeit. Kongressbeiträge zur 25. Jahrestagung der Gesellschaft für Angewandte Linguistik GAL e. V.* [C]Frankfurt/M：Europäischer Verlag der Wissenschaften，1995.

[4] Barkowski，H. *Esskultur，Subkultur，Kulturbeutel... Annäherung an einen Kulturbegriff im Kontext des fremdsprachendidaktischen Paradigmas Interkulturelles Lernen und Lehren.* In：Aguado，Karin；Riemer，Claudia（Hrsg. ）：*Wege und Ziele. Zur Theorie，Empirie und Praxis des Deutschen als Fremdsprache（und anderer Fremdsprachen）Festschrift für Gert Henrici zum 60. Geburtstag*[C]. Hohengehren：Schneiderverlag，2001.

[5] Barkowski，H；Eβer，R. *Wie buchstabiert man K-u-l-t-u-r? Überlegungen zu einem Kulturbegriff für Anliegen der Sprachlehr-und－lernforschung.* In：Duxa，Susanne；Hu，Adelheid u. a.（Hrsg. ）*Grenzen überschreiten. Menschen，Sprachen，Kulturen. Festschrift für Inge Christine Schwerdtfeger zum 60. Geburtstag*[C]. ，2005.

[6] Bering，K. *Bezugsfelder der Vermittlung visueller Kompetenz.* In：Huber，Hans Dieter；Lockemann，Bettina u. a.（Hrsg. ）：*Bild/Medien/Wissen：visuelle Kompetenz im Medienzeitalter*[C]. München：Kopaed，2002.

[7]Biechele，B. *Bilder als Kommunikate und Lernmedien im Fremdsprachenunterricht/ DaF*[J]. In：Info DaF 23/6. S. 746－757. ，1996.

[8] Biechele，B. *Visualisierung in Lehrwerken für DaF － ein Beitrag zur Gedächtnisschulung?* [J]In：*Materialien DaF*，H. 46/1997，1997.

[9] Biechele，B. *Wahrnehmen，Verstehen，Lernen － Implikationen für einen Paradigmenwechsel beim Arbeiten mit Bildmedien*[J]. In：ÖDaF-Mitteilungen，H. 1/1998，1998.

[10] Biechele，B. *Anmerkungen zum interkulturellen Bildverstehen* [DB/OL]. In：www. interculture journal. com Nr. 1/2006，2006.

[11]Bolten，J. *Interkulturelle Kompetenz*[M]. Erfurt：Landeszentrale für politische Bildung Thüringen，2007.

[12] Clapeyron，P. *Interkulturelle Kompetenz in der sozialpädagogischen Arbeit*[DB/

OL]. In Langholz, Claudia (Hrsg.) (2004): *Interkulturelle Kompetenz in der pädagogischen Praxis.* S. 5 – 15. http: //www. frsh. de/perspective/pdf/ Version26_ 05_ 04handr2. pdf , 2004

[13] Doelker, C. *Ein Bild ist mehr als ein Bild: visuelle Kompetenz in der Multimedia-Gesellschaft* [M]. Stuttgart: Klett-Cotta. 1997.

[14] Eβer, R. „ *Die deutschen Lehrer reden weniger und fragen mehr... ". Zur Relevanz des Kulturfaktors in DaF-Forschung und DaF-Praxis* [DB/OL]. In: Zeitschrift für interkulturellen Fremdsprachenunterricht 2006/3. http: // zif. spz. tu-darmstadt. de/jg – 11 – 3/beitrag/Esser1. htm, 2006.

[15] Glaboniat, M. *Profile Deutsch: gemeinsamer europäischer Referenzrahmen (mit CD Rom)* [M]. Berlin: Langenscheidt. , 2002.

[16] Goldstein, E. B. *Wahrnehmungspsychologie: der Grundkurs* [M]. 7. Aufl. Berlin: Spektrum Akademischer Verlag, 2008.

[17] Macaire, D. ; Hosch, W. *Bilder in der Landeskunde* [M]. Berlin, München, Leipzig, Wien, Zürich, New York: Langenscheidt, 1996.

[18] Oksaar, E. *Zweitspracherwerb. Wege zur Mehrsprachigkeit und zur interkulturellen Verständigung* [M]. Stuttgart: Kohlhammer, 2003.

[19] Peeck, J. *Wissenserwerb mit darstellenden Bildern* [C]. In: Weidenmann, Bernd (Hrsg.) (1994): *Wissenserwerb mit Bildern: instruktionale Bilder in Printmedien, Film/Video und Computerprogrammen.* Bern: Huber, 1994.

[20] Scherling, T. ; Schuckall, H. F. *Mit Bildern lernen: Handbuch für den Fremdsprachenunterricht* [M]. 3. Aufl. Berlin, München, Leipzig, Wien, Zürich, New York: Langenscheidt, 1994.

[21] Scholz, O. *Was heißt es, ein Bild zu verstehen?* [C] In: Sachs-Hombach, Klaus; Rehkämper, Klaus (Hrsg.) (2004): *Bild-Bildwahrnehmung-Bildverarbeitung: Interdisziplinäre Beiträge zur Bildwissenschaft.* 2. Aufl. Wiesbaden: Deutscher Universitäts-Verlag, 2004.

[22] Sturm, D. : *Das Bild im Unterricht* [J]. In: Goethe Institut (1991): *Fremdsprache Deutsch / Sondernummer.* München: Klett Ed. Deutsch, 1991.

[23] Sturm, D. *Visualisierung.* In: Kast, Bernd; Neuner, Gerhard (Hrsg.) (1994): *Zur Analyse, Begutachtung und Entwicklung von Lehrwerken für den fremdsprachlichen Deutschunterricht.* Berlin, München, Leipzig, Wien, Zürich, New York: Langens cheidt, 1994.

[24] Thomas, A. *Analyse der Handlungswirksamkeit von Kulturstandards* [C]. In:

Thomas, Alexander (Hrsg.) (1996): *Psychologie interkulturellen Handelns.* Göttingen: Hogrefe, 1996.

[25] Weidenmann, B. *Psychische Prozesse beim Verstehen von Bildern* [M]. Bern; Stuttgart; Toronto: Hans Huber, 1988.

[26] Weidenmann, B. *Bilder für Lerner.* [J] In: Goethe Institut (1991): *Fremdsprache Deutsch / Sondernummer.* München: Klett Ed. Deutsch, 1991.

[27] Weidenmann, B. *Lernen mit Bildmedien* [M]. Aufl. 2. Weinheim; Basel: Beltz, 1994.

[28] Weidenmann, B. *Informierende Bilder* [C]. In: Weidenmann, Bernd (Hrsg.) (1994): *Wissenserwerb mit Bildern: instruktionale Bilder in Printmedien, Film/ Video und Computerprogrammen.* Bern: Huber, 1994.

[29] Weidenmann, B. *Multicodierung und Multimodalität im Lernprozess* [C]. In: Issing, Ludwig; Klimsa, Paul (Hrsg.) (1995): *Information und Lernen mit Multimedia.* Weinheim: Beltz PVU, 1995.

[30] Weidenmann, B. *Psychologische Ansätze zur Optimierung des Wissenserwerbs mit Bildern* [C]. In: Sachs-Hombach, Klaus; Rehkämper, Klaus (Hrsg.) (2004): *Bild-Bildwahrnehmung-Bildverarbeitung: Interdisziplinäre Beiträge zur Bildwissenschaft.* 2. Aufl. Wiesbaden: Deutscher Universitäts-Verlag, 2004.

Culture and National Conditions

Reconceptualizing culture: A study of online hotel reviews[*]

Tian Youfei[**]

School of Foreign Languages, Yunnan University,

Kunming Yunnan

Abstract: This article is an Appraisal examination of American and Chinese travelers' rhetorical patterns in their online hotel reviews. Overall, the two groups of travelers display similar trends in global structures and linguistic realizations when evaluating their hotel stays. These similarities contradict the conceptualization of culture in contrastive rhetoric, which conflates cultures with national or geographic entities and hence assumes that different cultures entail different rhetorical patterns. Rather, these similarities are appropriately explained in view of the reconceptualization of culture in the newly-born intercultural rhetoric, which sees culture as dynamic and specific, and interprets rhetorical practices in terms of local contextualities. This article underscores the new reconceptualization of culture in the technology-facilitated globalizing world.

Keywords: reconceptualization of culture; online hotel reviews; similarity; evaluation; the globalizing world

1. Introduction

One defining characteristic of contrastive rhetoric has been its accentuated use of the notion of culture to explain differences in written texts since Robert B. Kaplan

---

  * 论文题目：文化概念之重构：对在线宾馆评价的研究。

  ** 作者简介：田有飞(Tian Youfei)，云南大学外国语学院英语系讲师，博士；研究方向：语言学。

(1966) published his "Cultural thought patterns" article, "which more or less single-handedly launched the field" (David Cahill 2003: 170). In this article, Kaplan conceptualized culture as something conflated with national or geographic entities, namely as values or norms shared by a nation or in a region, and as a result assumed that different cultures had different rhetorical tendencies, "doodling" the world of writing into five rhetoric patterns, with, for example, a straight arrow indicating the direct style in English whereas a whirlpool representing the indirect style in oriental languages. This conceptualization of culture "has inspired a very large number of cross-linguistic studies of rhetorical patterns" (Kaplan 2005: 383) and has even been accepted as knowledge into the university course on crosscultural communication (Ming Yan 2012).

However, this conceptualization, despite its influence, is a received view of culture (Dwight Atkinson 1999), which "has been severely critiqued for its top-down—that is, deterministic, essentializing, and stereotyping—character" (Atkinson & Sohn 2013: 670). The received view is inevitably biased toward the differences between languages or cultures, which is so strong that there has not been much recognition of the similarities over the years in either theorization or actual research. Kaplan (1987) later admits "having made the case too strong", stating that a language has various possible rhetorical patterns although it has certain clear preferences (ibid). And he proposes a framework by construing contextual factors in wh-questions and representing text at the core as a negotiated communicative achievement (Kaplan 2005). Nevertheless, the hypothesis behind this rubric, it can be argued, remains essentially the same as the old one as Kaplan denies any change of his mind about the basic cultural conceptualization, still contending, for example, that "English is more linear than many other languages" (ibid: 383). Thus, the purpose of his designing this framework is more to help empirical research give more detailed and accurate descriptions of differences to support the belief that "rhetorical organization of text does indeed differ across various languages" (ibid: 383) than to accommodate similarities. And in most of the actual research by Ulla Connor and others, concentrating on differences has been the motif despite her reiteration that contrastive rhetoric examines both the differences and similarities between languages (see Xiaoming Li 2008: 16). Arguably, the root of ignoring similarities and hence misrepresenting reality is the static or deterministic relationship assumed between culture and writing by the top-down conceptualization of culture, which fails to see a possible dialectics between difference and similarity. Such dialectics can be basically encapsulated in the Chinese philosophical *yin/yang* scheme: "Yin is found deep in the greatest citadel of yang, and yang in yin's. When tipped, yin can be transmuted into yang, and yang into yin" (ibid: 17). This model of fluidity indicates the existence of similarity in the domain of writing, a sphere that can not be missed if contrastive rhetoric aims to reproduce a fuller vision of the world of writing.

To that end, Atkinson (2004) reconceptualizes culture as dynamic, process, in the world, and small but not static, product, in the head, or big, as "that planless hodgepodge, that thing of shreds and patches" (Atkinson 2008: 6). This alternative conceptualization of culture stresses human agency: An individual assumes more or less a decentered or disunified self, being able to create ways of expression suitable for the immediate context. As Elinor Ochs (1996) points out, "members of societies are agents of culture rather than merely bearers of a culture that has been handed down to them and encoded in grammatical form", helping (re) define culture through their linguistic behaviors. Thus, the reconceptualization of culture inspirits examining individuals' hybrid, diasporic, and dynamic linguistic behaviors by underscoring the concept of context and discarding the essentialist view that it is their national culture which determines their behaviors in the context. By refusing a fixed embodiment of cultural differences across languages, the reconceptualization of culture assumes that a particular context would have its "indigenous language practices" (Atkinson 2008), and practices that the participants adjust to performing the social actions in that context. This suggests that individuals from so-called different national cultures would tend to display an overall rhetorical or linguistic similarity in a particular setting or context. The reconceptualization of culture, thus, bespeaks an exodus from contrastive rhetoric to intercultural rhetoric, with an emphasis on "the very situatedness of a given genre" (Connor et al. 2008: 5), and with "inter meaning 'between, reciprocal, shared by'—signifying contact, negotiation, complexity, relationality" (Atkinson 2008).

Theoretically, the reconceptualization of culture is inspired by a tidal wave of doctrines, among which are the text-in-context theory (Norman Fairclough 1992), the structuration theory (Anthony Giddens 1979), the accommodation theory (Howard Giles et al. 1991), the pragmeme affordability theory (Jacob L. Mey 2001), and the interaction theory (Srikant Sarangi 1995). These theories commonly view the contemporary world as one of "fragmentation, multiplicity, fluidity, plurality, and intensity" (Lester Faigley 1992: 15) and therefore highlight the nexus between text and context while recognizing, among other things, Michel Foucault's (1980) understanding of power as constructed in the ongoing discourse. To a considerable extent, the reconceptualization of culture contributes to reading Benjamin Lee Whorf as a critic of language and culture. As Kristopher H. Kowal (1998) argues, Whorf, who has long been criticized for assuming determinism between language and culture, actually promoted and defended cultural and linguistic pluralism with his analysis of the Hopi language as a disparagement of Western ethnocentrism. Noticeably, the world today is not as Western ethnocentric as it was, but rather is a postmodern, globalizing one, which is crisscrossed by well-known global flows and forces of people, knowledge, money, and popular culture, and where individuals adapt, resist and even subvert their national cultural norms (Atkinson 2008; Dianne Belcher 2014). Therefore, the reconceptualization of culture, given its stress on stiuatedness and similarity, is particularly appropriate for explaining cultural transitions, individual actor behaviors, and minor social phenomena, where a top-down or bipolarized conceptualization of culture would display weaknesses considering its concentration on isolating national cultural features(Kyle McIntosh et al. 2017).

To date, there have been a few empirical studies of offline discourse that lend support to the reconceptualization of culture in one way or another (Linda Beamer 2003; Haiying Feng 2008; Junhua Wang 2010; Mianjun Xu et al. 2016). These studies do not only expand the purview of cross-cultural research of writing, but also challenge the widely accepted generalization in the contrastive rhetoric literature that Americans prefer direct communication (beginning texts with their main ideas at the macrolevel and using explicit language at the microlevel) because of their highly individualist culture, whereas Chinese prefer indirect communication (using implicit language at the microlevel and ending texts with their main ideas at the macrolevel) due to their dominantly collectivist culture(Carol M. Barnum & Huilin Li 2006; Ringo Ma & Rueyling Chuang 200; Edward C. Stewart & Milton J. Bennett 1991; Fons Thrompennaars 1994; Yanyin Zhang 1995; Yunxia Zhu 2000). However, little research from a cross-cultural perspective has been paid to computer-mediated communication(CMC) despite the fact that cyberspace infuses increasingly people's daily lives, creating various contact zones or third spaces where communication takes place. Thus, the present study aims to highlight the reconceptualization of culture in CMC context by documenting how American and Chinese travelers behave similarly in their online hotel reviews at both macro and micro levels when evaluating the hotels where they have stayed.

The rationale behind the selection of hotel reviews for this study is that such texts, a regular and noticeable feature of a travel website, are naturally occurring, unbiased, and relatively short commentaries in which travelers, through evaluating their hotel stays, show concern for other consumers, engage in social interaction, enhance own self-worth, among other things. In other words, hotel reviews are of aparticular genre because they display the content, the form, and the distribution conventionally associated with some socially established task (see Diana M. Lewis 2003: 96). Though not much studied in applied linguistics, they have become a vibrant topic in the academic fields of opinion mining and e-marketing(Ellen Eun Kyoo Kim et al. 2011; Magnus Neimann et al. 2008; Viktor Pekar & Shiyan Ou, 2008; Asunur Cezar & Hulisi Öğüt, 2012; Maite Taboada & Jack Grieve, 2004)given their significant communicative values in hotel related industries. Evaluation, which conveys what the writer feels or thinks about the entities or propositions that he is talking about and, as a result, interacts with or elicits change in the reader(Geoff Thompson & Susan Hunston 2000: 5), has to do with the issue of"face"and is an interpersonal dimension of writing that can be construed in terms of directness and indirectness as far as the present study is concerned. Thus, the use of unbiased and naturally occurring hotel reviews can help produce (more) reliable information about Americans and Chinese, revealing their"true faces".

For the same purpose, this study examines American and Chinese travelers' evaluative behaviors at both macro and micro levels. This fits in well with the widely accepted conceptualization of rhetoric as a pragmatically grounded text linguistics which studies both linguistic and structural choices, and therefore lives up to the usual expectation of both global rhetorical and internal linguistic trends when talking about either directness or indirectness(Beamer 2003: 201). As a result, it helps shun the risk of forsaking an appropriate understanding of individuals' behaviors in a particular context. For example, Yu-Ying Chang & Yi-Ping Hsu(1998)find that, constrained by the unequal student-professor power relation, American students tend to be direct in structuring their email request texts but to be linguistically indirect in constructing the request per se, whereas the reverse would be true of Chinese students. Had the researchers not examined the global structures of the request emails in their data, they "might have mistakenly concluded that Chinese tend to make requests more directly than Americans" (ibid: 144). In view of the above considerations, the current study has the potential to be an exemplar of showing how American and Chinese travelers behave in the CMC context. Specifically, it is guided by two questions. 1) Do American and Chinese travelers display overall similar trends in the global structures of their hotel reviews in terms of where the main evaluation is placed? 2) Do American and Chinese travelers display overall similar trends in evaluating linguistically their hotel stays or experiences in writing hotel reviews?

2. Theoretical framework

This study is informed by mainstream research one valuation in applied linguistics in order to reveal a possible overall similarity of evaluative behaviors in American and Chinese travelers' online English hotel reviews at both macro and micro levels. The importance of evaluation to discourse was probably first recognized by William Labov (1972), who maintains that, in narrative, evaluation is "perhaps the most important element in addition to the basic clause". According to him, evaluation occurs throughout a story, forming a "secondary structure" along the narrative one, and meanwhile tends to cluster at various points, preempting the hearer or reader's "So what?" question about the story by putting its "point" across as funny, amazing, and so on. Such understanding indicates that evaluation is an interpersonal system for a central kind of meaning making in discourse.

The idea that evaluation tends to cluster at various points in discourse has been absorbed into later research looking at evaluation at the macrolevel. John Sinclair (1988), for example, argues that evaluation occurring at boundary points in a text plays a "monitoring" function, indicating that an assumption of the hearer or reader's acceptance of a point has been made while the text is unfolding. Similarly, Thompson and Hunston (2000) hold that evaluation, besides expressing the writer's opinion and hence maintaining relations with the reader, can organize the discourse: The writer does not only express an opinion, but also tells the reader that "this is the beginning of our text, this is how the argument fits together, and this is the end of our interaction". And one model to identify textually important elements of evaluation in written text is Adrian Bolívar's (2001) Lead-Follow-Valuate (LFV) triadic structure, where turn L initiates (usually with a comment on) a topic, turn F continues with the topic, and turn V gives an opinion of it. This model involves an understanding of text as social interaction whereby evaluation emerges for achieving a global coherence of the text, but meanwhile is rooted in and varies with context: As Bolívar's analysis reveals, the three structural turns are far more constant in newspaper editorials than in academic conference abstracts (where, for example, turn V has a fairly low occurrence) because, as far as communicative purpose is concerned, the former evaluate events or states of affairs whereas the latter are promissory (usually sent before the actual writing of the papers).

Thus, from a macrolevel perspective, some evaluation in a text can be construed as a main evaluation which has a semantic scope, cataphoric or anaphoric, over and therefore organizes the text. Although this understanding develops out of studies mainly about the evaluation in offline written texts, it sheds light on the present study in identifying certain evaluations as main ideas in American and Chinese travelers' online hotel reviews for a comparison of global structures along the directness-indirectness dimension.

Besides organizing discourse, evaluation, as mentioned above, also articulates interpersonal meanings throughout the text, which indicates that any clause conveys two kinds of fundamental information, what is known and what is felt about it (see Eugene Winter 1982). The present study's microlevel analysis of American and Chinese travelers' linguistic evaluations in their hotel reviews is based on Jay R. Martin & Peter R. R. White's (2005) theory of Appraisal.

The theory of Appraisal, "the most fully developed model of evaluation" (Thompson in press), is a significant extension of the interpersonal metafunction of systemic functional linguistics. It comprises three interacting semantic domains of attitude (the expression of evaluations or feelings), engagement (the introduction and management of the voices to whom evaluations are attributed), and graduation (the amplification or mitigation of the strength of evaluations). Formulated as such, the theory enables a comprehensive analysis of the construction of evaluative stance in discourse. However, for reasons of space, the microlevel analysis of the present study focuses on the domain of attitude in American and Chinese travelers' hotel reviews. This domain includes affect, judgment, and appreciation, three kinds of values "covering what is traditionally referred to as emotion, ethics and aesthetics" (Martin & White 2005: 42). Affect, the expression of emotional states, is arguably at the heart of this domain "since it is the expressive resource that we are born with and embody physiologically from almost the moment of birth" (Clare Painter 2003, cited in Martin & White ibid: 42), and judgment and appreciation are institutionalized affect:

Judgment reworks affect as proposals about people's behaviors, while appreciation reworks it as propositions about things (ibid: 45). These categories and their subdivisions are described in Appendix A, with illustrating examples taken from the American and Chinese subcorpora of hotel reviews for this study.

The reason for locating the microlevel analysis in the attitude domain of the Appraisal theory is that it approaches attitudes in discourse by recognizing that people do not only express positive or negative attitudes, but express them in either direct or indirect ways. In this theoretical framework, a direct attitude is one that is expressed through a lexical item within a clause, whereas an indirect one is most likely to be expressed by a string of words in a clause or even by one or more whole clauses: They tell the reader something about the entity or state which is intended as a whole to make him supply an evaluation. Judging by this, the writer's direct or indirect expression of an attitude flags his way of negotiating and establishing interpersonal relations with the reader. Thus, an analysis of American and Chinese travelers' attitudinal meanings in their hotel reviews in terms of directness and indirectness tallies with the aim of the present study.

3. Methods

Two subcorpora with a total of 360 hotel reviews were established, each containing 180 such texts written in English and posted by American or Chinese travelers on the travel website www. asiarooms. com. Excluding the appended information (the traveler's name, the traveler's country origin, and the month and year of publication) as a separate section to a published hotel review, the American subcorpus amounted to 16, 484 words, each hotel review carrying 91. 57 words on average, and the Chinese subcorpus totaled 13, 792 words, averaging 76. 62 words per text; no correction was made to any grammatical or orthographical errors in the hotel reviews, and each review was numbered, with "1A" for example standing for "hotel review 1, the American subcorpus", and "1C" for "hotel review 1, the Chinese subcorpus".

One reason for gathering hotel reviews from www. asiarooms. com was that this website claims to be the No. 1 of its kind in Asia and has a noticeably regular feature of publishing unbiased hotel reviews and hence promoting the hotels at issue. Partly because of this, it has become a locus of hotel room booking for Americans traveling to Asia and Chinese who are beginning to travel out of their "national gate" to other Asian countries as they are becoming financially well off.

In establishing the subcorpora, the possible tension between the travelers' operation over the cyberspace of travel website and their expectations of privacy was considered (see AoIR Guidelines, http: //aoir. org/reports/ethics2. pdf, p. 6). Since a traveler's name is a legally recognized identifier, the website's appending the information of a traveler's name, country origin, and the month and year of publication seems to suggest the traveler's intellectual property rights over the hotel review, but meanwhile the act of publishing indicates the traveler's motivation for it to reach other travelers. Thus, American and Chinese travelers' hotel reviews were considered public when collected into the subcorpora, but their names were hidden when their reviews were used as examples in this study.

The variable of travelers' names was controlled in the gathering of hotel reviews since the present study examined whether Americans and Chinese from their respective, so called national cultures demonstrated overall similar trends of evaluative behavior in their hotel reviews at both macro and micro levels. In this study, assisted by a professor of English from the United States, an American traveler was identified to be one who used an English name and therefore distinguished from someone bearing, say, a Spanish name; and a Chinese was someone from mainland China whose name was spelled in pinyin, which is different from the phonetic alphabet system popularly used by the citizens in, for instance, Hong Kong and Taiwan. This study was aware that not all Americans bear English names nor do all Chinese have their names in pinyin; its purpose was to get a sample of only Americans and the other sample of only Chinese.

At the macrolevel, the global structure of a hotel review in the subcorpora was identified by deciding if its main evaluation was stated in the beginning or toward the end of it. Thus, a hotel review beginning with a main point of evaluation was categorized as rhetorically direct, and one ending with a main evaluation was classified as indirect. However, there were some hotel reviews that did not have a main evaluation, suggesting that they had no point in governing the text; as a result, such hotel reviews were classified as "out of focus" (Kaplan 1966).

At the microlevel, the instances of evaluation in the subcorpora were coded in terms of broad fields rather than separate and specific entities or phenomena. Hotel reviews are short commentaries that travelers write on their hotel stay experiences, and naturally they are the appraisers who express their affect, judge service related people's behaviors, and appreciate the quality or worth of things, which include hotel features like location, food, room, facilities, and price(Pekar & Ou 2008: 150). As Susan Hood(2004)points out, coding occurrences of evaluation in terms of broad fields"facilitates the identification of patterns in the orientation of ATTITUDE across the texts". Thus, the appraiser(the traveler), the service related people, and things served as broad terms in the coding and contributed to measuring the range of evaluations which the genre of hotel reviews draws on to achieve its goals.

In the coding, direct evaluation was kept for more restricted cases where the context was not adetermining factor, that is, "direct" was in the lexical item but not in the discourse. Thus, words like "big", "small", "far", and "close" were not identified as intrinsically attitudinal because they could be positive or negative and whether they were positive or negative would involve a process of adjustment to the context: For example, "big" was positive in the context of hotel rooms but negative in that of cockroaches in hotel rooms, and"close" was most likely positive in"the hotel is close to the beach,"and yet was negative in"the hotel is close to a noisy KTV hall." Words of this kind were treated as descriptive and therefore served as tokens of indirect evaluation.

The data were intercoded and then interrated by the researcher and one colleague in applied linguistics, with discrepancies being solved through discussion. Major quantitative results were chi-square(χ^2) tested to see if particular characteristics of evaluation were the same or homogeneous for both American and Chinese travelers, with the critical p value set at the 0.05 level of confidence. To supplement the quantitative analysis, a short questionnaire was conducted, involving 30 Americans attending a Chinese language class at an American university(via the help of another colleague of the researcher on a Chinese teaching tour program at this university)and two classes of 67 Chinese MA postgraduates in English and literature from the researcher's university in China.

4. Results

4.1 Global structures

A macrolevel analysis reveals three types of global structures, direct, indirect, and out of focus, in American and Chinese travelers' hotel reviews. Table 1 summarizes the frequencies of these global structures in the subcorpora.

Table 1. Global structures in American and Chinese travelers' hotel reviews

	Direct	**Indirect**	**Out of focus**	**Totals**
Americans	84	65	31	180
Chinese	66	66	48	180

Overall, American and Chinese travelers manifest a homogeneous distribution of these three global structures, $\chi^2(2, N=360) = 5.8259$, $p = .05432$. In other words, both American and Chinese travelers belong to the same population as far as the global structures of their hotel reviews are concerned. Specifically, each group of travelers display an almost balanced distribution of the direct and indirect global structures in organizing their online reviews to evaluate the hotels where they have stayed, for American travelers, $\chi^2(1, N=149) = 2.423$, $p = .120$, and for Chinese travelers, $\chi^2(1, N=132) = 0.000$, $p = 1.000$; both groups manifest a homogeneous distribution of the out of focus structure, $\chi^2(1, N=79) = 3.658$, $p = .056$, suggesting that its appearance across the two subcorpora is not due to chance.

Following are examples illustrating how American and Chinese travelers unfold their hotel reviews in terms of the foregoing three global structures, with expressions where main evaluations appear being underlined.

(1) I've had a great holiday at this hotel, the experience was just FANTASTIC! It has its own private beach, and the beach was quite clean. The hotel was nicely designed with a beautiful big pool, plus a children's pool. Our room has pool view, but can see little sea through palm tree leaves. And it's very easy to get taxi from hotel. Definitely I'll stay there again if I go to Langkawi in the future!!! (60C)

Example(1) shows how the Chinese traveler frames his hotel review in a direct global structure, regardless of several language proficiency problems. The traveler begins by evaluating his holiday at the hotel as "great", which he reevaluates as a "fantastic" experience in the second clause within the same sentence. Evaluation always involves the evaluated, and the evaluations of the general entities "holiday" and "experience", two instances of reaction under appreciation, signal an overall positive valence of the review, commanding semantically the upcoming evaluations: The rest evaluations of hotel features are also positive, evidencing the values conveyed through "great" and "fantastic" about staying at the hotel. Note that the traveler's evaluation of the worth of the room with "[a] pool view" as the token is still positive, though somewhat mitigated or counter expected by the neighboring negative expression signaled by "but", and hence contributes to the main evaluation in the beginning sentence. Following these evaluations, the traveler concludes his hotel review with an expression of his feeling of satisfaction through the sentence "Definitely I'll stay there again..." , which echoes the main evaluation in the beginning line.

While example (1) exemplifies how a Chinese traveler unfolds his hotel review in a direct global structure, example (2) illustrates how an American traveler frames his hotel review in an indirect structure.

(2) From the efficient and professional manners of Karen Tan in Reservations to the disarmingly kind and accommodating charm of Nordiana and the world-class enchanting beauty and friendly smiles of impossibly lovely Nur'Aina at the Front Desk—and including the staff in Housekeeping, the spa, and breakfast restaurant——the personnel here must surely rank among the tip-top in Asia! You'll be smiling, too! There is simply a lot to smile about here, really... Of the rooms on the 9th (Club) floor, while nicely appointed, the ones I saw seem to harbor a musty smell that by the second day had me sneezing and wanting some relief. Nordiana graciously showed me another, but the same smell greeted us there—and she agreed, and it made her want to sneeze as well! She had Housekeeping bring up a dehumidifier, and they ran it a couple hours, and it seemed to help. My stay was only 2 nights, so I was gone the next day. Short-term it might be okay. Long-term, it might be worth it to personally visit and check a given room before settling in... However, though full, the environment seemed quiet, and restful sleep felt guaranteed. I liked it! Since—sadly—the days of opulent rooms at bargain prices are definitely gone in Singapore, it is getting harder and harder to find value. Given the perfect location and flawless staff—and far better Wi-Fi than most other spots in SE Asia—this hotel is a great choice. I hope to return! (49A)

In example (2), the traveler begins by judging positively the hotel personnel, particularly Nordiana, which takes up the lion's share of the review (from the start to "and it seemed to help" in the middle). Following that, the traveler evaluates the hotel in terms of long-and-short-term stays on the basis of his two-night stay, the worth of examining the room before settling in, and the value of the environment and of the bargain price. Finally, the traveler, mentioning other strong points in passing, summarizes by saying "this is a great choice. I hope to return", which serves as the main point of evaluation for his review.

Different from examples (1) and (2), example (3) does not contain a main point of evaluation that commands the whole text.

> (3) The free shuttle pickup to and from the airport was very convenient. Shopping and skytrain stations were about 15 minutes away by taxi ride (about 100 ~ 120 baht). The rooms were very large and clean. There weren't any good restaurants outside of the hotel in walking distance, but the hotel restaurant was alright. (6A)

The traveler appreciates the hotel from several aspects: transportation (shuttle pickup), location (in relation to shopping and sky train stations), room, and facilities (outside restaurants versus the hotel's restaurant). However, from the start, he does not have a leading evaluation to which he anchors these evaluations, nor does he boil down these evaluations to one general point with a valence about the hotel toward the end.

From the standpoint of contrastive rhetoric, example (1) would represent the direct or linear rhetorical pattern dominating American communication, whereas example (2) would stand for the indirect rhetorical structure dictating Chinese communication; for Americans, neither example (2) nor example (3) would be favourable in communication as the former would strike them as "unnecessarily indirect" and the latter, as "lack [ing] organization" (Kaplan 1966). However, this understanding appears debatable in the face of the homogeneous distribution of the three kinds of global structures across American and Chinese travelers' online hotel reviews.

4.2 Expressing attitudes

Evaluations have been touched on in passing in Subsection 4.1 in relation to the global structures of the two groups of travelers' hotel reviews. Nevertheless, their evaluations of affect, judgment, and appreciation are examined in more detail starting from Subsection 4.2. The overall results of evaluations in the subcorpora are summarized in Table 2.

Table 2. Overall attitude distributions in American and Chinese' hotel reviews

	Affect		Judgment		Appreciation		Totals
	Direct	Indirect	Direct	Indirect	Direct	Indirect	
Americans	210	61	195	100	1074	532	2172
Chinese	192	50	153	84	886	524	1889

As Table 2 shows, both American and Chinese travelers' hotel reviews have the lowest frequency of affect, lower frequency of judgment, and the highest frequency of appreciation. This overall distribution conforms generally to the one that Taboada & Grieve(2004) found although they ignored indirect evaluations when presenting their automatic method for calculating the semantic orientation (SO) of a corpus of hotel reviews and of other kinds of online reviews, and therefore testifies to Martin's(2000, p. 146) assumption that different text types foreground one or another of the three broad kinds of affect, judgment, and appreciation. And the two groups of travelers, as can be seen in Table 2, display an overall tendency toward directness over indirectness across these major kinds of attitudinal meanings.

4.2.1 Affect

Although affect accounts for merely a small number of the evaluations in each of the subcorpora, it is important as it is the basic set of choices having to do with emotional responses, and an examination of these choices can help reveal how emotional American and Chinese travelers are in evaluating their hotel stay experiences.

On the whole, the two groups of travelers display a homogeneous distribution of direct and indirect affects in their hotel reviews, χ^2 (1, N = 513) = 0.258, p = .612: Both American and Chinese travelers tend to be direct in expressing their emotions about their hotel stays. This homogeneous tendency is even found in the four kinds of affect values: for dis/inclination, $\chi^2(1, N = 76) = 1.007$, p = .316, for un/happiness, $\chi^2(1, N = 124) = 0.487$, p = .485, for in/security, $\chi^2(1, N = 94) = 1.524$, p = .217, and for dis/satisfaction, χ^2 (1, $N = 219$) = 0.011, p = .917.

Table 3　The Affect values in American and Chinese travelers' hotel reviews

	Dis/inclination		Un/happiness		In/security		Dis/satisfaction		Tls
	Direct	Indirect	Direct	Indirect	Direct	Indirect	Direct	Indirect	
Americans	49	2	51	1	43	1	67	57	271
Chinese	25	0	69	3	46	4	52	43	242

Tls: Totals

As Table 3 reveals, in American and Chinese travelers' hotel reviews, un/happiness and dis/satisfaction are more frequent affect values compared to dis/inclination and in/security, indicating that, when it comes to hotel stay, a traveler's emotional response mainly has to do with whether he has had a happy stay or is satisfied with the stay. Note that while the two groups of travelers show a preference for directness in the case of un/happiness, they show a virtual balance between directness and indirectness concerning dis/satisfaction.

　　Following are some examples showing how frequently used lexicogrammatical expressions construct affect values in American and Chinese travelers' hotel reviews (direct evaluations underlined, and expressions evoking indirect evaluations underlined and italicized; affect type and subcorpus indicated in the bracket).

　　　　(4) We had verbally requested the reception desk no less than 3 times to do something about it. (Direct inclination; 37A)

　　　　(5) I wanted to move to an airport hotel due to my early flight. (Direct inclination; 96C)

　　　　(6) We loved the Rainforest boutique. (Direct happiness; 25A)

　　　　(7) We really enjoy our stay here. (Direct happiness; 109C)

　　　　(8) Only surprise is that they don't have an English TV channel. (Direct insecurity; 49A)

　　　　(9) We can totally relax in that room. (Direct security; 55C)

　　　　(10) This was our first stay in Thailand and I would recommend this hotel for anyone starting out their travels in a new country! (Direct satisfaction; 129A)

　　　　(11) Considering the air-con and hot water are must, I don't recommend this hotel to you. (Direct dissatisfaction; 91C)

　　　　(12) I will definitely stay again on my future visits! (Indirect satisfaction; 67A)

(13) I will never stay in this hotel any more. (Indirect dissatisfaction; 43C)

4.2.2 Judgment

Overall, as Table 2 shows, American and Chinesetravelers also display a homogeneous distribution of direct and indirect judgments across their hotel reviews, both groups being inclined to realize directly their assessments of service related people's behaviors, $\chi^2(1, N=532) = 0.139$, $p = .710$. The two groups display even homogeneity in the breakdowns of judgment (Table 4): for normality, $\chi^2(1, N=14) = 0.294$, $p = .588$, for capacity, $\chi^2(1, N=77) = 0.660$, $p = .417$, for tenacity, $\chi^2(1, N=17) = 1.311$, $p = .252$, for veracity, $\chi^2(1, N=19) = 1.304$, $p = .253$, and for propriety, $\chi^2(1, N=405) = 0.524$, $p = .469$.

Table 4　The judgment values in American and Chinese travelers' hotel reviews

	Normality		Capacity		Tenacity		Veracity		Propriety		Tls
	Di	In	Di	In	Di	In	Di	In	Di	In	
Americans	10	3	21	16	4	6	0	7	160	68	295
Chinese	1	0	19	21	1	6	2	10	130	47	237

Di: Direct; In: Indirect; Tls: Totals

As Table 4 shows, propriety appears the most frequent compared to the other judgment values in the American and Chinese travelers' subcorpora. This ideational homogeneity suggests what counts most to travelers is whether or not service related people's behaviors are beyond reproach according to certain normative principles or traveler expectations in the particular context of hotel stay. While appearing somewhat balanced between directness and indirectness in capacity (the second most frequent affect value for each group of travelers), the two groups of travelers are skewed toward indirectness in tenacity and veracity, but display predominant direct realizations over indirect ones in normality and propriety. Obviously, the distribution of direct and indirect propriety occurrences contributes largely to the overall dominance of directness over indirectness in American and Chinese travelers' judging service personnel's behaviors.

Below are some examples giving a glimpse of how American and Chinese travelers realize judgment values through frequently used expressions:

(14) The location is great and the staff is <u>wonderful</u>. (normality; 64A)

(15) Good for <u>budget</u> travelers but not good for holiday. (capacity; 174C)

(16) Staff was <u>friendly</u> and <u>accommodating</u>. (propriety; 35A)

(17) Andrew and P. Neil are both very <u>friendly</u> and <u>helpful</u>. (propriety; 85C)

(18) He was really <u>great</u> for sure! (propriety; 47A)

(19) In summary, most of the workers were <u>nice</u>. (propriety; 21A)

(20) Front desk and customer service personal are very <u>polite</u>. (propriety; 40C)

4.2.3 Appreciation

Appreciation, as stated in Section 2, is the semantic domain that construes the evaluations of things. As Table 5 shows, in either the American or the Chinese subcorpus, the most frequent appreciation value is reaction, the less frequent is valuation, and the least frequent is composition. That the reaction value registers the most frequent suggests that travelers evaluate the quality of hotel features mainly according to whether these features caught their attention or pleased them.

Table 5　The appreciation values in American and Chinese travelers' hotel reviews

	Reaction		Composition		Valuation		Totals
	Direct	**Indirect**	**Direct**	**Indirect**	**Direct**	**Indirect**	
Americans	667	63	114	228	293	241	1606
Chinese	538	46	85	261	263	217	1410

Overall, both groups of travelers similarly prefer direct to indirect realizations of appreciation (Table 2). Specifically, as in Table 5, the two groups of travelers are homogeneous in reaction, $\chi^2(1, N = 1314) = 0.242$, $p = .623$, and in valuation, $\chi^2(1, N = 1014) = 0.001$, $p = .980$, two values where directness prevails over indirectness; contrarily, in the composition value, it is indirectness but not directness which dominates American and Chinese travelers' realizations even though this distribution is not homogeneous, $\chi^2(1, N = 608) = 6.430$, $p = .011$.

Below are some examples showing American and Chinese travelers' use of frequent lexicogrammatical expressions in realizing appreciation.

(21) The location is good for a holiday. (Direct reaction; 84A)

(22) The hotel appearance looks nice. (Direct reaction; 91C)

(23) However, the restaurants in the area were great. (Direct reaction; 96A)

(24) The new sunbeds are very comfortable. (Direct reaction; 28C)

(25) The rooms have always been perfectly clean. (Direct composition; 71A)

(26) Otherwise the rooms were spacious. (Direct composition; 8C)

(27) The main reason I continue to use Traders is that they provide free Wi-Fi. (Direct valuation; 117A)

(28) We found its a convenient place to go to beach, to surf-riding, to shopping. (Direct valuation; 146C)

(29) It is within walking distance to many places. (Indirect composition; 106A)

(30) It takes less than 3 minutes to walk to the beach. (Indirect composition; 13C)

(31) It is only 1/2 a block from the most tourist-useful trainline. (Indirect composition; 72A)

(32) There are so many water sports at the beach in front of the hotel. (Indirect valuation; 3C)

(33) Business center has only two computers. (Indirect valuation; 49A)

(34) No drinking water service after 10pm. (Indirect valuation; 61C)

5. Discussion

Section 4 shows that American and Chinese travelers, overall, display similar trends in their online hotel reviews at both macro and micro levels. At the macrolevel, both groups of travelers manifest a virtually balanced distribution of the direct and indirect global structures while using fairly frequently the out of focus structure. At the microlevel, the two groups manifest a general preference for directness over indirectness in constructing their evaluations, but in the subvalues of dis/satisfaction and capacity, they appear similarly almost balanced between directness and indirectness, and show a definite tendency toward indirectness in composition under the appreciation value. These findings throw doubt on the axiomatic, national culture based, and bipolarized view in existing scholarship that Americans prefer direct communication whereas Chinese prefer indirect communication. For one thing, neither group of travelers differ significantly in the distribution of direct and indirect global structures, and for another, Chinese travelers, like their American counterparts, display an overall inclination toward directness at the microlevel. Thus, the results of the present study testify to the reconceptualization of culture in intercultural rhetoric that individuals from different national cultures are more inclined to share than to differ in rhetorical or linguistic patterns in their performance of the social actions in a particular context. In other words, at least for American and Chinese travelers, the communication patterns teased out from the perspective of evaluation are, as it were, indigenous to or situated in the CMC context of hotel review writing.

The travel website context in which travelers communicate with readers (mainly potential travelers) by writing hotel reviews of their travel stays is an asynchronous one. This is because the traveler's act of writing a hotel review precedes the reader's act of reading it and, as a result, there lack kinesic and proxemic factors such as facial expressions, gestures, body postures, and distance, which in face to face (FTF) communication "are so critical in expressing personal opinions and attitudes and in moderating social relationships" (David Crystal 2001: 36). Critically, what this asynchrony affords is a kind of more egalitarian or much freer participation. In the circumstances, individuals are more willing to speak out in the CMC setting than in the FTF setting (Shirley S. Ho & Douglas M. McLeod 2008), and in a follow up survey of the present study, 94% of the Americans and 92% of the Chinese answered that they would feel free in writing online hotel reviews for any purposes as mentioned in Section 1. The asynchronous CMC context of hotel review writing thus "democratize[s] communication" (Joseph B. Walther 1996: 7), facilitates the expression and enhancement of feelings online (Walther 2012: 4), resulting in an informal and candid style on the part of travelers. Informality in a traveler's hotel review refers to not only his sloppy language use but also his off the cuff or casual organization at the macrolevel. This is why there emerges a homogeneous pattern where the direct, indirect, and out of focus structures are frequently used by American and Chinese travelers in the subcorpora. And in a traveler's hotel review, candor mainly has to do with his direct linguistic evaluations, and more significantly, it has a great impact on American and Chinese travelers' similarly dominant direct evaluations of their hotel stays.

The CMC asynchrony-afforded informal and candid style in American and Chinese travelers' hotel reviews has a close tie with the values to which contemporary society attaches importance. Arguably, it is through the asynchronous CMC context that these values are maximized, effecting casual behavior as the two groups of travelers demonstrate in the hotel reviews of the subcorpora. Naomi S. Baron(2003) summarizes three significant value changes in mainstream American society that lead to the decline of public face(diminished attention to how one appears to others), which in turn leads to informality over formality with respect to dress, affect, and language use: "reduced emphasis on social stratification and on overt attention to upward mobility, notable disconnects between educational accomplishment and financial success, [and]strong emphasis on youth culture". Although these values are said of American society, they also permeate, and play out in, the other parts of the globalizing world. For example, as Xiaoye You(2008) reviews, since China adopted the market economy oriented reform and opening up policy in the late 1970s, there has emerged a more hybridized value system, and writing themes and their treatment have become more depoliticized and diversified, standing in marked contrast to and challenging the opinionated perception (chiefly in Western scholarship) that Confucian and Marxist values dictate Chinese society such that it seems that all Chinese writers follow the same writing template(Li 2008: 18). There might be argument over where the values leading to the decline of public face are more noticeable, but at least in online hotel review writing, they dovetail and work well with the asynchronous context, inducing American and Chinese travelers to write such texts in an informal and candid manner, and rendering their respective national cultures dramatically irrelevant. In the follow up survey, 90% of the Americans and 87% of the Chinese answered"No"when asked if they could be influenced by their respective national cultures when writing reviews online to comment on hotels.

Extemporaneousness also contributes tremendously to American and Chinese travelers' similar rhetorical trends in their online hotel reviews. Studies suggest that writing other types of evaluative or persuasive texts such as quality newspaper editorials (Alireza Bonyadi 2010; Leila Khabbazi-Oskouei 2013), academic journal editorials (Davide S. Giannoni 2008; Youfei Tian 2010), and anonymous peer reviews (Inmaculada Fortanet 2008) typically involves heavy premeditation such that these types of texts tend to display meticulous global structures and cautious language use. By contrast, writing hotel reviews is extemporaneous in that travelers do not have a preset strategy to follow at both macro and micro levels. This is evidenced by the follow up survey where over 90% of the Americans and of the Chinese decided on"I will write extemporaneously"when questioned if they would write a hotel review with a prepared mind or just extemporaneously. As one Chinese interviewee explained, "I can speak my mind in a hotel review, but I don't care much about its structure or how I use language. It is something hasty online. "Thus, constrained by extemporaneousness, it is most likely a matter of coincidence in which global structure a traveler is writing a hotel review and, on most occasions, their language use tends to be emotional and hasty. Extemporaneousness, together with the asynchronous CMC context, leads to American and Chinese travelers' similar frequency balance between direct and indirect global structures(and a fairly high frequency in the out of focus structure), and their betrayal of"the imperfections and passions of human nature"(Zizi Papacharissi 2004: 279).

Although the two groups of travelers' similar trends in the global structures and their overall preference for direct realizations of evaluations can be understood in terms of the asynchrony of CMC context and extemporaneousness, there are still some local, yet fairly noticeable similarities, namely the close balance between directness and indirectness in dis/satisfaction and capacity, and indirectness over directness in composition, that are in conflict with the general preference at the microlevel. This suggests there is still another constraint on American and Chinese traveler's linguistic behaviors in their hotel reviews. In general, hotel reviews are evaluative discourse but meanwhile they are based on travelers' hotel stay experiences and, as a corollary, narrating these experiences forms a part of their evaluations. Charlotte Linde(1993) even argues that evaluation is the major criterion of narrative. In reviewing a hotel, the traveler's dis/satisfaction often has to do with, and is arrived at by, making a decision on whether they will stay at the hotel again, and this, as Section 4.2.1 shows, is mainly realized through the formulation of"first person pronoun + modal verb + come/go/stay(again)". On the other hand, to the traveler, capacity, besides having to do with how able the service personnel appear, covers whether the ways in which they behave are acceptable according to certain practices. Thus, it is natural for the traveler to relate the service personnel's doings as a way to provoke evaluations. All this makes the two populations' indirect realizations close in frequency to their direct ones concerning dis/satisfaction and capacity. But perhaps the most noticeable trend clashing with American and Chinese travelers' overall inclination toward directness at the microlevel is their similar dominance of indirectness over directness in composition. Composition in a hotel review is the attitudinal meaning which the traveler creates about the textual features such as the size of the room, and the location of the hotel relative to other venues. However, the rather limited reservoir of value laden lexical items for composition in this context (see Table 8) which drives the traveler to present the textual features in terms of descriptive items, and this becomes the most frequent means whereby the traveler invokes compositional evaluations. Thus, narrative plays a part in hotel reviews and is the resource of which American and Chinese travelers similarly make frequent use for triggering evaluations of dis/satisfaction, capacity, and composition.

To sum up, the overall similar structural and linguistic trends that American and Chinese travelers manifest in their online hotel reviews from the perspective of evaluation are ascribable to the local contextualities of asynchronous CMC context, extemporaneousness, and, in certain microlevel cases, narrative. These findings fracture the received view in contrastive rhetoric that a national culture has its unique rhetorical pattern and thus, for example, Americans and Chinese differ in their communication because of their contrasting national cultures; therefore, they indicate the importance of considering culture as dynamic and specific rather than static and wide-ranging in interpreting writing in particular contexts. That is, as advocated by the reconceptualization of culture in intercultural rhetoric, rhetorical practices should be looked at in terms of change ability rather than absolute difference. This approach is particularly significant for exploring the rhetorical practices in the proliferating spaces brought along by the internet technology facilitated globalizing world. However, it does not mean rendering differences in the world of writing invisible, for differences and similarities are dialectically existent. Rather, it means that writing is contextually situated, and therefore a sounder explanation should be mainly established on contingent factors, especially when it comes to answering why the taken-for-granted differences between two or even among more than two populations different at a national culture level have been transmuted into overall similarities.

This being said, the present study has its limitations. First, the subcorpora are relatively small such that they are not able to display in certain cases sure trends between American and Chinese travelers' hotel reviews. One way to settle such uncertainty is to enlarge the data, securing more reliable quantitative results and, as a result, a more convincing qualitative analysis. Second, the analysis at the microlevel has been conducted only along the dimension of direct and indirect evaluations while, for reasons of space, not incorporating the dimension of positive and negative evaluations. Under the circumstances, a broadened horizon of the two populations' evaluative behaviors in hotel reviews remains to be desired, and it follows that the conclusion drawn thus far is still tentative and should be accepted with caution, especially when projected into other contexts.

References

[1]Atkinson, D. *TESOL and culture*[J]. TESOL Quarterly, 1999, 33.

[2] Atkinson, D. *Contrastingrhetorics/contrasting cultures: Why contrastive rhetoric needs a better conceptualization of culture*[J]. Journal of English for Academic Purposes, 2004, 3(4).

[3] Atkinson, D. *Indigenous language practices: An exploration in intercultural rhetoric*[Z]. Paper presented at the Fourth Conference on Intercultural Rhetoric and Discourse, Indianapolis, IN. 2008.

[4] Atkinson, D., Sohn, J. *Culture from the bottom up*[J]. TESOL Quarterly, 2013, 47(4).

[5]Barnum, C. M., Li, H. *Chinese and American technical communication: A cross-cultural comparison of differences*[J]. Technical Communication, 2006, 53(2).

[6]Baron, N. *Why email looks like speech: Proofreading, pedagogy and public face*[C]//J. Aitchison, & D. M. Lewis. New Media Language. London: Routledge, 2003.

[7]Beamer, L. *Directness in Chinese business correspondence of the nineteenth century*[J]. Journal of Business and Technical Communication, 2003, 17(2).

[8]Belcher, D. *What we need and don't need intercultural rhetoric for: A retrospective and prospective look at an evolving research area*[J]. Journal of Second Language Writing, 2014, 25.

[9] Bolívar, A. *The negotiation of evaluation in written text*[C]//M. Scott, G. Thompson. Patterns of Text: In Honor of Michael Hoey. Amsterdam: John Benjamins, 2001.

[10] Bonyadi, A. *The rhetorical properties of the schematic structure of newspaper editorials: A comparative study of English and Persian editorials*[J]. Discourse & Communication, 2010, 4(4).

[11] Cahill, D. *The myth of the "turn" in contrastive rhetoric*[J]. Written

Communication, 2003, 20(2).

[12]Cezar, A. , & Öğüt, H. *The determinants of domestic and international visitors' online hotel booking*[J]. Procedia-Social and Behavioral Sciences, 2012, 58.

[13]Chang, Y. , & Hsu, Y. *Requests on e-mail: A cross-cultural comparison*[J]. RELC Journal, 1998, 29.

[14] Connor, U. , Nagelhout, E. , Rozycki, W. V. *Introduction* [C]//U. Connor, E. Nagelhout, W. V. Rozycki. Contrastive Rhetoric: Reaching to Intercultural Rhetoric. Amsterdam: John Benjamins, 2008.

[15]Crystal, D. *Language and the Internet* [M]. Cambridge: CUP, 2001.

[16]Ding, D. D. *An indirect style in business communication*[J]. Journal of Business and Technical Communication, 2006, 20(1).

[17] Faigley, L. *Fragments of Rationality: Postmodernity and the Subject of Composition* [M]. Pittsburgh, PA: University of Pittsburgh Press, 1992.

[18] Fairclough, N. *Discourse and Social Change* [M]. Cambridge: Polity Press, 1992.

[19] Feng, H. *A genre-based study of research grant proposals in China* [C]// U. Connor, E. Nagelhout, W. V. Rozycki. Contrastive Rhetoric: Reaching to Intercultural Rhetoric. Amsterdam: John Benjamins, 2008.

[20] Fortanet, I. *Evaluative language in peer review referee reports*[J]. Journal of English for Academic Purposes, 2008, 7.

[21]Foucault, M. *Power/Knowledge: Selected Interviews and Other Writings*, 1972 – 1977[M]. NY: Pantheon, 1980.

[22] Giannoni, D. S. *Medical writing at the periphery: The case of Italian journal editorials*[J]. Journal of English for Specific Purposes, 2008, 7(2).

[23]Giddens, A. *Central Problems in Social Theory: Action, Structure and Contradiction in Social Analysis*[M]. Berkeley: University of California Press, 1979.

[24]Giles, H. , Coupland, N. , Coupland, J. *Accommodation theory: Communication, content, and consequence* [C]//H. Giles, N. Coupland, J. Coupland. Contexts of Accommodation: Developments in Applied Sociolinguistics. Cambridge: CUP, 1991.

[25] Hennig-Thurau, T. , Gwinner, K. P. , Walsh, G. , Gremler, D. D. *Electronic word-of-mouth via consumer-opinion platforms: What motivates consumers to articulate themselves on the Internet?* [J]. Journal of Interactive Marketing, 2004, 18(1).

[26] Hinkel, E. *Second Language Writers' Text: Linguistic and Rhetorical Features* [M]. London: Routledge, 2002.

[27] Hood, S. *Managing attitude in undergraduate academic writing: A focus on the introductions to research reports* [C]//L. J. Ravelli, R. A. Ellis. Analysing Academic Writing: Contextualized Frameworks. London: Continuum, 2004.

[28] Ho, S., McLeod, D. M. *Social-psychological influences on opinion expression in face-to-face and computer-mediated communication* [J]. Communication Research, 2008, 35(2).

[29] Kaplan, R. *Cultural thought patterns in intercultural education* [J]. Language Learning, 1966, 16.

[30] Kaplan, R. *Cultural thought patterns revisited* [C]//U. Connor, R. B. Kaplan. Writing across Languages: Analysis of L2 Text. Reading, MA: Addison-Wesley, 1987.

[31] Kaplan, B. R. *Contrastive rhetoric* [C]//E. Hinkel. Handbook of Research in second Language Teaching and Learning. Mahwah, NJ: Erlbaum, 2005.

[32] Khabbazi-Oskouei, L. *Propositional or non-propositional, that is the question: A new approach to analyzing " interpersonal metadiscourse" in editorials* [J]. Journal of Pragmatics, 2013, 47(1).

[33] Kim, E. E. K., Mattila, A. S., Baloglu, S. *Effects of gender and expertise on consumers' motivation to read online hotel reviews* [J]. Cornell Hospitality Quarterly, 2011, 52(4).

[34] Kowal, K. H. *Rhetorical Implications of Linguistic Relativity: Theory and Application to Chinese and Taiwanese Interlanguage* [M]. NY: Peter Lang, 1988.

[35] Kubota, R., Lehner, A. *Toward critical contrastive rhetoric* [J]. Journal of Second Language Writing, 2004, 13: 7-27.

[36] Labov, W. *Language in the Inner City* [M]. Philadelphia: University of Pennsylvania, 1972.

[37] Lewis, D. M. *Online news: A new genre?* [C]//J. Aitchison, D. M. Lewis. New Media Language(pp. 95 -104). London: Routledge, 2003.

[38] Li, X. *From contrastiverhetoric to intercultural rhetoric: A search for collective identity* [C]//U. Connor, E. Nagelhout, W. V. Rozycki. Contrastive Rhetoric: Reaching to Intercultural Rhetoric. Amsterdam: John Benjamins, 2008.

[39] Linde, C. *Life Stories: The Creation of Coherence* [M]. Oxford: OUP, 1993.

[40] Ma, R., Chuang, R. *Persuasion strategies of Chinese college students in interpersonal contexts* [J]. Southern Communication Journal, 2001, 66: 267 -278.

[41] Martin, J. R. *Beyond exchange: Appraisal systems in English* [C]//S. Hunston, G. Thompson. Evaluation in Text: Authorial Stance and the Construction of Discourse. Oxford: OUP, 2000.

[42] Martin, J. R., White, P. R. R. *The Language of Evaluation: Appraisal in English* [M]. London: Palgrave, 2005.

[43] McIntosh, K., Conor, U., Gokpinar-Shelton, E. *What intercultural rhetoric can bring to EAP/ESP studies in an English as a lingua franca world* [J]. Journal of English for Academic Purposes. 2017, 29.

[44] Mey, J. *Pragmatics: An Introduction* (second edition) [M]. Oxford: Blackwell, 2001.

[45] Niemann, M., Mochol, M., Tolksdorf, R. *Enhancing hotel search with semantic web technologies* [J]. Journal of Theoretical and Applied Electronic Commerce Research, 2008, 3(2).

[46] Ochs, E. *Linguistic resources for socializing humanity* [C]//J. J. Gumperz, S. C. Levinson. Rethinking Linguistic Relativity. Cambridge: CUP, 1996.

[47] Papacharissi, Z. *Democracy online: Civility, politeness, and the democratic of online political discussion groups* [J]. New Media & Society, 2004, 6(2).

[48] Pekar, V., Ou, S. *Discovery of subjective evaluations of product features in hotel reviews* [J]. Journal of Vacation Marketing, 2008, 14(2).

[49] Sarangi, S. Culture [C]//J. Verschueren, J. Ostman, & J. Blommaert [C]. *Handbook of Pragmatics*. Amsterdam: John Benjamins, 1995.

[50] Sinclair, J. *Mirror for a text* [J]. Journal of English and Foreign Languages. 1988, 1.

[51] Stewart, E. C., Bennett, M. J. *American Cultural Patterns: A Cross-cultural Perspective* [M]. Yarmouth, ME: Intercultural Press, 1991.

[52] Taboada, M., Grieve, J. *Analyzing appraisal automatically* [C]//Proc. of AAAI Spring Symposium on Exploring Attitude and Affect in Text. Stanford, 2004.

[53] Thompson, G. *Appraising glances: Evaluating Martin's model of APPRAISAL* [J]. Word(Special Issue: The Realization of Interpersonal Meaning).

[54] Thompson, G., &Hunston, S. *Evaluation: An introduction* [C]//S. Hunston,

& G. Thompson. Evaluation in text: Authorial Stance and the Construction of Discourse. Oxford: OUP, 2000.

[55] Tian, Y. *"The author argues that..."*: *Reporting practices in Philippine journal editorials*[J]. Philippine Journal of Linguistics, 2010, 41.

[56] Trompenaars, F. Riding the Waves of Culture: Understanding Diversity in Global Business[M]. NY: McGraw-Hill, 1994.

[57] Walther, J. B. *Computer-mediated communication: Impersonal, interpersonal andhyperpersonal interaction*[J]. Communication Research, 1996, 23(1).

[58] Walther, J. B. *Interaction through technological lens: Computer-mediated communication and language*[J]. Journal of Language and Social Psychology, 2012, 31.

[59] Wang, J. *Convergence in the rhetorical pattern of directness and indirectness in Chinese and U. S. business letters* [J]. Journal of Business and Technical Communication, 2010, 24(1).

[60] Winter, E. *Towards a Contextual Grammar of English* [M]. London: George Allen and Unwin, 1982.

[61] Xu, M. , Huang, C. , & You, X. *Reasoning patterns of undergraduate theses in translation studies: An intercultural study*[J]. English for Specific Purposes, 2016, 41.

[62] Yan, M. *Intercultural Communication: University English Course* [M]. Beijing: Tsinghua University Press, 2012.

[63] You, X. *From Confucianism to Marxism: A century of theme treatment in Chinese writing instruction* [C]//U. Connor, E. Nagelhout, W. V. Rozycki. Contrastive Rhetoric: Reaching to Intercultural Rhetoric. Amsterdam: John Benjamins, 2008.

[64] Zamel, V. *Toward a model of transculturation* [J]. TESOL Quarterly, 1997, 31.

[65] Zhang, Y. *Strategies in Chinese requesting* [C]//G. Kasper. Pragmatics of Chinese as Native and Target Language. Manoa: University of Hawaii, 1995.

[66] Zhu, Y. *Rhetorical moves in Chinese sales genres*, 1949 *to the present* [J]. Journal of Business Communication, 2000, 37.

BIỂU TƯỢNG NỎ TRONG TRUYỆN KỂ ĐỊA DANH CỦA NGƯỜI THÁI Ở VIỆT NAM *

Nguyễn Thị Mai Quyên Li Meifang**

Tóm tắt: Người Thái ở Việt Nam là một trong những dân tộc thiểu số có dân số đông nhất. Họ có một kho tàng văn hóa, văn học dân gian hết sức phong phú. Bài viết này lấy biểu tượng chiếc nỏ trong truyện kể địa danh của người Thái ở Việt Nam làm đối tượng. Trên cơ sở phân tích 3 lớp nghĩa của biểu tượng nỏ để khẳng định vai trò của chiếc nỏ trong đời sống cũng như trong văn hóa của người Thái, từ đó khẳng định sự giàu có của nền văn hóa Thái đóng góp vào nền văn hóa Việt Nam đa tộc người.

Từ khóa:người Thái Việt Nam; địa danh;biểu tượng; nỏ

1. Giới thiệu khái quát về người Thái ở Việt Nam

Ở Việt Nam, từ những năm giữa thế kỷ XX trở lại đây, bên cạnh văn học dân gian người Việt, văn học dân gian các dân tộc thiểu số ngày càng được giới nghiên cứu quan tâm. Là một trong những dân tộc ít người có lịch sử cư trú lâu đời và dân số đông vào bậc nhất, dân tộc Thái có một nền văn học dân gian vô cùng phong phú và từ lâu cũng nằm trong luồng quan tâm đó.

Theo số liệu thống kê, đến ngày 1.1.1999, tổng số dân của người Thái ở Việt Nam là 1.328.725 người. Hiện nay họ là dân tộc ít người có dân cư đông thứ hai sau người Tày và phân bố tập trung ở bảy tỉnh, thành phố thuộc lãnh thổ Việt Nam. Họ là một trong 24 dân tộc ít người ở Việt Nam có chữ viết riêng đồng thời có một nền văn hóa – văn học – tri

---

* 论文题目：越南泰族人地名故事中弩的象征。

** 作者简介：Nguyễn Thị Mai Quyên，越南社会科学翰林院民间文学研究所助理研究员，云南大学外国语学院越南语系外教。研究方向：越南民间文学。李梅芳（Li Meifang），云南大学外国语学院越南语系讲师，研究方向：越南语言文学。

thức dân gian hết sức quý giá.Trên thế giới, người Thái cư trú ở nhiều quốc gia, trong đó *"các nhóm Thái ở Lào và người Thái ở Việt Nam kể cả các nhóm Shan ở bắc Mianma, Thay Khăm ti và Ahom ở Atssam Đông Bắc Ấn Độ và Thái Lan đều có nguồn gốc từ phía Tây Nam tỉnh Vân Nam, Trung Quốc. Từ thế kỷ VIII sau công nguyên trở đi, các cuộc thiên di của người Thái từ vùng Vân Nam (Trang Quốc) xuống phía Nam diễn ra liên tục. Trong các cuộc thiên di đó, có nhánh đi vào vùng Tây Bắc Việt Nam, có nhánh di cư vào đất Lào vốn trước đó là vùng đất thuộc các vương quốc Môn Khơ Me cổ"* (Vi Văn An 1994: 56). Khi đến Việt Nam, Mường Theng (Mường Thanh – tức Điện Biên Phủ ngày nay) trở thành trung tâm của người Thái.

Hiện nay ở Việt Nam, dân tộc Thái được công nhận có hai nhóm là Thái Trắng (Tăy Khao) và Thái Đen (Tăy Đăm).Những tên gọi khác như Tày Mười, Tày Thanh, Hàng Tổng, Tày Dọ, Tay Đeng (Thái Đỏ) … đều là tên gọi ở những địa phương khác nhau của hai nhóm Thái kể trên.

Câu chuyện tổ tiên người Thái từ những ngày đầu di cư đến Việt nam được ghi lại bằng chữ Thái trong những tập truyện kể như *Những bước đường chinh chiến của ông cha* (Tăy pú xớc) và *Kể chuyện bản mường* (Quăm tố mướng). Người Thái Đen ngày nay vẫn còn "những câu miêu tả về quê tổ xưa nhất của nhóm nói tiếng Thái, xem như lớp tổ tiên chung, ghi ngay ở phần mở đầu tập *Kể chuyện bản Mường*:

> *Kể từ khi đất sinh cỏ*
> *Sinh trời bằng chóp ấm*
> *Sinh đất có bảy vùng*
> *Sinh núi chụm ba hòn*
> *Sinh nước có chín dòng*
> *Sinh ra cửa Đà – Thao*
> *(Chiêm tế có pên đin pên nhả*
> *Có pên Phạ to thuông hết*
> *Có pên đin chết ton*
> *Có pên hin xam xảu*
> *Có pên nặm cảu que*
> *Có pêm Pák Tẻ - Tao)*(Cầm Trọng 1978 : 21,22)

Theo những phân tích nhà Thái học Cầm Trọng, việc người Thái ghi nhớ vùng đất mình sinh ra là nơi "sinh đất có bảy vùng" được chứng thực là bảy vùng lưu vực sông được hình dung theo thứ tự:

" Nặm Khong (sông Mê công) – vùng lưu vực 1;

Nặm Rốm - Nặm Núa -Nặm U (sông Rốm -Núa -U) -vùng lưu vực 2;

Nặm Ma (sông Mã) – vùng lưu vực 3;

Nặm Te (Sông Đà)   vùng lưu vực 4;

Nặm Tao (sông Thao) – vùng lưu vực 5;

Nặm Cháy (sông Chảy) – vùng lưu vực 6;

Nặm Xang – Nặm Lò (sông Gâm – sông Lô) – vùng lưu vực 7

(Cầm Trọng 2005 : 22,23)

Ở mỗi vùng, người Thái tụ cư và lan tỏa theo những cách khác nhau nhưng họ luôn ghi nhớ một cội nguồn chung. Tục ngữ Thái còn lưu lại câu "Đôi ta sinh ra vốn chung dòng sông Đà, Thao, U, Khong" (Xong hau cựt mã huôm me nặm: Te, Tao, U, Khong)...là vì vậy.

Trong ký ức của người Thái Việt Nam, Mường Then huyền thoại (nay thuộc tỉnh Điện Biên) là một trong những vùng đất Tổ. Đất Mường Then thuộc ngọn nguồn của ba con sông Nặm Rôm, Nặm Núa, Nặm U (là một nhánh của Nặm Khong – sông Mê Kông) thuộc vùng lưu vực 2. Người Thái từ đây vượt sang phía đông tới lưu vực sông Mã, rồi tiến hành những cuộc chinh phạt mở rộng địa giới của mình sang tận đất Lào, hình thành nên những vùng Chiềng Đông, Chiềng Tòng (tức Xiêng Đông, Xiêng Thong – nơi trung tâm của Luông Prabăng bây giờ). Từ sau năm 1954, người Thái Việt Nam hầu như đã sinh sống ổn định trên các vùng đất mà cha ông dày công khai phá và gây dựng. Họ duy trì những luật tục riêng, những sắc thái văn hóa – xã hội riêng theo từng nhóm.

2. Truyện kể địa danh của người Thái ở Việt Nam

Như đã nói ở trên, người Thái ở Việt Nam có một kho tàng văn học dân gian vô cùng phong phú. Trong kho tàng ấy, những truyện kể có yếu tố giải thích tên gọi của các sự vật tự nhiên (như đồi, núi, dốc, đèo, sông, hồ, gò, đầm...) và những điểm dân cư (như làng, bản...) hoặc những công trình liên quan trực tiếp đến đời sống, sản xuất của nhân dân (như mương, phai, mó, ruộng…) mà tên gọi đã được xác định như một địa điểm đánh dấu địa danh trên hầu khắp các vùng lãnh thổ Việt nam có dân cư Thái sinh sống được chúng tôi chọn lọc và tập hợp trong một công trình chung có tên là *Truyện Huổi Pú Nặm Mương(Truyện kể địa danh của dân tộc Thái ở Việt Nam)* (Nguyễn Thị Mai Quyên 2018).

Công trình này bao gồm 116 truyện kể được sắp xếp theo vùng địa lý. Số lượng truyện đương nhiên mới phản ánh một phần nào kho tàng truyện kể địa danh vô cùng phong phú của tộc người. Sở dĩ chúng tôi có thể khẳng định như vậy bởi lẽ trong điều kiện hiện tại, nguồn truyện mà chúng tôi có được chủ yếu là từ các công trình đã xuất bản. Thực tế cho thấy với những địa bàn mà người nghiên cứu có điều kiện điền dã nhiều lần như khu vực Mường Xang (thuộc Mộc Châu, Sơn La), Mường Mùn (Mai Châu, Hòa Bình), Mường Vạt (Yên Châu – Sơn La), số lượng truyện kể thu thập được từ thực tế là rất phong phú. Điều này cũng hứa hẹn trong thời gian tiếp theo, nghiên cứu còn có thể tiếp tục bằng việc mở rộng phạm vi điền dã và khảo sát để làm phong phú thêm số lượng truyện kể đồng thời có điều kiện tiệm cận hơn nữa những giá trị văn hóa của tộc người trong một tập hợp truyện dân gian.

Khi đã thu thập được một số lượng tương đối các truyện kể, có một vấn đề nảy sinh, đó là câu chuyện phân loại. Từ trước đến nay, khi tiếp xúc với truyện kể dân gian, mọi nghiên cứu gần như ngay lập tức nghĩ đến việc xác định thể loại của chúng.Về mặt phương pháp, chúng tôi ý thức được rằng đó là một việc làm hết sức tương đối - một dạng giả thiết. Bởi lẽ việc phân chia truyện kể dân gian nói chung và truyện kể địa danh nói riêng thành các thể loại khác nhau phụ thuộc rất lớn vào thái độ văn hóa đối với truyện cổ và các nguyên tắc phân loại truyền thống truyền miệng theo tiêu chí địa phương. Hơn nữa, khi các câu chuyện của một tộc người được kể lại bằng tiếng Việt tức là chúng đã đi từ một nền văn hóa này sang một nền văn hóa khác. Quá trình đó chắc chắn đã làm cho truyện thay đổi rất nhiều yếu tố hình thức thuộc về nguồn gốc khiến cho việc phân chia thể loại cũng như suy nghĩ về chúng trong bối cảnh văn hóa tộc người trở nên hết sức khó khăn.Tuy nhiên, trong điều kiện hiện tại, chúng tôi vẫn buộc phải sử dụng tiêu chí này làm một căn cứ để nghiên cứu đối tượng truyện kể này.

Do tính chất phong phú của tập hợp truyện kể, ở Việt Nam xung quanh vấn đề thể loại của truyện kể địa danh cũng còn nhiều quan điểm không thống nhất. Dưới đây chúng tôi thực hiện việc thống kê, phân tích các quan niệm về thể loại của truyện kể địa danh, mục đích cuối cùng là lựa chọn một quan điểm làm cơ sở cho quá trình khảo sát.

Xuất phát từ chỗ xác định tập hợp truyện kể địa danh chỉ bao gồm những truyện lấy việc giải thích địa danh làm mục đích, trong hai cuốn giáo trình *Những đặc điểm thi pháp của các thể loại văn học dân gian Việt Nam* (Đỗ Bình Trị 1999),và *Thi pháp văn học dân gian* (Lê Trường Phát 2000), các tác giả Đỗ Bình Trị, Lê Trường Phát đều gọi những truyện giải thích tên gọi hoặc nguồn gốc của các sự vật địa lý là truyền thuyết địa danh. Cùng quan điểm đó, tác giả Nguyễn Thị Bích Hà khẳng định *"Trước hết truyện kể địa danh không phải là thần thoại, mặc dù có nhiều môtip thần thoại tham gia vào truyện kể địa danh (...) truyền thuyết và những truyện kể địa danh cùng hướng sự phản ánh vào những đề tài rộng lớn, mang tính chất địa phương, tính chất dân tộc. Chúng được gắn với những yếu tố xã hội, lịch sử xác thực và có chức năng minh giải các vấn đề lịch sử xã hội. Những đặc trưng của truyện kể địa danh không nằm ngoài truyền thuyết, nó gần gũi với truyền thuyết ở những tiêu chí căn bản về thể loại và cũng khác cổ tích ở những tiêu chí đó. Như vậy truyện kể địa danh không thể nằm trong thể loại cổ tích (...) dựa vào cơ sở tư liệu và tiêu chí phân loại chúng tôi có thể khẳng định chắc chắn chắn rằng truyện kể địa danh nằm trong thể loại truyền thuyết và là một bộ phận của truyền thuyết"* Nguyễn Bích Hà 1983: 9).

Các tác giả khác như Kiều Thu Hoạch dù vẫn cho rằng trong loại truyền thuyết có truyền thuyết địa danh ("chỉ loại truyền thuyết giải thích tên gọi, tức là nói về nguồn gốc tên gọi của các địa danh ở các địa phương mà có gắn với các sự kiện, nhân vật lịch sử có liên quan" nhưng có chú ý thêm: "đã là truyền thuyết địa danh thì nhất định nội dung truyện kể phải được gắn với nhân vật hoặc sự kiện lịch sử đặc biệt nào đó, nếu không thì đó chỉ có thể đơn thuần coi là một câu chuyện giải thích địa danh theo thần thoại suy nguyên hoặc một kiểu giải thích theo từ nguyên học dân gian hoặc từ nguyên học thông tục mà thôi" (Kiêu Thu Hoach 2005: 9). Như vậy, với ý kiến này có thể thấy truyện giải thích địa danh đã được nhắc đến bao gồm cả những truyện thuộc thể loại thần thoại (thần thoại suy nguyên).

Các tác giả như Trần Thị An , Trần Tùng Chinh… lại có quan điểm tương đối khác. Trong bài Truyện kể địa danh - từ góc nhìn thể loại, Trần Thị An khảo sát truyện kể địa danh từ ba góc độ: thiên nhiên trong quan hệ với thiên nhiên, thiên nhiên trong quan hệ với lịch sử và thiên nhiên trong quan hệ với xã hội, theo đó lần đầu tiên vấn đề thể loại của truyện kể địa danh được nhìn nhận từ nhiều góc độ. Những truyện kể địa danh nói lên mối quan hệ giữa thiên nhiên với chính nó trong buổi sơ khai - khi mà "tên gọi của núi sông trong rất nhiều chuyện được giải thích bằng quá trình kiến tạo tự thân của vũ trụ, và những bí ẩn của quá trình kiến tạo đó được hình tượng hóa bằng hành động của các vị thần" (Trần Thị An 1999: 51) - được xếp vào thể loại thần thoại. Những chuyện phản ánh mối quan hệ giữa thiên nhiên với lịch sử, đáp ứng "nhu cầu rất lớn của tác giả dân gian là gắn truyện kể địa danh với cảm hứng về lịch sử" thuộc thể loại truyền thuyết.Còn lại những truyện phản ánh thiên nhiên trong mối quan hệ với chuyện đời thuộc thể loại cổ tích.

Gần với ý kiến của Trần Thị An, trong luận văn Bước đầu tìm hiểu truyện kể địa danh Nam Bộ, tác giả Trần Tùng Chinh (Trần Tùng Chinh 2000), cũng xác định truyện kể địa danh thuộc ba nhóm: nhóm truyện kể địa danh về đề tài con người đấu tranh với thiên nhiên; nhóm truyện kể địa danh về đề tài con người đấu tranh chống thù trong giặc ngoài; nhóm truyện kể địa danh về đề tài con người với những quan hệ xã hội thế sự đời thường tương ứng với ba thể loại thần thoại, truyền thuyết và cổ tích, đồng thời lấy đó làm cơ sở để tiến hành việc khảo sát nội dung và thi pháp truyện kể.

Chúng tôi nhận thấy ý kiến cho rằng truyện kể địa danh không thuộc thể loại thần thoại mà chỉ "lượm lại những mảnh vỡ của thần thoại để đưa vào những sáng tạo mới" chỉ đúng phần nào với truyện kể dân gian người Việt. Trên thực tế, kho tàng thần thoại của các dân tộc anh em hết sức phong phú, (sự ra đời của *Tổng tập văn học dân gian các dân tộc ít người Việt Nam* (Nguyễn Thị Huế 2007), có thể coi là một minh chứng, trong đó nhiều thần thoại mang trong nonhưng đặc điểm hoàn toàn phuhợp với tiêu chi cua truyên kểđi a danh vacothênăm trong tập hợp nay. Đây cũng là cơsở để chúng tôi khẳng định trong tập hợp truyện kể địa danh các dân tộc nói chung và dân tộc Thái nói riêng có những truyện thuộc thể loại thần thoại.

Mặt khác, cũng không thể nói trong tập hợp truyện kể địa danh không có truyện cổ tích. Tác giả Nguyễn Thị Bích Hà ngay trong công trình của mình cũng   công nhận: "có một số truyện địa danh gắn với đề tài sinh hoạt xã hội, vấn đề về đạo đức, đề cao tình cảm của cá nhân con người như tình yêu, tình vợ chồng (…) Nhân vật của truyện mang những triết lý sâu sắc về hạnh phúc, về đạo đức, đồng thời nó đặt ra những vấn đề có giá trị nhân sinh lớn (…) đặc biệt về thi pháp, một số truyện còn đưa nhân vật của mình thoát khỏi thế giới loài người (…) thoát khỏi thực tại là một nét độc đáo của thi pháp cổ tích" (Nguyễn Thị Bích Ha 1983 : 19). Mặc dù vẫn cho rằng cội nguồn của những truyện kể này là truyền thuyết, và bởi "trong quá trình lịch sử, do những nhu cầu mới của nhân dân, những người sáng tác và thưởng thức văn hóa dân gian mà truyện được bồi đắp thêm những lớp nghĩa mới, lấn át ý nghĩa giải thích địa danh ban đầu", nhưng sau cùng chính tác giả cũng công nhận "có một số nhà nghiên cứu coi những truyện trên là truyện cổ tích không phải là không có căn cứ" (Nguyễn Thị Bích Ha1983:20).

Truyện cổ tích là những truyện được khởi nguồn từ cảm hứng thế sự và mang nội dung thế sự. Trong khi đó "với cảm thức tên gọi, nhiều truyện kể địa danh đã lồng vào đó rất nhiều truyện đời (…) Mỗi một địa danh đều mang chở biết bao tâm sự của người kể truyện về sự éo le, trắc trở, về nỗi khát khao hi vọng hoặc niềm ân hận chua xót. Và thông qua đó tác giả gửi gắm một bài học nhân sinh" (Trần Thị An 1999:54).Những câu chuyện như thế hoàn toàn đáp ứng được yêu cầu của thể loại cổ tích và phải thuộc về cổ tích như bản chất của chúng vậy.

Đến đây có thể nhìn nhận, nếu lấy thể loại làm tiêu chí nhận diện các câu chuyện dân gian về địa danh (đã được kể lại bằng tiếng Việt) của người Thái thì truyện kể địa danh Thái tộc tồn tại cả ba thể loại: thần thoại, truyền thuyết và cổ tích. Kho tàng truyện kể này có nội dung hết sức phong phú, dưới đây chúng tôi xin phân tích một biểu tượng tiêu biểu của dân tộc Thái ở Việt Nam xuất hiện trong các truyện kể địa danh, đó là biểu tượng "nỏ".

3. Biểu tượng "nỏ" trong truyện kể địa danh của người Thái ở Việt Nam

Nếu như ở nhiều nền văn hóa, cung "là một vũ khí vương giả (…), một biểu trưng đế vương"(Jean Chevalier, Alain Gheerbrand 2015: 221) thì với văn hóa Thái, chiếc nỏ đi liền với mũi tên - một dạng thức vũ khí tương tự - dường như ít mang dấu ấn của vương quyền mà gắn bó nhiều hơn với đời sống thực tế của tộc người. Tuy thế, tên – nỏ cũng mang không ít tính biểu trưng, đặc biệt khi đi vào truyện cổ.

Trước hết, xuất phát từ thực tiễn, nỏ là biểu trưng cho nghề săn bắn và sức mạnh tiêu diệt kẻ thù.Người Thái là cư dân lúa nước, tuy thế trong đời sống, nguồn thịt quan trọng được cung cấp nhờ săn bắn (chứ không phải chăn nuôi), và bởi vậy trong xã hội Thái, những người đàn ông giỏi săn bắn rất được coi trọng. Quan sát tập hợp truyện kể địa danh, những nhân vật như nai phan – người đứng đầu phường săn (truyện Tạo Mường Phe và bản Na Tòong), ông Pú Quán Muôp (Truyện Pú Quán Muôp), người đàn ông trong Sự tích bản Tà… đều là những người có tài dùng nỏ và săn bắn. Dân tộc học Việt Nam cung cấp thông tin về việc người Thái có rất nhiều hình thức săn bắt trong đó đặc biệt quan trọng là săn tập thể."Săn tập thể còn gọi là săn gióng được tiến hành ở các gò săn (đon húa). Dưới sự điều khiển của thầy săn (nai pan), toàn thể dân bản được chia thành từng tốp gọi chung bằng tên đoàn người chuyên kêu đuổi (mú phủ téng khék). Bên kia gò săn gồm các tay thiện xạ gọi chung là đoàn người chuyên đón chặn (mú phủ téng lặt). Nếu dùng súng, nỏ có tên tẩm thuốc độc, giáo, mác thì bố trí vào các điểm phục sẵn. Nếu không dùng các khí cụ đó thì tổ chức đặt bẫy lao (cạt háo), bẫy sập hầm (cang kẹo khum) hoặc chăng lưới (cang xái). Khi nghe tù và thầy săn cất tiếng báo lệnh thì cuộc săn suối bắt đầu, đoàn chuyên kêu đuổi cũng bắt đầu gào thét, đập thanh la, gõ mõ, vừa tiến vào rừng xua đàn chó săn rượt đuổi thú. Hoảng hốt, thú vội chạy phóng khỏi gò săn, lọt đúng ổ phục kích đón đầu, lập tức bị diệt gọn" (Cầm Trọng 2005: 86, 87). Trong những cuộc săn như thế, người trực tiếp bắn được thú sẽ được hưởng thêm thủ như là một kỷ niệm của chiến công. Đọc truyện kể địa danh của người Thái sẽ thấy hình ảnh chiếc nỏ đi liền với người đàn ông tài giỏi xuất hiện trong 13 câu chuyện bao gồm cả truyền thuyết và cổ tích. Điều này cho thấy phần nào ý nghĩa của cây nỏ, từ chỗ có vai trò quan trọng trong đời sống vật chất, vật dụng săn và người sử dụng nó cũng có vai trò quan trọng trong đời sống tinh thần của cộng đồng.

Bên cạnh lớp nghĩa nói trên, cũng xuất phát từ thực tiễn, cây nỏ cùng ống tên, đặc biệt là tên độc còn là dấu hiệu nhận biết tài năng, nói cách khác nó là biểu tượng của tài năng. Truyện Tạo Mường Phe và bản Na Tòong kể về chàng thuồng luồng ở Mường Phe lấy được nàng Tòong xinh đẹp, giọng hát hay như tiếng chuông đồng. Nhưng cũng vì chuyện đó mà chàng bị tạo ngược mường Hy ghen ghét. Chàng lo lắng vì nước nhỏ, dân không đông, lực lượng kém, bản thân lại không có tài nên hóa thành người trên đầu đội khăn xanh, ngày nào cũng trèo lên cây sung trên bờ Văng tò ong, gặp ai cũng hỏi kế chống lại kẻ thù. Khi nai phan (người trưởng phường săn) đi qua, "thấy nai phan vác nỏ lớn, mang ống tên đầy, tạo đoán là người có tài". Với ông Pú Quán Muôp ở mường Ca Da, sở dĩ người mường nước biết được ông là người tài có thể giúp họ chiến thắng kẻ thù cũng bởi ông chính là người đã dùng tên độc giết được con cáo mèo do mường nước cử lên. Truyện kể rằng: "Một hôm giữa trời quang mây tạnh, nhìn thấy con cáo mèo đang ăn sung chín trên cây, ông lập tức giương nỏ lên bắn. Phát thứ nhất con cáo không chết, thì ra ông bắn bằng tên thường, mũi tên xuyên qua đùi mà cáo vẫn nhởn nhơ ăn sung, được một lúc tên tự rơi ra. Ông vừa thấy lạ vừa sợ hãi, rút mũi tên thứ hai tẩm thuốc độc ra bắn.Lần này cáo trúng tên độc chết ngay". Giống như vậy, người thợ săn trong Sự tích bản Tà cũng được kể là người giỏi dùng nỏ và tên độc, bởi thế mà rồng sông Mã chọn ông là người giúp đỡ trong cuộc chiến chống lại rồng sông Đà.

Phải chăng trong văn hóa tộc người, việc dùng tên tẩm thuốc độc hàm chứa một ý nghĩa? Vì sao mũi tên ấy đi cùng cây nỏ lại là biểu trưng của tài năng? Viết về chi tiết này, nghiên cứu dân tộc học của các tác giả Lã Văn Lô, Đặng Nghiêm Vạn cho biết "Ngoai viec săn băn băng nỏ vasưng, đông bao thương dung cac loai bây. (...) Đông bao Thai rât ít khi dung notâm thuốc độc. Conơi tâm thuốc thi thương lây nhưa cây xui (anharis toxicaria moraceae), nhưng phôbiên lamua cua ngươi Xahay Lao" (Lã Văn Lô, Đặng Nghiêm Vạn 1968: 213). Trong nhiều lần thăm hỏi trên các địa bàn cư trú của người Thái Đen ở Sơn La, người Thái Trắng ở Mộc Châu hay người Tày Mường ở Nghệ An, chúng tôi được biết ngày nay người Thái vẫn còn truyền nhau kinh nghiệm dùng nhựa cây "co nòong" để làm tên độc. Có điều loại tên này xưa nay thợ săn đều rất ít dùng bởi nếu chẳng may bị trúng tên, dù chỉ là vết xước nhẹ mà không được giải độc kịp thời thì kẻ xấu số nhất định sẽ chịu cái chết rất đau đớn. Bởi thế người đã biết chế ra và dùng tên độc ắt phải đồng thời biết cách làm thuốc giải để phòng khi gặp sự không may. Ông Vi Văn Việt - người giỏi nghề săn bắn có tiếng ở bản Chiềng Ve, xã Chiềng Ve huyện Mộc Châu (thuộc Mường Xang cũ) cho biết cả đời ông có chưa đến chục lần dùng tên độc và trên thực tế thường chỉ những tay nỏ rất lành nghề mới dùng đến loại tên này, còn lại đa phần người đi săn đều chỉ dùng tên thường. Từ một vài thông tin trên có thể hình dung một phương án trả lời, việc dùng nỏ và tên tẩm độc trở thành một trong những tiêu chí quan trọng để nhận biết người tài bởi trước hết nó gắn với thực tế khắc nghiệt của nghề săn - việc người ta phải trả giá đắt, có thể là tính mạng con người nếu chẳng may "sơ sểnh". Chỉ những người tài giỏi, đủ tự tin vào tay nỏ vì thế mới dám sở hữu loại vũ khí này, bởi vậy trong truyện kể, đây lại trở thành tiêu chí quan trọng để nhận biết mức độ tài giỏi của người dùng tên, nỏ. Tuy vậy, sự giải thích này phải chăng đã lý giải được hết cội nguồn của ý nghĩa biểu tượng? Mối băn khoăn ấy đưa chúng tôi đến với lớp nghĩa thứ 3 của cây nỏ - đi kèm với nó là mũi tên độc.

Cây nỏ và mũi tên độc là vũ khí để hạ thủ một con vật biểu trưng. Ý nghĩa này có phần tương đồng với ý nghĩa của cây cung và mũi tên ở nhiều nền văn hóa (Jean Chevalier, Alain Gheerbrand 2015: 223). Đối với người Thái, con vật biểu trưng ấy chính là tô ngươk – tô luông sự tổng hòa của niềm kiêu hãnh và nỗi khiếp sợ, của cái thiện và cái ác, hạnh phúc và khổ đau. Theo đó, ý nghĩa hạ thủ một con vật biểu trưng của biểu tượng nỏ đi cùng với mũi tên độc được hình thành khi trong truyên kêđịa danh Thại corất nhiều truyện kể về ngươ đàn ông tài ba dưng novà tên độc bắn chết con vật hung dữ trong cuộc giao tranh (thường là con rồng hay tô ngươk hung ác) để giúp đỡ phe còn lại.

Trở lại lịch sử, bên cạnh giả thuyết comôt lợp cư dân Tày – Thai cô cư trutại môt sôvung ơmiên Băc Viêt Nam, con lai nhữ ng ghi nhận, chứng tích chủ yếu ơnhiêu nơi cho thấy holanhưng cư dân đên sau. Nhiêu truyên kể địa danh cũng băt đâu băng motip thời gian "khi ngươi Thai đên, nơi đây đât đacochurôi". Nhưng chunhân nay được biêt đên langươi Xa (tên goi cac tôc người bản địa như Xinh Mun, Khơ Mú... theo cach goi cua ngươi Thai), holachunhân cua nhiêu vưng đât đai, đông thơi cung lachunhân cua văn hoa cu, văn hoa hai lươm vasăn băn. Tư liêu của các tác giả Đặng Nghiêm Vạn, Lã Văn Lô cho biết ngươi Thai ngoài việc tự làm tên độc còn dung cac loai tên tâm thuôc đôc cua ngươi Lao hay ngươi Xạ điêu này có nghĩa rằng ở các cộng đồng ấy (mà ở đây chúng tôi nhấn mạnh đực biệt đến cộng đồng người Xá - những cư dân lớp trước), việc dùng nỏ tầm thuốc độc phổ biến hơn, tới mức nó trở thành một sản phẩm để trao đổi. Điều này liệu có liên quan gì đến hình ảnh những ngươ đan ông giơ dưng tên tâm độc trong các câu chuyện kể?Phai chăng những hình tượng đó không chỉ là hình ảnh của người Thái mà còn lasưhình tương hoa những con người thuộc lợp cư dân đâu tiên cua nhưng vưng đât vốn nay thuộc về người Thái? Truyện kể có một chi tiết rất đáng chú ý là nhờ việc giỏi dùng nỏ và giúp được cư dân mường nước (hay người trồng lúa nước) mà những người tài giỏi được trả công bằng đất đai, mương phai, được "cho ơlạ" hoặc mường bản được mơmang. Như thê, ngươi trông lua nươc, đên sau, tươi a vike"nhơvạ' bước lên đi a vike"ban ơn" vađươc đơi sau ham ơn (đi a danh ban Taở Môc Châu, Sơn La, cach gơi tăt cua Ta Ơn tưc Ta Ơn cho thây rât rọđiêu nay).

Nói cách khác, trong hai lớp nghĩa cả biểu tượng - biểu tượng của tài năng và hạ thủ theo nghi lễ một con vật biểu trưng - có sự dung hòa của ý nghĩa thực tế là tính nguy hiểm của việc dùng tên độc đòi hỏi tay nghề của người sử dụng. Xét từ góc độ nào đó, có thể nói người Thái – cư dân gắn với nước – đã "nhờ vả" hay thu phục được sức mạnh của những cư dân săn bắn, biến họ thành những trợ thủ đắc lực cho công cuộc mở mang mường bản. Môt cach kheo leo, ngươi Thai biên cư dân ban đi a tươi a vi kelam chusang đi a vi kebi phuthuôc, muôn ơlai đêu phai chi u thân phân phai ham ơn. Tât canhư ng kiên tạo kyvi, sư mơrông ruông đông, mương phai, lang ban đêu lacông lao cua ngươi mương nươc, "kenhơvaban đải". Điêu nay cho thây vi sao khi khảo sát hầu như toàn bộ kho tàng truyện cổ Thái đã được xuất bản cũng như trong các câu chuyện gặp trên thực địa, việc dùng tên nỏ giúp đỡ cư dân mường nước hầu như chi xuât hiên trong những câu chuyên giai thi ch đi a danh. Và hẳn không phai ngâu nhiên khi ngươi Thai được đanh gia la "uyên chuyên khôn lương như nươc, cohi nh dang cua moi bơbên".

Đến mỗi nơi, cư dân Thái dùng sức mạnh quân sự và trí tuệ của mình để tìm đất sống. Chiếc nỏ đi liền với mũi tên - vũ khí không chỉ để săn bắn mà còn dùng trong chiến đấu - vì thế mang thêm một lớp nghĩa là biểu tượng cho sức mạnh chiến đấu nhằm thiết lập trật tự thế giới. Trong những truyên thuyêt đi a danh như Sự tích Mường Mùn, Mường Xang khi ngươi Thai vangươi Xađanh nhau không phân thăng bai, hotôchức thi băn nỏđêdanh quyên ơlai. Cuộc thi diễn ra vào lúc giữa trưa, hai bên cùng bắn tên, bên nào bắn được mũi tên "xuyên qua" vách đá sẽ là kẻ dành chiến thắng. Trong những câu chuyện, người Thái luôn dùng chiếc nỏ bằng tre, đầu bịt sáp ong. Giữa trưa, khi cuộc thi diễn ra cũng là lúc vách đá đã bị mặt trời đốt nóng, tên của người Thái bắn lên vách núi, sáp ong gặp vách đá thì chảy ra mà dính lại, trong khi ấy người Xá dùng mũi tên đồng, gặp vách đá sẽ rơi xuống nên tất yếu gặp thất bại.

Ở một số câu truyện khác, người Thái ở hai bản mang tên Nà Ngà (thuộc xã Mường Sang huyện Mộc Châu và xã Chiềng Hặc, Yên Châu) đều kể trong cuộc giao tranh với người chủ cũ (người Xá), người Thái ban đầu gặp nhiều bất lợi bởi bản của người Xá có cây tre nà ngà thân màu vàng óng rào kín xung quanh. Trong khi dân Xá ở bên trong đóng kín các lối vào bản rồi dùng tên nỏ bắn ra thì người Thái lại không thể nào bắn vào bản được. Về sau họ nghĩ ra kế dùng mũi tên đầu bịt bạc bắn vào luỹ tre, người Xá vì tham của, chặt tre để lấy bạc, vậy là mắc mưu người Thái và trở thành kẻ thua cuộc (xem Sự tích bản Nà Ngà). Câu chuyện này không chỉ được kể trong cuộc giao tranh Thái – Xá ở trên mà khi trong quá trình điền dã ở vùng lòng chảo Mường Thanh, chúng tôi cũng được nghe người Thái ở đây kể về cuộc chiến của người Thái để dành đất từ tay người Lự. Ở đó, người Lự thua cuộc cũng vì họ tham chỗ bạc mắc ở bờ rào tre mà triệt đi bức thành lũy tự nhiên đáng giá ngàn vàng. Vậy là một trật tự mới được thiết lập, kẻ mới đến bằng sự khôn ngoan của mình đã trở thành chủ nhân của đất đai, làng bản đẩy những kẻ kia hoặc buộc phải dời đi nơi khác hoặc trở thành cuông nhốc, phụ thuộc.

Trên những hành trình tìm kiếm vùng đất mới, trong lao động sản xuất, và cả trong những cuộc chiến chống lại kẻ thù, chiếc nỏ từ chỗ là vũ khí đã tham gia vào các sự kiện lịch sử, xã hội của tộc người mà trở thành biểu tượng. Với người Thái, nỏ luôn là hình ảnh tượng trưng cho sức mạnh chinh phục, cho sự mưu lược và khôn ngoan.Và ở những câu chuyện ấy, các lớp nghĩa của biểu tượng nỏ được thể hiện thông qua nhiều motip. Tiêu biểu nhất có thể kể đến motip người giúp rồng/ngươk thể hiện trong những câu chuyện như Sự tích bản Tà, Truyện Pú Quán Muốp, Phai đá suối Vì, Tạo Mường Phe và bản Na Tòong… Ở đây, con người luôn được kể là người đàn ông tài giỏi gắn với cây nỏ, nhờ giúp rồng/ngươk chiến thắng kẻ thù mà cuối cùng được đền ơn. Những địa danh được hình thành như bản Na Tòong, bản Tà, Hát Chạng Ca, Mó Tôm… vừa là sự ghi dấu chiến công của con người trong việc giúp đỡ/ chinh phục các thế lực của mường nước đồng thời cũng là sự ghi nhớ lòng biết ơn của con người trước sự kiến tạo của rồng/ngươk với chính các công trình như thửa ruộng, mó nước hay mương phai. Motip thứ hai xuất hiện giúp mang chở biểu tượng là motip thi tài xuất hiện trong những truyện như Sự tích Mường Mùn, Sự tích Mường Xang… Trong những truyện kể này, những địa danh như Pom Phả Khí Xút, Pú Đán Đanh, Đán Cặc… là nơi ghi dấu cuộc thi tài giữa người Thái – kẻ mới đến và những người chủ cũ, và ở đó chiếc nỏ chính là phương tiện để kẻ dành chiến thắng thể hiện tài năng và sự mưu trí.

Biểu tượng nỏ chỉ là một trong nhiều biểu tượng xuất hiện trong truyện kể địa danh của người Thái ở Việt Nam, mặc dầu vậy sự khảo sát biểu tượng này cũng cho thấy phần nào sự phong phú của văn hóa tộc người. Những lớp nghĩa của biểu tượng không phải là yếu tố tĩnh tại và đóng kín, chúng được hình thành, di truyền và trương nở trong quá trình người Thái cũng như bất cứ tộc người nào duy trì vô vàn các mối quan hệ xã hội với cộng đồng trong/ngoài mường bản, với nội tộc, ngoại tộc, với tự nhiên và xã hội, để biểu hiện một nhu cầu tự nhiên là khẳng định và khuếch trương văn hóa. Họ sử dụng các cách thức khác nhau để phóng chiếu nghĩa của biểu tượng (tức là những hạt nhân văn hóa của cộng đồng) lên các thực thể nhằm khẳng định chính mình đồng thời thể hiện sự ảnh hưởng với những cộng đồng giao tiếp khác. Với người Thái, bên cạnh việc xây đền, thờ phụng núi non, bỏ nhiều công lao để chinh phục mường nước/dòng nước phục vụ cho mường bản; dùng cây nỏ và mũi tên để chiếm lĩnh/bảo vệ đất đai… thì kể chuyện cũng là một cách thức để phóng chiếu văn hóa. Hầu như đến bất cứ bản làng Thái nào, người thăm hỏi cũng sẽ được nghe những câu chuyện về tên gọi núi sông, mường bản. Truyện địa danh Thái nói chung với hệ thống biểu tượng phong phú vì thế vượt ra ngoài ý nghĩa tự thân của nó, thuộc về giấc mơ mang tính cộng đồng với sức mạnh của một "trận lụt" mang tên Phủ Táy.

TÀI LIỆU THAM KHẢO

[1]Cầm Trọng.*Người Thái ở Tây Bắc Việt Nam*[M]. Nxb Khoa học xã hội, H;1978.

[2]Cầm Trọng.*Những hiểu biết về người Thái ở Việt Nam*[M].Nxb Chính trị quốc gia, Hà Nội: 2005.

[3]Đỗ Bình Trị.*Những đặc điểm thi pháp của các thể loại văn học dân gian Việt Nam*[M]. Nxb Giáo dục, Hà Nội: 1999.

[4]Jean Chevalier, Alain Gheerbrand. *Từ điển biểu tượng văn hóa thế giới*[M]. Nxb Đà Nẵng, Đà Nẵng: 2015.

[5]Kiều Thu Hoạch (chubiên).*Tổng tập Văn học dân gian người Việt, tập 4 - Truyền thuyết*[M]. Nxb Khoa học xã hội. Hà Nội: 2005.

[6]Lã Văn Lô, Đặng Nghiêm Vạn. *Sơ lược giới thiệu các nhóm dân tộc Tày – Nùng – Thái Việt Nam*[M]. Nxb Khoa học xã hội, Hà Nội: 1968.

[7]Lê Trường Phát.*Thi pháp văn học dân gian*[M]. Nxb Giáo dục, Hà Nội: 2000.

[8]Nguyễn Thị Bích Ha *Tìm hiểu truyền thuyết địa danh qua những truyền thuyết ven Hồ Tây*[D]. Trường đại học sư phạm Hà Nội: 1983.

[9]Nguyễn Thị Huế chủ biên.*Tổng tập văn học dân gian các dân tộc thiểu số Việt Nam*[M]. tập 3 - Thần thoại (song ngư), Nxb Khoa học xã hội, Hà Nội: 2007

[10]Nguyễn Thị Mai Quyên.*Truyện Huổi pú nặm mương (Truyện kể địa danh của người Thái ở Việt Nam*[M]. Nxb Văn học, Hà Nội: 2018.

[11]Trần Thị An.*Truyện kể địa danh từ góc nhìn thể loại*[J]. Tạp chí Văn học, số 3, 1999.

[12]Trần Tùng Chinh. *Bước đầu tìm hiểu truyện kể dân gian về các địa danh ở Nam Bộ*[D]. Trường đại học Sư phạm thành phố Hồ Chí Minh. 2000.

[13] Vi Văn An.*Về mối quan hệ nguồn gốc và những nét tương đồng văn hóa giữa ba nhóm Thay Đăm,Thay Khao và Thay Đeng ở Lào với người Thái ở Việt Nam*[J]. Tạp chí Nghiên cứu Đông Nam Á, số 1, 1994.

Hiện trạng và tương lai của tuyến đường sắt Vân Nam - Việt Nam *

Jin Min**

Tóm tắt: Tuyến đường sắt Vân Nam - Việt Nam (gọi tắt là đường sắt Điền – Việt) là đường sắt thứ nhất của tỉnh Vân Nam, đường sắt quốc tế thứ hai của Trung Quốc, đường sắt khổ 1m (ray dài 1 mét) dài nhất trên thế giới, nó đã ghi lại lịch sự quật khởi của dân tộc và cách mạng Trung Quốc, đã chứng kiến lịch sự bắt đầu của văn minh công nghiệp Trung Quốc. Nó là một hành lang du lịch vàng chung của nhân dân hai nước Trung Việt. Hiện nay tuyến đường sắt Điền – Việt đón chào lại cơ hội phát triển mới sau một trăm năm, nhưng lại đang bị hỏng hóc, xuống cấp và chờ đợi trùng tu. Tương lai của đường sắt Điền – Việt ra sao?Đối với tương lai của nó, người ta có nhiều mong đợi.Luận văn này xuất phát từ góc nhìn mà cho đường sắt Điền – Việt trở lại sức sống, tìm ra hướng mới cho đường sắt Điền – Việt một lần nữa thịnh vượng.Dựa vào tuyến đường sắt Điền – Việt có thể xúc tiến giao lưu và hợp tác về các mặt như văn hoá, kinh tế và chính trị giữa hai nước Trung Việt.

Từ khóa: Tuyến đường sắt Vân Nam-Việt Nam; hiện nay; tương lai

CHƯƠNG I Lịch sử phát triển của tuyến đường sắt Vân Nam - Việt Nam

1.1 Nguồn gốc lịch sử của tuyến đường sắt Vân Nam - Việt Nam

Hơn 100 năm trước, khi tiếng còi lần đầu tiên vang lên ở vùng sâu xa của Vân Nam, và đã chấn động mọi người từ trước kia chưa hề có.

Đường sắt Điền – Việt là con đường sắt đầu tiên của tỉnh Vân Nam, đồng thời cũng là một trong những đường sắt khổ 1m (đường có

---

* 论文题目：滇越铁路的现状与未来。

** 作者简介：金敏(Jin Min)，云南大学外国语学院越南语系助教，研究方向：越南语言文化。

ray dài 1m) trong cả nước, ngày 01-04-1910, đường sắt với chiều dài 854km, nối liền Hải Phòng - Lào Cai - Hà Khẩu - Côn Minh đã chính thức đi vào hoạt động. Vốn là do thực dân Pháp theo điều ước bất bình đẳng xây dựng. Điểm xuất phát của đường sắt này từ Côn Minh-Vân Nam-Trung Quốc, qua Hà Khẩu rồi vào biên giới Trung Việt đi vào Việt Nam, đến Hải Phòng-Việt Nam thuộc địa của thực dân Pháp trước mới là xong, vì thế gọi là đường sắt Điền – Việt, hiện nay đoạn đường sắt từ Hà Khẩu đến Côn Minh gọi là đường sắt Côn Hà. Đường sắt Điền – Việt cùng với kênh đào panama, kênh đào suez được coi là ba công trình khó khăn nhất trong lịch sử nhân loại.

Đường sắt Điền–Việt cũng là một trong ba đường sắt trên cao nguyên cả thế giới, có danh tiếng tương đối rộng rãi và giá trị nhân văn vô cùng lớn, lại là tuyến đường sắt khổ 1m duy nhất của Trung Quốc cho đến nay mà vẫn được sử dụng, đó là những văn vật sống, hóa thạch sống quý báu của lịch sử phát triển đường sắt Trung Quốc cũng như lịch sử phát triển đường sắt thế giới.

Năm 1903, chính phủ nhà Thanh Trung Quốc với chính phủ Pháp ký kết "Trương trình đường sắt Điền Việt Trung-Pháp", ngay sau đó người Pháp cắt cử những người đi thăm dò tuyến đường, vẽ ra bàn vẽ thiết kế, đồng thời thành lập chính thức công ty đường sắt Vân Nam - Việt Nam nước Pháp. Đoạn từ Hải Phòng Việt Nam đến Lào Cai gọi là "Việt đoạn", đoạn từ Hà Khẩu đến Côn Minh, gọi là "Điền đoạn". Năm 1901 khởi công, "Việt đoạn" được xây dựng xong trước. Năm 1903, chính phủ Pháp phê duyệt quy hoạch tuyến đông, vào năm sau chính thức khởi công, ngày 15 tháng 4 năm 1909 thông xe đến Bích Sắc Trại, một năm sau toàn tuyến được thông xe.

Tuyến đường sắt Điền – Việt có ràng 1m, chiều dài toàn tuyến là 854 km, trong đó đoạn ở Việt Nam dài 386km, đoạn ở Vân Nam dài 468km, tổng kim ngạch xây dựng tuyến đường là gần 159 triệu franc, số tiền này nhiều hơn 1 lần so với tổng kim ngạch xây dựng đường sắt tiêu chuẩn 1,435m của Trung Quốc, qua đó có thể thấy công trình có quy mô lớn đến mức nào. Hiện nay dọc đường sắt Vân Nam-Việt Nam vẫn bảo tồn rất nhiều dấu tích cũ mà có liên quan, như nhà ga Bích Sắc Trại, trạm bưu chính cũ Hà Khẩu, hải quan cũ Hà Khẩu, giới thuê cũ Mông Tự v.v...

Đường sắt Điền – Việt được xây dựng trên giá trị "một chiếc đinh chốt một giọt máu, một khúc gỗ tà vẹt một mạng người". Những nơi đường sắt Điền – Việt đi qua là những nơi hầu như không có người nào cả, trong đó rất nhiều núi cao vùng sâu, công trình xây dựng trở nên cực kì khó khăn, 446km đường sắt mà cần phải xây dựng 3628 cây cầu, hầm chui và các hang núi yêu cầu trình độ kĩ thuật cao, như cây cầu chữ nhân ở Ba Đọ Tinh, bắc qua hai vách đá, đồng thời cũng không có trụ cầu, cách mặt đất 90m, hai bên tiếp giáp là hang động dài 65m, khiến cho người xây dựng phải mất hơn một năm mới hoàn thành được. Sau khi thống kê, Công ty đường sắt Điền – Việt đã từ Vân Nam và các tỉnh láng giềng chiêu mộ 230,000 công nhân để thi công đường sắt, do tính nguy hiểm của công trình này và đãi ngộ phi nhân của công ty đường sắt Pháp, nhiều công nhân bị chết vì nhiễm bệnh. Hơn nữa là bị Cắt xén tiền lương, không có tiền để ăn uống, còn nhiều người chết vì bỏ chạy và đói bụng. Theo số liệu thống kê, trước năm 1910 đã có trên 60-70 nghìn công nhân tử vong.Giữa khu vực đồi núi hiểm trở của phía nam Vân Nam. Đường sắt này được miêu tả trong "Vân Nam thập bát quái" - " Xe lửa không nhanh bằng xe hơi" hoặc "Xe lửa không thông vào trong nước mà thông sang nước ngoài".

1.2 Vị trí của tuyến đường sắt Vân Nam - Việt Nam trong mối quan hệ giữa tỉnh Vân Nam Trung Quốc và miền Bắc Việt Nam

Ngay từ giai đoạn đầu được xây dựng, đường sắt Điền – Việt đã tạo ra một cảnh tượng mới cho vùng biên ải xa xôi của hai nước Trung Việt. Đối với Việt Nam, tuyến đường sắt từ Hải Phòng đi lên Lào Cai (LaoKay xưa) được ví như mạch máu giao thông nối liền cảng biển Hải Phòng với trung tâm kinh tế Hà Nội và vùng miền núi xa xôi Tây Bắc. Tuyến đường sắt này đã đóng vai trò to lớn với phát triển kinh tế - xã hội vùng Tây Bắc Việt Nam cùng với miền Tây Nam Trung Quốc. Hầu hết các thị trấn vùng biên giới Lào Cai - Vân Nam đều hình thành và phồn vinh gắn chặt với thịnh vượng và phát triển của tuyến đường sắt này.

Từ xưa đến nay, tỉnh Vân Nam là một con đường quan trọng của dân tộc Trung Hoa để giao lưu và mậu dịch với nhân dân trong vùng Đông Nam Á và Nam Á. Đến cận đại, đường sắt Vân Nam - Việt Nam là con đường sắt thứ nhất của vùng Tây Nam, sự thông xe của nó là dấu hiệu bắt đầu phát triển của Vân Nam, đồng thời đã gây nhiều ảnh hưởng sâu sắc đối với chính trị, kinh tế và văn hoá xã hội của Vân Nam. Đặc biệt là sau khi Trung Quốc mới được thành lập, đường sắt Vân Nam - Việt Nam là một trong những động mạch lớn của sự phát triển văn minh kinh tế của tỉnh Vân Nam trong một thời gian dài, trở thành một trong những con đường chính để giao lưu với thế giới của Trung Quốc.

Từ đây chúng ta có thể thấy rằng, tuyến đường sắt Vân Nam-Việt Nam có góp phần quan trọng trong việc hình thành một Lào Cai sầm uất như hôm nay. Vào đầu thế kỷ XX, thủ phủ tỉnh Lào Cai mới có 17 đường và ngõ phố. Năm 1978, trước chiến tranh biên giới, thị xã có 25 đường phố. Nhưng đến năm 2007, thành phố Lào Cai đã xây dựng được 175 đường phố. Hệ thống hạ tầng đô thị (như: điện, nước sạch, thông tin, giao thông, xử lý rác thải, dịch vụ công cộng v.v…) được hiện đại hoá. Đồng thời khu vực thương mại cũng được mở rộng trong khu vực cửa khẩu, mở thêm khu kinh tế Kim Thành. Đường sắt Vân Nam - Việt Nam đã đánh thức vùng Tây Bắc đang ngủ yên hàng nghìn năm được bừng tỉnh, làm cây cầu lớn cho một vành đai kinh tế đầy triển vọng mà cầu nó chính là Lào Cai - cửa ngõ biên giới phía Bắc của đất nước đang trên xu thế hội nhập và có vị thế mới.

1.3 Tác dụng và ảnh hưởng của tuyến đường sắt Vân Nam-Việt Nam đối với mối quan hệ hai bên Vân Nam Trung Quốc và miền bắc Việt Nam

1.3.1 Tác dụng và ảnh hưởng của tuyến đường sắt Vân Nam-Việt Nam đối với Vân Nam

Nửa đầu thế kỷ 20, Vân Nam diễn ra 3 sự kiện lớn được quốc tế đều chú ý đến: sự kiện thứ nhất là đầu thế kỷ 20 xây dựng được đường sắt Điền-Việt, hai sự kiện lớn khác là đường bộ Điền Miến và tuyến đường vận tải hàng không Đà Phong trong thời kháng chiến chống Nhật. Ba sự kiện này đã khiến cho thế giới bắt đầu hiểu biết vùng tỉnh biên cương Vân Nam, nơi hẻo lánh hoang vu của Trung Quốc. Đồng thời cũng khiến cho người Vân Nam nhận biết thế giới bên ngoài. Đường sắt Vân Nam - Việt Nam bất cứ kể đến thời gian hay quy mô công trình, sức ảnh hưởng phát triển xã hội của Vân Nam v.v...cũng phải xếp đầu của 3 sự kiện trên.

Chính sách đối ngoại của Vân Nam chính là từ khi đường sắt Vân Nam-Việt Nam thông xe, cũng chính là tuyến đường sắt này mang lại sự phát triển kinh tế và những chuyển biến trong quan niệm nhận thức của người Vân Nam, đem lại văn hoá giáo dục tiên tiến và tư tưởng khoa học dân chủ của phương Tây, cũng chính vì trên cơ sở đó, mới được có cuộc khởi của Tôn Trung Sơn ở Hà Khẩu, mới có phong chào vạn người ủng hộ vận động bảo vệ tổ quốc. Hơn nữa, giống lửa đảng Cộng Sản Trung Quốc tại Vân Nam được gieo trên tuyến đường này vào lúc ban đầu.Từ đó, công nhân đường sắt dưới sự lãnh đạo của Đảng, trước sau tiến hành 13 cuộc đình công bãi công lớn nhỏ.Có góp phần lớn cho sự nghiệp giải phóng Vân Nam.

Đường sắt Điền – Việt không chỉ rút ngắn khoảng cách trong không gian giữa cao nguyên Vân-Quý (Vân Nam + Quý Châu) với biển, mà còn đem đến những hơi thở của biển, quan niệm mới của xã hội văn minh cận đại. Các trường học như đào mỏ, nông nghiệp, thương ngiệp, đường sắt, nữ giới, giảng võ thậm chí cả trường đại học Đông Lục v.v..., đều được triển khai tại Vân Nam. Trong đó Chu đức, Diệp Kiếm Anh, Chu Bảo Trung v.v... là những nhà quân sự do trường giảng võ đào tạo ra.Vân Nam cũng bởi đường sắt Điền – Việt mà được ghi vào lịch sử cận đại Trung Quốc: 1908 Tôn Trung Sơn đặt "cơ quan bộ" tại biên giới Trung Việt Hà Khẩu là trung tâm chỉ huy cuộc khởi nghĩa Quảng Nam, Sau khi cuộc kháng chiến chống Nhật bùng nổ, một nửa nước non Trung Quốc rơi vào tay giặc, tuyến đường Điền – Việt trở thành con đường nối liền với nước ngoài duy nhất, hàng quân dụng và thuốc men của nước ngoài được viện trợ qua tuyến đường Điền – Việt vận chuyển đến hậu phương, các giáo sư và học sinh của trường đại học Bắc Kinh, Thanh Hoa,

Nam Khai như Chu Tự Thanh, Văn Nhất Đa, Từ Bi Hồng, Phùng Hữu Lan cũng từ tuyến đường Điền – Việt này đến Vân Nam, thành lập "Đại học liên hợp Tây Nam". Có thể nhìn thấy, sự ảnh hưởng của đường sắt không những mang lại đến Côn Minh và tỉnh Vân Nam, mà còn đêm lại sự biến đổi sâu sắc về các mặt của xã hội, sự ảnh hưởng này không thể thống kê bằng con số.

1.3.2 Tác dụng và ảnh hưởng của tuyến đường sắt Vân Nam - Việt Nam đối với Việt Nam

100 năm trở lại đây, tuyến đường sắt Vân Nam - Việt Nam đã trở thành cây cầu nối liền đặc biệt giữa nhiều nền văn hóa.Giúp văn hoá Trung Hoa, các dân tộc thiểu số, người Pháp và văn hóa Việt Nam có đan xen và hòa trộn với nhau.Chính nhờ có sự giao thoa giữa các nền văn hóa đã khiến cho tuyến đường sắt Điền -Việt trở thành tài nguyên văn hóa dân tộc có một không hai.

Năm 1910, sau khi tuyến đường liên vận quốc tế khai thông, để giúp nhân dân Việt Nam xây dựng kinh tế và kháng chiến chống Mỹ tuyến đường sắt đã trở thành tuyến đường tiếp viên quan trọng của Trung Quốc đối với Việt Nam, một lượng lớn nhân lực vật lực đã thông qua tuyến đường này chuyển đến Việt Nam. Tháng 8 năm 1965 dưới sự chỉ đạo của trung ương, tỉnh Vân Nam đã giúp đỡ 3 tỉnh Việt Nam: Lào Cai, Hà Giang và Lai Châu hàng triệu nhân dân tệ và 50 nghìn tấn gạo.

Đường sắt Điền -Việt được xây dựng trở thành 1 cửa khẩu đối ngoài, Việt Nam không chỉ trở thành đối tác kinh tế, giao lưu văn hóa của tỉnh Vân Nam, mà còn trở thành con đường giúp tỉnh Vân Nam bước ra thế giới. Hơn nữa, tuyến đường sắt Điền -Việt giúp thúc đẩy sự phát triển kinh tế cả Việt Nam và Vân Nam. Không chỉ vậy, tuyến đường sau khi hoàn thành đã giúp người dân trong tỉnh Vân Nam giao lưu buôn bán dễ dàng hơn. Sau khi tuyến đường khai thông, việc giao lưu buôn bán giữa Vân Nam và Việt Nam trở nên thuận tiện hơn nhiều, quy mô cũng lớn hơn.

Sau khi Việt Nam và Trung Quốc thiết lập lại quan hệ hữu nghị ngoại giao,tuyến đường sắt Điền -Việt có tác dụng không nhỏ trong việc thúc đẩy giao lưu kinh tế giữa Vân Nam và Việt Nam, chủ yếu được thể hiện dưới mấy điểm sau: vận chuyển hành khách, vận chuyển hàng hóa...

Việc xây dựng của đường sắt Điền -Việt đã đáp ứng nhu cầu về sản xuất, sinh hoạt của hai bên, đồng thời cũng thúc đẩy sự phát triển kinh tế, xã hội của song phương.

Chương II Phân tích hiện trạng của tuyến đường sắt Vân Nam - Việt Nam

2.1 Sự chấm dứt hoạt động của đường sắt Vân Nam - Việt Nam tại Vân Nam và tiếp tục được sử dụng trên lãnh thổ Việt Nam

2.1.1 Sự chấm dứt hoạt động của đường sắt Vân Nam - Việt Nam tại Vân Nam

Bởi vì sự biến đổi của thị trường vận chuyển và con đường đã cũ đi, khả năng vận chuyển truyền thống của đường sắt Vân Nam - Việt Nam ngày càng yếu đi, cho nên dịch vụ chở khách bị dừng lại trong tháng 5 năm 2003, chỉ còn lưu lại một đoạn dài 42 km để chở khách, giá vé chỉ là 2,5 tệ, là giá cả rẻ nhất trên thế giới. Tuy nhiên dịch vụ chở khách vẫn còn tiếp tục, nhưng hàng năm đều bị lỗ vốn 3 - 4 tỷ tệ, cho nên hiện nay đoạn Vân Nam của đường sắt Vân Nam - Việt Nam sắp bị chấm dứt.

Sự chấm dứt của đường sắt gây ra ảnh hưởng to lớn đối với sự phát triển trong xã hội kinh tế của tỉnh Vân Nam, nó không những kết thúc thói quen đi ra ngoài hàng trăm năm của cư dân dọc đường sắt, làm cho hành động đi ra ngoài của cư dân dọc đường sắt thành một vấn đề to lớn, mà còn khiến cho sự sầm uất ngày xưa mất đi mà không trở lại, tháng 1 năm 2010, một phần nhân viên và chuyên gia của tổ chức Hội nghị Hiệp thương Chính trị tỉnh Vân Nam chỉ ra; " Đường sắt Điền -Việt trên thế giới có một không hai đang rơi vào tình hình sống còn, tuyến Đông của đường sắt từ Ngọc Khê đến Mông Tự dự tính được thông xe vào năm 2010, ngày thông xe của tuyến Đông trong đường sắt xuyên Á tức là ngày chấm dứt hoạt động vận chuyển của đường sắt Điền -Việt."

2.1.2 Đường sắt Vân Nam - Việt Nam tiếp tục được sử dụng trên lãnh thổ Việt Nam

Tuy nhiên đoạn tại Vân Nam đã bị chấm dứt, nhưng đoạn tại Việt Nam vẫn được tiếp tục sử dụng đến hiện nay, tác giả từng được đi Việt Nam bằng xe lửa. Trên đường này, tuy tốc độ của tuyến đường sắt này không nhanh, nhưng đã có cảm giác đặt biệt. Ga Hải Phòng hiện nay là một trong những ga lớn và hiện đại nhất trên Việt Nam. Hiện nay một ngày có 4 đôi tàu chở khách chạy tuyến Hải Phòng - Hà Nội và ngược lại vận chuyển hành khách bằng các toa xe ngồi cứng, ngồi mền, toa xe 2 tầng có điều hoà nhiệt độ. Ga Hải Phòng khai thác hệ thống đường sắt tại nhà ga và hệ thống đường sắt trong Cảng Hải Phòng, Cảng Chùa Vẽ, Cảng Viconsip.

Năng lực vận tải hàng hoá đáp ứng thường xuyên từ 3000 đến 4000 tấn xếp, 2000 đến 3000 tấn dỡ/ngày, bằng các toa xe có mui (GG) trọng tải từ 25 đến 36 tấn, toa xe không mui thành cao (HH) trọng tải từ 25 đến 40 tấn, toa xe không mui thành thấp (NN) trọng tải từ 25 đến 35 tấn, toa xe xitec (PP) trọng tải từ 25 đến 35 tấn, toa xe thành thấp (MVT) trọng tải 50 tấn, toa xe chuyên dùng vận chuyển container (M cd) trọng tải từ 25 đến 35 tấn.

2.2 Sự ảnh hưởng của tuyến đường sắt xuyên Á đối với tuyến đường sắt Vân Nam - Việt Nam

Năm 2006, các nước Đông Nam Á đã bắt đầu quảng bá để huy động khoảng 5 tỷ USD vốn cho dự án xây dựng tuyến đường sắt Xuyên Á. Đường xuyên Á nối liền 8 nước với chính tuyến chạy từ Singapore qua Maylaysia và Thái Lan tới Côn Minh, trong đó có các chi nhánh Myanmar, Campuchia, Lào và Việt Nam. Đường sắt xyên Á được đánh giá là một trong những dự án giao thông chủ yếu của ASEAN nhằm thúc đẩy sự phát triển mạnh mẽ về kinh tế, văn hóa và du lịch của các nước trong khu vực. Chính vì tuyến Đông của đường sắt xuyên Á từ Côn Minh đến Hà Khẩu sẽ đi qua đường sắt Điền -Việt.Hiên nay, đoan Vân

Nam, đoạn phi a Đông của đương sắt Xuyên Atư Côn Minh đến Singapore đang xây dựng. các cơ quan có liên quan của tỉnh Vân Nam cho rằng, thông xe đoạn phi a Đông đương sắt Xuyên A, tất sethay thểchức năng vận tải truyền thông của đương sắt Điền -Việt. Cho nên nhiều nhân dân lo lắng về tương lai của đường sắt Điền -Việt, sợ đường sắt Điền -Việt sẽ bị vứt bỏ và bị người đời sau quên đi.

Tác giả cho rằng sự lo lắng này cũng có lý, bởi vì hai tuyến đường sắt này đa số đi song song với nhau, chỉ là đường sắt Xuyên Á đang xây dựng càng ngang hơn, tốc độ và năng suất của đường sắt Xuyên Á là không thể so sánh được, đường sắt này là đường sắt cao tốc thứ nhất của tỉnh Vân Nam, sau khi đường sắt này được xây dựng xong, từ Côn Minh đến Hà Khẩu chỉ cần mất 3 tiếng thì sẽ đến. Hiện nay, đường sắt Xuyên Á đã được khởi công toàn diện, để cho đoạn Vân Nam của đường sắt Xuyên Á có thể nối liền với mạng lưới cả đường sắt, người thiết kế chuẩn bị xây dựng một đường sắt tiêu chuẩn hiện đại hoá tại biên giới Trung-Việt, để thực hiện vận chuyển hàng hoá liên vật quốc tế một cách thuận tiện và dễ dàng.

Thực ra, cứ nhìn bản đồ thì sẽ hiểu ra: khởi công xây dựng đoạn Ngọc Khê - Mông Tự không phải là biến đổi hoặc mở rộng trên cơ sở vốn của đoạn Côn Minh - Hà Khẩu, ngược lại là lấy Ngọc Khê làm điểm xuất phát, dựng một đường sắt mới, đường sắt này là đường có ray tiêu chuẩn. Cho nên đường sắt Vân Nam - Việt Nam không bị thoái bỏ, mà là được giữ gìn và tu sửa, miễn là có một ngày thì kiên quyết không thoái bỏ. Lịch sử lựa chọn một lần nữa Vân Nam, Vân Nam một lần nữa đi tới tuyến đầu có phát triển lớn.

Chương III Những suy nghĩ về tương lai của tuyến đường sắt Vân Nam - Việt Nam

Đường sắt Điền -Việt trong lịch sử hiện đại, đã đóng một vai trò quan trọng trong "Vân Nam thập bát quái", có hai kỳ lạ đến từ nó, nó đã cùng được xây dựng với các kênh đào Panama, Suy-ê bảy kênh rạch và được gọi là phép lạ "của thế giới ba dự án lớn" đế quốc đã được báo chí mô tả như là "hút máu" của Trung Quốc "sau một thế kỷ thăng trầm, nó đã trải qua các bài hát và sẽ đối mặt với số phận của sự chú ý của con người.

Nếu theo quan điểm của lịch sử và duy vật biện chứng đường sắt Điền -Việt, nó chỉ là một cái phương tiện quan trọng khi người Pháp quản lý nó. Đường sắt Điền -Việt thực sự là một bằng chứng nhục nhã rõ ràng của cuối triều đình nhà Thanh. Khi nó trở về tay của người Trung Quốc, nó đã trở thành phương tiện quan trọng đóng góp phần lớn về phát triển kinh tế của 1 thế kỷ, đồng thời cũng có giá trị lịch sử, văn hóa, du lịch phong phú. Chúng tôi không thể quên những đóng góp xuất sắc cho đường sắt Điền -Việt, chúng tôi tự tin vào nó, tôn trọng nó, bỏ qua những gì trong quá khứ và nhìn tới tương lai.

Cho nên tác giả sẽ suy nghĩ về những quan điểm của người ta, đồng thời cũng tha thiết hy vọng có thể rút ra một kết luận hữu hiệu về tương lai của tuyến đường sắt Vân Nam-Việt Nam.

3.1 Tương lai đáng lo lắng của đường sắt Vân Nam - Việt Nam

Bởi vì nhiều nguyên nhân, tương lai đáng lo lắng của đường sắt Điền -Việt. Tuy nhiên, đường sắt Điền -Việt tất nhiên không thể bị vứt bỏ một cách dễ dàng, nó là chứng kiến của lịch sử, chỉ cần tìm ra một tư duy mới để phát triển, nó vẫn có khả năng sinh sống. Hiện nay có nhiều người suy nghĩ về tương lai của nó, và đặt ra nhiều ý kiến, ví dụ như: một số người đề nghị phát triển đường sắt thành đường sắt tham quan du lịch. Năm 2003 và năm 2004 chủ tịch của tỉnh Vân Nam và bộ trưởng đường sắt đều đến khảo sát đề án đường này, và hai người đều rút được kết luận mà tiếp tục sử dụng đường sắt này, không lâu nữa đoạn Trung Quốc được bảo vệ một cách tốt nhất.

3.1.1 Thời đại kêu gọi một "đường sắt Vân Nam -Việt Nam" mới

Khi bước vào thế kỷ mới, quan hệ kinh tế chính trị giữa Trung Việt không ngừng củng cố và phát triển, chính quyền cấp cao của song phương giao lưu với nhau rất thân mật, hợp tác mậu dịch không ngừng tăng thêm. Hiện nay, qua hiệp thương quyết định của hai nước, Trung

Quốc và Việt Nam đang tận sức vào việc xây dựng quy hoạch "Hai hành lang, một vành đai kinh tế", để cho hợp tác kinh tế đi tới sâu sắc hơn. Dưới bối cảnh quan hệ Trung Việt phát triển ổn định, quan hệ mậu dịch giữa Vân Nam và Việt Nam được tiếp tục phát triển. Việc giao lưu hàng hóa và giao tiếp của nhân dân ngày càng tăng thêm giữa Vân Nam và Việt Nam, cùng với sự triển khai hợp tác trong khu vực tiểu vùng sông Mê Công, đều gửi gắm hy vọng cho đường sắt Vân Nam - Việt Nam.

Thật không may, bởi vì những khuyết tật bẩm sinh, chỉ dựa vào sửa chữa đã không thể khiến cho đường sắt Vân Nam - Việt Nam đổi mới hoàn toàn và có thay đổi mang tính đột phá. Thời đại kêu gọi một "đường sắt Vân Nam - Việt Nam mới", kế hoạch xây dựng đường sắt xuyên Á đã tạo cơ hội tốt cho đường sắt Điền - Việt mới.

3.2 Hai nước Trung Việt nên có thái độ coi trọng và xây dựng lại tuyến đường sắt Vân Nam - Việt Nam

Trung Việt hai bên đã từng nhiều lần thảo luận về việc tuyến đường sắt Điền - Việt, nhưng tại sao cứ không được thực hiện? Theo tác giả, nếu phương án này được thực hành sẽ là một công trình to lớn, không những tiêu tiền mà còn lãng phí thời gian, phải mất nhiều năm để cải tạo lại. Nhưng nếu không cải tạo lại thì có phải là hy sinh của những người đã chết và có cống hiến của thời đó sẽ mất ý nghĩa? Hình như đáp án là "có". Rất may là đường sắt Xuyên Á đang xây dựng có thể thay thế công dụng của nó tại đoạn Vân Nam. Đồng thời Việt Nam nhằm phối hợp với chương trình mới của đường sắt Xuyên Á, bây giờ cũng chuẩn bị nâng cấp tuyến đường sắt Hà Nội - Lào Cai.

3.2.1 Tuyến đường sắt Xuyên Á

Tuyến đường sắt sẽ giúp hình thành mạng lưới giao thông đường sắt nối liền miền Nam Trung Quốc và các nước trong khối ASEAN. Xe lửa khởi hành từ tỉnh Vân Nam (TQ) sẽ đi qua Lào, Thái Lan xuống tới tận Singapore. Mục đích thứ hai của tuyến đường sắt là chở hàng. Nghiên cứu tiền do chuyên gia Trung Quốc thực hiện cho thấy tàu hàng có thể chạy với vận tốc 120 km/giờ, giảm chi phí vận chuyển hàng hóa, tăng khối lượng mậu dịch buôn bán.

Theo giới chuyên gia, mục đích chiến lược của tuyến đường sắt này lớn hơn nhiều so với lợi ích kinh tế do trao đổi mậu dịch mang lại. Thông qua tuyến đường sắt này, Trung Quốc sẽ tăng gia ảnh hưởng đáng kể về chính trị và kinh tế tại những vùng sâu vùng xa của khối ASEAN. Công nhân Trung Quốc sẽ được đưa sang xây tuyến đường sắt này và lúc cao điểm có thể lên tới 50.000 người. Trước mắt chính phủ Trung Quốc nhấn mạnh đến lợi ích kinh tế của dự án, qua việc thúc đẩy giao lưu mậu dịch giữa Trung Quốc và ASEAN.Tuyến đường sắt này cũng góp phần đẩy mạnh việc tìm kiếm khoáng sản tại vùng chưa có mậu dịch nhiều với thế giới bên ngoài.

Hiện nay, đoạn đường sắt Côn Minh - Hà Khẩu, ngoài việc nâng cấp tuyến đường sắt khổ 1m, đang xây dựng một tuyến đường mới khổ 1.435 m đạt tiêu chuẩn quốc tế từ Côn Minh đi Mông Tự, đến năm 2011 sẽ hoàn thành tuyến này đến Hà Khẩu.

3.2.2 Việt Nam sẽ cải tạo nâng cấp đoạn đường Việt Nam của tuyến đường sắt Vân Nam - Việt Nam

Ngày nay, trong điều kiện mở rộng giao lưu kinh tế qua biên giới, đường sắt Hải Phòng - Lào Cai - Vân Nam trở thành tuyến đường giao thông vô cùng quan trọng, là "cầu nối" của vùng Tây Nam rộng lớn .

Tuy nhiên, qua khảo sát thực tế, hệ thống đường sắt tuyến Lào Cai - Hải Phòng khổ 1m từ thời Pháp thuộc với công suất thiết kế 1,5 triệu tấn hàng hoá/năm, đã vận chuyển với 200% công suất cũng không đáp ứng được nhu cầu vận tải hàng hóa và hành khách trong thời điểm tăng trưởng nhanh chóng của hoạt động mậu dịch, du lịch như hiện nay. Ngành đường sắt hai nước đang hợp tác tổ chức liên vận quốc tế trên tuyến này, cho nên việc cải tạo kỹ thuật đối với tuyến đường sắt Vân Nam-Việt Nam phải được đặt trong khuôn khổ quy hoạch tổng thể hệ thống đường sắt toàn châu Á.

Theo Tổng Công ty Đường sắt Việt Nam, tuyến đường sắt này dài khoảng 285km, Sau hơn 100 năm sử dụng, tuyến đường này hỏng hóc nghiêm trọng nên vận tốc chạy, có đoạn chỉ đạt 10 - 15 km/h. Trong khi đó, tuyến đường sắt này được ngành đường sắt đánh giá là tuyến đông khách nhất hiện nay (mỗi ngày có từ 20 đến 22 chuyến tàu) (孙灿2005.7).

Việc cải tạo nâng cấp tuyến đường sắt Hà Nội-Lào Cai sẽ góp phần đáp ứng nhu cầu vận chuyển trên tuyến đến năm 2020 khoảng 5 triệu hành khách/năm và khoảng 7,5 triệu tấn hàng hoá/năm.

3.3 Hai nước Trung Việt hợp tác trình báo UNESCO xin tuyến đường sắt Vân Nam - Việt Nam là một di sản văn hóa thế giới

Bên cạnh sự dựng lại đường sắt Vân Nam - Việt Nam, điều quan trọng nhất là bảo vệ môi trường xung quanh của nó và đường sắt bản thân, cho nên những tác giả đề nghị Trung Việt hai nước hợp tác trình báo UNESCO xin tuyến đường sắt Vân Nam - Việt Nam là một di sản văn hóa thế giới. Năm 2010, tại Vân Nam, Trung Quốc đã diễn ra Hội thảo nhân dịp 100 năm tuyến đường sắt Việt Nam - Vân Nam.

Do năng lực vận tai, tốc độ chạy xe khá thập, nghề vận tai chở khach cua tuyên đương sắt nay đã toan bông ngưng vao năm 2003, vận tai chở hang nhưng năm gân đây liên tục giam xuông. Doc tuyên đương sắt Điền -Việt có nhiêu công trinh độc đáo, cảnh quan thiên nhiên, kiến trúc có lich su văn hoa cổ điêu kiên xin công nhân la di san văn hoa thê giơi .

Phát biểu tại hội thảo, Tổng lãnh sự Việt Nam tại Côn Minh Nguyễn Hồng Hải cho biết, tuyến đường sắt Việt Nam - Vân Nam giàu giá trị văn hoá lịch sử, là tài sản quý báu chung của nhân dân 2 nước; 2 bên cần tăng cường trao đổi, tiếp xúc, phối hợp vận động UNESCO sớm công nhận tuyến đường sắt này là di sản thế giới. Sở Văn hoá Vân Nam-Trung Quốc đề nghị hai bên cần sớm tiến hành điều tra toàn diện đối với các điều kiện đăng ký di sản của tuyến đường sắt, đồng thời tiến hành ghi hình, chỉnh lý các tư liệu liên quan để chuẩn bị cho công tác lập hồ sơ.

Có thể nói, trở thành di sản văn hóa thế giới đối với đường sắt Vân Nam-Việt Nam có nghĩa là sống lại, đây là một điểm xuất phát mới.

3.4 Đường sắt Vân Nam - Việt Nam sẽ trở thành một đường du lịch vàng

3.4.1 Bối cảnh và ý nghĩa của việc khai thác văn hóa du lịch của đường sắt Vân Nam-Việt Nam

Đường sắt Việt Nam tương đối mạnh về giá trị lịch sử và văn hóa, đã luôn luôn được người trong và ngoài nước biết đến như một nét văn hóa quan trọng.Tất nhiên sự phong phú của nguồn tài nguyên đó không thể tái sinh, là dễ dàng thấy được. Tích cực phát triển giá trị khai thác về du lịch và văn hóa của Đường sắt Vân Nam - Việt Nam có ý nghĩa rất lớn trong thực tiễn, vì nó có những nét đặc trưng sâu sắc về lịch sử và văn hóa.

Hợp tác giữa Vân Nam và ASEAN ngày càng toàn diện và trưởng thành.Vân Nam đã sơ bộ đổi thành tháp cầu quan trọng nhất đối với Đông Nam Á kể từ khi cải cách mở cửa. Sau nhiều năm không ngừng phát triển, Đông Nam Á đã trở thành đối tác mậu dịch toàn diện, đa dạng và mở rộng lớn nhất của tỉnh Vân Nam, kinh tế của tỉnh tiến bộ trong những năm gần đây, xuất khẩu mậu dịch song phương chiếm khoảng 35%, thương mại của các nước ASEAN cũng là thị trường chính, hơn 90% các dự án của Vân Nam hợp tác kinh tế nước ngoài tập trung ở khu vực này. Từ phía Tây Nam đến Côn Minh là trung tâm và tập trung vào khu vực Đông Nam Á, mở ra một mô hình mới, Vân Nam - Trung Quốc - ASEAN là khu vực mậu dịch tự do cung cấp điều kiện nền tảng tốt.

3.4.2 Việc thực hiện các chương trình và phương pháp xử lý

Đẩy nhanh việc xây dựng "hành lang du lịch" giao thông hiện đại để đặt nền tảng cho đường sắt Vân Nam - Việt Nam phát triển,việc thực hiện các chương trình và phương pháp xử lý cụ thể như sau: Thứ nhất, trong quá trình xây dựng phía đông của đường sắt xuyên Á, đặt biệt là đoạn từ Mông Tự đến Hà Khẩu phải ra sức tăng cường sự bảo việc đối với tài nguyên văn hóa dọc đường, sáng tạo cơ hội cho khai thác lợi dụng sau này.

Thứ hai, phải tích cực tranh thủ sự ủng hộ của nhà nước, gắng sức vào công tác trình báo UNESCO xin tuyến đường sắt Vân Nam - Việt Nam là một di sản văn hóa thế giới. Thứ ba, phải kế thừa di sản quý báu này, đi theo quy luật tiến triển của di sản độc đáo, lấy Đường sắt Vân Nam-Việt làm nút để thúc đẩy phát triển toàn diện của xã hội kinh tế.

KẾT LUẬN

Tuyến đường sắt Điền -Việt vừa thuộc về Vân Nam, cũng thuộc về thế giới, nếu bạn dần dần tìm hiểu lịch sử một trăm năm của đường sắt, bạn sẽ cảm nhận được lịch sử này là một kỳ tích hiếm thấy. Do đường sắt và người dân sinh sống trên đường này, cùng với người ủng hộ cộng đồng sáng tạo ra kỳ tích này.

Đây là việc thật đáng mừng, nó không bị át mất vì đồn đại của môi giới; nó không bị chấm dứt vì lời bàn của một số lãnh đạo không có cảm giác trách nhiệm.Đây là đường sắt khổ 1m của nhân dân Vân Nam, cũng là đường sắt của nhân dân cả nước.Không có người sẽ huỷ diệt nó, cũng không có người vứt bỏ nó.

Đường sắt Điền -Việt tương đối mạnh về giá trị lịch sử và văn hóa, đã luôn luôn được người trong và ngoài nước biết đến như một nét văn hóa quan trọng, là một dấu hiệu văn hoá quan trọng để nhận thức Vân Nam, tính phong phú và tính không thể tái sinh của nguồn tài nguyên của nó. Tích cực phát triển giá trị khai thác về du lịch và văn hóa của Đường sắt Điền -Việt có ý nghĩa rất lớn trong thực tế, vì nó có những nét đặc trưng sâu sắc về lịch sử và văn hóa.

Giữ lại hiện trạng của đường sắt Vân Nam-Việt Nam để trở thành chương trình quan trọng của sự phát triển Vân Nam, đồng thời có thể đưa tuyến đường sắt Vân Nam - Việt Nam lên thành di sản văn hóa thế giới. Vì thế, người ta hoàn toàn có thể tin rằng đường sắt Điền -Việt từng trải nhiều gian nan khó nhọc sẽ qua phương thức khác biệt sáng tạo kỳ tích mới trong thế kỷ mới. Đây không chỉ là một tình tiết, mà còn là một khát vọng đối với đường sắt, nhân dân.

TÀI LIỆU THAM KHẢO

[1] Chiêm Toàn Hữu. Văn hoá Nam Chiếu - Đại Lý [M]. NXB Văn hoá
Thông tin. Hà Nội: 2004

[2] Liên hiệp đường sắt Việt nam. Lịch sử đường sắt Việt Nam [M]. NXB
Lao động, Hà Nội:1994

[3]云南省政协文史资料委员会．法帝国主义利用滇越铁路侵略云南三十年
[C]．云南文史资料选辑第16辑．昆明：云南人民出版社，1982.

[4]陆韧．云南对外交通史[M]．昆明：云南民族出版社，1997.

[5]李开义、殷小俊：彼岸的目光——晚清法国外交官方苏雅在云南[M]．昆
明：云南教育出版社，2002.

[6]孙代兴、吴宝璋．云南抗日战争史[M]．昆明：云南大学出版社，1995.

[7]段锡．滇越铁路—跨域百年的小火车[M]．昆明：云南美术出版社，2007.

[8]孙灿．泛亚铁路建设与滇越铁路历史文化保护[J]．云南民族大学学报，
2005，7.